A STAR BOOK

SCOUTING ON TWO CONTINENTS

BY
Major FREDERICK RUSSELL BURNHAM
D. S. O., Chief of Scouts under Lord Roberts

ELICITED AND ARRANGED BY
MARY NIXON EVERETT

GARDEN CITY PUBLISHING CO., INC.
GARDEN CITY, NEW YORK

COPYRIGHT, 1926
BY DOUBLEDAY, PAGE & COMPANY
ALL RIGHTS RESERVED
PRINTED IN THE UNITED STATES AT
THE COUNTRY LIFE PRESS
GARDEN CITY, N. Y.

Major Frederick Russell Burnham, D.S.O.

TO MY WIFE
BLANCHE BLICK BURNHAM
MY DEAR COMPANION OF MANY A MILE
I DEDICATE THIS BOOK

"In real life he is more interesting than any of my heroes of romance"
SIR RIDER HAGGARD

"I have seldom been as much taken with a narrative"
REAR ADMIRAL WM. S. SIMS, U.S.N.

"I have read it all with enthralled interest"
THEODORE ROOSEVELT

"England was never made by her statesmen; England was made by her adventurers."—GENERAL GORDON.

THE ADVENTURERS

They sit at home and they dream and dally,
   Raking the embers of long-dead years—
But ye go down to the haunted valley,
   Light-hearted pioneers.
They have forgotten they ever were young,
They hear your songs as an unknown tongue,
But the flame of God through your spirit stirs,
   Adventurers—O adventurers!

They tithe their herbs and they count their tally,
   Choosing their words that a phrase may live—
But ye cast down in the hungry valley
   All that a man can give.
They prophesy smoothly, with weary smile
Fulfilling their feeble appointed while,
But Death himself to your pride defers,
   Adventurers—O adventurers!

—MAY BYRON

Extract from a letter from LT. GEN. SIR ROBERT BADEN-POWELL, K. C. V. O., K. C. V., *written from Africa to his mother, in 1896:*

"12th June, 1896. . . . Burnham is a most delightful companion . . . amusing, interesting, and most instructive. Having seen service against the Red Indians he brings quite a new experience to bear on the Scouting work here. And while he talks away there's not a thing escapes his quick roving eye, whether it is on the horizon or at his feet."

FOREWORD

SOME years ago, Sir Rider Haggard said to me, in regard to Major Burnham: "Burnham in real life is more interesting than any of my heroes of romance." This appreciation by the author of "King Solomon's Mines," "Allan Quatermain," and "She" was no idle comp'iment, but was earnestly expressed, and I know that the readers of this book will agree with the famous novelist that truth can be stranger than fiction.

Haggard also told me that he tried his best to induce his friend Burnham to give him material for writing a series of magazine articles, and that Lord Northcliffe had offered Major Burnham £2,000 to dictate broadly his exploits, but that Burnham, from excessive modesty, had firmly turned this offer down. Such characteristic refusals account mainly for the fact that Major Burnham remains relatively unknown to the American public while his fame is spread throughout England and the English Colonies, where no modesty on his part could possibly suppress the record of his exploits in South Africa, the scene of his many extraordinary adventures.

Of the many Americans who have contributed service to the winning of South Africa from barbarism, no one is held in higher esteem than Frederick R. Burnham. His extraordinary accomplishments, unblemished character, and winning personality fully earned the high praise bestowed upon him by the people of South Africa and the patriotic pride of his fellow Americans in that country.

I recall a conversation with Cecil Rhodes when discussing the winning of Rhodesia, that great territory about the size of California, which lies south of the Zambezi River and contiguous to the Transvaal on the north. Rhodes had been reading a letter which he passed over to me with the explanation that it was in reply to one that he had written to Burnham after the first Matabele War in 1894. Rhodes said that he had asked Burnham to suggest some way in which the British South Africa Company, the owner of the country afterward called Rhodesia, could recognize the invaluable service he had rendered as a Scout in that war. Burnham's reply, and I well remember it, was to this effect: "While I appreciate the honour you pay me, in your generous estimate of the service you consider I have rendered, and your offer of recompense, I must frankly tell you that the part I played was not with the object of promoting the interest of your company but was in defence of the lives of the people who were at that time besieged by hordes of savages under Lobengula. For that reason I cannot consistently accept any reward, but I sincerely hope that I shall be able to retain the appreciation you have expressed by what I may be able to accomplish in the future." Rhodes exclaimed, "What an extraordinary letter! It is a rare experience to have an offer of that kind turned down." I said, "Yes, but you respect him the more for having done so." Later, Rhodes persuaded Burnham to accept a concession of mineral land as a token of his appreciation.

One of the most enthusiastic admirers and devoted friends of Major Burnham was the late Lord Grey, at one time Administrator of Rhodesia and subsequently Governor General of Canada. Lord Roberts, Lord Milner, General Sir Baden-Powell, identified with South African history, were among his many admirers and friends. Lord Roberts had a special admiration and fondness for Major Burnham, and whenever I happened to visit London, would call to see me particularly to make inquiry regarding his health and welfare.

While I have said his fame has not reached the American public generally, Burnham was, nevertheless, well known to Theodore Roosevelt, Hopkinson Smith, Richard Harding Davis, Thomas Nelson Page, and other prominent Americans who greatly enjoyed his company. Hopkinson Smith, not a mean judge, once told me that he regarded Burnham as the

FOREWORD

best story-teller he had ever met. I recall spending several hours with Roosevelt and Burnham after a luncheon at the White House, to which we had been invited by President Roosevelt, and no higher tribute could be paid to the absorbing interest of Burnham's narrative of South African adventures than the mute admiration of Roosevelt as he listened without interrupting.

In addition to the fund of thrilling experiences that some of his intimates could by skillful manœuvring induce Burnham to recite, his comprehensive, clear, and original views, his picturesque exposition of great national and international problems were in themselves a source of edification and enjoyment to those privileged to discuss such matters with him.

No life of Major Burnham would be complete without a reference to his wife. She has been an ideal helpmate in his career, often sharing great hardships and dangers in his field of strenuous activity. An inspiring and sustaining influence in his life, she is held in the highest esteem by his host of admirers.

The writing of this book has long been delayed, and it is only after years of persistent endeavour on the part of a few friends, of whom I am proud to be one, that Burnham has been prevailed upon to write this autobiography.

JOHN HAYS HAMMOND.

WASHINGTON, D. C.
June 5, 1925.

CONTENTS

CHAPTER		PAGE
I.	THE MAKING OF A SCOUT	1
II.	FIRST LESSONS IN SCOUTING	12
III.	THE TONTO BASIN FEUD	21
IV.	MY SMUGGLER FRIEND	34
V.	UPS AND DOWNS IN GLOBE	49
VI.	THE NECKTIE PARTY	63
VII.	GOLD MINING	73
VIII.	THE CALL TO AFRICA	79
IX.	THE LONG TRAIL	86
X.	THE TREK NORTH	97
XI.	THE WAR CLOUD	108
XII.	MASHONALAND	121
XIII.	THE FIRST MATABELE WAR	131
XIV.	WHEN THE COMPASS FAILED	139
XV.	CARRYING DISPATCHES	152
XVI.	THE DASH TO CAPTURE THE KING	163
XVII.	WILSON'S LAST STAND	174
XVIII.	FORBES'S RETREAT	189

CONTENTS

CHAPTER		PAGE
XIX.	AFTER THE WAR	200
XX.	THE JAMESON RAID	217
XXI.	THE SECOND MATABELE WAR	227
XXII.	RHODESIA'S DARKEST HOUR	240
XXIII.	THE M'LIMO	249
XXIV.	KLONDIKE	259
XXV.	AN OPINION OF THE BOERS	272
XXVI.	PAARDEBURG AND MODDER RIVER	280
XXVII.	THE PIETERSBURG FAILURE	290
XXVIII.	CATTLE LIFTING NEAR BRAKPAN	302
XXIX.	TAKEN PRISONER AT SANNA'S POST	309
XXX.	ESCAPE FROM THE BOERS	321
XXXI.	CUTTING THE RAILROAD	329
XXXII.	WOUNDED	338
XXXIII.	REWARDS	349
XXXIV.	THE GREAT WAR AND THE PROSPECTOR	358
	THE LATEST ADVENTURE	368

INTRODUCTION

It was a dozen years ago, during a motor trip with Mr. and Mrs. John E. Marble of Pasadena through the park-like country around Paso Robles, that we were joined by a certain Major Burnham, gold miner, hunter, and explorer, as well as Chief of Scouts under Lord Roberts in the Boer War, whom Mr. Marble knew and the rest of us had long wished to meet.

We saw a rather short man dressed in gray, the colour of his thick wavy hair; with the fair skin and regular features of the typical Anglo-Saxon, resolute cleft chin, excellent teeth, firm but expressive lips, large, well-shaped head well poised on an erect, broad-chested frame, strong, compact-looking hands—emphatically a man's man, able, active, alert.

His way of striding up and down while talking, his step as elastic and noiseless as that of prowling lion or competent burglar, seemed peculiarly characteristic of his abounding vigour of mind and body; yet this quiet, unassuming gentleman would never pass unnoticed in a crowd did one but glimpse his eyes, blue eyes of startling keenness and brilliancy, eyes that see everything without seeming to see, eyes that at times are as cold and fierce as the steel of a drawn sword, yet, when laughing with his wife, as tender and merry as a boy's.

To the mere physical outline must be added the impression he makes on all of force and self-control, leading one to visualize his true nature; not merely that "infinite capacity for taking pains" which marks the genius or the scout, but that delicate soul balance of experience and judgment which is, perhaps, man's highest achievement, and which shines forth to be recognized even by those who have no knowledge of the actual record of accomplishment. All this I saw then and continue to see in the Major's personality, and the divine fires of my hero worship have never dimmed through the everyday of pleasant friendship that has followed.

As we drove along the lovely wooded country of San Luis Obispo County, the Major sharing the rear seat with Mrs. Marble and me, we were given sudden and vivid proof of the famous readiness and resource of our new companion. My husband was at the wheel, and we were starting down a steep, narrow hill road when the brakes began to slip. At that instant, around a curve, over a light bridge at the foot of the hill, we saw coming toward us a very old man driving a pair of skittish horses. High tragedy seemed inevitable—when out of the tonneau without touching the sides sprang the Major and had a boulder lodged under the wheel and the perilous car stopped in the very nick o' time! Never have I witnessed such quick action.

That same day, after a picnic luncheon together, beneath a great sycamore in a broad dry arroyo, my husband had the temerity to ask our new acquaintance to tell us how he killed the M'Limo in South Africa. I caught my breath until, with a cordial smile, the Major had consented, and held us all spellbound by the charm and interest of his recital. Just as he was describing the awful suffering of the children from improper and insufficient food during the siege of Bulawayo and the tragic loss of his own little girl, he said quickly: "We'll kill that snake when I finish the story." We followed his glance, and there, only a few yards away, a big rattler was coiled. So absorbed were we all in the Major's narrative that we were as if hypnotized, and no one stirred until the end, when the Major seized a stick and, with the litheness of a boy of twenty, made for the snake.

This, then, was the beginning of a friendship that led on to the moment when I said solemnly: "It is very, very wrong, Major, not to preserve the account of a life so full of value and interest as yours. If only for the sake of your lovely young granddaughter, Martha, the whole story should be told." The Major replied, "Will you help?"

INTRODUCTION

To say that I was deeply gratified ill describes my satisfaction. I knew well how the reticence of a brave man too often proves an insurmountable barrier against either admiring personal persuasion or the clamour of public curiosity; and a further obstacle in this case had always been the perpetual motion of the object pursued, since the Major is such an unusually active person, leading a tremendously busy life, flying here and there and back and forth on important missions; and when called in consultation on momentous matters thousands of miles from Los Angeles, starting off at a moment's notice, so that the moss of memoirs could hardly be looked for on this rolling stone. But at last the moment had come! To be sure, my competence for my proud task was much like that of the Irishman when asked if he could play the fiddle at a dance: "Shure an' I wull thot! Fer isn't it mesilf is afther *watchin'* it many's th' toime?"

Thus a joyous adventure began for me, while the Major found himself driven along a hard road with a relentless whip ever on his flanks, having learned straightway that it was himself and not I who was writing his story.

He would sit at his desk with the air of a determined martyr while his merciless prodder kept urging, "Tell about this!" and "Tell about that!" and when he handed the pages over with a patient sigh, my reproachful voice would keep on prodding: "You have neglected to put in the best part!" "Why do you leave out that?" "Where is the liaison between this adventure and the next?" "Fie! Fie! Major, you are too modest! Back must go every one of those I's you are eternally dodging"—for, alas! I discovered that even a superlatively courageous man has his fallibility. The Major, the brave Major, is in abject terror of the small pronoun I. Yes, I have seen my hero fairly squirm, and his teeth almost chatter at sight of that diminutive black object, but I have remained adamant on that point, for well I know that if the Major were to be given his way with that little pronoun, this book would have been written so that the dear Dumb Reader would never get so much as the ghost of an inkling as to whom it is all about.

INTRODUCTION

Of the Major's comrade-at-arms through all his wars and wanderings, he wrote to me:

In boyhood it was my greatest good fortune to meet a girl who truly believed in me and that I would carry out the wild schemes and plans which I confided to her. Fantastic as those dreams were, nearly every one has come true. The vision of all she would be called upon to endure amid appalling circumstances was mercifully hidden from her young eyes, nor could she foresee how tragedy and sorrow would some day test her soul as by fire; yet, throughout all the hard experiences of our years together, no resentment of destiny ever showed in her manner or crossed her lips.

A gentle heart, a pleasant voice, a loyal nature, with a wide understanding of life as it is—she has indeed met every situation with supreme courage and continues to be a clear fountain of inspiration to me and to all who know her.

Heartily can I echo my young daughter's dictum after a visit we had enjoyed from the Burnhams—"Yes, Mother, the Major *is* very wonderful, but Mrs. Burnham is *still more wonderful.*"

MARY NIXON EVERETT.

ARDEN ROAD,
   PASADENA, CALIFORNIA.
     June 1, 1925.

SCOUTING ON TWO CONTINENTS

SCOUTING ON TWO CONTINENTS

CHAPTER I

THE MAKING OF A SCOUT

MY ADVENTUROUS ancestors, migrating from England during the turbulent religious wars, carried a fierce love of freedom and great physical energy into the New World.

My father, Edwin Otway Burnham, was born in Kentucky, his Connecticut grandfather with his Virginia bride having already pioneered "across the Ridge." The family of my mother, Rebecca Russell, did not reach America from England until after the Black Hawk War. They pioneered to the then extreme frontier beyond the Mississippi, where, at a hamlet called Le Clair, my mother studied the three R's in the same little log schoolhouse with Colonel Cody—"Buffalo Bill."

In 1862, the black tornado of the War of the Rebellion was sweeping the land, and the young and strong were being sucked into its path from all parts of the country. Out on the frontiers of Minnesota, the few settlers who remained kept their holdings in constant peril from hostile Indians. Emboldened by the depleted condition of the settlements and stung by repeated deceptions and injuries suffered at the hands of the whites, two thousand Sioux under Chief Red Cloud swooped down on the Minnesota pioneers at New Ulm, setting fire to the town and killing and scalping the inhabitants.

At this time, my parents had just moved from Tivoli, on the Indian Reservation where I was born, to our new homestead some twenty miles from Mankato. As our home lay in the path of the raiders, my father left at once for Mankato for powder and bullets to protect his family, in case of need. He found three thousand terrified settlers, scantily armed, huddled in the town in instant expectation of attack. He was, therefore, unable to procure any ammunition to carry away for his own use.

Left alone in the log cabin except for myself, an infant of two years, my mother was keeping a sharp lookout for any sign of hostiles. Not many nights earlier, she had seen the sky turn red and learned soon afterward of the burning of New Ulm, where three hundred men, women, and children had been tortured and slain. Early one evening, as she stood in the doorway brushing her hair, she suddenly spied with horror a band of Indians moving out of the timber along the creek, not far away. Realizing that she could never escape if hampered with her baby, she decided instantly to hide me in a stack of newly shocked corn. The corn was too green to burn, and if I should make no outcry, I might escape discovery. So she tucked me into the hollow depths of a shock and earnestly adjured me to keep perfectly still, not to move or make the slightest sound until she should return. As she was young and strong and exceptionally fleet of foot, she managed to reach some hazel bush on the edge of the clearing just as the Indians surrounded the cabin. She saw the hostiles hunting all about, and then some of them started on her trail, but she was hidden by the cottonwoods as she moved swiftly along the stream. Through the increasing darkness and her desperate speed, she succeeded in outdistancing her pursuers and reaching a barricaded cabin six miles away, but long before she reached safety she saw the flames of her own home rising to the sky.

At daybreak the next morning, she returned with armed neighbours to look for her baby. She found me, as she often loved to tell, blinking quietly up at her from the safe depths of the green shock where I had faithfully carried out my first orders of silent obedience.

The burning of New Ulm and other horrors perpetrated by

THE MAKING OF A SCOUT

the Indians were promptly avenged by the pioneers. Under Governor Sibley of Minnesota, punitive measures were taken, the details of which are celebrated in Minnesota history. On December 26, 1863, thirty-eight Sioux chieftains were tried and condemned to death by hanging at Mankato. I remember hearing my parents relate vividly how the braves met their fate singing the Sioux war song; undaunted, exultant, and defiant to the end. A pioneer of New Ulm, whose sick wife and children had been burned alive by the Indians, was given the precious privilege of cutting the ropes that let the thirty-eight warriors drop into Eternity.

Those were rough days and fierce resentments. To-day, recalling all the crimes of the Indians, which were black enough, one cannot but cast up in their behalf the long column of wrongs and grievances they suffered at the hands of the whites. Then hatred dies, and I can entertain the honest hope that they have all reached the Happy Hunting Ground of their dreams.

But the dark side of the lives of the pioneers, measured in terms of tragedy and hardship, violent feuds and religious intolerance, and Indian massacres, does not tell the whole story. The daily tasks, the hours of relaxation, the eternal love theme woven by joyous youth into the scheme of things —these made up the sunshine of those days.

The years following the return of the soldiers from the Civil War brought to Minnesota strong and able hands to assist the settlers. New houses, barns, roads, fences, made their appearance. My father, having constructed a house of sawn lumber, decided to tear down our log cabin and build it over into a barn. A recent flurry of snow covered a shallow, icy pool lying between the cabin and the barn site. My mother suggested hitching up the team to move the logs, but for answer, Father, who was a very strong man, swung a log on his shoulder and started with it toward the site. Mother and I turned away toward the house. Glancing back, I saw Father slip on the snow-covered ice and, as he went down, the great log fell upon him. It crushed his lung so that he spat blood, yet a few days later he insisted that he was quite well enough to go into the timber with the team. He drove home in a howling blizzard, and a cold settled on the injured lung and persisted so long that he was finally persuaded to go to California for a cure.

Our little family of four started west in the winter of '70, crossing the state line in January, 1871. It was a two weeks' trip from the Mississippi River by the new railroad. Buffalo were still to be seen along the way. Extra provisions were carried by each train in case it should be snowbound indefinitely. Considering all the difficulties that had to be overcome and the meagre equipment for the task, that first railroad to California was and still is a monument to the builders. Constructive courage of the highest order was called for in every mile of its length.

How shall I write of California, the new world into which I dropped as from a cloud at an age when every scene and every event left its vivid imprint on my memory? The rugged qualities acquired in Minnesota found themselves expanding in a glorious atmosphere of ease. Yet soft and golden as life in California appeared to be, I soon found that it would require just as much energy to succeed there as in the sterner land of my birth. Moreover, every phase of my new experience seemed impelling me to take desperate chances. Years later, I found much of the same recklessness prevalent in South African life. I sometimes wonder if this pioneer spirit of high adventure—what scientists might call our peculiar racial urge—has been swept away for ever by the vast wave of alien immigration in recent years. I hope not!

As my father was searching for health, we journeyed from place to place and at every ranch found hospitable doors standing wide open. Each hacienda was a principality in itself. To my boyish fancy, the whole world was bounded by the mountains at the back of us and the broad blue sea in front. The thousands of horses and vast herds of cattle move again through my memory as I saw them in those days. All the incidents of the new life keenly interested me—the fiestas and fandangos, the hard riding, and the great rodeos where the annual crop of beef hides was gathered and shipped in strange old vessels or small coast steamers to some distant region inhabited by Yankees, peculiar beings, of whom Californians thought vaguely or not at all. We lived simply. We had little money and cared less about it. Nature was bountiful, the acres were broad, the boundaries very dim. There seemed to be plenty for all. For the greater part of the year, California was one long summer afternoon.

I was first under fire when about ten years old. My father undertook to act as arbitrator between some Mexicans and Americans who were having a fierce contest over the boundaries of one of the old Spanish land grants in Contra Costa County. We drove to a Mexican rancho in an old buckboard, and my father talked to the Mexicans for some time, in an endeavour to bring about a peaceful settlement of the difficulty. One of the Americans concerned—an old man who was very keen to find out the result of the conference—had, without intending any harm, trailed along behind us and taken up a strategic position on a hillside, where he sat waiting for my father to come back with his report. On our return from the rancho, several of the Mexicans, mounted and with loaded rifles, followed along behind us. We had travelled perhaps a mile or two when we came to the old man sitting on the hillside. The suspicious Mexicans at once concluded that my father was in collusion with the Americans instead of acting as a disinterested go-between, and they immediately opened fire, both on the old man and on our horse and buggy.

The sharp crack of the guns and the little spits of dust flying up several feet in the air where the bullets struck all around us made a very vivid impression on my boyish mind, and when I saw the old fellow throw up his arms and fall down the side of the hill, I was quite sure I had seen my first man slain in battle. At the splatter of bullets and the ricochet of one that hit the buggy tire, our horse bolted down the road at a tremendous pace. Fortunately, some distance from the scene of the shooting, we were stopped by a gate in the road.

We then went back to pick up the corpse of the old man. We found him alive and unscathed. As he was unarmed he had simply adopted the ruse of throwing up his hands and falling over. The Mexicans, thinking they had killed him and not wishing to follow up the fighting any further, had retreated to their ranches. Although the little battle proved a bloodless one, it stirred my pulses in a most lively manner and indeed influenced my entire career. Assuredly no knight ever received his accolade with a more definite thrill.

The death of my father in 1873 compelled me to join somewhat in the new order of things and take up the strenuous life. My mother's health had broken, and as my brother Howard was but three years old and I not yet thirteen, there was no visible support for the family. But when some kind uncles offered us all a home in the East if we would return, I determined to stay in California and make my own way. A friend in Los Angeles, a Mrs. Porter, lent my mother the money to pay her fare east. I set myself the task of repaying this, to me, vast sum of money—one hundred and twenty-five dollars. At the age of thirteen, I became a mounted messenger for the Western Union Telegraph Company. Their wire ended in the old pueblo of Los Angeles, and their messages were carried by means of swift horses to all the outlying towns and haciendas within a radius of thirty miles. I supplied my own mounts for this work, and they paid me twenty dollars a month for the regular run; but when I had to ride outside and at the dead of night, as I frequently did, to Lucky Baldwin's Ranch or to Santa Monica, Anaheim, or San Pedro, I got extra pay. It was not long before I was able to wipe off the slate all but the lasting debt of gratitude which I still owe to the kind Mrs. Porter. While doing this work, I first discovered that I had more endurance than other boys. I found that I was able to change horses and stay in the saddle, not only all day, but far into the night, often tiring out four horses of my own in the course of the ride.

This experience did not last long, and served mainly, no doubt, to whet my appetite for adventure. My greatest pleasure was in wandering over the mountains in the country that is now bounded by the two lines of railroad running into Los Angeles.

At that time, the great wagon trains of bullion were coming in over the deserts from old Cerro Gordo. Along this route, I explored and hunted, often alone for weeks at a time. For sharpening the perceptions and enabling a man to concentrate his mind for hours on one thing without change, I believe a certain amount of solitude is necessary.

During this time, I came in contact with many of the old Indian fighters from Arizona and saw the famous General Crook. He chatted kindly with me and set me afire to reach the still little-known frontiers of Arizona and old Mexico. At this period, the career of the bandit Vasquez held a place in the attention of California similar to that once enjoyed by Captain Kidd on the Atlantic Coast or Jesse James in the West. On one of my hunting trips into the Tejunga when I was a boy of thirteen, I had staked my horse for the night in a little side cañon near my camp. About four o'clock in the morning, I left camp to watch a water hole for deer. Coming back after sunrise, I found that, while I was gone, someone had stolen my horse. Noticing the marks of small boot heels, I concluded that the thief was a Spaniard or Mexican; there was also evidence that the horse had been taken only a few minutes before my return to the camp.

The horse trail out of the cañon made a great bend. By climbing a steep ridge and running hard, I believed I could cut into the cañon again and reach the trail ahead of the horseman. So I climbed and ran desperately for two miles and reached the cañon probably not more than five minutes behind my horse and his new rider. Much chagrined, I slipped along the trail until I saw by the tracks that the horse was now being urged to faster speed than his usual running walk, so that I must abandon all hope of catching up with him. I then turned aside at a wood-chopper's camp. The Mexicans there had seen my horse and told me it was Vasquez who rode it. This did not tend to lessen my indignation, and had the famous Vasquez been five minutes slower, he would have been popped off his mount as quickly as any common horse thief.

From this time on, I nursed my grievance and felt a lively personal interest in the exploits of the bandit, who was then using Los Angeles as his base of action.

Not long after this, my friend Arthur Bent and I were walking along Figueroa Street, intending to go swimming in the zanca near by. Incidentally, most of the townspeople drank water from this same reservoir, but that was of no concern to us. The day was hot; the dust deep. We saw a farm wagon jogging slowly along. On either side of it rode armed men so covered with dust that we could not recognize any one. Inside the wagon, on some straw, lay a man with bloody clothes. Another knelt, fanning the wounded man.

Arthur exclaimed, "I'll bet they have caught Vasquez!" The officers would not tell us, whereat our suspicions increased. We forgot all about our swim in the zanca and trailed along in the dust after the wagon until we reached the old adobe jail on Spring Street. There we learned from the jailer, Mr. Clancy, that it was indeed the great Vasquez. We had the scoop on all the other boys and felt tremendously important over it. Clancy had a warm spot in his heart for boys and told us fully how the posse had cached in an old ox cart and had impressed the Mexican driver to take them up to the adobe house of Greek George, on the La Brea Ranch; where, as Vasquez jumped out of a window, the posse shot him full of holes before he could be captured. A jealous woman had betrayed his whereabouts to Sheriff Rowland.

Vasquez was taken into a large, comfortable room in the jail, and surgeons worked over him conscientiously for six weeks to get him into prime condition for hanging. This event came off in San Jose—the scene of his first killing. He would have needed a neck as long as a giraffe's to be hanged in every hamlet where he had snuffed out a life. While he was in the Spring Street jail, Clancy let a few of us boys in to see the celebrity. On one of these visits I asked Vasquez about my black horse which he had stolen in Tejunga and told him of my effort to cut him off. He assured me that he would not have taken the horse if he had realized it belonged to me, and laughingly added, "I will give you a better horse. Ride mine now. Some day you will be a great robber like me—but never trust a woman." To my immense satisfaction, Sheriff Rowland let me ride Vasquez's pinto horse around Los Angeles—sweet balm for the wound I had suffered in losing my own.

I have still in mind a boy's vivid picture of Montgomery Queen's circus in Los Angeles—still to me the greatest circus ever on earth! On its departure, a lot of us started violent circus stunts of our own. At that time, there were still big sycamores along Aliso Street, where we held forth, walking the tight rope and training our livestock to startling feats.

An old fellow who came to look on at our performances confided to me that he had been a scout—an intelligence officer under Zachary Taylor in the Mexican War. He showed me with sand and corncobs how forts were built "according to Vauban." Sober, he was a most taciturn man, but when plied with liquor he became very communicative and would recount amazing adventures I cultivated his friendship and naturally sought him in his expansive moods. He became a hero in my boyish mind, and I fed on his tales of fighting and scouting.

One day when he was very drunk, he got into a terrible fight on Alameda Street with another powerful man who finally threw him and started to beat out his brains with a cobblestone. I stood by so paralyzed with horror and fright that I never thought of doing anything to help. Suddenly Juan Abbott, a boy about my own age, rushed by me shouting, "Won't you help a friend?" He dashed into the scrap and pulled off the man with the cobblestone. Twice this aggressor jumped up to attack again and twice Juan tripped him. Meanwhile my old soldier friend, covered with blood, made his escape. My humiliation was intense. Juan had saved my friend while I had played a miserable, cowardly part in the affair. That query of Juan's, "Won't you help a friend?" burned into my brain like a hot iron and I believe has caused me to act quickly many times in later life when help was needed.

There came a time when I realized that I must have some education, so, when an uncle living in the Middle West sent for me, I set forth, at the age of fourteen, and landed in a little town on the banks of a great river. Lest my statement about its good people should even now wound their feelings, it shall be called Montville. It was a flesh-and-blood replica, including the cuticle, of many little Puritan villages, but without the broader vision which New England communities acquired through having as citizens retired seafaring men or men of wide affairs from such places as Boston or New York. The town was just old enough to have lost its rugged pioneers and Indian fighters and had become a strange combination of materialism and intolerant religiosity. When the inhabitants were not trying to reform one another, they were wholly bent on making a lot of money. In this town I remained long enough to get one year of schooling.

In order to carry on any sort of normal boyish activities, it seemed necessary to lead, not merely a double life, but a quadruple one. Sunday was an awful day. No one dared swim in the river, fish, or go boating. Baseball or football on that day would have led to immediate arrest. The youth of the village were like steam in a boiler with a big fire underneath and no safety valve. They were at the point of explosion, and I was the ready firebrand. I offer my apologies to-day to the mothers of that village for completely shattering their nerves. What with the fleet of dugout canoes built by the Trappers' League and our secret Indian Tribes formed for special raiding, those women never knew what might happen next. A strange new cult was introduced as a substitute for the Sun Dance of the Indians. We hardened ourselves by lacing each other with hickory or hazel switches until we were able to take any ordinary flogging without moving a muscle or shedding a tear. We made moccasins, dug caves in the sand pit, bought twenty-two pistols, got hold of several rifles, waged war on the paper-mill gang, and carried on other momentous affairs too numerous to recount now.

Through all this nonsense, matters were coming to a real

crisis with me. Games began to pall. I felt an urge to do bigger things. I had my own living to make, and I realized that the dreams of great African adventures that I had secretly dreamed from childhood could not yet be made to come true. My numerous relatives all wanted to plan my life for me, while I had definite and different ideas of my own. The consensus of opinion was that I should have a strong-handed guardian who would see that every hour of my day should bring its appointed task and who would give constant attention to my spiritual instruction; that I must abandon all connection with the "Tribe" and adopt what would be, for my nature, the equivalent of a monastic life. I conscientiously tried this for a time, for I was under moral obligation, as well as financial, to repay to my uncle the cost of a year's schooling and my transportation from California. I was then started out on a commercial line about as fitted to my taste and talents as composing music or making lace would have been.

I cut the knot of all my difficulties by taking to the great river in a canoe, one dark night. Then, abandoning the river, I headed for the plains—the Southwest and Freedom.

CHAPTER II

FIRST LESSONS IN SCOUTING

WITH my ruling passion for life in the open and for the wild and beautiful in nature, no charm could hold me long against the lure of New and Old Mexico and Arizona—fascinating regions then on the outskirts of civilization and with a picturesque life of their own, now past and done with.

It was on the frontier of Arizona that I met the man who first gave me definite instruction in scouting. His name was Holmes—a peculiar and erratic character who had served under John C. Fremont, Kit Carson, and other great scouts. He was an old man then, and physically impaired, but his mind was exceptionally keen. He was given to moments of violent temper and seasons of moroseness; largely the result, I believe, of certain terrible sufferings he had endured in the deserts of Altar, in Mexico.

Fearing his end was not far off, and having lost his entire family in the Indian wars, he was desirous of finding someone to whom he might impart the frontier knowledge he had gathered throughout his long life. He chose me, then a boy of eighteen, as his companion and pupil. For six months he took me into the mountains of Arizona, New Mexico, and Sonora, Mexico, and with infinite patience taught me the details of trailing and hunting that make up a scout's work.

He impressed upon me that in the performance of even the simplest thing there is a right way and a wrong way. This truth he applied to such things as putting on or taking off a saddle, hobbling a horse, drawing a nail, braiding a rope, tying a knot, making a bed, protecting one's self from snakes or from forest fires, from falling trees or from floods. He showed me how to ascend and descend precipices, how to double and cover a trail, how to time myself at night, how to travel in the direction intended, and how to find water in the deserts. All this instruction was given with endless detail. We spent hours around our camp fire at night while he related tales and incidents, all bearing on the scout's life he had led from boyhood. Much of this information, unfortunately, I could not absorb, but many of the golden grains he so patiently offered me I hoarded carefully. Many times, in emergencies, his remembered words proved the deciding factor between my destruction and my survival, and I have gratefully given credit to his wisdom whenever I have been able to save lives entrusted to my leadership.

About all that is left in our memory of such old pioneers are some of the more dramatic incidents in their careers, but I feel that it would be of more real interest and importance to us to recall their methods of meeting their problems as they arose day after day and the deep romantic and philosophical ideals wherein they entrenched their hearts. Such characters are worthy to be remembered as long as the nation endures, not only for what they did, but for what they knew and thought.

In Prescott, Arizona, I met another old scout named Lee, who taught me many things. He had a prospect down in the Santa Maria country, and wishing to get some samples for assaying, he took me along with him. It was a rough desert land of wide mesas covered with boulders or lava and cleft by tortuous cañons hundreds of feet deep. At the bottom of these cañons were small streams making deep holes under the cliffs, never touched by the sun's rays. The trout in these holes were almost as dark as the basalt walls that held them. Along the shoulders and benches, protected from the cold winds of the mesa, grew acres of mescal; and in among the rocks and boulders was much gramma, or bunch grass, with here and there clumps of cedar and many desert shrubs. To hunt the wily Apache in such a labyrinth was no easy task.

Lee was one of General Crook's scouts, and his success in locating these bands of hostiles was due to his intimate knowledge of their mode of life, and especially of their method of preparing mescal. This is a species of aloe with a heart about the size of a very large turnip. It is the duty of the squaws to gather the mescal, trim off the thorny leaves, and pile bushels of the hearts into great mounds of boulders on which a fire is kept burning for about five days. The heat of the boulders gradually roasts the mescal, bringing out the sweetness and nourishment. These baked hearts are then patted out in cakes, dried on racks of small cedar poles or willow sticks, and made ready for carrying in fibre bags or rawhide lacings. They taste somewhat like baked turnip, but are sweeter even than sweet potato. They are very nourishing, but are full of fine fibres which the Apache chews and spits out, much as sugar cane or sorghum is eaten and disposed of by the negroes. It is also a custom of the Indians to gather each year one big pit full of mescal to be fermented into a strong drink, called tiswin, and to wind up the harvest season with one grand, glorious drunk.

Lee had made a careful study of the air currents that sweep through the deep cañons, and although the Indians found ways to conceal the telltale smoke clouds, they could not prevent the odour of burning mescal from hanging in the air and drifting for miles up and down the cañons. By tracing these odours, Lee could mark the most secret hiding places of the Indians. As they could not delay the harvest of the mescal or be content to live without it, they were inevitably spied out by him, then surrounded by government troops and captured. Sometimes the odour of the mescal could be detected as far as six miles from its source. The chewed fibre was another evidence to the scout of the whereabouts of the Indians; but if the Apaches were suspicious of pursuit, they would not drop a single thread of mescal and would step from boulder to boulder, leaving so faint a mark on the rocks that only the most highly trained eye would ever notice the trace. With a little dried venison, beef, or horse meat and his roast mescal, the Apache seemed to be supplied with a balanced ration. On this slender fare, as frugal as that of the Bedouins of Arabia, they managed to lead their enemies a maddening chase and to inflict many defeats.

It is imperative that a scout should know the history, tradition, religion, social customs, and superstitions of whatever country or people he is called on to work in or among. This is almost as necessary as to know the physical character of the country, its climate and products. Certain people will do certain things almost without fail. Certain other things, perfectly feasible, they will not do. There is no danger of knowing too much of the mental habits of an enemy. One should neither underestimate the enemy nor credit him with superhuman powers. Fear and courage are latent in every human being, though roused into activity by very diverse means.

If, as a nation, we had the courage to write the pages of history as the events really occur, there might be some changes in value very startling to our cherished beliefs; but many errors are so firmly planted in the public mind that it is sacrilege to disturb them, and where they are harmless, it is probably better to let them rest. The idea that the Sioux Indians could fight the modern soldier without any training is an error of the same cloth as the recent pronouncement of the late William Jennings Bryan that "an army of a million men can leap to arms between the rising and the setting of the sun." Armies are not made in that way. The old Sioux warriors who pitted themselves against such generals as Custer, Reno, Miles, and Crook all passed through much preparatory training. To begin with, they hardened the body systematically. They controlled the mind and set it on a definite object unswervingly. They well knew the uses of both love and hate in all their shades and degrees. Around the council fires, traditions and tales were poured into the ears of the Indian boy until the time arrived when he demanded to become a warrior. Each spring, a class of candidates would come before the medicine man for physical examination. If not strong enough, the youth would be sent back to the care of the squaws for another year. Those who passed the tests were put in close training, both mental and physical, until, on some clear, sunny day in June, the whole clan or tribe would gather on a slope of the prairie near a stream and pitch their tepees for the Sun Dance of the young braves.

When the exhausting test was ended, the youths were carefully tended by the squaws and nursed back to full strength in a few days. They were then passed over to the hands of older warriors for training with bow or gun, lance and horse, and in all the intricate lore of the plains. When they became proficient, they were divided into bands and sent to ambush each other's horses and equipment, also to manœuvre on a large scale under the orders and eyes of the great chiefs. If to the qualities and training possessed by these men had been added modern artillery and weapons, one would hesitate to guess how many of our troops would have been necessary to conquer them.

In the literature of the West, the hero, bad man, or sheriff is usually endowed by high Heaven with superhuman powers and has not found it necessary to go through long dreary months and years of training, like ordinary mortals; but I have never, in my experience, met either savage or white man whose natural traits without careful development would have made him distinguished. There are, however, great differences in ability, even among Indians. Those who become famous add to their natural inheritance long training in many things, especially in the hardening of the mind and body to stoical endurance. The great Indian chiefs were men of iron will as well as iron bodies.

I have often thought it would be well for the nervous European to cultivate a little of Oriental calm and self-control and with "Kismet" as his password, relax both mind and body at times and learn to sleep soundly even in the midst of danger. Lord Roberts had this rare power, and it was one of the things that enabled him to devote forty-one years to the service of India and at the age of sixty-eight to take active command of a great army in a new field. In the anxious hours when all Europe seemed combining to wage war on England, Lord Roberts could retire to his camp wagon in the midst of an action and sleep dreamlessly for six hours. To sleep at will is a fine art.

I have often been asked how it happens that I neither drink

nor smoke. My answer is that both liquor and tobacco have their uses, but I am of a nature that has never required a stimulant or a sedative. As a scout, I needed all my five senses and every faculty of my mind at highest efficiency at all times. There is nothing that sharpens a man's senses so acutely as to know that bitter and determined enemies are in pursuit of him night and day. In many lines of endeavour, errors may be repeated without fatal results, but in an Indian or savage war, or in a bitter feud, one little slip entails the "Absent" mark for ever against a man's name. I recall one scout who forfeited his life by his neglect for one instant to keep in the shade of a small oak tree. He was safe from sight so long as he kept in its shadow, but he became so intent on using his field glasses that he allowed a shaft of sunlight to betray him to the enemy.

The senses and actions of every animal, bird, and insect, if studied, can be made to pay tribute to our store of human knowledge, and our own rather dull wits can be wonderfully informed. Solitude intensifies the perceptions. The herd with a thousand eyes trusts itself to a solitary sentinel with only two. Yet there comes a point where solitude, which entails total repression of the social instinct, turns upon its victim and destroys the alertness of brain it has built up; when, like a great wave, it uplifts only to engulf. I have met solitary sheep herders in the West whose eyes clung to the ground and who mumbled unintelligent words for hours at a time. Solitary confinement in prison brings insanity. Overtrained athletes become muscle-bound, and solitude in excess may make one thought-bound.

I am sometimes asked how it is possible for a scout to live for months in an enemy country, and how horses can travel the astounding distances they do. A volume could be written on the training of a scout—and many volumes have been written on the care of horses. In every country, food can be found if the scout knows how to get it and if his stomach will lend itself to such adjustments as are sometimes necessary. When changing from a cereal diet to one wholly of meat, there is asually a terrible craving for bread that may last for six weeks, and when living on cereals alone, there is likely to be a constant desire for meat or fats in some form. But man's stomach, like his hand, can be trained to adapt itself to many strange uses.

In the Arizona days, one of our favourite ways of preparing food for long hard rides without fire in dangerous country was to dry venison and grind it to a powder, then mix it about half and half with flour and bake in a loaf that would fit our cantenas or leather saddle pockets. Ten pounds of this concentrated food would, at a pinch, last a man ten days and keep him in strength, albeit lean and hungry. In the North, the great stand-by of Indians and trappers is pemmican. This is dried meat, finely powdered and put up in animal fat. In the Boer War the iron ration given us was made of four ounces of pemmican and four ounces of chocolate and sugar. On this, a man could march thirty-six hours before he began to drop from hunger. All American frontiersmen are familiar with the Indian's bag of parched corn and with pinole, a Mexican preparation of corn differing but slightly from the "johnnycake" of Colonial times.

In Africa, even in the tropics, one can live very well on a diet of three parts milk to one part fresh blood drawn from cattle. This ration, with a little biltong, enables the Masai to raid a thousand miles. Camel's milk, goat curds, and dates give to the Bedouin of the desert his wonderful endurance. In the jungle of the Ashanti, the native survives on nothing more nourishing than bananas, yams, and fruit, but he is no match for the man of the desert or the meat-eaters of the high veldt.

A scout knows that a horse can thrive on most of the food that man eats, even cooked food. One of the reasons why I was sometimes able to outride the cowboys and frontiersmen of the West was that I gave infinite care to my mount. In Alaska and the Klondike our horses would eat bread, all kinds of dried fruit and vegetables, crackers, sugar, prunes, raisins, candy, syrup—even bacon, dried meat, and dried fish in very small quantities. They also ate raw eggs when obtainable, dried milk, and other

FIRST LESSONS IN SCOUTING

things not ordinarily thought of as fodder. The twig ends cut from willow and cottonwood give roughage and some strength. In the deserts a man may save his mount by gathering the fig-like fruit from the tops of the Pitahaya or Sahauro. The "Spanish bayonet" also has a good fruit. Horses will eat crushed mesquite beans, acorns soaked and ground, and other desert shrubs and seeds in season. There are bunches of gramma and other grasses clinging to the cliffs that can be gathered for the scout's faithful friend in time of need.

Water is sometimes found in deep, almost impenetrable cañons. It can be carried to the horse in a hat, a Navajo blanket, a piece of good canvas, or a bit of rubber cloth. If none of these is at hand, it is well to remember that a saddle blanket will absorb a gallon or two of water, and by turning it over and over in a ball as one walks or climbs, not much will be lost, and the greater part of the water collected can be wrung out into a hat or a cavity in the rock. If there is no rock at hand and the ground is sandy, the procedure is to mix some stiff mud at the water hole, carry it up to the horse, dig a hole in the sand and line it carefully with the mud; then soak the blanket or even one's clothes and wring the water into this improvised bucket. The horse will drink it gratefully. He can also easily be taught to drink from a canteen or bottle.

In timbered country at night, if bitter cold, a camp fire saves the horse as well as the man. Once, several of us were caught in a terrible blizzard in the Panhandle of Texas. We happened to have some green buffalo hides and we tied some of these over our horses. The skins froze as stiff as boards, but the thick hair saved the team, as other similar skins saved us, although many experienced plainsmen and their stock perished in this same storm. It is always well to save the strength of one's horse for that one last mad gallop which may mean success after long days of struggle, or escape when all seems lost. Nick Calvarabbias of California was one of the best judges I have ever known of the strength and mental power of a horse. He was the man who first taught me to look a horse in the face as I would a human and leave the search for obscure blemishes to the veterinarian. Courage and endurance make up for light weight and other defects. Many years later, in the Boer War, this schooling in the selection of mounts enabled me to make a three-day raid into the enemy country with a force of Colonial troops and bring back a great herd of beef cattle sorely needed by the main army, as well as many remounts and some prisoners. It was our horses that enabled us to accomplish the impossible.

CHAPTER III

THE TONTO BASIN FEUD

MY ABRUPT escape from my youthful perplexities at Montville was followed by a period of glorious wandering into Missouri, Kansas, Texas, and Mexico. For part of that time, I was joined by a Montville boy, Homer Blick, whose sister had been my boyhood sweetheart. His people had migrated farther west, and, after a while, Homer and I rode together from the cow country to see his new home. The schoolgirl sister still remembered me, and when again I rode into the wilderness, there was much in my heart to disturb my plans for the future—but I rode alone and far.

The buffalo were then disappearing from Texas. The silver camps of Arizona were opening. I made a small stake by driving a bunch of wild Texas ponies up to Missouri and selling them, and for a time thereafter revelled in spurs, sombreros, and all the picturesque equipment and life of a cowpuncher.

At last I found myself in Santa Fe. The place was dead and times very hard. I was soon broke and started on my last pony into the bad country that lay between Santa Fe and Arizona. Through my own carelessness, my mount was stolen from me in broad daylight on the outskirts of a town. I made a five-hundred-mile trip on foot and alone to Prescott, Arizona; much of the time travelling by night and sleeping by day, as the Indians were out on the warpath. The Mogollon Mountains were covered with snow. Food was scarce. The Indians had raided and driven off all settlers and stock. They almost had me, and the snow and cold of the Mogollons gave me a still closer call. A little creek filled with melted snow water across my track compelled me to swim. It was only about twenty feet wide, but my famished and exhausted condition made the feat seem as arduous as swimming the Hellespont. In spite of hardships, I found much in that trackless wilderness of intense interest to me—the Painted Desert, the forests of solid stone, and the curious cliff dwellings of the Verde.

My first work, after I reached Prescott, was with my friend the old scout Lee, already mentioned. About this time I met still another remarkable character, whom I shall not name on account of a certain blemish in his record and because his descendants are living, prosperous and respected, in Los Angeles at the present time. The fever for mining was now running strongly in my blood, and whenever I was not working for ready cash, I roamed the mountains, prospecting. From my new acquaintance I learned to assay ores and to handle a horn spoon and gold pan, as well as blasting powder and explosives of all kinds. The Mogollon Mountains fascinated me. Although they had almost conquered me, I determined to wrest from them their hidden treasure. From the days of Coronado, many had tried to do this, in vain. So far as I know, all, even to this day, have failed. Others have ridden, as I did, to the rock rim of the world and gazed into the depths below, climbing and delving into every cranny—to no end. My own venture cost me all I had made, and I came down into the warm valleys of Tonto Basin and Salt River to begin life anew.

There I ran across a family that had also been driven out of the Mogollons by the hard winter. Of their great herd of cattle not more than a hundred or so of the strongest had survived. They had taken up a homestead of land on Salt River and had built a brush house and a few corrals. Poor as they were, my wretched condition excited their sympathy and I was cordially invited to camp with them and rest my horse. My mount surely needed it; Don Quixote's steed was obese by comparison; if I had thrown my hat at him it would have caught on some projecting bone! As for myself, I must have matched my horse in appearance. My boots clung to my feet by courtesy only, and my clothes cried for help at every seam. My intended destination had been the new silver strike at Globe, but the kindly invitation to rest, with pasture for Rosinante and a square meal for myself, was gratefully accepted.

This hospitality and the consequent turning aside from my purpose forged the first link in a chain of events that for years I could not break. I became a thread woven into a strange and intricate pattern—a pattern sometimes bright and cheerful, but never altogether free of the black warp of crime and the red woof of bloodshed which made up so much of the fabric of life in Arizona and northern Mexico in those days. Trouble had long been brewing. Not only were the Apaches always sullen and often at war, but the cattle men were trying to drive out the sheep men—a cause of strife as old as the Eternal Triangle. Certain powerful politicians secretly encouraged a feud centring in Tonto Basin and extending into Mexico until it developed into a long and bloody conflict, resulting in the almost complete extermination of one faction. Into the main issue were injected many personal grudges. It was impossible to remain neutral, especially for one young, vigorous, and quick to champion the oppressed.

The family that had given me shelter on Salt River soon became my fast friends. The father and mother were elderly but rugged. There were a number of daughters, but there was only one son, so the main range riding had to be done by him with such assistance as his sisters could give. They were quite competent, and their aid was at times necessary to protect or to save the herds, for in those days range was held only by the very strong or the very swift. I soon became conscious of a strange undercurrent of mischief at the round-ups or in the dance halls of Globe. I sensed the growing struggle among the officials and politicians as to whether Arizona should be run by a few great cattle barons or by certain wealthy sheep men backed by allied interests in the towns. The worst thing about a feud is its unexpected ramifications; its confusing crosscurrents of passion. My life seemed no more than a twig of driftwood in a whirlpool. It was easy to believe in Kismet or to accept the iron march of events as portrayed in Greek plays.

I made friends especially with the old man—the father—who

was an expert rifle shot and used a double-trigger, long-range buffalo gun. I was constantly perfecting myself in rifle practice, and he gave me much valuable information as to light, shadows, windage, etc. While my horse was recuperating in pasture, I borrowed a mount from the old buffalo hunter and pushed on to Globe, where for a time I took part in some mining developments, but every few weeks I would return to the River and Tonto Basin to see my new friends. The feud was increasing in fury, and there were frequent killings. My friends tried to remain neutral, but at last it became impossible to do so.

They had borrowed money in Globe to carry over their cattle, and were ordered by their backers to join a certain faction and to kill or drive off all the stock of the other, or their own herds would pay the forfeit. The old man stoutly refused to obey, whereupon a certain faction bought up his store debts and, failing to get instant cash, attached his cattle. I turned over to him the little money I had made in the mines, but it was only a drop in the sea of his troubles. He decided to cache the cattle away in the mountains, and I left town and came out to help him. The only son, John, and I rode point and flank with the main herd; the girls, with the dogs, bringing up the gentle stock. The old man covered the trail with his long rifle. But two sharp young deputies, keen to make a name for themselves and possibly get a bunch of the cattle in payment, followed hot on our trail. They caught up with the girls. The barking of the dogs reached the ear of their brother. We let the herd go and galloped back. Needless to say, we would not let the deputies take away the girls' cattle. We had a wordy war; the girls claimed the animals as their personal property. One of the deputies dismounted. A dog promptly bit him. He shot the dog. Everybody drew—but only one more shot was fired. The deputy dropped dead and the other one threw up his hands. It was not known who fired—one of the girls, or John, or myself.

It is all ancient history now, but the fact is, it was none of us. It was the old man. He had trailed the deputies, and, with his long rifle, had killed his man at the astounding range of eight hundred yards. It would be a wonderful feat with a modern flat trajectory, high-power rifle. He was an old buffalo hunter—yet it was in all likelihood a chance shot with his black-powder rifle.

Thus Fate dealt us all a terrible blow. In that one act, a whole family and their best friend crossed the Rubicon that divides the law-abiding citizen from those who live beyond. The hour had now struck when, to gain protection from the law, it was indispensable to join one of the factions. This was done; arrangements were made to give up some of the cattle to the captured deputy, and, with his connivance, a tale was built up for the officials at Globe. It was not long before help was needed again by the feudists and had to be given, both in money and in personal service. At this time, I used to practise incessantly with the pistol, with both right and left hands, and especially from a galloping horse.

Our friends were being rapidly killed off. To my sorrow, I found that many of them deserved it. Sordid motives and black treachery are rampant in every gang of feudists, cattle thieves, and outlaws; although here and there great characters stand out—both the good and the evil. A feud is a terrible eye-opener to youth. It reveals the seamy side of life at the time of a boy's highest enthusiasms, and is very apt to make him cynical and pessimistic. He sees the cowardice in high places; the secret dread that follows a man like his shadow but, unlike the shadow, does not depart at night.

A feud is hard, too, on the women involved, and even the little children absorb the fear around them and show pathetic furtiveness. I recall a day when three of us, all heavily armed, rode up to a cabin on Tonto Creek and saw a little girl, about five years old, carrying a white pitcher of water from the spring to the house. When the child sighted us, she gave a scream, dropped the pitcher, and ran—not to the house, as a child ordinarily would, but to the creek bottom, shouting at the top of her voice, "Daddy! Here they come to kill you!" She already understood that her own presence in the cabin might deter her father from shooting an enemy. Fortunately, Daddy was not an impulsive man and was not disposed to open fire until quite satisfied that it was against a foe, but the little girl refused to come out of hiding until her mother's voice called with just the right ring of assurance.

In order to know life as it really is, it is necessary once in a while to be the under dog. In this Arizona trouble, I found myself on the losing side. After a time, as the legal authorities got control of things, some of the treacherous deputies were ousted and matters began to swing back to their normal status; but the scars of that Tonto Basin feud still mark the second generation, as any old Arizonian will acknowledge. More than forty years have passed since those days, but for fear that it might even now bring tears to some and rage to others, I shall not repeat names or assign blame. It was a harsh school of life—yet from this same belt of the West, Teddy's immortal Rough Riders were largely recruited. All that was really needed was a good cause and a good leader to transform outlaws into heroes.

A new condition now confronted me. Even in defeat, I still had enemies. A cloud hung over me. I moved warily and changed my name often. Throughout the Tonto feud, I kept one complete outfit in Prescott, where I not only had good clothes but loyal friends and a place where I could safely disarm and rest. I became liaison to certain men in Prescott, Globe, and the Basin. Here and there, I had glimpses of the highest powers of government in that region, and I saw that all of us were only pawns in the game. I made use of all the craft and cunning I had learned among the Indians, as well as the methods employed by such bandits as Vasquez. In those days, every little detail of a man's equipment was observed and remembered by those whom he met, and, of course, his horse and brand were especially noted. I took care never to ride a horse from one district to another, but established a cache and a friend in each district. I found that I could travel long distances on foot and very swiftly. I had worked in mining camps and knew the lingo. I could drive ox teams well enough to get a job. At times, I was a prospector with burros. Again,

I was a hunter of game on the Black Mesa. I learned by bitter experience to conceal whatever skill I had at arms. On more than one occasion, my boyish boasting had nearly cost me my life. The hardest things for me to disguise were my height and my eyes. Being young and slightly undersize, my best rôle was that of a tenderfoot from back East—a mere careless, harmless kid.

Throughout this period, there were many hours when I had leisure to clarify my thoughts, and, looking into the future, see a far different life from that which I had pictured to myself in California. As compared to Arizona, California seemed a free and happy country where Law reigned but, at that time, was not carried to the point of prescribing what one should say, write, think, eat, drink, love, or hate. The Reformers had not arrived, but if a crime was committed, the offender was usually captured and punished. Doors were not locked and women were safe always. But, in Arizona, my every turn was enmeshing me more completely in a network of rustlers, smugglers, and feudists. It was the twilight before the terrible night wherein stalk murderers, bandits, and all the grim underworld, which, once entered, grips a man in bonds that at first seem light as cobwebs but later have the cruel strength of steel.

About this time, a fine, hard-riding young Kansan, whom I had met on an Indian raid and whose nerve I had greatly admired, came to see me in Globe and asked me to ride out with him on the hill overlooking the town. He told me he had come to a momentous decision, after deep thought. He had been working hard for many months as night herder for a big outfit in the mining camp, and had held their horses and cattle, at great personal risk, against both rustlers and Indians. He had thriftily saved his earnings, as he thought, by not drawing them on payday. Now he had discovered that the company was a stock swindle and the property already mortgaged. Broke, penniless, and outraged, he was determined to reimburse himself. He said he knew where the superintendent of the mines had cached some good horses and quite a bunch of cattle; also, where any number more were to be found, of various brands. An emissary to him from the Curly Bill outfit in San Simón Valley had promised a cash market in Tombstone for any brand north of Globe and Phoenix. The Kansan needed a partner and proposed that I join him. In three weeks, he said, we could clean up a thousand dollars.

It looked easy. He was a cool, sober-minded young fellow who did not fall for the usual mining-camp diversions. In fact, his dream had been to save every dollar, go back to Kansas, and buy a farm. There was a girl waiting for him there. I believe the man would have carried out this plan if the mining swindle had not broken his faith in his employers and in big business men generally. The directors were men of standing in their home towns, but their bad faith was responsible for the desperation of this youth in Arizona and for blighted romance in Kansas.

We talked for two hours. He was convinced that there was no use in trying to make a stake in any legitimate way. "Six months of success, and then me for the farm for ever," was his declaration. I listened to him attentively I, too, was a financial failure. I had made quite a little pile, but it had all gone in tearing over the country in the Tonto Basin row. Even now, men were looking to "get" me. What matter if a few more were added to the list? There was much to consider, and I wanted to think it over. As we rode back to town, neither of us spoke. We were boys no longer. All that we had done before, even our fighting, had been romantic—incidental. Now, life had suddenly become real. Up to this time, we had been adventurers but not criminals. Our decisions had been made, not by our minds, but by our environment and the quick blood of youth. But this was different. We must decide as men.

I put my horse in a livery stable and took a room at a locally famous hotel. I walked along the street, trying to get his talk out of my mind, but the bright lights seemed dim; the town dull. At ten o'clock, I mounted my horse and rode up a lonely trail into the Pinal Mountains, then covered with pine trees. Here I off-saddled and lay down on my saddle blankets, but I could not sleep. I got up and paced to and fro in the night, and as I did so, pictures and visions rose before me. I saw Vasquez as he lay wounded in the Los Angeles jail and heard his clear voice telling me that some day I would grow up to be a great robber like himself, and never to trust a woman. Again, I saw the kindly features of one of the finest old-time citizens of Los Angeles, H. K. W. Bent, as he put his hand on my shoulder one day and asked, "Freddy, are you a good boy?" Many friendly faces drifted across my inner vision—relatives and others. If they knew what I was contemplating, how would they feel? I saw the dear eyes of one who had such wonderful confidence in me, such abiding faith, that no matter what ill reports flew about in that puritanical little town on the big river, she never ceased to believe that I was sound in mind and heart and would some day return and prove to the world that her intuitions had been right. Turning from these memories and thoughts, I confronted the possibilities of the future and visualized the grim fighting without quarter which lies before the man who, in the end, is cornered. I even decided that I would carry a small, keen stiletto, Spanish fashion, so that if I should use my last cartridge unwittingly, I could still end my own life by one quick thrust. I felt something of the swank and power that goes with supreme indifference to death. I had observed the dominance of fear over ordinary men; how the hearts even of the stout deputies would fail them at times, so that a rustler could ride them down without a gun leaving the holster on either side. As for the women, in every hamlet and town, they were then, as they have been throughout all history and ever shall be, responsive to the personal appeal. The very ardour of their assistance and confidence has often been a man's undoing. It is more often a woman's love than a woman's treachery that is the downfall of the outlaw. . . . By midnight I had repudiated the life of a horse thief, after picturing myself as hanged and all my relatives and friends disgraced. By one o'clock, I had become master of a mighty gang in an impregnable valley in Mexico, with the officials in the towns eating out of my hand. Did I not have before me the example of the great robber barons of days gone by and their successors of the present who somehow control the law? Yet, through all my arguments, I felt ill at ease. I had no fear of the Law, or Death, or the Hereafter. Long ago, one stern relative had told me that I feared neither man, God, nor Devil, and that I would inevitably come to a bad end. Perhaps my scruples were really a product of my blood—some ancient memory of refusal to do wrong—a message from honest ancestors in time of great mental stress.

The night wore on. I changed the picket of my horse and tried to sleep, wishing the darkness would last for ever, for it seemed to shelter me and delay the hated morning when I must look into the resolute eyes of my friend and give him my answer. More pictures came: my beautiful day dreams of following Stanley to the Mountains of the Moon and the inland seas of the Nile, through vast jungles and endless deserts to the lost cities of ancient tales; to say nothing of shooting big game amid the wonderful savage life of Africa Pages could be written of all that revolved through my mind during that long, long night, but in character it was probably what might pass through the mind of any normal, healthy youth suddenly confronted by a great, alluring temptation. From over San Carlos way, the first streak of dawn told me that my hour was at hand. Yet I had made no decision. This, in itself, was a new and painful experience, for by nature I make my decisions as quickly as the complete picture is flashed on the brain.

I rode slowly into town. The stage from Camp Bowie drove up. The Wells Fargo shotgun messenger, stiff with cold, climbed down. As I watched the mail sacks thrown out, I thought of loved ones and their letters. There might be one for me. It would come as an enclosure, addressed to the editor of the Globe *Silver Belt*. This man knew my real name and my people. He was a famous character in the old days of Globe, and the unsuspected well wherein a thousand personal secrets were safely hidden by citizens and citizenesses. He could be trusted to the grave. I decided to watch the delivery at the *Belt* office for what might easily be the last letter I should ever receive.

The editor handed me one short missive. It was not from mother or sweetheart, but from the puritanical uncle of the town by the big river. I had always corresponded with him through the editor of the *Silver Belt*. In some mysterious way, he had sensed through my guarded and optimistic letters that things were not going as well with me as they should. His few sharp sentences went through me like knives. "Duty before all," he wrote, and wound up with these words: "Remember you come of the wrong stock to make a villain." How did he guess that I stood with one foot on the Bridge of Sighs?

Now my mind began to clarify. I saw that my sentimental siding with the young herder's cause was all wrong; that avenging only led to more vengeance and to even greater injustice than that suffered through the often unjustly administered laws of the land. I realized that I was in the wrong and had been for a long time, without knowing it. That was why I had suffered so strangely in the Pinal Mountains.

When the hour came to meet my friend, we had another long talk. At one time it looked as if he might be persuaded to give up the whole enterprise, but his sense of injury had rankled too long. He turned away to the south, where he became the guiding mind of the San Simón Valley rustlers and made much more than his thousand dollars The end of the trail came for him in less than two years. Instead of the Kansas farm and his faithful sweetheart, he won a nameless homestead in the desert, two feet by six.

After this, it was only natural that I should turn to my friend, the editor of the *Silver Belt*. He did not know all that I had been up to, and I was loath to tell him, but his own career had made him wise and sympathetic. He advised me to throw off my Northern connections, gave me some helpful names in Tucson and Tombstone, and arranged to throw as much dust as possible on my trail. Most important of all, he put me in touch with some of the genuine though often obscure men who, in that land as in all others, are called "the salt of the earth." To one in particular he wrote a letter in such a way that, by tearing the sheet in two, neither half was intelligible by itself. The two pieces had to be fitted together in order to be read. He gave me one piece and sent the other by another route to his friend. This was much the same method of secrecy and safety as that employed in Rhodesia and other wild places in Africa, when we used to cut the Cape notes in half and send them to the Cape Town banks for collection. The two halves of a note were sent by different routes on different dates and nothing was paid until both arrived at the bank. Robberies and forgeries were made nil by this method. It was a modification of the split-stick of the savage and the ancient treasurer's receipt for taxes as given in England.

Tombstone was a wild and romantic camp. On presenting my letter, I found that I was in touch with a quiet, soft-voiced man—a gambler of the old type. Nowadays, he would probably be a realty broker. His games were all of skill and chance; his word was his bond; his percentage of profit was measured like any broker's on the stock exchange. His vaults held money in safe keeping for many friends and customers who would not trust the banks of those days. I found that he hated all stage robbers, rustlers, claim jumpers, smugglers, feudists, and criminals in general. He had a vision of the Arizona of the future as a land where no one would use a gun; where a child could carry a purse of gold untouched, and women could go anywhere unguarded. It sounded to me like the patter of some evangelist or utopian reformer. Yet I knew here was a man, practical and successful, who had disarmed one of the worst desperados in the country not a week before. There was in him some rare quality like that of Chinese Gordon who led a victorious army, himself unarmed. Possibly his immunity and his power were due to the very dislike felt by most armed men, unless totally depraved, for shooting an unarmed and fearless man, especially one whose demands are just and right.

He kept me as his guest for days and showed me the practical, common-sense way of looking at life. He convinced me that there were many quiet, decent folk who were getting more out of life than others were aware of. Finally, he won me completely by telling me how close he had come once to becoming a bandit and stage robber—describing just such mental turmoil as I had lately gone through on the big mountain. He showed me how to avoid trouble and wisely provided means for me to join the forces of law and order. I had a chance to make a good turn as guard for some of the silver mines discovered by the famous prospector, Dick Schieffelin. The owners needed quick and nervy men to keep off claim jumpers, and I could make worthy use of the unusual strength and endurance inherited from my ancestors.

But in one respect I failed to follow the advice of my friend of the *Silver Belt*. I wanted to hear the underground news of the Tonto feud, so I again put myself in touch with my friends there by mail. Very soon I received a long, pleading, tear-stained letter from one of the girls whose lover was in serious trouble. This sent me flying back over the long trail—only to find the tears all dried up and forgotten and another star shining in the sky. When I returned to Globe, the editor of the *Belt* gave me a terrible calling down, showing me how weak and silly I had been. His words stung like salt in a wound. In shame and desperation, I turned my horse's head again toward the Tombstone country.

CHAPTER IV

MY SMUGGLER FRIEND

WHEN I rode away from Globe, I did not know that a new thread, and an important one, was soon to be added to the pattern which fate and my own desires were weaving during those vivid years. As I was crossing the desert, I saw a slow-moving buckboard ahead of me and gradually overtook it. When about two hundred yards away, I saw that the driver was walking beside his rig—a sure sign that the horses were dead beat. But a more ominous sign was that the driver walked around the rig, placing it between us. I knew he had picked up a rifle—and he might be an excitable person and use it. So I rode parallel, thinking I would pass him and not hail. We watched each other for a time; then he beckoned me with his hat. I turned my horse around, showing my rifle on the saddle, dismounted, and led my horse up to the buckboard, which had stopped.

I found myself facing a man who looked the counterpart of Abraham Lincoln. Lying in the buckboard was a second man, seriously wounded—a brother, as I learned. Finding that my horse was gentle and could stand a rope, we tied an end to the buckboard tongue, and I took the turns on my saddle horn and thus saved the stranger's jaded horses on every sand patch and hill. It was eight miles to a water hole, but, fortunately, we had ample water for the wounded man and ourselves in our canteens. It was late at night when the staggering horses reached a little oasis. All the next day we rested.

The man told me his name was McLeod, and after one night's camp together, he explained many things to me. I learned later that he was the most noted and successful smuggler along the Arizona frontier. His brain directed men who never saw him. His agents reached from Mexico City to San Francisco. He had silent partnerships in several stores in Tombstone and Tucson, as well as interests in livery stables, stage lines, mail contracts, and mines. How he could carry on such diverse businesses and yet find time to pit his skill against the government sleuths of two nations is still a marvel to me.

The reason for this particular jaunt into the desert was that his brother, who lived in Nevada, had killed a man in a fight over what men have always fought for since the dawn of creation and probably always will. The woman in the case, being beautiful, had, like Helen of Troy, precipitated a local siege. McLeod's brother had escaped, well loaded with lead, from the burning jail, and had hidden for weeks in the Ruby Range of Nevada until a whisper of his situation reached the smuggler in Arizona, who had at once come to his rescue. It was no light undertaking for a man to escape from Nevada when once its wide-awake sheriffs had set out to get him. McLeod sent three outfits into the mountains with buckboards and stock, and his cleverness in having two of the dummies chased and captured while he and his brother made good their escape in the third was one of the most adroit pieces of strategy I have ever known. It baffled some of the best officers in the West.

McLeod did not conceal from me that a reward was on his brother's head. He was a man who could tell very much in a few sentences, and could extract from another the most essential knowledge by a few quiet questions. They would be asked in such a casual manner that one answered truly without stopping to think. The complete trust that he placed in me, not demanding an oath or hinting at any revenge for possible treachery on my part, gave me a new insight into the life we were leading in our little corner of the world.

It was decided that it would be best to leave his brother in Tucson while McLeod went on to Tombstone. So we exchanged outfits—clothes, names, horses—every scrap of paper and even our weapons. I may say here that, eventually, an able frontier doctor took the brother in hand and worked wonders. Meantime, I rode on again to Tombstone, then the most famous camp in America. There were strong cross-currents of interests in that region. Rich silver mines gave the life blood to a rapid development of railroads and other lines of enterprise. Curly Bill found here a market for his stolen stock, as did the smugglers for the goods they brought in from Mexico. The merchants, in turn, vied with the ancient and honourable pueblo of Tucson in supplying such smuggled goods as Mexico might require. The Earp Clanton feud was in full swing, as well as several mining fights over claims. The Old Bronco had, I remember, more than a dozen shallow graves around it, though the irony of fate decreed that it should prove the most barren claim on the hill.

By the whispering of the leaves, it came to me again that my good friends, the feudists of Tonto, needed me, and that a certain enemy was out to get me. I was warned that I should seek sanctuary at Dripping Springs, if possible, but that to remain in Tombstone would be perilous, perhaps fatal. I knew the men after me were hard-riding and relentless. The chances of remounts from Tombstone to Globe were not good, for it was the dry season, when range horses are in poor condition.* Besides, unshod horses cannot stand hard ground. The solution of my problem resolved itself into a one-man, one-horse proposition. My friend McLeod gave me an excellent horse and added a second rather poor one, with a small supply of jerky and pinole and a canteen of water and most minute instructions for my welfare.

It is difficult to explain and perhaps would be tedious to read all the details of a long, serious chase when both parties to the affair are skilled and determined men. To the hunted the first question is, *Who is in pursuit?* If a white man and of the towns, he may be counted on to do certain things; if an Indian of the plains, certain other things; if an expert frontiersman, his actions and movements will be quite different, and if a mountain Apache he will employ yet other strategy. The Malay, the savage of Africa, the Mexican—all differ in their actions, whether as hunter or hunted. In this instance, I knew I was followed by two very keen white frontiersmen. The inciting motive of one was to get me before I could give evidence in court concerning the sale of a certain stolen brand. I was an inconvenient connecting link, and my destruction might save him from prison. The fact that I was a close friend of his bitter enemies added zest to the chase. Besides, he had to make good his frequent boast that when he once took the trail he always got his man. My other pursuer had a still stronger driving power to send him over mountains and deserts—an insane jealousy, which is almost as potent and enduring as inherited hate.

It was fortunate for me at this juncture that I had a friend in McLeod. Smuggler that he was, he knew well the hearts of men and their weaknesses. His instinctive acuteness was similar to that possessed by Marion of Revolutionary fame and by Mosby and Quantrell of the Civil War. Some of his methods were baffling in their very simplicity. He instructed me to make inquiry openly of the road I intended to take and secretly about the one I did not intend to take, for my trailers had many sources of information and would probably be told of my secret inquiries. In any case, they would not suspect a youngster like myself of taking the trail over an openly avowed route. It was very important that I should gain a few hours of the night over them. Every horse in the town had been spotted by my enemies, and when McLeod's disappeared, they would learn for the first time that he was my friend. The darkness would cover my movements till morning, for, as was well known, I was not one to leave a trail that could be picked up by match, lantern, or torch.

McLeod gave me minute instructions how to make use of my led horse. The animal's home was in Tucson and he would, if turned loose, go direct to a certain corral there. I was to bring this about in the following manner. I was to take the road toward Pantano until break of day, then pick a rough gravelly ridge where I could feed my horses and cook and eat. There I was to take the shoes from my good horse and put them on the unshod and inferior steed. This done, I was to tie a few bits of cactus in a stout piece of canvas, fasten this securely to the latter's tail and head him toward Tucson. Said McLeod: "As the cactus hits against him, he will give a series of mad jumps, then he will settle into a run and finally slow down to walk without stopping until he reaches his corral in Tucson. You should allow three hours to change shoes and eat. By seven, you should have sent your spare horse on his way. Then mount your own horse, who will then be barefoot, set spur to him, and jump him off down a little cañon and into a sandy wash for about a mile. Then stop. In your pack you will find a set of shoes quite different from the ones you have just taken from this horse, yet made to fit him. Put the new shoes on him, then make a detour and turn toward the San Pedro River. You will gain it, with luck, in two days—or it may be four. Do all this so it will look as if you had been surprised by Indians just as you saddled up after resting and your barefoot horse had bolted while you had barely been able to head your own horse, plunging with fear, toward Tucson. Be sure to pick a gravelly point so there will not be left a discernible change in the shape of the barefoot tracks, and yet a clear tale of all that happens to the shod horse."

These instructions were carried out. I kept the food and barley left over from my first meal, and the next night camped on the San Pedro. My trailers did precisely as McLeod had foretold. They did not consider me old enough or wise enough to make use of the shoe-changing trick, and all that seemed written at the camp could be accounted for by a fright from Indians or any other cause, for even a pot of coffee spilled on a camp fire will sometimes stampede a pack train. They had followed my runaway horse clear to Tucson because, being badly scared, he had circled around every outfit and ranch house he sighted, which was just what they would expect me to do.

Meanwhile, by long and careful riding and great vigilance, I arrived in the Dripping Springs country, hid out my horse, made the agreed smoke signal, got the correct return signal, and came in to meet my friend John of the first Tonto episode. Instead, I found one of his sisters awaiting me. She had ridden across the shoulder of the Pinal Mountains. On the way, a bear had frightened her horse, which had plunged down the mountain through heavy brush, driving a dry stub of pine clear through the calf of the girl's leg. She was in agony and the leg terribly swollen. To add to the chapter of woes, she told me that John was under arrest and being railroaded to Yuma for cattle-stealing. It was because of this that she had ridden to meet me in his stead. Her old father had died suddenly. It was surely the "last of the Mohicans" for that family and brand. Because of her injury, she could not ride. She had already lain in hiding three days watching for my signal and had determined to delay appearing at the Dripping Springs stage station until the last possible moment.

On the Gila River there was a copper prospect owned by the Tweeds, and a bull train was camped there, resting the cattle, as feed was very short. One of the drivers, a California boy, recognized me. I persuaded him to take his lightest freight wagon and a few of his gentlest and strongest oxen on to the main road and camp there. Together we made a canvas stretcher and proceeded to carry the wounded girl out of the hills. Next day, the stage, in passing, halted at the sight of a woman on a rough-slung canvas bed being jolted over the uneven road. In the stage were two gay girls from the Bird Cage in Tombstone, en route to Globe. They quickly made arrangements with the driver and took our wounded girl along with them to their apartments in Globe, where they tenderly nursed her back to health.

One evening, as we drove back to the Gila River, my enemies rode past, but they had not counted on my travelling south attired as a cowpuncher, and did not recognize me. My California friend, who had cut signs for miles around, learned soon after that they had located my horse but left him where they found him, as bait, to catch me. They watched him patiently for two weeks while he ranged around to the south side of the Pinal Mountains and finally joined some miners' horses at the head of Mineral Creek. It was heart-breaking to have to abandon so well-trained and so swift a mount. The temptation to recover a favourite horse is so strong that foolish and even fatal risks are often taken. It needs infinite patience on the part of trackers to camp on a horse range in secret and keep careful tab on every man, afoot or mounted, who comes near a certain horse, on the chance that the owner may try to drive the animal off in the night or entice him to hand with a lump of sugar or with salt or grain. Most amateur sleuths and scouts would quit the vigil after three days, and many after one day, but an Apache will lie on a rocky point for many days and make no trail or sign. His whole equipment consists of a gourd of water, a piece of dried meat or jerky, and a little mescal, mesquite beans, or a handful of parched corn meal. Every film of smoke, dust cloud, or glint of light on the desert below will be noted, as well as the flight of every bird and the movements of the few desert animals. Patience, patience, and then more patience! The Indian scout will make a little buried fire of smokeless dry twigs, warm up the ground all the afternoon, bury the embers under the earth, and then lie on the warm spot until toward morning, when it will have cooled again. Then he will make a tiny fire of two crossed sticks, wrap his blanket around him, if he has one, and doze and freeze by turns until the sun once more brings warmth and another day of silence and watching.

What the white scout has to learn from the Indian is the power to endure loneliness, as well as stoical indifference to physical pain. The Boers of the high veldt, the Tauregs and Bedouins of the desert, and the Apaches, have this power in a superlative degree. Negroes and most savages, as well as many of the white races, are town dwellers by nature and have not the inner strength to meet this test of solitude.

I joined the freighters and returned to Globe, but was too late to help my friend John of the Tonto Basin. He died in Yuma. The mother soon afterward died in Globe. As I have said, the father was already dead. The younger sister married a Tonto Basin cattle man and died in childbirth. The wounded girl, finding the first real friends of her life, took up their mode of meeting the world. Three years later, the California friend who had helped me fetch her from the hills on the canvas stretcher met her in Tucson. They buried the past together and are now prosperous ranchers in California, with several children and many friends. Hers is the only happy ending I can record for any member of that unfortunate family caught in the toils of the Tonto feud.

Again I sought my friend, the editor of the *Silver Belt*. He insisted upon bringing about a meeting between my implacable and jealous enemy and myself, whereby a truce could be arranged and the dogs of the vendetta called off. This was not easy to accomplish, for I was bullheaded and vengeful. I had been hunted to the point where fear was dead and the lust to meet and finish my foes grew stronger every hour. The settlement finally effected gave me a still deeper view of the pit around whose crumbling edge I daily walked.

Returning to the South, I met McLeod and was offered a chance to carry messages for him along the front from Nogales to Guaymas and far into the mountains of the Sierra Madre and to the head of the Yaqui River. He did not ask me to do anything that would get me in wrong with the law, but eventually it would have tied me to a group of smugglers and gun-runners operating between El Paso and Los Angeles. I greatly admired McLeod. He knew I was loyal to him and a fast worker, not to be caught by the bottle or click of ivory. It is to his credit that he did not make use of me for his own purposes in his endless plots and schemes.

McLeod had the most amazing information in regard to frontier affairs. No fact seemed too small for his attention. He knew all the ordinary ruses to get letters and codes past the customs guards, and in addition had other methods that would do credit to the spies of any first-class European power. One of his means of communication was to put a few childish marks with a lead pencil on certain post-office boxes or on doorposts of hotels, railway stations, and tank houses. Shotgun shells loaded with different-sized shot, each one marked, conveyed a whole chapter of instructions to ships at Guaymas or to officials in Mexico City or the United States. "Adobe" dollars (Mexican) shipped in payment for goods often carried long messages and reports pricked on them with a steel needle and read by someone with the key to the code under his hat. It would be interesting to compare the elaborate modern military codes with some of the simple methods devised by McLeod in those frontier days, but at that time his knowledge of events always seemed to be days ahead of that of the customs guards of either nation. Light flashings with a mirror were known to both Indians and whites, but the late General Miles brought the first perfected helio into the Indian wars in 1886.

McLeod once said to me: "There are so many better ways of talking to your friends than by letters. I never write anything that couldn't be published in the Tombstone *Epitaph* the next morning. And quite a lot of news is sent out by way of that funny paper every day." This was the most boastful remark I ever heard him make.

I was always the last link in the chain with McLeod. One day, he called me into his place in Tombstone and, in a casual way, said: "The Apaches are on the warpath. I am anxious to send a message to some friends in Sonora beyond Fronterras, and I want you to carry it for me. Get ready for a ten-day ride and come to see me about dusk. You will start to-night."

There is an idea abroad in these days that the usual mode of procedure for an Indian scout was, after eating a hearty breakfast, to saddle up his broncho and, equipped with an extra belt of ammunition, a rifle, two six-shooters, and possibly a spy glass and a canteen of water, gallop over the mountains until he ran across some Indian sign; then dismount, hide his horse, and with incredible stealth creep up on a large band of deaf Indians. He would probably pot a few of the fiercest, and might then be chased for a mile or two on foot. On reaching his horse, he would vault to his back without touching stirrup and ride gallantly away, still carrying all his equipment and no lighter than when he started, except for the lead in the bodies of the dead Indians. A truer idea of what often occurred may be gathered from an account of my experience when McLeod sent me on this scout into Mexico.

At the appointed hour, McLeod equipped me with a swift but lean and bony horse, a comfortable but old and ragged saddle, an American bit with rope bridle reins, a bag of pinole in one cantina and a lot of pinoche and jerky in the other. Altogether, it made a queer-looking outfit for Arizona. He said: "You are a friend of George Woodward at Moctezuma and expect to work on his ranch. He is planting some California fruit trees. You have never seen him but knew his people in San Francisco." (This happened to be true.) "You must not have an outfit worth following, but in spite of looks, your horse is grain-fed and very tough. You can turn him loose anywhere and catch him with a piece of pinoche."

He instructed me to ride unarmed except for a sawed-off Colt to be carried under my arm or in my boot-leg. Finally, he handed me a match box made of an empty government rifle shell with a pistol shell for a stopper. Inside this were a lot of the little old-fashioned sulphur matches that came in square blocks, but these were all picked loose. Glancing at them, he said: "These are not for use. All you have to do with them is to go to Cabeza Borago, that little hill where you camped on your last run south. On the top of the hill dig a hole about six inches deep and bury this match box. After sundown make a fire over the box. Build it of mesquite sticks of fairly good thickness so it will burn for many hours. After lighting the fire, do not go back to it or try to see who visits the hill. Watch this hill and all the others around, and if you see an answering fire, consider your message delivered. If there is no answering blaze, then you must build a fire every night for five nights before you abandon the hill."

I rode easily, carrying some extra barley for horse-feed. In all the distance, I saw not even a moccasin track. So far as hostiles were concerned, I might have been riding along the banks of the Thames. In due time, the match box was buried and the fire lighted on the hilltop. I hid my horse in a little clump of brush where there was some grass and worked my way to a point where I could keep watch of the fire, my horse, and all the peaks around. No answer came. I slept most of the next day, and when darkness fell, I built another fire over the message buried in the grass and passed another lonely and fruitless night. But on the third night, within an hour or two after lighting my beacon fire, there suddenly leaped up on an adjoining peak a bright flame that flared about four feet high and lasted for more than two hours. My message had been delivered, and I knew that each little match would be taken from the shell—by whom I knew not—and put under a strong magnifying glass, and every needle-point and mark on it interpreted in a code of which I knew nothing.

About eleven o'clock that night, I mounted and rode carefully west of Fronterras, as McLeod did not wish my outfit and face to become familiar in that part of the country. Some Mexicans driving cattle tried to halt me, but by daylight I had filled my canteen at a Mexican ranch, watered my horse and hidden him where he could get a little gramma grass, and was ready to take a nap on the top of a rocky, brushy ridge about half a mile beyond. The proper procedure when travelling in this way is, after hiding your horse for the day, to cache your little bit of food near by, and, if possible, your saddle and boots; so that, in case your horse is captured, you still have something left, along with the chance of finding a new mount. You keep with you your light shoes or Mexican tawas (a kind of moccasin and legging combined, and very useful in a thorny country), some food, a canteen of water, and your gun and field glass.

On reaching the ridge I had selected, I found its top covered with rather larger trees than usual and a dyke of rock several feet thick running along it like a broken wall. Creeping under some bushes and snug against the rock, I soon fell asleep. Around eight or nine o'clock I awoke, swept the whole country carefully with my glass, crawled down beside my rock, drank from the canteen, ate a good bit of jerky and pinole, and slept again.

When next I woke it was with a sense of trouble, vague and undefined. I looked over a hot mesquite plain with the sun of Mexico beating down on it as it only can at midday. Yet there was not a sign to arouse suspicion. The buzzards were circling calmly; a few little lizards panted on the rock near me, and not a puff of dust made by man or beast was visible. I swept the hills and valley with my glass and tried to sight my horse, but he was doubtless in deep shade and as motionless as the trees. I reached for the canteen and took a long drink, and just as I set it down, I sensed the faint sound of a heavy body moving slightly on my rock. The possibility of such a sound being made by any wild animal was instantly eliminated from my mind. It was the dreaded Apache! As he was so close, he had doubtless picked up my faint trail and was just on the point of getting a clear shot at me at a range of a few feet. I could almost feel the lead. The physical impulse of fear ordered me to jump for life like a startled rabbit, but the training of years, while it did not for an instant decrease the fear, sharpened and steadied my wits.

It dawned upon me that this unseen adversary was a scout like myself; that by some strange chance he had taken this same ridge as a point of vantage from which to overlook the country, but had come up from the east and therefore had not seen my tracks. With every sense alert, I waited several minutes, not daring to move lest I startle a lizard or stir a pebble. Then I heard the faint tinkle made only by a cloth-covered metal canteen as it comes gently in contact with a rock. This told me many things in the fraction of a second. The Indian was probably a Reservation Apache and would have a United States rifle. Moreover, he certainly had not seen my tracks. He was probably getting data for a raid on the Fronterras ranchers to obtain a few horses and kill a few Mexicans. I knew the ranchers were creeping back to their holdings, and no Indians had been reported in the neighbourhood. This scout would stay on the ridge until sundown. He would suffer from the heat just as I did and would shift around on the rock to keep himself in the shade and invisible, taking care to avoid the skyline and the eye of any stray cowboy or vaquero. All I needed to do was to keep perfectly quiet until he went away.

Again I heard a slight sound—then the faintest crunch of gravel. The Apache was coming around and down the rock to my place of hiding. Probably the hot sun was driving him to seek shelter. I would most willingly have turned over to him my apartment with shade—free of charge, if possible! To fire a shot would be dangerous. I might not drop my Indian. There might be two of him, though this was not likely. The circumstance of this hill being used as an outpost told me plainly that Geronimo or some of his band would be near by; therefore, a meeting with the scout must be avoided, if in any way possible. It occurred to me that, as he came down the rock, I would slip up and around the other end and take the place he had just vacated. By the time he had seen my tracks and worked them out, I would be some distance away down the eastern side of the hill.

I carried out my scheme perfectly, moving like a shadow, and gained the top of the rock just at the instant when the Apache slipped into the spot I had used as headquarters. Everything so far had gone as planned, but as I took a few light steps down the eastern side of the hill I found myself right among a group of Indians. Two of them were lying on a bright coverlet with lace trimmings, evidently the loot from some ranch. One was industriously killing vermin from a shirt spread over his knees; others were mending juaraches. All had their guns lying beside them. The tiny little cañon with its scrub timber seemed to be alive with Apaches!

One of the Indians walking up the cañon toward me was the first to see that I was a white man. When he espied my white face he froze—but only for an instant. Then he let out a shrill yell and started to raise his gun, but I already had mine in hand and it had been cocked since the time of the first faint sound behind the rock, so I fired before he could level his. What happened in the next few seconds is still a bit sketchy in my mind. So long as you are facing a foe or going toward him, your legs will act very well, but once you start running, you race as madly as any little child dashing down a long hall to escape the bears that spring out from the dark.

I gave a yell and fired a few shots at jumping Indians, then tore off through the brush like a hunted stag. I felt the whole Apache tribe was after me. There was much shooting and shouting. For a few moments, I tore through brush, over boulders, and down the hill. A ledge of rocks lay below me. I made a terrific leap and landed in some mesquite brush, which broke my fall. I lost my canteen and my hat. The shots and yells had ceased, but this added to my fear, for now I could imagine several silent, fast-running Apaches spreading out, with a couple of trackers racing directly behind me. It was still several hours before dark. I had turned along the ridge, so as to keep from view, but could not risk circling around to my horse. If I left the hill and ran out into the valley, I would be seen and the Indians might easily have some horses hidden and so be able to run me down.

As soon as my cowardly legs would obey me, I slowed down a little, well knowing that I had a long race before me. On second thought, it seemed best to chance it if the Apaches did not have horses very near. Before me lay a rough valley with brush and much of the dreaded cholla cactus through which no one can run, not even an Apache. Many varieties of cactus can be endured, though painful, but the cholla is impossible. Luckily, I struck a stock trail through it, winding and crooked, but bearing away north and east, the direction in which I wanted to go. Now I slowed to a jog trot, for no one could outflank me. The dreaded chollas were in a way an advantage, for my enemies could do nothing but follow exactly on my trail.

I had been in the thorn belt about five minutes when I heard the shrill Apache yell that for hundreds of years has frozen the blood of the Indian tribes with whom they have been at war, as well as of the Mexicans and Americans of their wide frontiers. Again my legs took command—and no Apache could compete. I ran with a strange sense of strength, clinging to the trail, and at dark I reached a sandy arroyo where I doubled on my trail for a hundred yards and then threw myself flat on my back and put my heels on a bit of driftwood a few inches higher than my head. This relieves blood pressure better than anything else I know, and eases the breathing.

Darkness, that godsend of the scout, was a welcome shield that night. I lay there thinking that I had outdistanced the fastest running Indians in the West—and that fear is a wonderful accelerator if it does not hold sway entirely or last too long. Later, the commandant at Fronterras told McLeod that Geronimo's band had raided more than one hundred horses and killed several ranchers the day after I made my sudden departure.

It was a hard-looking, sunburnt, thorn-scratched youngster who arrived at Tombstone with scarcely enough clothes left to avoid arrest. But I reported to McLeod that the brass match box had been delivered on Cabeza Borago.

Like the immortal Stonewall Jackson, McLeod was eventually killed accidentally by his own men. This happened in a smugglers' camp near Fronterras. I have tried for years to get this information to Gus (trainer of the famous horse, Bullet Neck), who was McLeod's close friend in Tucson in 1882. If these lines ever reach his eye, they will ease his mind, for McLeod's grip on the heartstrings is not loosened by lapse of years or death.

CHAPTER V

UPS AND DOWNS IN GLOBE

I TURNED back once more to Globe and made my entrance on another field. My friend of the *Belt* had introduced me to the two Johns of that town—both sheriff's deputies and with legitimate use for just such an active youngster as I. My past was not exploited, neither was it revealed, but I began now to see life from another angle. Life worth living depended on property, and property on law, and these three factors were necessary to lift men from chaos and savagery. The county taxes were hard to raise, the territory vast; trailing criminals was difficult and expensive. By preliminary scouting, I could often save a posse of men from wasting their time—in fact, I could do most of their work. My youth was an asset which I gladly cashed in. I worked with such men as Pete Gabriel of Florence, Paul of Tucson, and Buckey O'Neal of Prescott, later one of Roosevelt's Rough Riders. Thatcher, the famous Wells Fargo guardian of bullion shipments and treasure, taught me many simple things that everyone is supposed to know but usually does not. He sent me to distant points in California, mining camps and ranching counties, sometimes into towns, and into all the underworld life. Occasionally, I guarded Wells Fargo treasure out of Globe, crouching with a sawed-off shotgun in the rear boot of the coach instead of beside the driver. The bandits shot some good men off the high seat without warning, but they quit the Dripping Springs line after they had been given a salute from the great leather boot at the rear.

On one of my missions, my horse was stolen from me by Mexican horse thieves. This hurt my pride and taught me that I still had much to learn about certain phases of Mexican life. I followed the robbers, two of them, into Mexico, back to Tucson, then out on the deserts south of Casa Grande, in and out of Mexico again; lost their trail, recovered it at Weaver Station, and followed it over the Apache Trail to a tragic capture in Tonto Creek. Like many other things that happened in that wild country, the capture took place at a point that is now under the placid waters of the lake at the back of the Roosevelt Dam.

Many years have passed since that day. The great dam itself is a dream come true. In retrospect, I see myself sitting on the hard quartzite reef, the solid rib that holds all the weight of this mighty masonry, and beside me is a white-haired man named Sirine—a Mormon engineer—trying to visualize to my young eyes this very structure. He it was who turned the old Mesa City canal, lower down the river, into the prehistoric channel of the ancients, using their same gradients, and puddled the gravelly points by hauling thousands of wagon loads of clay into the channel, then turning in a little water and driving herds of cattle up and down the canal. The trampling hoofs firmed the clay until it held water as well as modern cement does.

As we sat on the reef, Sirine said to me: "It is beyond the span of my life, but you will live to see a great dam here and all Tonto Creek and Salt River for twenty miles a beautiful lake."

Now, the mirror of the Sierra Anchas lies before this rocky point, and deep under its smiling surface are certain closed chapters in the lives of some of my old friends and enemies, as well as in my own life. Here, by the strange irony of fate, Al Sieber, the noted scout, was crushed to death by a fragment of the mountain that he was moving in building this dam, and his assistants in the labour were the same Indians that he and I had chased and been chased by in the 'eighties—the terrible Tonto Apaches.

The Apache War began during the Tonto feud, and in 1882— a year that will long be remembered in Arizona—the savages broke out in force. What dare I write about the Indians?

UPS AND DOWNS IN GLOBE 51

Every page of American history from coast to coast for a hundred years teems with controversy over this subject. It can stir up as much rancour as a discussion of religion or prohibition. Although I was born on an Indian reservation and have been among many tribes, from the Chilkoot in the far North down to the small, silent, stealthy, wooden-arrowed tribes of Mexico still, I feel that I know little about the race and am disposed to refrain from giving my views and opinions except as they may leak out in anecdote.

The San Carlos Reservation, to which most of the Apaches had been sent, was not under military administration, but was in the corrupt hands of the Indian Bureau, whose agent at that time was an ex-parson named Tiffany. This man robbed the Indians unscrupulously and broke faith with them so persistently that the wise and humane policies of General Crook could not find fulfilment. As one old chief said, to excuse his depredations: "The Great Father at Washington is the head and General Crook is his right hand, holding all the soldiers. General Crook is a good man. But the left hand, Tiffany, steals from the Indian all that the Great Father gives him. Then how can the head—the Great Father—be good? All white men are liars. It is better for the Indian to die fighting than to be starved to death by that man Tiffany."

General Crook, who had been recalled from the Black Hills and the Sioux country, was a very remarkable man. If he had been left to carry out his own plans, he would doubtless have brought all the Apaches under control at small cost of money and life. Crook was a good man for the taxpayer, the honourable settler, and the Indian; but he roused bitter antagonism among all those merchants, ranchers, and traders who made their profits by fat contracts through the Indian Agency and the Military Posts. He was asked to perform an impossible task; namely, to reinstate the confidence of the Indian in the white man's word and written pledge after treacherous and thieving treatment extending over years by the local traders as well as by the Government's Indian agents.

To-day, at Washington, the most complete and scathing arraignment in this case can be read in a report made by a Federal Grand Jury to Judge Hoover in October, 1883. It is an historical document. For such misdeeds, the prophets of old demanded of their people repentance in sackcloth and ashes and prayers for forgiveness. Even the good offices of General Crook could not hold all the fierce Apaches in leash, and some of them broke back into Mexico. The public clamour for sharper action was too strong, and Crook was relieved of his command, to be succeeded by the brilliant Miles. From a military point of view, General Miles carried out one of the most difficult campaigns in the annals of the Indian wars. A number of men afterward famous for courage and wisdom here won their spurs. Generals Leonard Wood, Chaffee, the beloved Lawton, and many others, pitted their brains and strength against the crafty and clever Apaches. Their strategy and swift campaigns against the wiliest savage on earth are not myths; they are of official record.

The common conception of Indian fighting is of continuous action, either galloping madly in retreat to save one's life or gloriously charging to victory. The sober facts are that in a very active campaign the actual fighting may last but a few moments, and even a glimpse of the elusive enemy is seldom attained. There may be day after day of fruitless marching and counter-marching with not so much as a moccasin track or a shoe mark to urge on the chase. Most frontier settlements, when the Indians are out, huddle together in the towns and call for government troops or gallantly send out a body of armed men who chase the Indians at long range until their grub and their horses are exhausted, when they return to town and reëquip. Experienced Indian fighters like Crook or Miles, or great scouts like Colonel Jack Hay of the Rangers or King Woolsley of Arizona, carried on their campaigns very differently and far more effectively.

It was my good fortune to find service, at one time or another, under such remarkable men as Al Sieber, Archie McIntosh, and Fred Sterling. Every commanding officer in the Apache wars suffered from lack of information as to where the Indians were and from the difficulty of getting in touch with them. It was for this reason that Crook, Miles, Chaffee, and Lawton made frequent use of fast-running Indian scouts. It is a mistake to suppose that a cowboy is a fleet man in the mountains. He is a superb horseman, but he will trudge miles to catch a horse so that he may ride a mile. There are very few white men who can or will make long runs on foot, and no horseman can overtake an Apache on foot in rough mountains such as those of Arizona. Through the Indian games of my childhood and my hunting afoot in the mountains of California, I had developed a swift and silent pace which enabled me to scout in the Apache country without fear of being caught, even if sighted. For an untrained white man to be seen in an Indian country is to be caught if the Indians so mind. There were a few old-time trappers who could outfoot the Apaches, but they were already old men when I was on the frontier.

The Apaches were very treacherous, differing greatly in this respect from the Pimas and the Maricopas. Any one of our Apache scouts would go into the mountains and hunt down a hostile of his own tribe and bring in his scalp, even though the victim were a blood relative. A fancied wrong or an injury to their pride would start them killing one another even in the presence of their enemies, and would bring on a tribal war. Since they were so treacherous among themselves, how could we be astonished when an Apache robbed or killed a settler, even though the settler had treated the Indian with kindness for years? They had robbed and raided for many generations before the white man came to America.

The Apaches delighted in torture. The squaws, especially, were like the women of certain hill tribes in India—in love with cruelty. Once, in the Tonto Basin, I saw a group of children playing in front of one of their bear-grass huts while some squaws were grinding corn near by. The children had captured some young turtle doves from a nest and were intent on sticking large thorns into the birds' eyes, much to the amusement of the squaws. And on a hunting trip for deer in the Sierra Anchas I saw a young fawn being skinned alive by the squaws. No wonder it was the chief determination of the whites in those days never to be taken alive by the Indians.

Knowing all these things, it is not surprising that the settlers, in such fights as that of the caves of Salt River and some others, killed squaws as well as bucks. Yet, admitting all that is worst in the Indian, there is still much that I admire: his unconquerable spirit, his love of freedom, his infinite patience and unflinching stoicism. They were, after all, a mere handful, fighting the world and holding themselves accountable only to the Great Spirit. Some of the chiefs had a wonderful flow of language and poetic imagery.

I recall an incident when I was supposedly killed but was rescued and nursed back to life by a good squaw, the wife of Archie McIntosh. One day, while he was away on government service, his squaw left the house to go to the near-by hills to gather Spanish bayonet, whose root makes an excellent soap for washing the hair and is much used by Indians and Mexicans. She discovered me lying in a little gulch quite unconscious, as the result of a terrific thump on the head administered by the barrel of a Winchester. (This slight unpleasantness was a souvenir of the Tonto feud.) She took me to her house and cared for me faithfully until I was fully recovered.

During the Apache outbreak of 1882, Fred Sterling was Chief of Scouts and had under his command about twenty Indians who were employed in scouting the country immediately around Globe, from Tonto Basin to Dripping Springs. There were all kinds of volunteer companies formed of rangers and settlers. Many of these never got outside the barrooms, where elaborate plans were outlined to capture the hostiles. Not all the citizens, however, were so foolish as to think that untrained men were capable of meeting the rigours of an Indian campaign, and Sterling, knowing the helpless position of the miners, ranchers, and freighters, did all he could to modify the unpopularity of the army and to protect the citizens.

I was appointed to assist Sterling and to report my findings

UPS AND DOWNS IN GLOBE

to Captain Burbridge. There were some mining camps still working on Mineral Creek and some prospectors on Pinto Creek to be guarded from possible raids by the hostiles. It was my duty to cut for tracks from Dripping Springs around the south side of Pinal Mountain to Pinto Creek and down that creek to a point near Salt River where Scar-faced Charley, a Modoc Indian, would meet me with another scout or two and bring me any instructions they might have from Sterling. I would then, by devious ways, retrace the whole long series of mountains back to Dripping Springs. This was all footwork of the hardest kind.

The Modocs of California were more like the Apaches than any other Coast Indians. Scar-faced Charley would kill any Indian as quickly as he would a rabbit if ordered by Sterling to do so. Sterling always took great chances with his Indian scouts. His word to them was his bond, like General Crook's, and every one of them was under obligation to him, yet, in the end, they treacherously slew him. Soon after that, his successor as Chief of Scouts was also murdered by his own Apaches only a few miles from Globe.

When news reached us that the settlers on Cherry Creek were attacked by Indians, volunteers were called for, to be under the command of Captain Burbridge. We set out on a long and trying march. Salt River was in one of its periodical floods and formed a raging torrent half a mile wide. A chilling rain beat on weary men and horses. Many of our mounts were from the desert and could not swim well. Fortunately, there were a few Northern horses as well as a number of Northern men, who were at home in rain and in cold, swift water. This was where the Northerners were able to show the men of the desert some new wrinkles in woodcraft. Rafts were put together and the great river crossed at a point now under the lake made by the Roosevelt Dam. Several horses and mules and one of our men were drowned.

All the settlers found alive on Cherry Creek were rescued. The Indians did not give battle, though I am sure they could have wiped out our entire force if they had chosen to attack.

We were under the eyes of their scouts all the way from the wheatfields just outside Globe until our return. Among those we saved was a small boy named Charley Meadows, famous for many years afterward as Buffalo Bill's leading cowboy.

Not long after this, a report reached Globe that not only were the White Mountain Apaches out, but that the Chiricahui of San Carlos had joined them, making an army of seven hundred hostiles—enough warriors to sack and burn the town. The settlers were greatly agitated by the tidings and felt helpless to meet this crisis. I was detailed to scout the ground between Pinal Mountain and Globe. Arrangements were made for the women and children, in case of attack, to gather at once in a big feed corral with sheds on all sides in the centre of the town. Pickets and guards were posted on the outskirts. About eleven o'clock one night, I reported in and was ordered to patrol the entire picket line until morning. By midnight, I had finished one round and found all in order, awake, and alert. On the east side of the town, we had posted some Mexicans. A bunch of horses from a wood camp got loose; the pickets, hearing them and receiving no answer to a challenge, fired. The Mexicans galloped through the centre of the town shouting "*Los Indios! Los Indios!*" The parson rang the alarm bell frantically, and all Globe had a thrill that lasted until daylight. One famous evangelist ran into the corral with the women and children and was compelled by the women to climb up on top of a shed, where he lay in a blue funk till morning. In justice to the cloth be it said that two stouter-hearted parsons were on the job with guns and ammunition at the expected point of attack.

In an alarm of this kind, more funny incidents can happen in an hour than would ordinarily occur in a year. Even the dogs, horses, and mules get the infection of fear and do unheard-of silly things. One woman lit a candle (contrary to orders) and started sewing on a torn curtain to hide the light and could scarcely be convinced that if she would blow out the candle the curtain would not be needed. Another woman arrived at the corral barefooted but well armed with broom and rolling pin. But the majority moved silently and with such arms as they had to their appointed places. Probably, for many, it was neither their first fight nor their first scare.

Globe had many ups and downs and colourful events in those days and only needed a Mark Twain or a Kipling to make of its happenings treasures of literature. Like the neighbouring camp of Tombstone, it had in its history all the elements of comedy, melodrama, and too often the grimmest tragedy. Life was lived intensely, and the lure of silver, gold, and copper, drew the strong and adventurous youth of a lusty young nation. As I remember it, we were all perennially on the crest of some little mining boom or else all dead broke and waiting for capital and a railroad to come along and develop the vast copper mines we knew existed but which were of no profit to us so long as we had only oxen and mules for transportation and our picks and shovels as tools. Whenever the Indians became active, all the miners and prospectors for miles around were driven into the little camp, and this congestion for a time made society, such as it was. Globe was the only place where youth could find any social amusement, and when a few hundred miners arrived in camp after months of ceaseless toil, they felt it was up to the town dwellers to assist them in celebrating the holiday.

I remember one Fourth of July when the principal mines were shut down and the merchants especially hard up. The town seemed stone dead. There was no firing of cannon, no dancing or speech-making, and no parades or picnics had been planned. Down the gulch just below Burns's blacksmith shop stood a big cottonwood tree which had not infrequently been used as a gallows to assist certain undesirable citizens out of their troubles. Some wag suggested that we all go down to the cottonwood tree and hang ourselves as a protest to the dead-in-the-shell and unpatriotic townspeople of Globe. We compromised by spending a couple of hours trying to honour our great national holiday by mock-heroic speeches, wrestling, and horseplay, all in a spirit of boyish fun. But one of our number, a husky young miner named Dick Bilderback, took himself very seriously. After absorbing a bottle or two of red liquid, he got hold of a twenty-five-pound box of dynamite and a lot of fuses and caps which he carefully attached to the sticks of powder, and then proceeded to have a Fourth of July celebration of his own. Walking up the main street of the town he nonchalantly tossed his charges behind him in the middle of the road. Each shot, as it went off, tore a considerable hole in the ground and raised a tremendous lot of dust, besides rocking every store and shack in the place.

The local policemen were not overanxious to arrest a man holding in his hand a sizzling fuse attached to a stick of dynamite, especially as Dick solemnly threatened to blow up the whole box and himself along with it if any one interfered with him. By the time the third charge had gone off, most of the population had fled to the hills, but we youngsters realized that some of the irate citizens had taken their guns and might kill Dick from afar, so we formed ourselves into a committee of the whole to keep him from being shot while he shot up the town, but when I saw Benbrook, a cool deputy sheriff, striding down the street Winchester in hand, I thought Dick as good as dead. Just at that instant, a white-haired old woman stepped briskly toward Dick. She was the Irish landlady of a miners' boarding house and feared no man.

Dick shouted to her to keep back or he would blow her to Kingdom Come.

"Yis!" she retorted, "an' the whole worruld wud be sayin' ye did it to kape from payin' me the week's board ye are afther owin' me! An' me your partner in a silver claim wid yersilf an' the Chilson boys over in Richmond Basin," etc., etc. Her tongue flew fast, always putting Dick in the wrong and on the defensive, until finally he suggested that they talk it all over. Then she asked him if he would be "afther kapin' a lady shtandin' in the middle av the strate in the blazin' sun—now wud he?"—and at that Dick stepped with her into the shade of a near-by porch where he put down his box of dynamite, keeping the fuses and the burning candle in his hands.

The old lady promptly sat down on the dynamite, covering

the box entirely with her ample form and wide skirts. Dick was now like the pirate captain in the "Houseboat on the Styx"; he could not proceed with his plans without insulting a lady. Soon the gallant Irishwoman took the opportunity to blow out Dick's candle, and so his celebration of the Glorious Fourth came to a peaceful end. But the incident seemed to wake up the whole burg, and that night everybody celebrated in quite the regular old-fashioned way, and we boys felt that the day was saved.

While trailing the Mexican rustlers who stole my horse, I met at a desert station the famous Major Pauline Cushman, the only woman given a commission in the United States Army for secret-service work inside the enemy's lines during the Civil War. She had married a great six-footer named Jerry Fryer, a noted character throughout the territories. As both of them were tired of civilization, they had established themselves in this odd corner of the world, where they offered me a hearty welcome and a much-needed rest, with feed for my horses. Major Pauline told me many things about her secret work and gave me inside information about the men I was after, as well as a list of "don'ts" for a scout which have stood me in good stead many times since. Both the Fryers were interested in mines and fired my imagination with desire to explore the deserts from the Gila River to Altar, in Mexico—a desert country four hundred miles across with no living stream between those two points. Yet, by those who have the key to its hidden water holes, rock tanks, and dampened sands, it may be crossed and recrossed in safety. Out of it, in those days, came glowing tales of copper, silver, and gold.

In Globe I met some expert desert prospectors who, like myself, had the gold fever. Soon we all rounded up at the desert station of Maricopa, equipped for a long hunt for the dry placers. At last we found them and actually winnowed gold from the surface gravel by tossing it in the wind with canvas and blowing the sand concentrates with the breath until only black sand and gold remained. This we accumulated until we had our pack horses loaded, then packed it many miles to a water hole where we washed it in gold pans. We were always millionaires until the final clean-up, when we generally found we had much black sand and little gold. By a good deal of hard labour, we cleared just about enough to buy supplies sufficient to enable us to go at it again.

My particular job much of the time was scanning the desert from a hidden cleft in some peak, so as not to permit our camp to be raided by day or night. My vigils were long, lonely, and silent, but gladly made, for I knew that these men trusted their property and lives to my sleepless eyes. From time to time there came to our ears tales of lost mines far toward Altar —tales, for the most part, with little foundation. Among the miners was a certain young Texan optimist who, like myself, always "fell" for these romances. Together we left the dry placers and visited Major Pauline that we might hear from her lips further stories of the great strikes such as the Plancha La Plata, the Gunsight, Ajo, and Vekol mines. These all had their romantic lure and were to some extent trustworthy; therefore, we argued, other similar stories might have a basis of truth.

We outfitted in Tucson and never ceased our wanderings until we touched the salt marshes of the Gulf of California. Here our horses perished. We saved ourselves by distilling salt water with the aid of a few ollas found in a deserted Indian camp, but were not able to freshen enough water to save our poor animals. We finally arrived in Yuma clad in such bits of rawhide and canvas as had withstood the thorns and cactus. Our tattered appearance made us the laughing-stock of the town. My Texas friend met an old freighter who knew him and from whom he secured a job as swamper with a sixteen-mule team going to the Silver King mines.

I again sought out my friends, the Fryers. Major Pauline would not hear of my leaving the station until I had regained my lost weight. Many youths from off this desert, exhausted by heat and perishing for lack of water, had she nursed back to health and strength at one time or another. When, a few years later, taps were sounded in San Francisco for Major

Pauline, there were men whom she had befriended all the way from the Golden Gate to the banks of the Rio Grande who deeply grieved to hear of her passing.

Leaving the station on an outfit borrowed from Fryer, I turned north to the then active mining camps of Tip-Top, Black Warrior, and the Bradshaws. I was worse than broke, for I owed the Fryers for my outfit. The superintendent of the Tip-Top mine, Jefferson Clark, was a grandson of the great Roger Clark of the Lewis and Clark expedition of 1804, which really brought under our flag the states of Oregon and Washington. He showed some interest in me, but said he had no job to give me, as only the best single-jack miners could break rock in the Tip-Top mine, for the vein was narrow and harder than flint to drill. He asked, "Can you shoot?" I demonstrated. He then told me that he would give me ten cents a pound for venison, as it was a dry year and the cattle were too poor for beef. The Bloody Basin and Black Mesa country teemed with game, as I knew, and before long I developed such proficiency that I hired two Mexican Indians to trail me and carry in the deer, which I marked for them by setting a red flag near each kill. Already there were two experienced hunters trying to supply Bradshaw and Tip-Top camps with venison. One was an old Californian and the other an ex-buffalo hunter—both splendid shots, seldom missing a buck, but they were old men. I was trained in the then new school of the repeating rifle and running shooting and my ability to travel on foot rapidly from daylight to dark gave me a great advantage over them.

Clark, the superintendent, foolishly boasted to my competitors of my shooting, as I was sending in four deer to their one. He bet one hundred dollars that I would beat them at a target. A match was arranged. They used hair-triggers and a rest, and their bullets almost touched each other in the centre. They beat me easily and made me look ridiculous in the eyes of Tip-Top. Clark himself was a quick shot of the Bogardus type. Years later, when we were both in Africa, he greatly astonished the Boer hunters by hitting coins tossed into the air and performing other feats with the rifle such as they had never seen.

The lure of the desert again came upon me. I met in Globe one of the Chilson boys; we outfitted and again made the Fryers' desert station of Casa Grande. I was now able to repay my good friends what I owed them and have a good stake besides. Another one of the Chilsons was already in that country. They were wonderful prospectors. The younger brother had the patience of an Indian. We traced minute particles of float, fine as dust, and worked for weeks in the burning sun, using magnifying glasses and carrying water many miles in canteens that we might test the ground with the horn spoon instead of the batea or gold pan.

Finally, after wandering hundreds of miles across the deserts, we found a gold pocket in most unpromising rock within thirty-six miles of Casa Grande, our starting point. We shot out over a thousand dollars with the first stick of dynamite. The news of our strike spread quickly, and we had to put on guards to protect the dumps from enthusiastic visitors who might absent-mindedly carry off a hundred dollars' worth of specimens in a coat pocket. There were exaggerated reports as to the amount of wealth we took out. Nevertheless, it was sufficient for me to carry out my fixed intention to change the name of a certain girl who lived beside the great Mississippi and place her in charge of a home in an orange grove in Pasadena, California.

CHAPTER VI

THE NECKTIE PARTY

A GREAT daydream of years was now realized. Although I had turned down a chance to go to long-desired Africa with Stanley and had chosen instead to marry my boyhood sweetheart, Fortune smiled on me, and I now owned a home and an orange grove in Pasadena. My mother and fourteen-year-old brother joined us in California, and I was able to make a small allowance for the declining years of my grandparents. I give all praise to the goddess Fortune, for very few of our family have the dollar-making instinct, even in mild degree.

It was not long before I realized that a successful orange grower, like a poet, must be born, not made. I believe it takes more gray matter to outwit the vagaries of an orange tree and coax it into productivity than is required for a railway president, governor of a state, or manager of a life-insurance company. As near as I can recall, my oranges cost me twenty-five cents apiece and sold, if very carefully packed, for less than one cent each.

As the charms of the orange grove palled, the mountains and the desert began calling again, and in the dim distance returned my lifelong vision of Africa. I still had some mining interests of promise in Arizona, but it was a time of depression in the United States, so I exchanged mining claims for land and took part, in a small way, in the development of the old Mesa Canal near Phoenix, Arizona. This brought me in contact with the Mormons of the valley, the most successful desert farmers in America. The preliminary agitation for what afterward developed into the great Roosevelt Dam grew in intensity and led me to the study of irrigation. My wife and brother joined me, preferring the active life of Arizona to a sleepy, pleasant existence in sheltered Pasadena.

An aftermath of the turbulent days of my teens was now interjected into my peaceful pursuits of water development in Arizona. That old trouble led to a duel between my friend E—— R—— and a man who had been a member of the opposing faction in our famous Tonto feud. This faction was now in the political saddle and controlled public opinion through two local papers. To add to the black outlook for my friend, there was a beautiful woman involved who knew well how to stir up excitement in a frontier community. The preliminary trial showed strong evidence in E—— R——'s favour, wrung even from reluctant witnesses, but this seemed only to inflame the mob spirit more violently than ever. The woman in the case was a wonderful firebrand. Moreover, there had not been a lynching in Arizona for a long time. Humanity seems still to demand a blood atonement once in so often, no matter who or what the victim or the crime, and it was obviously my friend's fate to appease this community appetite, now whetted to a point where men were eager to disregard law. They demanded blood.

But there is another equally strong force let loose at such times—the fear of the mob to shed its own blood. Out of a gathering of a hundred furious men, there are seldom more than two or three who will rush against the muzzle of a gun held by a man who shows fight.

Hearing of the peril of my friend E—— R——, I rode rapidly across the desert to the county seat. There I found a strange undercurrent of intensely bitter feeling. The local paper was, perhaps unconsciously, rubbing salt into old wounds. I saw men carrying cigars in their mouths unlighted or striking matches for cigars already lighted. There was elaborate talk about the weather and the calf crop, but the unspoken question was, "Will E—— R——'s friends actually fight if we hang him? And if so, will they do it at the jail or mark us down to be potted later as we ride the trail or range?" It mars the pleasure of a hanging bee to foresee that half of those who grasp the rope may be dead within a few months.

Upon hunting up my friend's friends, I found that there were only four in town who would, if properly led, make a desperate effort to save him. Fortunately, one of them was an ex-sheriff, B——, a strong character who had been much dreaded in Nevada by criminals and mobs. He asked us to meet at a little ranch in the willows about two miles out of town where he would join us at dusk, which he did. The ranchman was an old Tejana, a friend to all of us for years. He contributed both aid and good advice, but as he had cataracts on his eyes and suffered from rheumatism, we refused his gallant offer to join us with his old gun and make it a real party. We were informed that the town had worked itself up to fever pitch and that about the third night from then the mob would be primed for the killing, but that the sheriff of the town would be against any mob. Our informant knew all the symptoms and diagnosed the mental state of the town just as a physician would diagnose a case of chills and fever. A vain appeal for mercy to the woman in the case had been tried, through one of the cleverest and handsomest men in town, but the report brought back was that, like Salome, she would be appeased by nothing less than the head of her victim.

Our leader was living at the hotel, a one-story adobe structure just across the street from the jail, and it was his plan that we should use his room as a rallying point from which to attack the mob in case they stormed the jail.

Said B——, "I have a rifle and six-shooter behind the bar, but they have already been inspected, and if they were removed, I should be shadowed and covered, as they all feel I would be at the bottom of any effort to help E—— R——. Therefore, you must take the buckboard and drive to X——, forty miles, and get two hundred Winchester shells, two rifles, and two shotguns and buckshot, so that with what we have here we shall have plenty to last us through."

With a pair of tough little Mexican mules, I made the eighty miles and reported back inside twenty-four hours. While being unharnessed in the corral, one of my mules bucked the harness off and but for the closed gate would have run away with the precious ammunition.

That day I rented a room from a Mexican woman whose backyard adjoined the rear of the hotel. In this way, it was easy to transfer all our weapons into B——'s room, including those I had brought from X—— and others borrowed from our Tejana friend. We ripped a seam in the ceiling cloth and laid our store of arms carefully across the rafters, then drew the edges of the cloth together. It was planned that every evening we four should be within a few steps of B——'s room, whose two shuttered windows directly faced the jail at a distance of about sixty feet. The slats of the shutters enabled us to observe without being seen from the street.

The chief mob leaders were mostly so-called "solid citizens" who prated of law and order to cover up their elemental blood lust. There seemed to be about four ringleaders. They were, for the time, monuments of good citizenship and indubitable heroes. They felt so secure of their victim and so confident of the fury of the mob that they were loath to shorten the hour of their glory—for after a hanging, everyone slips away. No honours or bouquets accrue to the leaders or even to the crusading orators, once the cowardly deed is done.

That afternoon, a young man named G——, whose real home was in a near-by mining camp, appeared and began exhorting. He was even more bloodthirsty than Salome, and by evening had quite a following of corral-keepers, miners' boys, and many of the satellites of the Big Four. G—— demanded instant action—that very night. He cornered two of the Big Four in the lobby of the hotel and fairly roasted them as quitters. No one chose to resent the taunt, for G—— was over six feet and had a beady, treacherous eye that made others hesitate to oppose him.

That evening our leader, B——, called us together, and outlined the situation. He said G—— was making a bid for Salome's favour by urging the immediate hanging of E——

R——. This pressure would force the hand of the Big Four, and to-morrow night would certainly be set for the necktie party. It was almost a relief to us to know that this abnormal strain of uncertainty was to end so soon. B—— warned us that we need expect little help from the sheriff as he was not a personal friend of E—— R——'s and knew, if he should oppose the mob too strongly, they would simply kill him and then hang E—— R——. It is asking a lot of one mere human sheriff to face a determined mob of his own "best citizens" in anything but a perfunctory way.

This talk worried me greatly, as the sheriff was known to be a fearless man and had declared that no one could take any prisoner from him without a stiff fight. I told B—— I had known that sheriff in my boyhood in California; we had ridden the hills together at times. I said he was a hard man to sway, drive, or coax in any way, but I would try to enlist his sympathies for our stand. B—— at first objected to my telling the sheriff that we intended to fortify the windows and pour buckshot into the mob the instant the keys were surrendered or the jail stormed; but he finally gave in to my urging; although he thought the natural thing for the sheriff to do would be to tip off the Big Four to all of us, after which they would take our guns and keep us under guard. The sheriff's point of view would be, he argued, that after one hanging bee, agreeable to most of the townspeople and soon forgotten, he would in two years be sure of reëlection; whereas, if there should be a division, it would be followed by a long sectional fight and the sheriff's opponent would be cocksure to be elected.

But I insisted that the sheriff was not a Texan and the Tejana feud traditions would mean nothing to him. After much argument, B—— suggested that I go to the sheriff and ask him to ride out on the desert for an hour. Said B——, "As he passes the old stage corral you can join him on a mule you will find saddled there. Tell him all we have planned and find out if he is really for us or not. Do not overpersuade him for old friendship's sake or exact impossible assurances from him. After stating our side, listen and let him talk. As you go out, walk slowly in the streets. You will notice the women are all indoors to-day."

The sun beat hot on the adobe walls, and I knew many eyes watched me as I entered the sheriff's office and quickly came out again, making an angry and disappointed gesture and striding away to my room. An hour later, the sheriff and I were on the desert, riding through the greasewood. It was a terrible half hour for both of us. His code and mine, under which each of us tried falteringly to live, had many points of difference. I did not appeal to our boyhood acquaintance. Its only use was that it gave us ground for mutual frankness. I found that he knew more about all of us than I had suspected, and as to the Big Four and G—— and Salome, he knew almost certainly along what lines their past actions would now compel them to move, for they had started fires they could not control. He told me that two of the Big Four could be bluffed, but Number Three was a killer and would undoubtedly fire the first shot—but that he was the kind of poker player who always wants four aces.

Finally, the sheriff said: "I will hold the mob for a final argument at the doors of the jail. I will, when I see Number Three about to draw, touch my hat, and you fellows across the way may then turn loose. The Big Four are not sure of all their men and are afraid some of them will get shot if they shoot me, so I will play this as my last card."

We parted on the mesa, and by five o'clock I was at the Texan's ranch reporting to B——. He, in turn, had learned that G—— had made his boasts to Salome that before midnight he would give her a piece of the rope that had hanged E—— R——. By eight o'clock, three of us were in B——'s room in town. We loosened up a few adobes from the old chicken coop and laid them in the window, taking out the sash to give greater freedom of action and prevent our being hit by shattered glass. B—— sat in the bar-room playing solitaire, well knowing that some of the gang would be sent to cover him, as he was suspected. Sure enough, Big Hank, the gambler, and his pal Frosty came in and said, "B——, where do you stand to-night? You know what the fellows think."

"Yes," replied B——. "I am a friend of E—— R——'s. You don't expect me to go out and help hang him, do you?"

"No, but, by God, we don't want you to take a hand for him! If you don't mind, we want to borrow that artillery of yours to-night. We are a bit short."

"All right," said B——. "I feel damned bad over this, and I am going right off to my room till the thing is over. One man can't fight a hundred. You fellows will be sorry after you have finished this job."

They took his guns and went out to report to their leaders. B—— joined us in his room and fixed up the adobes in the window casings so as to make crude loopholes. "Boys, take your boots off," he said. "I'd hate to die with 'em on." This was in deference to the old frontier belief that bad men died with their boots on. Evidently, the ex-sheriff did not think we were in that class. He then turned to me, saying, "Now, son, take this place beside me, and when the mob comes, keep them covered, but don't you pull till my gun cracks."

We laid out our shells on the broad window sill, and, before long, the mob that had been gathering back of the hotel came marching grimly down to the doors of the jail. The sheriff was inside. One of the Big Four called to him, "Come out, Sheriff! We want to talk to you!"

The jail was a thick adobe building flush with the street. The front rooms were the sheriff's offices; the entrance was through large wooden double doors leading into a hall, at the end of which was a very modern iron-celled jail containing the worst prisoners. In answer to the shout, the sheriff threw open the wooden doors and stood in the doorway, asking, in a bantering way, "Why the honour of this visit, gentlemen?" (As if he had not slept in the jail for two weeks expecting just this delegation!)

I cannot remember all that he said, but there was a flat evenness of tone and an ominous spacing between words that sent a chill up and down my back. When he finished, there was a silence. He had told them that he would shoot the first man who stepped inside the jail door. Then, raising his voice a little, he called Number Three of the Big Four by name, and G—— also, saying, "For your especial information, gentlemen, I may tell you that at the first crack of a gun, a dozen bullets marked with your names will start toward you, and they are in the hands of men who will place them right. This is no easy job you have undertaken. Getting me is easy enough. But you are starting, over nothing, another Tonto Basin. Do you want it?"

The sheriff had played poker with Number Three, and he knew that gentleman would now begin to doubt whether he held four aces for a necktie party; he would begin to wonder who was marking a bullet for him. Quick as a flash, he turned and would have scurried off but for fear of a quick gun, ready for such Judases, which might be poking him from behind. "It's B——!" shouted Number Three. "Where is he?"

"Wrong again!" laughed the sheriff. "B—— is in his room and you have his arms. E—— R—— will have friends when a lot of you fellows will be sorry."

G—— ripped out an oath and his hand went to his gun, but the sheriff said to him, "Don't reach for it, G——; a little kid has you covered." G——'s face turned white and his eyes rolled. There were five seconds of tense silence. In the street a hundred fingers rested on as many triggers. Inside our room, my own lay along the double triggers of a shotgun. One cannot hold one's breath, ready to fire, indefinitely, and I was compelled to let some of the air out of my lungs. This made it seem as if the whole street and all the mob were moving gently up and down past the end of my gun.

From a window in the upper story of the big hotel a woman's voice rang out: "What are you all waiting for?"

Right beside me B—— boomed out, "Waiting for you to kiss the sheriff!"

This, to the mob, was like putting a handful of salt in the mouth of a balky horse. It gave them something different to

THE NECKTIE PARTY

think about. Some of the boys tittered, but there was in that tone of B——'s a sinister timbre of hate and power. The mocking words seemed to shout "Jezebel!" to the woman, and she shrank back. It seemed to confirm the sheriff's warning that there were bullets ready for Number Three and for G——. It made everyone instantly *afraid of the man behind him.*

The mob hesitated. In reality, it was groping for some way to save its face, to prevent ridicule, and—most important of all—to save each individual hide from puncture. The sheriff sensed their state of mind and began talking to them almost casually.

"You believe E—— R—— is guilty and that there have been too many killings of late in this county. You believe you are law-abiding people, but that, in this instance, you are warranted in acting outside the law. You may not know, but I know, that the judge who will try E—— R—— is —— ——, a Texan, and you know well his reputation for sentencing all killers. My suggestion is that in this one instance you give that famous judge a chance, and at the same time show the world that this community stands for law and order," etc., etc.

It was the usual appeal to a mob, and if it had been offered when they first rushed up to the jail would have led to the immediate shooting of the sheriff, but now that the bombshell of personal danger had burst among them, along with the deadly apprehension that there might be traitors standing armed within their own ranks, they were relieved to hear the slogan "Law and Order" and eager to lay hold of any suggestion that could hoist them out of their own peril.

Several voices rose: "Reckon the sheriff is right," and on his further advice that everyone should go directly to his home and not advertise the night's doings abroad, the whole mob melted away. I confess I turned limply from the window and sat on the floor for some minutes with my cocked gun across my knees, holding my head in my hands.

The first word was spoken by B——. "Boys, let's pull on our boots and get a drink."

Salome left town within two days, her power and popularity

broken by a mocking word. But, before she left, my Mexican landlady had told her that it was *my* voice which had shouted the insult to her on the night of the party; whereupon Salome wrapped a pistol in a veil and sallied forth to get me on the street, but I was warned and kept out of her way. She had no grievance against me, for I had neither the wit nor the knowledge of mob psychology to seize on just the right moment and the right method of attack as B—— and the sheriff had done.

Two weeks later, the judge complimented the jury on the acquittal of E—— R——, saying he was glad he had been transferred as a Federal judge to such a law-and-order-loving community, etc., etc. He little dreamed that some of that jury had only fourteen days earlier been members of the necktie party, thirsting for E—— R——'s life!

Years later, when I was in London, there had been in the papers too much about some of my South African adventures, followed by much sympathy expressed for my wife and myself over the loss of our little boy who was drowned in the Thames. This brought us many kind visitors, some of them total strangers. What was my surprise, one day, to recognize a very beautiful woman, handsomely dressed, who arrived in a fine equipage, and for whom my wife poured tea while I listened to warm-hearted expressions of sympathy—*from Salome!* By some strange whirligig of fortune, our paths had crossed again! I suspected that she recognized me—probably knew beforehand who I was—but neither of us alluded to the little sunlit Arizona town, the frustrated necktie party, or the furious woman with her gun wrapped in a veil, vainly hunting for my humble self with intent to kill!

CHAPTER VII

GOLD MINING

AFTER the acquittal of my friend E—— R——, I sold my Mesa City interests and water stock. A journey into Mexico was followed by a longer one into California, when my brother Howard and I drove some very valuable horses across the desert to Los Angeles. We were three weeks in making the crossing, and the mercury each day stood around 120 degrees. Another party who tried it just ahead of us fell by the wayside and are still lying somewhere under the shifting sands. This was the same trail over which many of the early settlers of Los Angeles had crossed successfully with their wagons, stock, and families; but from June to September it invariably took cruel toll of life, both of man and of beast.

In Los Angeles, I met some old Arizona and Texas friends, and, as times were hard and dull, we decided to take a whirl for fortune in the Northwest. We were mostly of the Southwest and had much to learn of Northern frontier ways. The Mounted Police of Canada, who were the Rangers of the Northwest, had much to show us as to the management of dogs, deep snow, and cold, swift water. We had some sturdy and spirited ponies that would flounder through snow and across bogs that none of our Southern horses would attempt. They would even walk logs, but the one thing we could never teach them to do was to crouch down and pass under a fallen log as a cow or a deer will do. Once, when caught in a timber fall with a forest fire raging around us, we found a way out by digging under a huge tree trunk, then throwing our horses, tying their legs, and rolling them under the log, releasing them on the other side. We all enjoyed our sojourn among the salmon eaters and webfeet, and I gained much information that I was to use later in the Klondike. The Northwest is a world in itself and well worth the time we took to study it. When it came to following the faint traces of minerals, the men of the Southwest found they had the edge on the Northerners. We discovered several valuable mines in both Washington and Idaho. Like most scouts and prospectors, I did not find a fortune, but did uncover a hidden vein of silver that produced ore at a profit for many years.

Not long after this, I turned back to the orange grove in Pasadena, because my wife and young son were there. Besides, in those years, I had recurring fits of aberration in which I persuaded myself that I could run an orange grove at a profit. It was not long, however, before I was seized with another attack of mining fever. An old Tejana friend and I went prospecting into the San Jacinto Mountains. Here, far above the beautiful Hemet Valley made famous by the tale of Ramona, we discovered a thread of gold in quartz and opened up a little mine. Some of the ore was worth about a dollar a pound— the only trouble was that the pounds were scarce. My brother, who was just recovering from a wound received in fighting Indians on the desert, joined me at this mine, and with him came a young man who had followed me in the Northwest and who was destined to cast his vote in Congress for many years as the representative of all this mountain country—William Kettner. Here under old Tacrish (the mountain that roars) we dreamed dreams and planned expeditions into the wilds of Africa. Charley Thomas was to mount us all on his race horses. Bill Kettner was to be one of our band. But the Democratic Party caught him in its grip, and Washington, D. C., was as near Africa as he ever got. Four of us managed to elude Washington and see Africa and many other lands. But I believe Bill and I are, at this writing, the sole survivors of that lively little mining party.

Once more in Pasadena, another obsession took firm hold on me, and this one was shared equally by my wife. We believed our first child, Roderick, was a wonder whom it was our mission in life to exhibit. We took him and a doting aunt on a wide tour which lasted several months. It carried us Northeast, South, and finally wound up among the descendants of our Colonial ancestors who were still sitting quietly in New England listening, perhaps, for Paul Revere to ride by again.

Soon after our return from this trip, all my wife's family (the Blicks) came to California, and all were land hungry. There were eight of them eligible to take up government land, but the nearest bit available was about one hundred miles away on the desert. Like thousands of others, we all took up desert claims, timber claims, homesteads, homestead pre-emptions, and various other opportunities of securing the right to starve without let or hindrance. Among us we controlled several thousand acres. We had a good time building our cabins, but my most vivid recollection of that year is of the constant effort necessary to keep our horses from being stampeded and carried off among the wild horses that roamed the range. We had to tie up even our gentle old saddle horses and plough horses to keep them from joining their wild free brethren. There was one magnificent stallion with silver mane and tail that would dash up within quarter of a mile of our corral and call and cavort for an hour at a time. Great efforts were made by all of us to capture this wild leader, but when hard pressed by many riders, he would turn away into the sinks of the Mojave River and so escaped for years. A persistent cowboy named Rooney Crane became his final captor.

It was different with old Roany, our one and only milch cow. She had no fancy at all for the lonely desert, so unlike her Pasadena orange grove and alfalfa patch home. So addicted was she to civilization and society that every time a cabin door was left open she would walk in, and at times all the furniture had to be carefully carried out so she might be turned around and headed for the door without danger of wrecking the place.

While the desert land scheme was at the peak of its activity, my brother returned from the North and again infected me with the virus of mine hunting. He did not have the usual documents or maps but actually brought along an old "desert rat" who, at the close of the Civil War, was prospecting from Nevada into Death Valley and, with two companions, was driven off by hostile Piutes. The story sounded convincing, for I knew that Colonel Jack Hays of the Rangers had been called upon to subdue the Piutes at that very date. I outfitted my brother, and he, with Guesford the prospector, disappeared into the desert via Owens Lake and the State Range. They returned in about two months. The old prospector had justified himself, for after days of work he had retraced his trail to the very spot and the very pile of galena ore dug out by himself and his companions on the morning when the Piutes fired on them and drove them from the region. The richness of the find had increased in the old man's imagination through the years, but the essential facts were clear, and the ore brought back assayed eighteen ounces in silver and forty per cent. lead—good enough to be commercial if the deposit proved reasonably large.

Now all thought of desert claims and orange groves was forgotten. Roderick was big enough to walk, therefore big enough to ride. So we planned to take him along and develop the "lost mine." We outfitted for the desert with burros, as well as with buckboard and horses, for the final location of the mine could be reached only by trail over dry mountains where no horses could survive. Leaving our horses at Independence, we succeeded in reaching the lost mine and making camp. My brother's job was to run the burro train and fetch water many miles. My wife ran the commissary, and Guesford and I blasted out the shaft to test our deposit. For several weeks we were millionaires.

Suddenly, the bottom dropped out of our ore chute. As in many other Western mines, the dynamite had ruined it. For about twenty-four hours we enjoyed the glooms. There was no use turning south, as the land boom had burst and the bunch of mortgages and notes I had acquired in selling lots from my Orange Grove in Pasadena was about as valuable as the tumbleweeds on a Kansas farm. My brother, being young and adventurous, proposed to turn pirate. Guesford, being a true prospector, wished to sink the shaft deeper and would have spent a million of his own money, if he had had it, in demonstrating that there was plenty of ore there.

Finally, we separated. Guesford went on to the mines in Bodie. My brother went back to Independence, crossed the Sierras in winter, losing his horse over a snowslide, and eventually came out afoot into Yosemite Valley and went on into the old camps of the Mother Lode. I turned south with my wife and child to see if the financial blizzard had blown away every crumb of my life savings. Upon our arrival in Pasadena we found the same sun shining as of old and the same acres still in place. Everything that had happened was in men's minds. The decimal point had hopped over on the wrong side of some of the valuation figures; therefore, certain people had to go to work. Most of us had been claiming equities we had never earned, although we made a great outcry when our paper profits vanished. There was hardly a soul of us who had not lost a million.

The next few years were spent in hunting lost mines and opening up prospects from Colorado to Mexico, with occasional backslidings to ranching. One snug little fortune went up in smoke when our modest quartz mill on the desert burned just as we had melted out the first bar of gold bullion. During this period I came in contact with many young men who later became leaders in the mining world. Some of them had been hard-riding youngsters in the old days in Globe, Tombstone, and other camps—Vosberg, Mason, Murphy, Clark, Rickett, Douglas, and a hundred others of similar quality, whose unconquerable spirit helped to bring about such a rich outpouring of metallic treasure that the "Man with the Hoe" had betaken his sad visage from our American landscape.

Many strange characters eddied into our little camp on the whirlwinds or floated in from nowhere on a moonbeam: Indians, smugglers, miners, writers—even a poet, a missionary, and several criminals hiding from deputies. There was always time to study this flotsam and jetsam of the desert tides, and much of interest could be gleaned because the contacts were so much closer than is possible in the life of cities.

Vivid pictures come crowding on memory's page. There was Andy Hammond who, as a boy, fought Quantrell—Hammond lying in the streets of Globe with a dozen buckshot in him, and the man who had fired them stepping up to fire again when a passing Spanish girl jumped between the two and covered Hammond with her skirts. In those days of chivalry, no man would fire to endanger a woman, so Andy's life was saved, and in due time he recovered from his wounds. He was killed later on the Gwelo River in Africa. At that time, he had with him three companions who had adopted the foolhardy custom of the colonists and did not carry weapons, but Hammond could not so easily shake off the habits of a lifetime and carried a six-shooter, though he kept it concealed When the party were suddenly attacked by about two hundred natives, Hammond whipped out his revolver and with six shots killed five natives before they speared him. He was then more than seventy years old. His bones were among those we gathered for burial on the high veldt after the Matabele War—brave relics, surrounded by the skeletons of five of the savages who had attacked him.

CHAPTER VIII

THE CALL TO AFRICA

AFTER the combat between England and Holland for sea control had been settled, the sturdy Dutch pioneers of South Africa turned their faces to the black hinterland where, outnumbered a hundred to one by savages, for nearly two hundred years they waged a war for existence that reads like a saga of the Norsemen. At the determined advance of these uncouth, bearded, blue-eyed men who called themselves Boers, fear seized all black Africa, and the native chiefs gathered together to drive the white invaders back from Matabeleland.

To this end, the wily Lobengula enlarged and strengthened his kingdom, but by the year 1890 he was startled to learn that still another white had appeared with whom he must reckon— a ruddy beardless man of great stature and light eyes. This new menace was softer of speech and more plausible and reasonable than the harsh Boers. King Lobengula found the newcomer strangely just in his dealings, ready to pay for what he required, and faithful to his word. This was the fine strategy of Cecil John Rhodes in his dealings with the blacks: "that they should find in his tongue no fork, in his heart no hatred, and in his hand no sword."

While the trek of the English was in some ways like the Boer trek of earlier years, yet their movements were not so much aimed to dispossess the blacks as to head off the Dutch in the Transvaal from gaining the great plateau which is now Rhodesia. The extreme animosity of this struggle between Boer and Briton was somewhat analogous in spirit to the strife in Kansas and Nebraska, in the United States, when slavery or free soil hung in the balance. Between the two independent

Dutch republics and the English colonies jealousy and rancour persisted, and the bitter seeds were sown which later bore fruit in the Boer War.

Upon the shining page of South African history stand out the names of many "Vans" and "Sirs," but over all are writ in large, bold strokes the three greatest: Hoffmeyer of Cape Colony, Kruger of the Transvaal, and Rhodes of the British holdings. These were leaders of superior acumen and iron will, prepared to contend to the uttermost for what they considered their rights in the new land. Each believed firmly in the justice of his cause, and, thus armed, they pursued their course with equal courage, faith, and devotion; heroic figures, striving together like warring gods for the world destinies depending upon them.

In 1890, the power of Rhodes had grown from a nebulous wisp on the political horizon to a mighty cloud whose volume not only spread over Africa but overshadowed the whole British Empire. His superbrain evolved schemes far beyond the wildest imagination of a Hoffmeyer or a Kruger, for Rhodes possessed the most masterly mind that ever dominated the Black Continent.

At about this time, while I was mining for gold in Arizona, my attention was vigorously caught by the personality of Cecil Rhodes. In newspapers and magazines I followed the incidents of his rise with intense interest, and the more I learned of his character and achievements and aims, the more infatuated I became with the man who "thought in continents." Half a world away, I caught the glory of his splendid vision which was leading him on to rescue the vast areas of Africa from the grasp of savages and mould them into one of the great nations of the earth—surely a colossal dream of empire.

Thrilled to the core of my being, I was as one summoned by an irresistible call, and I determined to go to Africa and cast my fortune with this unknown leader who so constantly fired my imagination. I believed that my knowledge of scouting, gained on the American frontier and in fighting Indians, could be made of value to him. So I made my plans to start in 1893, when I was thirty-one years old and in what I then considered the prime of my strength and usefulness, one of the thousands who landed in Africa that year to become as grains of sand shaken by the hand of Fate across the freshly written page of events to fix the record.

This brings to mind a day on the march to Iron Mine Hill when, riding far in advance of the column, I met Major Wilson on his big buckskin, accompanied only by a Hottentot horse boy. He said he would halt the column, and we need scout no farther to the west, but might rest our horses for an hour. Then he told me that he had wanted to have a talk with me ever since I joined his command, and the burden of his inquiry was to find out just why a stray Yankee should have come all the way to Africa to join the British in their struggles. He could understand such a move on the part of any one in the British Empire, whether Tory, Liberal, or Home Ruler, but "Why an American?"

Then I explained to him that, like others of my countrymen, I had a profound admiration for a great man, and the personality of Cecil Rhodes had drawn me strongly and persistently. His aims and character were so far above those of the ordinary swashbuckling adventurer that I could not resist the call to cast in my fortunes with this unknown empire-builder, and I had hoped my experience as a scout might be of service to him in the task of conquering this great land to which he had set all the energies of his life. Wilson confessed to me that he shared my hero-worship, and we made many plans for present and future devotion and loyalty to Rhodes.

Good fortune brought me into close contact with my chosen leader, and I was never disappointed in my first enthusiasm. Many of my countrymen, knowing of my close relations with Rhodes, have asked me about the man, and before I could answer, they would begin to describe him to me as a monstrous land grabber, a greedy capitalist, and so on; accusing him of wickedly and cruelly conquering inoffensive natives and of destroying the noble Free Republic of South Africa.

Perhaps the easiest and most rational way of replying to such accusations would be to begin to decry Lincoln as the ruthless destroyer of the noble South, or to arraign Marshall for limiting liberty by law, or to blame Monroe for scheming the subjection of South America. If the causing of pain is itself a sin and an evil, then no one should ever have been born. Nations, like human beings, always experience pain at birth. It is a law as immutable as gravity. The conquest of South Africa caused much pain to conquerors and conquered, but from that event came a beautiful new life, a wonderful nation, a flower of civilization where once grew only rank weeds of savagery and ignorance, and the chief credit for that noble result should be given to the prophetic genius and wise efforts of Cecil John Rhodes.

Hoffmeyer was a trusted, patriotic, and much-loved man in the Cape Colony. He held the esteem of both English and Dutch. He had a vision of final peace between Boer and Briton, and would gladly have followed Rhodes in all his plans for the development of South Africa. But his policy did not reach beyond the Zambezi River and certainly did not contemplate absorption into the British Empire, even though assured sovereign rights. There came at last a parting of the ways between Rhodes and Hoffmeyer or rather a slackening of the pace of Hoffmeyer, who could not keep step with the Colossus. Yet these two men almost persuaded Oom Paul to clear the road to the north and to join in a great confederation of the white colonies of Africa, whose northern bounds were not set and might not be for generations.

But the thought of contact with other great nations and the ruling of a hundred million blacks; of railways, armies, navies, cities, and a vast commerce, drove Oom Paul back to his Bible and the narrow paths of his youth. His desire was for a solitary, hermit nation where no stranger should ever set foot and where every Dutchman should own a farm of three thousand morgen —about nine square miles. Because of this let no one think Oom Paul a simple man. He was crafty and resourceful, as many a shrewd speculator and trader found to his cost. His massive body carried a massive brain, and his deep, booming voice spoke with a fixity of purpose as hard as flint. He loved his people and, according to his lights, he fought for them with all his strength and all the resources at his command. It required unusual qualities to withstand the march of modern civilization so long as he did, especially when the forces of progress were marshalled and led by such a man as Rhodes. It was the trek-tow against the railroad, the English language against a patois spoken by less than half a million people. As an American, I felt for Oom Paul as I had felt for some of the great Sioux chiefs who were my boyhood enemies. They belonged to another age; they could not adjust themselves. Most of the Boers in Cape Colony and other coast lands had long ago joined with the British colonists, and their position was an honoured one, corresponding to that of the Dutch who transferred their citizenship when New Amsterdam became New York. But in the two Boer republics of the Orange Free State and the Transvaal it was the intention of Oom Paul to call a halt for ever to the British advance. There, for thirty years, this Lion of the North indeed crouched across the trail and no Rooinek passed.

And now what can I write of Rhodes? Many volumes have already been printed and there will be more to follow, long after those of us who knew him have passed away. I feel it is a great presumption on my part to write anything; yet, as I recall the daily happenings of my life in Africa, its hopes, fears, and ideals, the spirit of Rhodes, like the strong breeze across the high veldt, is ever present though unseen. It would be hard indeed to describe all that I believe to be essential to a true leader or to analyse what attracts other men to him. A frontiersman like myself is perhaps especially keen to read and study the inner mind and find out the sources of the strength or weakness of his leader. Perhaps any one who has always been obliged to make his own decisions swiftly and accurately may demand that ability to be paramount in one whom he is willing to follow. In all my dealings with Rhodes, he stood this test, but it was only one of his many superior qualities.

It is not enough to say, although it is true, that Rhodes was unusually constructive and practical and that he was clearly dominated by a high and kindly philosophy, for that description could be fitted to lesser men. Just where his remarkable superiority lay would be hard to determine. In his personal tastes and habits he was a model of simplicity, yet his mentality was exceedingly complex. He had an extraordinary combination of romantic vision and hard common sense; the indomitable force of the virile Norseman tempered by the thoughtful humanity of the Oxford don and infused with the subtlety of a born master of statecraft. In some with whom he came in contact he roused an immediate and singularly violent antipathy, while in others he lighted such a fire of enthusiasm that they fairly burned to do or die for any cause he might espouse. The word "superman" best describes him, for the great qualities he possessed seemed irradiated and strengthened by the very essence of the man. His inspiration could best be understood by meeting his eye or hearing his voice—a purely personal illumination.

Rhodes had the courage of a lion. He hated bloodshed. He did not believe in lordship over subject races, but admitted that backward races should be guarded, conserved, developed. Scrupulous justice and unlimited mercy were shown in all his adjudications. He was never misled by slogans, nor did he believe that the Voice of the People is the Voice of God. He recognized too well the crimes that have been committed by popular vote, from the Crucifixion to the present day. He did believe that the civilization of the English-speaking world was to become the pivotal point around which all peaceful nations might safely rally. Under the administration of Rhodes, there were the fewest laws, the widest freedom, the least crime, and the truest justice I have ever seen in any part of the world.

Though the colonists were high-spirited men, used to arms and impatient of control, and although money was plentiful and valuables were inviting to the pilferer, yet crime was almost unknown; doors were left unlocked and the jails were empty. The nearest approach I have known to the Rhodesian condition of things was in the early days of the Klondike rush, when tons of gold were carried down the creeks and shipped without guard, and cabins and tents were wide open. Some unseen spirit of good government must have ruled Alaska during those first days; some exquisite Ariel of Law, as subtle and intangible as the bouquet of the vintage of '84. In Alaska, we said, "It is in the air—this marvellous, pure, still Arctic air!" In Africa, all men would have agreed that it lay in the magnetic and forceful personality of Cecil Rhodes.

A hero worth worshipping is so seldom found in this world that a journey to the ends of the earth to find and serve such a one is well repaid. Knowing this, I, an American prejudiced by ill-written histories to feel sharply antagonistic to the English, deliberately set out for unknown Africa to put myself into the hands of an Englishman I had never seen; who yet so completely fulfilled and satisfied all my ideals of what a real man should be that I gave him my enthusiastic devotion and service, which did not end until, in 1902, the wild ceremonial death chant of the Matabele echoed over the kingly sepulchre of Cecil John Rhodes in the far Matoppo Mountains of Rhodesia.

CHAPTER IX

THE LONG TRAIL

OUR journey to Africa began at San Francisco on January 1, 1893. My wife and I did not expect to see the United States again for many years; indeed, we might never see it again. This statement is amusing now, since we have run back and forth across continents some thirty times, but our first leave-takings from friends and relatives were as solemn and final as ever those of the pioneers of the Santa Fé trail or the English colonists who sailed away for wildest America in their little wooden ships in 1620.

We turned north, touching at Vancouver and the Sound, then across Canada, the Lakes, and on to Washington, D. C. My son Roderick, then aged six, will always remember Washington as the place where something bit his ears when the sun was shining brightly, though he had managed to traverse Canada without recognizing the sharp nip of Jack Frost. Soon after this we sailed from New York, landing at Liverpool, whence we wandered for a while around England.

To those Americans who feel pride in their own history, the British Isles must always make a strong appeal. It set our hearts to bounding to recall that out of those harbours, for a thousand years, had sailed the rulers of the world and the builders of many nations, including our own. It was flattering to my self-esteem to find the family name of my remote forbears carved in stone on ancient monuments, as well as perpetuated in the naming of one of the few bits of primeval forest left in the kingdom, Burnham Beeches. Every acre of those little islands anchored off the coast of Europe seemed saturated with romantic history. To the unemotional and self-contained Englishman, I must have appeared an animated interrogation point, asking questions about as relevant to his orderly mind as those of Alice in Wonderland.

It was not long before a good many settled convictions had to be taken out of remote corners of our minds and readjusted and retabulated. Worse yet, and more humiliating, we had to discard from our mental attics a lot of very dear, dusty prejudices. Parting with prejudices is always painful, especially if they are of the inherited or heirloom variety, as many of mine were.

England was delightful and absorbing, but the time came to resume our trek.

It is unnecessary to recount in detail the personal experiences of a small American family suddenly picked up from the far West and dropped into the midst of the crowded civilizations of Europe. All that happened to us has happened to thousands of other Americans and is best recorded by such historians as Mark Twain. Every hour, we had cause to laugh at ourselves. As a substitute for the spoken word, I sometimes made use of the Indian sign language, and, strange to say, it often worked quite well. A little study of the local customs of the people, and care taken not to offend in any way, resulted in many favours being shown us, sometimes demanding much time and thought and done without hope of tips or reward.

The winter of 1893 was severe. We had a wardrobe selected for tropical Africa and found it a poor one with which to meet the rigours of France and Switzerland. We suspected why our forerunners, the Goths, had been in such a hurry to cross the Alps and reach the warm shores of Italy. But even in Italy it was cold, so we were glad to glide out of the Bay of Naples and see the feathery plume of its volcano fade away, and at night watch the molten lava flow down the cliffs of Stromboli into the sea. Hurrah! We were on our way!

The inactivity of steamer life gave us our first pause since landing at Liverpool in which to catalogue the impressions so rapidly gained. The mind seemed like a steamer which had taken on a mixed cargo during the last thirty days. Now we must clear the deck by sorting out all valuables and storing them away in cabin and hold, while useless stuff must be heroically jettisoned before the next port. Unfortunately, mental cargo is not easily stowed away and often refuses to be discarded. One night, while passing the Island of Cyprus, all the sounds that had been vibrating during the past month seemed to return and orchestrate themselves in my mind. In America my ears had been attuned to catch natural sounds, from the hum of insects to the peal of thunder, but the sounds of crowded Europe were all man-made. There were the crash and grind of street cries and noises, there were bands, cathedral music, solemn chants, bugle calls, laughter, and dancing—all dominated by the rhythm of marching feet audible to one who, like the buffalo hunter, presses his ear to the ground.

After a great storm, ridden out by the help of oil bags, we neared the coast of Africa, toward which all eyes were strained. I was the first to sight land. How I had longed for this moment! Here at last, after years of striving and many defeats, lay the kingdom of my heart's desire before my eyes! Its dream shores stretched before me, inviting exploration of the unknown. However the adventure might end, I felt I could die content. Those who know me intimately will understand why I was more thrilled by the first low, sandy dunes of Africa than by all the wonders of Europe. The lure of this oldest yet newest of lands had held me in thrall for many years. It was hard to leave the shores of Egypt almost immediately, but we promised ourselves a sure return.

At Suez, that universal joint of the Eastern and Western worlds, the working of the huge German war machine first came to my notice. Several tall, grim-looking German officers came on board, filling the lower decks with Soudanese recruits and their families, all being transported to Dar-es-Salaam, the capital of Germany's new and vast East African possessions.

The contact with Asia at Aden opened fresh avenues of thought and led to more throwing overboard of useless mental cargo. I happened to meet a retired United States Army officer, a Westerner by birth, who was in some dim way connected with the Intelligence Department of our government. He gave me a laughable five-minute rehearsal of my own beliefs and imaginings in regard to Asia and the Asiatics as they were at that moment, to which I was forced to assent as ninety per cent. correct. He admitted that those same ideas had once been held by himself. Then, in an illuminating thirty minutes, he explained wherein nearly all the objects and ideals we had both attributed to these Eastern people were erroneous. Ten years in Asia had given him mental glasses of another colour through which to observe their life history and study their thoughts and their reasons for certain lines of action. But he added quickly, "Even now I may have to change again half of what I believe of these people. In a thousand ways they are like us— and in a thousand others as different from us as the colours of the rainbow are from one another, though all blend in white."

We were surprised to find that Aden is more important than Gibraltar as a vantage point in the trade routes of the world. It would take a volume in itself to describe it fully and justly. Most travellers gaze on its great rocks under the pitiless sun, and pass on as unaware of its hidden power as the plodding camels that wind over its trails to the desert beyond. But the silent Arab swaying on the camel's back gazes at the Unbeliever with inscrutable eyes, and one is vaguely conscious of a hatred born of a thousand years of alien thoughts and aims. The British officers here are mostly those who have had long Indian experience. They resent the questioning of tourists, and seem in a way to live like turtles inside a very hard shell. As they bump against representatives of every nation and class in the world, this shell is probably a necessary protection; yet, once in a while, they open up to an unobtrusive stranger, and then their portrayal of things Oriental is vivid and illuminating. What they imparted to me gave me a new and priceless insight into the soul of the East.

At this point I witnessed the first meeting of German and British forces joined in a campaign against the slavers of Nyassa. The Soudanese had poured on deck, to the loudly shouted commands of their German officers, with a confusion and jabbering that reminded me of roosting time in a poultry yard. But I was not even aware that the British were embarking their forces until I glanced down on the deck and saw that already half their company of turbaned Sikhs were gliding noiselessly to their quarters. They were tall, slender, silent men and they moved in perfect order to the commands delivered in conversational tones by one solitary British officer. Embarking on a strange ship for an unknown land might have been an everyday matter to them for all that their appearance or manner betrayed. Their officer was only a first lieutenant—Edwards, then starting on that brilliant career which was so soon to win him a colonelcy, fame, honours, and—alas, death!

This was my first close contact with a British officer, and he proved to be the opposite of all my anticipations. I was charmed by his graceful manners, his high sense of duty, and the simplicity and directness of his mind. We became fast friends and together studied our crude maps of Africa and promised each other that we would meet again in the near future, as I then hoped to join one of the expeditions of Cecil Rhodes and come up from the South. Two years later we approached within a hundred miles of each other, but never actually met again, although at that time we exchanged greetings and messages by runners. Lieutenant Edwards's career was truly remarkable. Sir Harry Johnston, High Commissioner of Nyassaland, in his absorbing book, "The Story of My Life," pays high tribute to the qualities of this gallant officer. With his hundred Sikhs and the aid of the local police force of Nyassaland, Edwards drilled a large force of natives and defeated the powerful Wahi again and again.

On the other hand, the Germans, new at the colonial game, spent large sums of money and lost fifteen hundred of their native levies as well as many trained officers, before they succeeded in controlling this same tribe.

Crowded in the narrow confines of our ship were representatives of ten nations and several races, each group clinging with tenacity to its own traditions, its own beliefs, and its own conventions. There was the rigid, sword-clanking German; the reserved, confident Britisher; the ceremonious, caste-bound

Sikh, and the childish yet ferocious Soudanese. Each lived his daily life as near to his accustomed habit as possible, and each doubtless in his own heart derived satisfaction from criticizing the absurd ways of the others. Very likely the secret memoranda of their various opinions as to the strange little American family on board would have proved illuminating—and perhaps humiliating! One morning, I stood on the upper deck watching the Sikhs below as they prepared their food. Suddenly one, glancing up, saw my absorbed attention, whereat he promptly threw his ration overboard. Immediately the whole assembled soldiery followed his example. I stood dumbfounded, when Lieutenant Edwards appeared and asked me gently to turn my back and walk away, explaining that I had outraged one of their conventions. For me, an unbeliever, to gaze upon them as they prepared their food rendered it unfit in their eyes, and they had just discarded their polluted rations without a moment's hesitation. Needless to say, I never offended in this respect again, and I learned an invaluable lesson as to the political importance of considering the notions of other races by which I have profited ever since.

Every hour from Aden grew in interest. Here before my eyes were working specimens of the policies of those European nations dealing with Asiatics and Africans. Assuredly, the German officers had a forceful way with them, exercising a grim discipline which recalled that of Cæsar's Tenth Legion. They insisted on drilling the poor seasick Soudanese daily on the crowded decks of the *Reichstag*. Persistent, tireless, inflexible, these officers devoted hours to the deck work and then turned for mental relaxation to the study of maps or their great war game, "Kriegspiel." In my individualistic and independent American mind, their manners and methods roused a strong antagonism in spite of my profound respect for their industry, their excellent mental equipment, and the firm resolution which seemed to enforce every move they made. It amazed me to see how rapidly they managed to instil the rudiments of drill into the raw Soudanese. Even the little boys took to it and were used as instructors to drill the more awkward. Yet, through it all, there seemed to me something lacking in their method. They did not hold their men in the same spirit which the British maintained.

The thought kept recurring to my mind that some day we must clash with these Teutons. Wherever the Germans put their feet they seemed to rouse antipathy. Just what set every one against them, I could not have told. They were large, powerful men, and in moments when they could dispense with the click of heels and their formal courtesies, they tried to unbend and sometimes would become quite human and jolly over a mug of beer and a good song. Nevertheless, I always sensed a potential enemy in them. They seemed so different from the German neighbours and friends I had known and liked in America. One night, as they were looking over their maps, news came on board from a passing steamer that the British fleet lay off Salonika. It seemed as if the Day of Reckoning had come. A hush fell on the Germans. Soon they were closeted with the ship's officers, and when they reappeared, every face wore the mask assumed by all military men in time of stress and danger. I recognized it through all their smiles and jokes. Every move betrayed the strain and that they were mentally as taut as the sinew strings on an Apache bow. Then word was brought that the British fleet had sailed away. The Turk was left dreaming on the shores of his wonderful sea, and on our ship the German and British officers saluted gravely as usual and agreed to work in unison in defeating the Wahi slavers on Lake Nyassa.

It was on this voyage I made the discovery that I could play chess. Indeed, it was the first really idle time I ever remember having. The German officers played often, both chess and the war game—and these games have much in common. Sometimes a game would last far into the night, or even until dawn.

The steamships of the Ost Afrika Line, being new in the Eastern trade, called at many obscure ports for freight, and this gave us opportunities to see strange sights along the coast. Each port had its surprises for us, and doubtless we were of some interest to the staring inhabitants. Perhaps some of them wondered if we were fair samples of the Yankees or Americans and just how our peculiarities had been acquired; while we marvelled at the Somalis, whose long, kinky hair, bleached to a tawny yellow, stands straight up like that of a circus Albino and, with their dark skins and gleaming white teeth, gives a startling effect. They cleanse their teeth with the twig of a certain plant and after each using cut off an inch or two, so there is a brand-new toothbrush ready for the next occasion. This method is at least sanitary. It was said of Montezuma of Mexico that he had a new spoon for each mouthful of beans; doubtless, that finicky monarch would have appreciated the Somali toothbrush.

A rocky headland was pointed out to me with the information that within a few years five ships had been wrecked there and that in each case the wreck had been looted by the natives and every soul on board hideously slain. Africa is distinctly temperamental.

Among the passengers taken on were six missionaries, so it appeared we were doing something to keep up the tradition of our race—that every cargo landed on the African coast includes "rum, gunpowder, and the Bible." The native bids fair to withstand even this combination, judging from the ancient ruins which indicate that his civilization twenty thousand years ago was as far advanced as it is to-day.

Past headlands austere and arid we glided into warm seas alive with dolphins, flying fish, and the beautiful sailing nautilus. It was at night, with the water full of fire, that the first faint breath of spice blew softly to us from the shores of Zanzibar. It was the height of the clove season and the aromatic odour was pure and penetrating; the more so as the British who now control the island had passed laws forbidding adulteration. An Arab dhow, loaded to the limit, had been condemned, run on shore, and set afire, cargo and all. As it burned slowly, the pungent perfume drifted for days far out to sea. In the light of morning, the glistening water and the graceful sails made a picture as beautiful as a poem.

We arrived just after the Sultan of Zanzibar had declared war on the British. It was probably the shortest war in history. It lasted forty minutes. At the end of that time, the Sultan's navy was sunk, his palace a ruin, and the white flag was flying in token of surrender. In a few days, a new Sultan was enthroned and all was well This strange old Arab city has been the end of the trail for all the great caravans of slaves and ivory that through the centuries have come down from the far mountains and the inland seas of Africa. In modern times its streets have been trodden by the great explorers, Stanley, Livingstone, Speke, and McKinnon; by Emin Pasha the soldier and Tippoo Tib the slaver. Many nations have held this coast but none for long: Phœnicians, Semites, Egyptians, Arabs, Portuguese, Germans, and now the British. On the mainland at Mombasa, long ago, Vasca da Gama built one of his massive forts, still a marvel of construction. What a man he was! Four hundred years after his passing, his works still dot the islands of two oceans and the shores of four continents. Far inland, for two thousand miles, I was to tread the trails of men sent out by him on explorations from these vantage posts. Yet all this wealth of empire he laid in vain at the feet of his sovereign. Poor little Portugal could not see beyond her narrow borders or appreciate the gifts her great son brought home.

We discharged our cargo in part at Dar-es-Salaam, Germany's African capital. The Soudanese warriors with all their wives and children were duly landed, and from here they went forward to their undoing by the Wahi and the jungle fever. They, like hundreds of others, never saw again the yellow sky of their own Soudan. Mozambique was our next call. This was another outpost built by the Portuguese in their Golden Age. Here, under the pink and rose coloured walls, we parted with Lieutenant Edwards and his tall, silent Sikhs. His fate was to fight the Wahi very successfully and then to lay himself down in the jungle for his eternal rest. Three years later, I was to see the landing at this port of eight missionaries en route to their inland station. They were inexperienced youths from America who knew nothing of African life. The savages they went to teach knew more than they of the essential things. In twenty-two months, all were dead from fever. Their story was, in its own way, as pathetic as that of the children of Europe, marched by Peter the Hermit across the continent to capture the Holy Sepulchre from the fierce Saracens and within a twelvemonth leaving their little bones dotted along the frozen passes of the Balkans.

The landing of our small family was to be at the next port, Beira, on the shore of Africa due east of Mashonaland (now Rhodesia)—our destination. But when we reached Beira we learned that the Pungwe River was in flood and all communication up-country cut off, so we decided to go on to Durban, Natal, and trek via the Transvaal and Johannesburg to Mashonaland, an extra thousand miles. After playing a farewell round of chess with the officers of the *Reichstag*, I was ready for the landing.

Durban was a surprising little city, more English than England, yet a very independent colony. Our astonishment at the beautiful shops, great stores, parks, gardens, and homes only proved how little we knew of the world. My wife had a good laugh over the precious things she had purchased in London thinking that, of course, nothing could be bought in Africa. Among these things was a tea set. Almost the first day in Durban she saw in a shop window a set of the identical pattern and at the exact London price.

We fell quite in love with this quaint colony and its friendly people. It seemed to us in spirit much as some of the American colonies must have been before the Revolution. Here we outfitted for our trek north. The extra fare to Durban had drawn heavily on our little store of money, and we found, to our dismay, that everything was at boom prices. The great gold rush to Johannesburg had absorbed all the spare oxen and the black labour as well. A full span of oxen—eighteen head—with good wagon and equipment, would now cost a small fortune, and we were more than a thousand miles from our destination, where I might or might not find employment when I arrived.

What if Rhodes, with his empire-building schemes, should find no use, after all, for a stray American from the Far West?

But on the faintest hint that I might leave my wife and Roderick in the comfortable town of Durban while I should go up country with some freight outfit to get a foothold, my wife's pioneering blood began to tingle, and I knew there was no hesitancy on her part to venture on the long trek north.

CHAPTER X

THE TREK NORTH

OUR first few days in Durban were disheartening. Everything on wheels was ponderous and built to last a hundred years. It took six mules or oxen to move the lightest Cape cart or Scotch cart and the smallest up-country trek wagon took ten oxen and required a fore-loper to lead them, as well as a driver. I knew how to drive oxen in the American fashion, but these African beasts are broken to drive with a light pole yoke and are managed with "rims," and I found that either the oxen or I would have to be broken over again before I could drive them. To handle the African whip, which is from thirty to forty feet long, and make proper use of all its signals, is nearly as difficult as learning to throw the lasso; both are arts that need to be acquired in early youth.

Fortunately, in the suburbs of Durban we found the kinsmen of our old American friend, the burro. Had not his blood brothers carried us over miles of mountain and desert in America, facing blizzards and sandstorms and, though hating water, swimming flooded streams, pack and all? Burros for us! Best of all, they were cheap—only fifteen dollars each. Now, if we could only find an American buckboard, we would soon be off!

All the next day I searched the go-downs. The only light vehicle I found was a rickshaw used to carry local passengers. This was designed to be pulled about town by a big Zulu boy and could not by any stretch of imagination be converted into a trek wagon. At last, I found in a warehouse the running gears of an American buckboard that had at some time been sent out from the United States by an agent of the famous Studebakers. Straightway our hopes of continuing our journey took on a rosy hue. Nobody in Africa had been willing to trust himself in such a frail vehicle, so the gears were stored in a loft and forgotten. I purchased them for one hundred dollars and found a sympathetic workman who made the slat wagon bed and put on the spring seat according to the plans I sketched for him. Meanwhile, there was a search for harness. Nothing was suitable, so, to save time and money, I bought a hide of good leather and a few tools and rivets, and in short order made up a strong and serviceable breast-strap harness.

My wife packed all our necessary stores in small space, as she well knew how to do, and quilted a mattress for the floor of the buckboard, and when she had sewed a canvas cover for it, we were about ready to start. The four burros I had purchased had never been driven or hitched to a wagon, so we held an exciting dress rehearsal in the hotel yard, much to the amusement of the very polite guests, for in Durban "things are not done that way, you know." My performance was not brilliantly successful. Two of my burros, I discovered, were fairly intelligent; a third was rather mean-tempered, and the fourth was just plain feeble-minded and forgetful. He insisted, for instance, on turning round frequently and facing the driver. Reasoning with him was vain—he was too dull-witted to comprehend.

Time was pressing, hotel bills were mounting, and it was a long road to Mashonaland. The proprietor of the inn was a very kind-hearted woman, and when she saw the uncertain little outfit that was for months to carry us over deserts, rivers, and mountains in a land where we could not speak one word of the native language, she begged my wife to abandon the trek, with Roderick, and let me go on ahead. She suggested that there would be opportunity to follow later with more safety and comfort in some wagon train. As a last resort, when she found we were obdurate, she sent a Zulu boy with us for the first sixty miles, secretly believing that experience of a few days on the veldt would at least drive my wife and boy back to Durban. But she did not know my wife.

It so happened that our departure was on a Sunday morning.

THE TREK NORTH

The burros spent so much time moving up and down instead of forward that we got behind our schedule and found ourselves passing the church in Durban just as the worshippers were filing out. From their faces it was clear that they had never before seen just our kind of outfit starting for the north. I confess we felt embarrassed, and in almost any other land, unless it were altogether heathen, we would have been the butt of ridicule. But Durban is always dignified, for which we blessed her on that occasion. Nevertheless, we were glad to get away into the wilderness and away from so many curious eyes.

At Pietermaritzburg we paid off the black servant and sent him back with a note to our kind-hearted hostess; after which, I took the education of our burros seriously in hand. They soon learned that I spoke their language. They might fool with me in town, like spoiled children with company in the house, but out on the veldt I tolerated no nonsense, and they had to move ahead all together, not merely up and down and end for end. We were able before long to sell the absent-minded one, and for the fabulous price of five pounds I purchased a very strong burro which I soon broke in as leader. He was so wise we dubbed him "Doctor." Roderick had much fun in naming and riding the animals. He called them Doc, Ta-ra, Ah Sin, and Ty Wink.

Now we felt we were really off. Settlements were far apart. Clumps of blue gums and black wattle dotted out the ranches or farms of both British and Boers. We were climbing the great rounded hills of Natal (the Zululand of our old geographies) through air as balmy as that of California, and we exclaimed aloud that these natives passing along the roads were really Zulus!—those terrible blacks that broke the regiments of England! We were destined to see on this trek the famous Majuba Hill where, in 1881, the British were defeated by the Boers. It is rare to find such spots in the world and they are soon famous because of their rarity. They are especially worth studying in order to learn why the British were defeated. In this instance the Boers were the Minute

Men of their Lexington and Concord and animated by similar ideas.

As we climbed the great Drakensberg Mountains, the little burros hardened to the harness and pulled our earthly belongings at the rate of fifteen to seventeen miles per day. On the up grades we all walked, to spare our team. We always found good excuses for walking—because the air was so chilly, and so on. The order of the day was: up at dawn; cook a breakfast of bacon, coffee, and corn cakes; inspan at sunrise, trek about four hours and outspan three. The afternoon trek was usually three hours, making an average day of seven hours' actual travel but about fourteen of active occupation. We carried water enough to make a dry camp at night in case we should fail to reach a spruit or well. Roderick would herd the team where the grass was good and soon taught the burros to come at his call to get a handful of shelled mealies. This saved his young legs from running many a mile after the grazing stock. Our animals were now becoming very docile and drove to line and whip like carriage horses, except that two and a half miles per hour is good speed for burros in harness. In this mile-a-minute age that may seem slow, yet it was better time than an ox cart could make, and it enabled us to have a change of scene every day and to enjoy every minute of it.

Sunday was nominally a day of rest. All my wife had to do was to wash and mend clothes, cook an extra good big dinner in the Dutch oven, and write a long letter home. Roderick looked after the stock while I overhauled the harness, greased the buckboard, reloaded the rig, and tried to replenish the larder with game or bought supplies at near-by farms or kraals. Fuel was scarce and was carried with care. It always repays effort to have a good fire at night and to be able to sit around it for an hour or so before turning in. There is something very comforting in watching the glowing coals, but there were many weeks when this joy was denied us, buffalo chips being our only fuel. Probably the camp fire, rest, and peace were synonymous terms to our ancestors for thousands of years, and a little of the heritage of peace comes down to us now when we take time to sit by a fire and let fancy roam where it will. We are relieved from the need of conversation, and the silence is eloquent of good-will and repose.

After crossing the Drakensbergs we reached the rolling plateaus of the Transvaal; a country similar in topography to our own West along the eastern flank of the Rocky Mountains—a grass country, once the home of enormous herds of game but now sparsely settled by the Boers, whose farms are not unlike our own American cattle ranches. Each home ranch grows a little corn and stock-feed and here and there a more ambitious farmer cultivates a garden and raises ornamental flowers, shrubs, and fruit trees.

One day, as we were passing one of these farms, a gray-bearded Boer came out to chat with us. He informed us that he was quite wealthy and that he had trekked all over South Africa. On finding that we were bound for Mashonaland, he urged us strongly to lie over two weeks at his farm and join with him and some of his sons who were making ready to go north with their big wagons. He pointed out that it would be impossible for us to cross the rivers with our little burros; that the lions would surely eat them; and that for us to go into such a wilderness would be both foolish and dangerous. We appreciated his kindness, as well as the value of his intimate knowledge of African life, but we were set on going without delay. As we started down the road, he called me aside and said: "You are new in this land. You should not risk the lives of your wife and child this way. Some of my people were eaten by lions, and yours may be also. I will give you a Scotch cart and six oxen if you will go along with my sons and sons-in-law and our friends in a regular trek."

This was certainly a generous offer and showed the kindliness of some of these isolated and hardy people. The next day this same Boer overtook us, riding a fine horse. He again urged us to lie over and join him and his sons in their trek. But, with more determination than judgment, we pushed on until we reached the end of the first stage of our journey, at Johannesburg.

I have known nothing like this place in all the world. Boer government, English capital, and black labour by hundreds of thousands under the management of American engineers, using their superior methods of mining, formed a combination that had never before been brought about. However, there are many accurate descriptions to be read of this huge city with its miles of gold reefs and its thundering stamp mills, so I will not attempt to describe it. It made all other mining camps I had seen seem small. From here we trekked to Pretoria, the Boer capital—a most interesting town of about forty thousand people and distant forty miles from Johannesburg.

There, for the first time, I saw Paul Kruger, that forceful product of the soil of Africa, who, ignorant and densely superstitious, was yet to match his wits and power astutely against imperial Rhodes and make the name of "Oom Paul" a household word in many nations. His great booming voice ordering his burghers to war started armies moving in Europe and navies steaming at top speed. A world war was averted only by a hair's breadth.

In Pretoria, we found a rumour of smallpox and a rigid quarantine threatened, so we acted in haste. We laid in supplies for our further trek and purchased two more burros, promptly christened Babe and Chub. We built a cartel or bed of rawhide, bought a sawed-off shotgun and pounds of lead, to keep the lions from eating up Roderick or the stock, and galloped at top speed (fully three miles an hour) out of Pretoria just in time to escape the quarantine.

We now began to feel that we had a power plant sufficient to warrant our riding most of the time. The country grew wilder and more interesting; the great Blauburg loomed purple and blue in the distance. Every day was full of memorable incidents. Thousands of natives were seen moving south to work in the gold mines or in the diamond fields of Kimberley and De Beers. In a few days, we hit the edge of the bush veldt and for the first time had real wood for fuel instead of the buffalo chips of the plains. That day I shot several pheasants and we roasted them in a reflector before the fire. From now on the gun played an important part in sustaining the commissary. Gradually the farms disappeared and finally even the Kafir staats (settlements).

We were now entering the dry, thorny bush and jungle toward the Limpopo or Crocodile River. The sun was hot; sand flies and gnats in clouds ate into the tough hides of our burros and greatly annoyed us all. The sand was deep and we were obliged to walk. At last, we saw trees in the distance, and knew there must be a water hole there; but on arrival we found they were the pale, sickly, yellow-green fever trees, and in their branches sat that creature of ill omen, the Get-away bird—all just as the old Boer had foretold. He had warned me that my wife and little boy would die of fever, if they were not eaten by lions, before ever I reached Mashonaland. This was one of the few afternoons when we camped in silence and gloom. The doleful, reiterated cry of the Get-away bird was as persistent as the throb of an African drum and more nerve-racking than the "Nevermore" of Poe's raven. Even the game had left this fever hole. I shot only a small parrot, a killdeer, and one lone pigeon; not much of a meal for three hungry trekkers. The parrot proved inedible, as tough as whalebone, although it had been made into a pot-pie, but the killdeer and the pigeon were very palatable. At this place we saw our first black mamba: a six-foot member of the cobra family and the deadliest of all the snakes of Africa. It seemed appropriately placed by Nature in this dismal environment.

But next morning when we trekked away to more open lands our high spirits returned with a bound and every hill beckoned us on to the next. We came now to a fork in the road. The main route by way of Tuli was that most favoured by freight teams; the other was a dim hunter's road used by the Boers, which crossed the Crocodile River at Rhodes's drift. Although we knew that this ran through a long dry stretch of thorny jungle, it was much shorter than the main road, and we decided to take it. We would load our canteens with water and trek day and night with only short halts, until we reached the river.

We were now in the lion country—and we had been told

the lions were very fond of burro meat. Besides, there were leopards and hyenas about which might attack a child even in the daytime, so we did not dare allow Roderick to leave the buckboard. At night we built fires and replenished them often for fear the lions would kill the burros and leave us afoot on the veldt. When travelling at night I walked beside the burros or just ahead of them with a gun and let my wife do the driving. The natives, if compelled to move at night, usually carry a torch. The wise warnings of our old Boer friend often recurred to my mind on these night marches.

While crossing this long dry stretch we were joined by some trek wagons and felt much more at ease in their company. The night camps were wonderful. The ponderous wagons drawn up in laager (fortified camp) protected alike the great spans of oxen, the horses, and the people. Within their circle the blazing fires, the steaming coffee, and roasting biltong, chased away all fatigue. Outside, the wild animals sent up their cries, each according to his kind, while overhead the moon and stars—so marvellously clear and bright in that pure air—gave the illumination best befitting the scene. It is no wonder the Boer hates to have his country overrun by strangers. He loves his wilderness and feels no mad haste to conquer it. His great trek wagons, his good horses and oxen, and his numerous black servants give him speed and comfort enough in travelling. The cares of government do not oppress him. As he keeps most of the Ten Commandments from conscience, few police and no standing army or extensive law courts and jails are required. So it is not without regret that we see his day pass and the new era of silk and steel replace the trek-tow and the veldt schoen.

The Fourth of July found us in camp near the parting of our roads to the north. We were here visited by two young Americans who were trekking north with the big wagons. Their names were Bain and Ingram, and both were destined to play important parts in the development of Rhodesia. Reminiscing as to why, whence, and how this particular group of Americans should be gathered together in this bit of thorn bush in Africa, we found that the same lodestar had drawn us all—the reputation of Cecil John Rhodes. We also found that Ingram and I, strangers to each other, though later to become brothers-in-law, had both stood beside Lotta's fountain in San Francisco exactly one year before, watching the whole city at play, and had both left at the same time by different routes for the same destination in Mashonaland, Africa.

We had a great celebration of the Fourth, with doughnuts, pot-pie, and plenty of noise. The next morning we parted, but met again on the banks of the dreaded Crocodile River. The fording of this stream had for days loomed large in the mind of everybody along the road, although my youthful experience in crossing such rivers as the Missouri, Columbia, and Rio Grande gave me a certain confidence which the Boers thought the result of ignorance or conceit. The Crocodile, like many rivers in Africa and our own West, is dangerous only when in flood, but it was swimming water for our little burros with the floating buckboard. After firing into the water to scare away the numerous crocodiles, Roderick and my wife and our supplies were put on one of the big wagons. At the last, we added our small fox terrier, for the crocodiles would surely get her if she were left to swim. We had purchased the little beast from a native for twenty-five cents, but, as she had shared all our hardships without a whimper, her sentimental value was beyond price. All our treasures were landed safely, and Bain, Ingram, and I crossed my little Yankee outfit successfully, much to the amazement of the other trekkers.

Just across the river, we established camp at Ingongsloop. Some Boer hunters and English colonials were planning to have a hunt to lay in a supply of biltong for food up country, and I decided to join them. This region was too dangerous to allow Roderick to herd the animals, and I was so busy overhauling rifles and ammunition that I failed one night to bring the burros in to laager before dark. A little later, two came in of their own accord, and about seven o'clock a great braying and charging through the bush announced the arrival of Chub and Doc. Lions had nearly got them, and they were telling us all about it. Taking a rifle, I rushed out into the bush, thinking I could call in the other two burros. On glancing back, I saw my wife following me with a lantern and the sawed-off shotgun. I have always flattered myself she came out into the bush to save me from the lions. One of the Australians in the trek confided to me that he had been looking for a woman of that kind for many years.

An hour's beating about the veldt gave no results, so we returned to laager expecting to find at daybreak only the remnants of our two missing burros. At dawn, I scanned the sky for the great vultures, to mark down the kill. Not seeing any, I began circling for tracks, but Roderick and my wife, scouting on their own, discovered Ah Sin and Ta-ra in a little thornbush hollow near by. At sight of them, the burros gave a bray of welcome and almost ran over my family in their joy. Ah Sin showed some claw marks but evidently had eluded the lions by plunging into the terrible thorn bush.

I was now to compete with some of the best Boer hunters and for the first time had a chance to try my new big Martini-Henry, the popular rifle of all South Africa and the military weapon of England in 1893; a powerful gun with a frightful recoil, corresponding to our .45-70 Springfield. The first time I fired it, I allowed my thumb to rest on the stock in the customary way, instead of putting it on the top of the gun where is a little notch, and I got a jolt that was more damaging to me than was my bullet to the game I was after. However, with a little practice, I found it a reliable weapon. Anything struck by a bullet from the Martini-Henry was apt to hit the earth immediately afterward.

One of the favourite marksmanship tests of the Boers is to put up an empty bottle on an ant hill at one hundred yards. The losing man pays for the drinks. As a Boer hates to lose and loathes having to pay for the drinks, he shoots with careful accuracy and the scores are remarkable. Some Boers can shoot offhand and succeed in hitting a hen's egg three times out of five at one hundred yards. I insist that to do this with the average sporting rifle is first-class shooting and more difficult than most of the fancy tricks exhibited on the vaudeville stage.

One of the members of our party was an old man named Botha (a relative of the late Premier and former Commander-in-Chief of the Boer armies). He and his son spent most of their time on the veldt hunting for a livelihood. I learned from them much as to methods of spooring and the peculiar habits of African game. After ten days' hunting I realized that one great advantage of my Western training was in snap-shooting at running game. This enabled me to get a bigger bag in those ten days than Botha and his son combined. Many times afterward in hunting with the Boers, I found the case to be the same. Where the Boer scores is in his long-range shooting in the open veldt, which corresponds somewhat to the buffalo hunting on our own plains in the 'seventies.

I once saw my former employer at the Tip-Top mine—a well-known American engineer named Jefferson Clark—referred to in Chapter V—show the Boers some fancy shooting: hitting twenty-five-cent pieces thrown in the air, splitting cards put up edgewise, cutting threads that held swinging pieces, etc. He became the gun hero of Pietersburg and was looked upon as the most brilliant rifle shot that had ever struck the country. His reputation followed him into Rhodesia, and, for a time, the Boers believed him an American against whom it was absolutely useless to pick up a gun. Unfortunately, before very long, Clark had to take several treks into the veldt in the company of Boers, and, of course, it was up to him to bring down some game. When they discovered that at two hundred yards the game was generally safe from Clark, their respect for his superior skill began to wane.

Accurate snap-shooting is, nevertheless, extremely valuable to a man in night work, in firing from the saddle, or in the bush, or for a running shot; in fact, for anything at short range where he has only a fraction of a second to place the bullet. Many a time our camp would have gone hungry had it not been for a snap-shot from my rifle, so I was well repaid for the devotion I had given to this kind of practice from boyhood.

CHAPTER XI

THE WAR CLOUD

OMINOUS news came down to us from the north. Inyao, a general under Lobengula, had been killed in a fight at Victoria, and all Matabeleland would be sure to rise.

Lobengula was the Matabele king, and no story of South Africa is complete without some knowledge of his romantic and tragic career and the events leading up to it. Before the founding of the Matabele nation, the king of a small Zulu tribe sent his son Chaka south to the End of the World, where the great Rock reaches out into deep blue water that thunders unceasingly. Chaka was to bring back to his father exact information as to the number and kind of white men who had come into that land and who, it was said, wore flaming red coats in war and fought with guns fastened to spears. The young Zulu watched the soldiers of England drilling at Cape Town and saw that the principle of cold steel and close contact was the deciding factor in their method of warfare. After a few months Chaka returned to his own country and, upon his father's death, became king. He straightway formed his young men into companies and regiments and made them discard the throwing spear and use only the stabbing spear and shield. In the event of failure to accomplish an assigned task, the officer responsible and all his men were invariably beheaded by the king's orders. In a short time, Chaka conquered and united the surrounding tribes and built up a power in Africa that shook the continent for years and ultimately led to two great defeats of the British and some terrible massacres of the Boers, besides many lesser wars waged against Chaka and his successors to the Zulu throne.

M'Silikatze, a powerful general, was given ten thousand warriors and sent against the Swazi, a kindred tribe to the north of Chaka's dominions, but they fought fiercely and he could not subdue them. Calling his warriors together, M'Silikatze said to them, "Why return to King Chaka to be killed in disgrace? Let us conquer a kingdom for ourselves in the north," and, turning aside into what is now the northern part of the Transvaal, he conquered the natives there and established an independent kingdom. Contact with the Boers led to a long and bloody war. One of the early incidents of this struggle was the tragic destruction of a great Boer laager by the crafty M'Silikatze—a part of the heavy price which these tenacious and hardy people paid for their country.

The Boers had brought up some three thousand settlers. Their method of fighting, when the natives attacked in masses, was to form a laager of their wagons, put their women and children and horses inside, and fight from behind the wheels. On defeating the enemy, the Boers would mount quickly, rush out, and shoot the stragglers as long as their horses could gallop or any stragglers be found. M'Silikatze noted these tactics, and one day, after attacking the whites, he withdrew across the hills in one direction while a second and much larger impi (regiment) from another direction was secretly posted close to the laager. Upon the retreat of the savages, the Boers, as usual, immediately mounted their horses and dashed off in pursuit of the fleeing impi, leaving the laager occupied solely by women, children, and a few old men. When these were attacked by the Zulus of the second impi, they put up a desperate defence, the women using axes and knives to chop off the hands of the savages as they tore at the ropes and chains that held the wagons together or climbed over to get inside the laager; but the end of it all was that two thousand women and children were slaughtered and the wagons set on fire before the Boer men, who were only a few miles away fighting the first impi, became aware of what was going on in their camp. To this day, that place is called the Valley of the Rini, which means Valley of Weeping.

To avenge this deed, the whites started a relentless war against the Zulus, and strong as was M'Silikatze, the tenacity of the Boers wore him out. After two years of fighting, he drew off all his warriors and again marched north, across the Limpopo, into the country of the Mashonas, which he soon conquered. His influence and power now covered a wide territory, with a population of more than three hundred thousand blacks. As the first king of the Matabele, he modelled the nation very closely on the military plan of King Chaka of Zululand, gathering the young men into regiments and giving them a certain amount of military drill. Incessant war was waged on surrounding tribes.

Lobengula was the son of M'Silikatze and took the throne at his death. Every year, a huge feast and dance were held at his capital at Bulawayo, and at the conclusion of the dance the king would step into the middle of the kraal twirling a spear which he then hurled over his head. In whatever direction the spear pointed when it alighted, there the warriors were to wage a fierce war for the coming year. The very name of the town, Bulawayo, means "The Town of Killing (or Death)." The impis of Lobengula believed that they maintained their strength by keeping their spears always wet with blood, and they were a fair example of what a number of determined men can do against a much larger population of unorganized and cowardly people, such as the Mashonas. Possessed of equal natural resources, not inferior to the conquering Matabele in physique, and situated in impregnable granite hills full of gullies and caves and covered with heavy thorn bush, the Mashonas were yet enslaved by the impis of Lobengula and paid tribute to them. The Matabele fought with spear and shield, and they also had another weapon which the Mashonas lacked—courage.

I have already said something of the great trek of the English in South Africa, their conflict with the Boers, and the dealings of Cecil Rhodes with Lobengula, who had become the most powerful black monarch in Africa. The personal acquisition of great wealth from his diamond mines at Kimberley and his gold mines at Johannesburg never distracted Rhodes from his ambition to develop and civilize Africa. Though bitterly opposed in the home country by the army of Little Englanders led by Labouchere, Rhodes nevertheless succeeded in getting Parliament to approve a Royal Charter similar to that granted India and not unlike that of the old Hudson's Bay Company in America. It covered territory the size of our New England States, lying north of the Limpopo River and south of the great Zambezi. Rhodes did not have the hatred of the black that generations of war had instilled into the heart of the Boer. He was a man of his word, a representative of a great nation far over the sea, whose power touched every shore and every land. He sent plausible emissaries to the king and sought a safe way for the coming flood of white men to pass northward toward the other great sea without war.

King Lobengula fell partially under his spell and sold to Rhodes the great territory known as Mashonaland, demanding in payment a huge sum of gold and quantities of modern rifles and ammunition. These were faithfully delivered, and Rhodes thus gained the first step to the north, passing clear around that growling lion on the path, Oom Paul. He was now ready to send forward his first band of pioneers. There were more than five hundred of them, gathered from many parts of the Empire, and to his dying day Rhodes looked on them as the apple of his eye. They built roads, towns, telegraph lines, and for good or evil began turning savage Africa into a civilized community. The advent of the Union Jack automatically freed two hundred thousand slaves from the Matabele, but of this there came a terrible aftermath.

Lobengula's truculent chiefs did not approve the sale of Mashonaland. They complained that they had been deprived of their slaves and of their accustomed tribute, and as they now had thousands of the white man's deadly rifles, they asked only that they be allowed to march against the invaders. Reluctantly, Lobengula consented that a raiding party under Inyao should descend on the Mashonas, claiming that title to the slaves had not passed with sale of the land. Many of the

Mashonas were working for the white settlers in the town of Victoria when the impi of two thousand Matabele warriors swept down on them and slaughtered them before the very eyes of their masters. Some of them grovelled at the feet of their employers and clung to their knees as the warriors plunged their spears through them. Others were stabbed to death in the churchyard. The town was thrown into a panic; the whites, taken by surprise and unarmed, were powerless to protect their servants. War with the Matabele had been undreamed of, since all the terms of sale had been scrupulously carried out, the boundary lines agreed on without dispute, and there were no Matabele living in the country.

This overt act of savagery roused every settler in the community. A town meeting was called. Feeling ran high. Guns and cartridges were overhauled. Owing to the Dikop sickness, only forty horses were available, and white men on foot cannot compete with the fast-running Matabele.

Two days later, the insolent warriors of Inyao again swanked through the streets of Victoria with bloody spears and rattling shields, shouting a warning to the settlers that the next time they came they would stab whites as well as Mashonas. This stirred the community to a pitch of resentment that wiped out little local bickerings and united the colonists, extremely individualistic men though they were, into a company willing to take orders and resolved to avenge the insults and attacks on their servants. The Japanese have no monopoly of those qualities expressed by Bushido.

Sensing the coming storm, Vigers, the official in charge, urged Inyao to lose no time in crossing over the border into Matabeleland. He was answered with a flow of abuse, but Inyao moved his impi out of town, about two miles away, and there went into camp. It then became a grave question whether he intended to attack Victoria again that night. The colonists decided that, instead of awaiting the issue, they would take the initiative and attack Inyao. Forty horsemen mounted and rode out to the black encampment. Inyao's men could hardly believe that this little handful of pioneers purposed to attack two thousand Matabele warriors.

While the general was haranguing his braves, the Victorians galloped up, dismounted, and poured in their volleys. Inyao and some forty of his warriors were killed. To the astonishment of the whites, the Matabele immediately retreated over the border and returned to Bulawayo, although they could easily have enveloped the few white men and killed every person in Victoria within an hour. Afterward it was learned that what saved the town was the fact that Lobengula had given stern warning to Inyao and his fighting men when they started out: "If you shed one drop of the white man's blood on this raid into Mashonaland, I will have every one of you killed when you return," and they well knew he would carry out his threat.

It is easy now, after thirty years, to look back and say the colonists were a mad lot, and knew little of military tactics and nothing of strategy to invite war by such hasty action. But Africa is dotted with the landmarks of just such incidents of reckless courage and forlorn hopes. Perhaps they indicate the quality that enables two million whites to live surrounded by a hundred million fighting blacks. Men who are looking for a safe thing should keep away from Africa!

But this brave and foolish sortie had given Lobengula's indunas (chiefs) a political club to hold over him. They would protest: "We did not shed a white man's blood, but they killed our chief and forty men. Lead us to war! Lead us to war!" Rhodes and the king were on opposite horns of the dilemma. Neither wanted war, yet neither was afraid. But circumstances, or a power beyond their control, had set this day and hour for the contest for supremacy between White and Black.

Something of this situation we knew as we went forward on our trek; some of it we learned later. Meantime, all trekkers were advised to move in a body and to form laager every night, or turn back to the Transvaal if they thought best. A crisis of this kind is swift to sift out men according to their temperament and training. Of the little handful of trekkers whom we had joined, a few who had talked loudest about fighting slipped away in the night and never halted until they crossed into the Transvaal. But most were determined to go on. It was interesting to watch the effect of the news on the different colonists. I made the error in judgment, common at that time, of thinking all Boers cowardly who trekked south, but later I formed a more just estimate of them. This was not their own Transvaal or even their own trek. Kafir wars were no novelty to them. For generations they and their ancestors had fought the blacks. They were not scared, but knowing the full meaning of such warfare, they never entered into it either as an adventure or to prove their own prowess. They had everything to lose and little to gain. So they calmly inspanned and turned south, leaving the English colonials behind. A few Boers who had interests in the north stayed with us and later fought in the wars of Rhodesia with honour and credit.

When the Chartered Company established their colonies in Mashonaland, Rhodes built a telegraph line connecting with the Transvaal and Cape Town. This line passed through the jungle twelve to eighteen miles west of our laager on the hunter's road. We knew there was a white operator at a lonely station on this line, so scouts were selected to hunt up the station, get the latest news from the front, and rush it back to the laager so that we could then decide whether to try to trek north or fortify ourselves and await reinforcements.

A colonial named Black—a veteran of many Kafir wars, Der Huyter—a young Boer, two colonials from the Cape, and I were selected to find this outpost and return with news. We struck the line, followed it north, and found the station in charge of a youth named Dillon, only eighteen years old, blue-eyed and full of boyish pranks. He was a hundred miles from nowhere, and his only touch with the world was through his ticker. With that instrument, he kept passing on to Cape Town officials such pleasant tidings as, "Loben's impis can easily cut off all supplies and wagons north of the Crocodile."

THE WAR CLOUD

"Rush up every available horse from the Transvaal at once. Unmounted men cannot withstand the Matabele." "We are short of guns and ammunition. Rush by Cape carts and mules." "Send medicines and surgical instruments for Victoria forces. They have no supplies whatever."

Cheerful messages for Dillon to feed upon, alone in the wilderness, when all these hostiles were much nearer to him than were Victoria and Salisbury! He showed us all the wires that had passed since the outbreak, so, with this information in hand, at two o'clock in the afternoon, the colonials started back to the laager. Black, Der Huyter, and I waited for direct instruction from Doctor Jameson, the British Administrator in Salisbury, as to whether we should push north at once or fortify. The afternoon wore away and, for amusement, Dillon offered some of the natives from a near-by kraal a silver coin if they could pick it up from a basin of water. They, not knowing it was connected with a fairly powerful battery, got a sharp shock and let out a loud yell at each attempt. Dillon, who could speak their tongue, explained to them that this was merely a small sample of the white man's medicine; that he, being only a youth, was not trusted with the big medicine that came over the wire. This small circumstance may explain why, in both Matabele wars, the natives greatly feared to touch the wires. Dillon played a smiling part, little dreaming that the sands of his gallant young life were already nearly run.

It was night before the ticker gave us the answer from Jameson for which we waited. "Trek north rapidly. Form laagers. When outspanned throw out scouts." Signed L. S. J. Those initials, soon to be so famous in South Africa, sent the three of us out into the night to find our laager.

We had proceeded only a short distance when a difference of opinion arose as to where our laager might be. The commandant, or trek leader, had informed us just as we were leaving that morning that he would move up the hunter's road six miles or more to better feed and safer ground, and, in returning, this fact must be taken into consideration. In the end, we decided that each should choose his own way. I had occasion that night to thank my stars for the scoutcraft picked up among the Indian boys I had played with in my youth, for it brought me to the laager about midnight. The others had not arrived. Two shots were fired close together at regular intervals until dawn, and then scouts were sent out to find the missing men. Black had been treed by a lion and did not come down until daybreak. Der Huyter had lost his bearings on the stars, but as he had a good knowledge of watersheds, etc., he hit the road ahead of the laager and turned south, meeting our search party.

Our trek to the north was resumed at once. The Boers are the most expert drivers of ox teams in the world, and it is amazing with what speed sixteen or eighteen oxen can be inspanned and set moving in an emergency, as well as the distance they can cover on a forced march. A volume could be written on the great treks of Africa. It has been claimed that the invention of the wheel was a greater benefit to man than either steam or electricity. Next to fire, it gave him mastery over the wilderness, wild beasts, and savage men. The Goths, the Boers, and the Americans each conquered their country with a wagon train which served to carry their food, protect the women and children, shelter their stock, and on occasion became a formidable though quickly movable fort.

When the Boers are on trek, the usual orders of the day are given at two in the morning. The commandant shouts, "Upstandt!" and gives his great whip a crack as loud as a rifle shot. Every Kafir servant jumps from under the wagon wheels or the big bucksail, and fires are started quickly, while the fore-loper and the driver stir up the sleeping oxen. Each ox is tied to the trektow by a great band of rawhide called a reim (rim). The light pole yokes are laid over the neck, each held in place by two wooden keys about sixteen inches long, and all made snug by a rawhide throat latch. In thirty minutes, every wagon is inspanned and the cooks have made great kettles of coffee which each one drinks from his own pannikin. Then another crack of the great whip, and the order to trek is given. Each wagon in turn moves into line and off into the night, with much popping of whips and long, resonant cries as the drivers call each ox by name—sometimes many names! The loose stock is trailed behind. The commandant rides ahead, selects the outspan, and at sunrise, if possible, halts the trek and outspans for the day. When evening comes, again the crack of the whip! Everyone scrambles to get his kit into the big wagons. Even the chickens are herded into their coops by the whip. The oxen, now well fed with grass, are driven in from herd. Just as the sun is nearly down, the final order to trek is given. The next halt is called at nine or ten o'clock and, as before, the trek is resumed at two in the morning.

Under these conditions, the Boers will cross incredible stretches of sand and thorn bush without water and yet save their oxen. They have a saying, "Let not the sun shine on yoked oxen," and it is a good rule on all long, difficult treks. But under war conditions we had to modify this rule, though the result soon worked disaster. A few daylight treks, and the long hot hours seemed to shrivel the great frames of the oxen. Their eyes sank into their heads, for it was the dry season and there was little grass. The loud popping of the whips or the touch of the forelash gave way to the deadly swish and dull thud as the great lashes, now doubled, stung and flayed the struggling, staggering brutes. The voices of the Cape boys grew hoarse and raucous or ceased from exhaustion. Soon the colonials and Boers had to use their heavy sjamboks (hippo hide whips about six feet long) in all sandy spots, and in crossing rivers it was necessary to put thirty-six oxen to one wagon in order to make the opposite bank. The loose cattle became mere staggering skeletons and began to die off. On our flanks prowled hyenas and jackals. Overhead circled the great vultures, and each day their food supply grew while ours decreased.

There were many consultations between the commandant and the older men, and plans were discussed for abandoning the poorest cattle, wagons, and loads in order to save the most valuable. There was something to be considered above money value, for our train might easily be the last to reach the settlements of Mashonaland before the war cloud burst, and some of our supplies would be of vital importance. I now saw Boer and colonial under trying circumstances and began to form an opinion of them and a high regard which have never since changed. There is something vital in them that gives me the same feeling of respect I have for the Bedouin of the desert. They have taken root in the land and are a part of it. They will survive.

One day, as we were creeping northward, there came up from the south a Cape cart and six mules. In the cart sat a bronzed, alert, wiry man wearing a stiff-brimmed Stetson hat made from beaver fur. Noticing that I wore the same kind of headgear, he halted and asked, "When did you leave the West?"

"Just ahead of you," I answered.

His response was, "It was daybreak, as near as I can remember."

"Almost you are a Texan," I laughed, "and almost a short grass puncher."

So we exchanged jokes but, with Western reticence, refrained from asking names. He pulled from his jockey box a hat similar to the ones we both were wearing and said, "I am taking this to Captain Wilson at Victoria," and as he drove away he shouted back, "Go to see him—we shall need you. Hell is going to pop soon." And away dashed the Hon. Maurice Gifford, the Jack Hays of Africa. All that he prophesied came true.

As we drew near to Victoria, the Mashona kraals could be seen clinging like swallows' nests to the great domes and kopjes of granite. These harassed people had fled from the Matabele into the security of these rocky fastnesses where they lived on Kafir corn and a few patches of vegetables hidden away among the hills. They were wild for meat, and when one of our oxen would lie down to die, the poor wretches would not only fight off the hyenas and vultures, but would quarrel fiercely among themselves over the division of the miserable carcass.

My policy of feeding our burros, even hauling mealies for them, now showed results. We found we could easily out-trek all the wagon train, and were often able to find bits of sweet grass sufficient for the donkeys where the ox teams could get only the tall, African grass, three to five feet high, which stands dead in the dry season and gives little strength. As the oxen grew weaker and the treks shorter, I decided to leave the wagon train and push on to Victoria alone. The country was very wild, and night camps had to be hid from the road for fear of hostile Matabele, yet to camp without fires meant almost certainty of attack by hyenas or lions. So I adopted the Boer method and trekked at night and hid by day in the tall grass.

Sinister rumours reached us and urged us on. We met an outfit fleeing from Victoria. A woman told my wife that the Matabele were about to attack the town; that all women would be killed in a horrible manner; that they could cut out the tongue of our little boy, and other details of like cheerful nature. She advised us to turn south while yet there was time. But at dusk we inspanned the faithful donkeys and hurried them forward along the dim road. On either side, the rustling grass stood dry and yellow, higher than their backs. Dark night fell quickly. The huge hyenas of this part of Africa seemed to believe that our end was near, though none of us had been wounded to give them the scent of blood. They padded along persistently, sometimes just ahead, sometimes behind us. I knew with what suddenness they could attack, for I had a memory of Ingongsloop, when I had seen one tear down a saddle horse; so I carried the sawed-off gun at full cock as I walked beside the burros. My wife drove, and Roderick was not allowed to leave the buckboard. All went well until ten o'clock, when I found that one of the wheel bearings had absorbed too much sand. While I was struggling with the hot wheel we heard the measured thud of advancing feet. My wife handed me the gun, which I had relinquished. Then, close at hand, a big ox lifted his head over the high grass and looked at us. I never knew before that an ox could have so sweet a face.

At last, one happy night, we spied the lights of Victoria, that far-flung little outpost of the British Empire. We had trekked for four months. Another month, we thought, would put us at our destination—Salisbury, in Mashonaland—but the skein of our lives became kinked, and we never drove the little American buckboard through the gates of Salisbury. We found plenty to do in Victoria.

CHAPTER XII

MASHONALAND

AT THE time of the first Matabele war the English settlers in the province of Mashonaland (later Rhodesia) were separated by five hundred miles of wilderness from the Boer settlements of the Transvaal, then under the presidency of Paul Kruger. From the vantage of Bulawayo, his capital, Lobengula could throw regiments of many thousands across any possible line of British retreat.

When we arrived in Victoria, wild rumours were flying. War without quarter was upon us; King Lobengula and ten thousand men were in camp just outside the town; all the friendly natives were going to turn traitor; the British Government had sent an army; the British Government had sent a navy to Portuguese waters; the Portuguese had fired on the British flag, etc., etc. But under all the idle chatter things were being done. Fortunately, the whites were blessed with leaders of supreme courage and accurate knowledge of the habits of thought of the enemy. This courage and this knowledge were best expressed in the slogan, "When in doubt, attack." Every able-bodied white man in Mashonaland responded instantly to the call to arms. Able officers such as Wilson, Napier, Green, Kirtin, Gifford, and Lendy were drilling men, gathering cattle, trekking oxen, and fortifying Victoria; while De Forest, Brabant, and the native commissioners contributed the "low down" on the movements of the natives. The black man's brain is slow to act. His tongue has to wag and wag before an idea is brought forth. We heard by the native grapevine telegraph that great endabas or councils were being held by Lobengula in Bulawayo and that a large army was being formed. We must have horses and ammunition at all costs.

Certain Imperial officers proposed a fast march into Matabeleland with horsemen only, but it was decided to advance in Boer fashion with ox wagons and form laager when attacked. This was a wise decision. A thousand cavalry could not have taken Bulawayo, for at night they would have been at the mercy of the savage spearmen. The horses could not have been turned loose to graze at night, and the day's grazing alone would not sustain horses for hard riding. Moreover, our soldiers were not really cavalry but mounted infantry.

At the back of every move was the directing mind of Cecil John Rhodes. Doctor Jameson, the Administrator, secured permission from him to purchase such horses as would be required, in the Transvaal and farther south, and they were to be rushed into Mashonaland as fast as possible. There would be a delay of at least thirty days while we waited for horses and ammunition to come up from the south, and as I feared an outbreak of fever in the Victoria laager, I concluded to join some colonial acquaintances who were driving a hundred oxen to pasture in the green grass meadows of the Sabi River.

The region between Victoria and the Sabi is one of the most interesting parts of Mashonaland, and when I learned that the ancient ruins of Zimbabwe were only thirty miles away, I decided to visit them. This kind of exploring has always intrigued me from boyhood, when my taste was formed by digging into the hills of the mound builders and by investigating the cliff dwellings of our own Southwest.

It is an easy trip from Victoria to Zimbabwe, so I took my wife and little son with me, and we made our camp in the shadow of these ruins. In this picturesque country a traveller from the New World has strange thoughts as he stands on the granite tombs and looks down on the great walls and labyrinths of stone set without mortar by some energetic people of a past so misty that there exists neither legend nor tradition of them. We searched room after room, examined with interest the doors of rock that slid into place, and speculated about the curious conical sun tower. After a thorough exploration, I took a gold pan and worked over some of the débris near a little spruit (stream) which flowed through the ruins, and in a few hours I washed out more than a hundred small gold beads and other ornaments of the ancient inhabitants. My wife and little boy became intensely interested in this panning, so I left them to continue the search for treasure while I went hunting.

I wished particularly to get some specimens of the beautiful reed buck of the country, which I had heard was abundant here, and also of the oribi, a small gazelle especially prized for the delicious flavour of its meat. On a high ridge back of the main buildings was a series of walls and fortifications. After hunting nearly all day without success, I was standing on one of these walls looking out over the ruins and revolving in my mind the questions how were they built and for what purpose. I had on a pair of Boer veldt shoes, and as the grass through which I had been stalking was slightly damp, I was able to move along the top of these low walls without a sound and my elevation was probably sufficient to prevent my scent from reaching the ground below. I had stood still for three or four minutes when, glancing directly beneath my feet, I saw an oribi curled up fast asleep, with his head tucked around in the same way as that of a calf at rest in a pasture. I was so astonished that at first I could hardly believe the animal to be alive, for these creatures are so keen-scented and large-eared that they are difficult for even the wily leopard to capture, and impossible for the lion. Yet here was I, a clumsy human, actually within a few feet of a sleeping oribi. It was the first, last, and only time in all my hunting that this occurred, and I have yet to meet a man who has had a similar experience.

As I looked at the sleeping creature, I felt no desire to shoot him. For fully a minute I stood there, until either some faint odour or the sound of my breathing reached his senses. Like a flash, his lithe muscles lifted him from what was apparently the soundest sleep, and he was over the wall with a bound. At this, with the instinct of the rifleman, I threw my gun around and shot, but as the oribi was going downhill my bullet ranged high and he escaped with what was probably the biggest fright of his life, leaving me with the memory of one of the greatest surprises I ever met with in stalking game.

After exploring the ruins for another half hour or so, I turned down a slight declivity, intending to make just one more round before going to camp. This time, out of a clump of grass, an oribi leaped away like a streak of yellow light. A lucky shot from my rifle stopped him. That night we had delicious steaks, and the following day, the most appetizing Dutch oven roast that South Africa can offer.

A colonial friend named Main, and Ingram, the young American, had joined us, and within the next few days we got splendid specimens of the reed buck; several times shooting at the extremely long range of six hundred yards, with the Martini-Henry rifle. We also brought in and added to the bill of fare Namaqua partridges, guinea fowl, plover, rice birds, coran of two varieties, and a few of the African pigeons which feed mostly on wild figs and whose flesh is extremely delicate—indeed, of much finer flavour than the squabs we find in our home markets. We made quantities of biltong in preparation for future needs. While I was off hunting, my wife and little boy accumulated various trophies, including a cap box full of gold beads which they washed out of the ruins. As the objects of our outing were now achieved, we started back to Victoria. Before reaching town I shot a great wart hog with tusks fourteen inches long and extremely thick and solid from base to tip. These were exceptionally large tusks for that part of the country, but I have since seen larger ones both in East Africa and north of the Zambezi River.

Finding that our stock still needed more time to recuperate their lost strength after the great trek from the Cape, some friends made up a party with us for an expedition toward Gazaland. We took some of the best of the oxen and our little American buckboard, about which our British friends loved to joke, and five days' trekking brought us into good grass country full of game, where we had some excellent hunting.

For two or three weeks we were in the home of the Mashonas.

Although, as a race, these people are subject to the fierce Matabele, they are far more advanced in culture than their conquerors. Their methods of handling iron ore, of making their own hoes and weapons, tanning leather, etc., would lead one to infer that in the past they must have been in close contact with some more advanced race, possibly from Egypt or Asia. They outnumbered the Matabele about ten to one, and if they had had as much courage in their whole bodies as the Matabele warrior has in one finger, they would never have become his slaves. But the quality of courage has somehow died in the Mashonas, and there is left only a boastful truculence, a swaggering bounce, that poorly disguises their weakness. The country is full of kopjes, passes and vleys (valleys), groves and forests, and is well supplied with streams and impregnable caves, or caves that would be impregnable if held by Matabele with their shields and spears. But a slave mind makes a slave, irrespective of prowess or arms; and though the Mashonas are as strong physically and seemingly as intelligent as the Matabele, they prefer to hide in barricaded caves where they can store their food and flocks and women rather than meet the enemy in the open. When the Matabele war began, three thousand of these Mashonas danced themselves dizzy under the protection of our guns, swearing by all that was holy that they would march steadily into Matabeleland and fight the foe to the death. Yet when news came that a squad of Matabele herders with a small guard from one of their impis was camping in the next valley, more than two thousand of the Mashonas melted into the darkness that same night.

We had supplied ourselves plentifully with African trade stuff—a curious collection of small looking-glasses, blue beads with white eyes for one tribe, white beads with blue eyes for another, large blue beads and amber beads for still others; besides copper wire, iron wire, brass wire, Americana (*i.e.*, American sheeting), cheap calico, and a little black powder for use in antiquated muzzle-loading muskets which the Mashona chiefs always liked to sport at full cock. Often, when they had no powder, they would carry only the caps; and at other times, without either powder or cap, the empty gun at full cock remained a mark of social distinction, like the diamond ring of the bank cashier or the hotel clerk, worn for the sake of the deference it is supposed to inspire. We traded our beads, wire, and calico for garvanzos, that favourite chick-pea of the Mediterranean peoples; also for lentils, American and Kafir, and upland pink rice. The natives had flocks of goats and fowls and a few cattle and lived very well in times of peace. The valley of the Sabi is dotted with noble trees and flanked by bold granite kopjes and domes a thousand feet high, similar in some respects to Stone Mountain near Atlanta, Georgia. On these domes the natives wove their grass huts, shaped like candle-snuffers, and around the bases tilled their gardens. With these great hills for defence and this rich valley to supply food, why they should ever have become enslaved by the Matabele remains a mystery.

While we were camped on the Sabi, my thrifty wife took occasion to mount her little hand sewing machine and build our husky boy some clothes. Most of the Mashonas had never seen a white woman, and certainly none of them had ever seen a sewing machine. Whenever she started this mechanical wonder, sometimes as many as a hundred natives would come running from all directions and stand around in an awed circle so long as the needle moved. It was witchcraft of a high order, they decided; in fact, very strong medicine! Sometimes even the warriors would lend dignity to the exhibition by standing around the outer edge and staring at the marvel, meanwhile keeping their old muskets capped and at full cock. Adelina Patti's reception in the wild and woolly Cheyenne of long ago did not excel in enthusiasm the plaudits my wife received on the banks of the Sabi. Our pleasant experience ended all too soon. It was time the horses and men came up from the south, and King Lobengula's impis might be ready to invade. We must move faster than the king. It was our one hope of success.

On our return, we found Victoria humming with men. Hundreds of horses had made the long forced march, and with them had come some fine young colonial Boers who understood the Kafir thoroughly, as well as others from more distant lands. They had jumped north, moved either to extend the Empire or to save the handful of settlers holding this distant post. One of the joys of life on this frontier was the mingling of the adventurous and hardy from every corner of the world. If there was a single colony of the British Empire that was not represented, I have yet to hear of it. There was a brave contingent from Australia, placed by mutual consent under the command of their greatest and best-loved prospector, Thomas. His heroism, his whimsicality, and his almost impossible doings became a tradition. Quite appropriately, at his death, the monument selected for him was a huge uncut boulder of a peculiar white quartz—an expression of the tribute we paid in our hearts to the whiteness of his soul. We had Americans with the nasal Yankee twang and the soft Southern drawl as well as the Western slang, to match the quaint lingoes of the Britishers. Added to all was the large Dutch element, so similar to the men from our own West. The Honourable Sirs and Lords who joined us, fought with us, starved with us, and died as men should, doing their bit, were the least materialistic of all and often generous to their own undoing. Even our rotten wasters and ne'er-do-wells became for the time heroic and dependable. Probably there was never a more individualistic colony in the world, though we were amalgamated and held together by the pressure and the menace about us of overwhelming numbers of blacks, all latently dangerous and many openly hostile. They outnumbered us more than a hundred to one.

But if any stranger expected us to take our responsibilities seriously, he had only to observe the laughing, careless, casual way in which we assumed control of this part of the continent. In 1893, South Africa was a young man's land. When we marched into Matabeleland I was considered elderly by my companions—and I had just turned thirty-two.

All the settlers were drawn into laager, either in Salisbury or Victoria. The women and children were to be left behind in these improvised forts with the old men and boys as guards. This was long before General Baden-Powell organized the famous Boy Scouts, but the commander at Fort Victoria had a station and a duty for every boy and for every woman and girl as well. My seven-year-old son carried a bandolier of Martini-Henry ammunition, and his duty, in case of attack, was to pass out shells to the men in the loop holes. Other youngsters, too small to carry a rifle, were assigned to carry water and act as messengers from point to point. The danger of a Mashona uprising greatly complicated matters. Africa is dotted with Cherry Creeks, New Ulms, and Custer's defeats. The settlers happened to have a few small pieces of artillery captured from the Portuguese in a previous row over the possession of the town of Massikessi. One of these weapons was a Hotchkiss one-and-a-half pounder. A clever Holland gunsmith made shells for us, and we moulded bullets about the size of ordinary buckshot which we imbedded in a mixture of tallow and resin, thereby providing a fairly effective weapon for resisting attack.

I had reported to Captain Wilson, now Major, in command of the Victoria column. He smilingly showed me the Yankee hat given him by Maurice Gifford, and I plaited the band for him after the custom of the cowboys of the Southwest and Mexico. We were formed into companies, and I was assigned to a picked group of scouts under the temporary command of a colonial named Dollar—a good horseman and a crack shot. We threw a screen of scouts around Victoria for many miles, but the everyday circus was on the drill ground.

From daylight till dark, men were drilled and mounts inspected. As the new horses arrived, they were assigned to the amateur soldiers and the antics of a Western frontier rodeo were enacted daily. One morning, a hundred and twenty remounts were ready to be turned over to an equal number of men. After a rather tempestuous mounting and march, each man was ordered to turn his mount over to the horse guards to take on herd. The next day, when we were all on the picket lines, we were commanded each to pick out his own horse and lead by in review before Major Wilson. I was among the first to march by the Major. He had given me a small buckskin with a dark stripe down his back and striped markings on the legs like a zebra. He appeared a miniature of the big buckskin the Major himself rode. As he looked me over, Wilson said, "I think our mounts match these Yankee hats, and if you are as tough as that pony, you will make some hard rides."

"Probably in retreat!" I answered.

"That will do for you!" he laughed. "Fall in here on my right. Here come some men with the wrong horses."

Sure enough, about one third of the men did not know their mounts. One great powerful recruit weighing more than two hundred pounds led up a neat little bay pony. Wilson said, "Is that the horse I gave you yesterday?"

"I think it is, sir."

"Fall in on the left," Wilson ordered. "You would have to carry that horse into camp every night."

Of another he asked, "Do you like your mount?"

"He is a bit of a kicker, sir."

"If he is a worse one than you are, take him back to the lines—I will give you another horse."

It so happened that this trooper was a notorious grouch, though a good fighter.

The Major knew each horse, not only by colour and weight, but with a subtle understanding of its mental capacity, as he knew the characteristics of his men, so that he was able to fit horse to man with marvellous appropriateness.

Finally, the day came when Doctor Jameson reviewed us all. We formed in a great semicircle in full marching order, every horse as shining as we could make him. Doctor Jim made a great speech. I don't know what it was all about. It didn't matter what he said. We all yellfully approved. Already we considered ourselves seasoned veterans and capable of meeting the best troops in Europe, if necessary. The Horse Guards had nothing on us except their tin jackets and helmets. As I now look back through the years, I wonder at Jameson's hardihood in daring to invade an unknown wilderness, there to meet the strongest savage king in Africa, who greatly surpassed him in number of men and guns and in experience, and on ground of the king's own choosing.

The columns forming at Victoria and at Salisbury, two hundred miles to the north, were to decide the fate of all the whites in a section of country as large as all Western Europe. Major Allan Wilson commanded the Victoria column; Forbes, the senior officer, was in charge of the Salisbury united columns. The artillery was under Captain Lendy, a well-known British athlete, who won the hearts and confidence of all. Sir John Willoughby was military adviser to Doctor Jameson, the Administrator, under whose immediate authority the military acted. Salisbury furnished less than four hundred men and Victoria about three hundred. King Lobengula was believed to have twenty thousand gun men and eighty thousand spear men in the field. Our two columns were to advance into Matabeleland and unite at Iron Mountain, not far from the eastern border. We learned that many thousands of the enemy were gathered on the edge of the Samabula forest not far from Iron Mountain, or Iron Mine Hill as it was afterward called on account of the ancient iron workings discovered there.

When all arrangements had been made, Jameson marched his small force into the unknown wilderness to the west with the king's capital, Bulawayo, two hundred miles away, as his objective. Every mile had to be scouted in advance. By doing the impossible, there was just a chance of success. The stake played for was the life of every white settler north of the Limpopo River. The boundary of Lobengula's kingdom was the little Shashani River, and we managed to cross this Rubicon without declamation on the 12th of October, 1893.

"A mingling of the adventurous and hardy."—in Rhodesia. Standing: left, Ingram; right, Captain Charles White. Kneeling: Art Cummings, Stocker, Moffat, Bain, Burnham, and the Hon. Maurice Gifford

CHAPTER XIII

THE FIRST MATABELE WAR

THE hour of our actual march from Victoria had been purposely withheld from us, partly to prevent any information leaking out to native spies, and partly to shorten for all of us that black hour when we must look into the eyes of loved ones perhaps for the last time. Even if we should return safely, we realized with anxiety that we were leaving our dearest with only a handful of old men and boys and one old spluttering Gatling gun (a relic of the American Civil War—by way of Massikessi) to defend them against thousands of savages, should an uprising occur.

During this advance, our little column of twenty-odd wagons was driven in parallel lines, each wagon drawn by a span of sixteen Dutch oxen. They carried our commissary for man and horse, as well as spare ammunition and our wounded. When attacked, we could form into a hollow square and mount a gun at each angle within five minutes' time. On the march, our mounted men protected the wagons on all sides, and when in laager, the wagons shielded our mounted men. Our expert wagon masters were Boers or English colonials, and though we were moving in a country devoid of roads of any kind, we never lost a wagon on all the march over rocky river beds, or through heavy dust or deep vleys of mud. At night, some of the friendly natives would bring in large quantities of thorn trees and bushes and scatter them thickly over the ground for a number of yards on all sides of the wagons, as an additional impediment to the enemy, thus greatly strengthening our defence. We were, of course, careful not to build the barrier so high as to shut out the vision of the riflemen in case of attack.

A circumstance that aided in our conquest of Matabeleland

was the fact that the native army was in a stage of transition. Lobengula well knew that the white man's rifle was a very destructive weapon, and when he granted his concessions of territory in Mashonaland to Rhodes, he exacted as part payment thousands of military rifles and large quantities of cartridges. Probably one third of his warriors were armed with rifles, and, in addition, there were many muzzle-loading and antiquated weapons among them. Had the warriors thrown away the spear and shield altogether and learned to use the rifle effectively, their numbers alone would have defeated our column long before we reached Bulawayo. As it was, they still carried their old weapons and added the rifle and cartridges, to whose use they were not duly trained. The grim discipline of Chaka, who forced his warriors to close with the enemy and stab, had been relaxed, and the blacks did not drive their charges home with the same ferocity that Chaka's men would have shown. They would start their rushes with the old-time vigour, but, on encountering the deadly work of our guns, they would pause at a distance of two hundred yards and deliver their own rifle fire, or else would fire as they ran toward us, gripping their rifles with rigid muscles and thereby spoiling their aim.

It should be explained that the national weapon of the Matabele was the assegai or stabbing spear, generally not more than five feet long and rather light and slender. This could be thrown a few yards with great effect in an emergency, but the Zulu and Matabele, like the ancient Roman, relied for victory upon closing with the enemy. Like the Roman, the Matabele used a shield for defence; in this instance a curved oval of ox hide three feet or more in length and two feet in width. It was stiffened longitudinally by a light straight stick of hardwood about an inch in diameter. Along this stick were loops of hide in which the stabbing spear could be carried, and from the middle of the curved interior a firm loop of hide depended through which the left hand could be thrust in such a way that hand and fingers were free to grasp anything else needed on the march, such as an extra spear or a knobkerrie. The whole outfit of spear and shield was very light and perfectly balanced and would only slightly impede the movements of a fast runner. When, however, a nine-pound Martini rifle was added to this equipment, it slowed down the movements of the native considerably. In firing, the gun barrel was held in the left hand, from which were suspended the shield and spear by the loop I have described. This handicap to accuracy, added to the belief of the native that the harder he gripped his rifle the farther it would shoot and that if the sights were raised, the bullet would travel faster, helps to account for the fact that, although our patrols and sortie parties often encountered heavy fire from hundreds of guns at close quarters, we usually came through untouched.

On the other hand, if the Matabele had clung to their Zulu formation, rushing on us while we were on the march or catching us at night when the skill of our riflemen would have been of no avail against their vast numbers, they could have annihilated our entire force. Assuredly no Imperial aid, not even the potent arm of Rhodes, could have reached us in time had Lobengula's impis been directed upon us in full force.

We had an instance of the peculiar nervous organization of the natives one night when a friendly Mashona, running into the laager, got in the way of the fire of a Maxim gun and had his arm shattered about three inches above the elbow so that it simply hung by shreds. It was about nine o'clock in the morning when the surgeons got around to his case. There was no anæsthetic, as the numbers of our wounded had already exhausted our small supply, so two natives held the injured man while the doctors cut off his arm a little above the shattered part. The black stood the operation without a groan. He was then backed up against a wagon wheel and within three quarters of an hour was greedily devouring a big bowl of boiled meat brought him by his wife. That very afternoon I saw him marching along behind the commissary wagon, apparently no worse off than an ordinary lizard when he disjoints his tail and leaves it unconcernedly in the mouth of the pursuing snake. The lizard, however, has this advantage over the native, that he can grow a new tail while the black man cannot sprout a new arm.

One of the incidents of our advance is related in a letter I wrote home soon afterward.

November 8, 1893.

. . . My last letter to you gave news of the war and that I would take service with the British South Africa Company as scout and with the enlistment would get certain concessions of land, mineral rights, etc. I will try to give you as well as I can the events as they have occurred since.

Our column left Victoria, four hundred men with several Maxim guns, one seven-pounder and one Hotchkiss. On crossing the border of Matabeleland we learned that an impi of the enemy was within five miles. Our men stood to the guns and laager was formed until the scouts had cleared the country. We advanced slowly through a lovely well-wooded land, dotted with enormous buttes of granite of most fantastic shapes—the home of the Mashonas. They build their huts under and among these enormous rocks and till little patches of corn, rice, and beans in the surrounding valleys. We raided them for food supplies—goats, fowl, and cattle when they had them, and as we were fighting their lifelong enemies, they were told to charge the account to profit and loss. So mild was our raiding compared to that of the Matabele that they took it as a joke and followed our column in hundreds to live off the garbage and get a chance to loot the Matabele in case we should conquer. They are a cowardly, cringing, thankless lot of dirty beasts, to say the least; lacking even that one redeeming quality possessed by many savage races—courage.

We rode westward on the watershed between the Zambezi and Crocodile rivers, through land as beautiful as ever an English army traversed. We reached a mountain of iron used by the natives for ages to make their spears and hoes. The trails leading to it could be seen for thirty miles. Here we were to meet three hundred men with Gatling guns and Gardiners from Fort Salisbury, but the columns missed each other, and heavy scouting was required. At last I was successful in finding them, and we passed the camps of the Matabele, who did not attack the single column as, from their point of warfare, they should have done.

Then five of us took the trail of an impi driving a large herd of cattle. We followed them all night and at daybreak located them in a large valley not far from the Iron Mountain. As we were only a few miles from our column, I picked out one man who had shown that he was afraid to attack and sent him back for reinforcements. Looking down into this valley, we saw an interesting sight. Half a mile in advance of the herd of cattle were about one hundred savages; we could see their guns and shields. About the same number brought up the rear a mile and a half behind; while in the middle was a guard of about forty driving the cattle up the valley and into the mountains. I knew they would have them safe before aid could come to us, so made up my mind to attack and check them, at any rate.

We four scouts rode down off the mountain directly toward the rear guard

THE FIRST MATABELE WAR

in the lower end of the valley. The savages were armed with the same kind of rifles we carry and evidently did not think it possible that four men would attack them. We rode straight at them until within five hundred yards—then turned and went up the valley like a flash, and before the cattle guard realized what was up, we were upon them. We killed twelve in less than five minutes. We hardly missed a shot, while they were so excited that their bullets went wild. We rushed the animals out of the valley but were attacked by the advance guard. These we fought for some time, but they recovered about two hundred of the five hundred head of cattle. We got clear with the remaining three hundred and turned them over to our column.

Then, reinforced by ten more scouts, we returned to the attack and fought the advance guard until they suddenly brought up more than a thousand warriors over the mountain, who gave us volley after volley. Some of them were very plucky, and one of their chiefs singled me out. He walked coolly from cover, threw down his shield and blanket, and began to shoot at me. I dismounted, knelt on the ground with my bridle rein on my arm, and we poured lead at each other at a lively clip. He was a fairly good marksman and grazed my head and threw dirt in my face with his first and second shots but the fortune of war favoured me, and his shield and spears are now among my trophies.

The situation was getting serious, however, and we were forced to retire. We lost Captain Campbell and several horses that day, besides suffering wounds among ourselves. This was the opening fight, and from that time on I was in the saddle almost continuously night and day with more or less fighting all the time.

We crossed some beautiful plateaus dotted with gnu, hartebeeste, kudoo, and various other kinds of game, and camped on the headwaters of the Tekwe and Lundi rivers and others which are of size in the low country but here are only little streams rising in park-like valleys. We are in a wonderful mineral country; gold veins and ancient works abound and many fine samples showing free gold are brought into camp every day. We raid, burn, and destroy everything as clean as you did when you were one of Sherman's men marching through Georgia.

On the afternoon of October 24th, timber was sighted along a river, and at dark we camped about two hundred yards from its left bank. We afterward learned that this was the Shangani. We were in the heart of the Matabele country and knew we must be close to the king's Insucomene (always ready) regiment. We were about one hundred and sixty miles from Victoria, our starting place. Our laager was formed as usual with the artillery placed at the angles, our stock inside, and the camp of friendly natives close up under the protection of our guns. (We had with us several hundred Mashonas armed with spears and muzzle-loading rifles.) That night, it was my especial duty to reconnoitre around some Kafir kraals that lay in the granite hills a few miles from our camp. On my return, I decided not to go inside the laager but to lie down under some trees close by. At about half-past two in the morning, a shot and a wild yell from the camp of the "friendlies" roused the whole force. Then came several scattering shots followed by the terrific war cry of the Matabele as they rushed our laager, and the battle of the Shangani began.

This was one of the most spectacular night fights I have ever taken part in; what with the double line of fire from the men lying on top of the large African trek wagons and those crouching under the wheels, the roar of the Maxims, and the continuous crack of several thousand hostile rifles that rimmed our entire laager. Over and above all the din of the firing rose the shrieks and yells of the friendly natives as they were stabbed and slaughtered by the onrushing Matabele. It was on this occasion that some of the unfortunate friendlies got mixed up with the enemy and were swept against our laager, willy-nilly, to be shot down by our own Maxim guns. The firing continued until the light of day brought deadly accuracy to our rifles and enabled us to open the laager and with our mounted men sweep the grass and timber free of the enemy in the direction of Bulawayo.

This blow to our friendlies revealed to us one of the reasons why the Matabele had been able to enslave three hundred thousand Mashonas. One defeat, and their spirit was broken and their usefulness ended. They became an encumbrance to us, rather than an assistance, after that attack, and most of them had to be sent back under guard to Mashonaland. A certain number were retained to march beside our wagons, carrying large branches of the thorny mimosa to be utilized in forming laager, as we did instantly whenever attacked in force by the enemy.

We did not spend much time wondering what the Matabele were doing. We all had visions of those frail forts far away in Mashonaland with thousands of hostiles between them and us. Our defeat would mean death to those we had left behind.

THE FIRST MATABELE WAR

Swift action and continuous advance offered our only chance of success. The savage fights best when flushed with victory;

BATTLE OF THE SHANGANI

This map is copied from one in the British War Office which was made by Sir John Willoughby immediately after the battle. Had the natives abandoned their guns and rushed us with the assegai, the victory would have been theirs, although our laager was formed with consummate skill after the approved Boer method.

the white man when desperate or when fighting for his own in a cause he deems right. Then there is a grimness about him that strips away all the conventions of ordinary life, and no savage is his equal.

As we went on, the Matabele hovered constantly on our

flanks, impeding our advance and cutting off any stragglers in the rear. Daylight scouting became extremely difficult, both on account of the roughness of the country and because of the harassing presence of the enemy. We were in country absolutely unknown to any of us; no man could even guess what the next hill or ridge might show. It became extremely important that the exact location of Bulawayo should be ascertained.

CHAPTER XIV

WHEN THE COMPASS FAILED

ALL our contacts with natives and with wounded prisoners had failed to reveal the supposed open road to Bulawayo, nor had we sighted the famous Mountain of the Chiefs, called by the natives "Thabas Indunas"—a flat-topped mountain or hill about ten miles from Bulawayo. Jameson had hazarded all on native reports of a fairly open series of vleys from Iron Mine Hill direct to Bulawayo by way of Matchum Slopé (the White Rocks). Only by this route could we hope to make use of our horses and protect our ox wagons loaded with supplies and ammunition. If our mounted column should be attacked in the Samabula forest, which stretched from Bulawayo nearly to Salisbury, all would be lost. In times past, Bulawayo had been visited by many traders and by Jameson himself, but from another direction. No one had ever crossed by the route we were now taking from Mashonaland.

Some of our best scouts had been killed and others were worn out from loss of sleep. Our Commander of Scouts was Captain Charles White, an Imperial officer of generosity and courage, held in high esteem by the Colonial troops. He ordered me, after I had been thirty-six hours on constant duty, to report to Doctor Jameson, and I was given an outline of what was expected of me. I asked Jameson if he would allow me to take as my companion Maurice Gifford, but, to my disappointment, he refused this request. Gifford was about the only effective scout left in the Salisbury column and could not be spared. He had been for eleven years on the American frontier and had fought in Reil's Rebellion in Canada and in many other fields of action all over the world. He was destined to do many great deeds in South Africa, and was well qualified for just such a difficult mission as that before us. Jameson, however, decided that a hard-riding colonial named Vaversol should be detailed to ride with me. Our objective was to find Bulawayo, the capital of Matabeleland.

Jameson's instructions to me in this particular instance were, "If one of you should be wounded and unable to ride, he must be left to fight it out alone. If the open route should be found by either of you and then lost through one trying to save the other, all our people would be sacrificed; while if either one of you can find the trail and guide the troops into Bulawayo, we shall win the war."

Vaversol and I left the column in the bush on the morning of October 28th, starting by daylight on our scout through unknown country swarming with hostile savages. Using many stratagems to avoid the Matabele, we came, two hours later, into a fairly open rolling land, resembling the foothills of the Rocky Mountains, with clumps of brush and many dongas (gullies). Bands of black warriors could be seen crossing in long lines or driving herds of cattle in all directions away from the advance of our column. They saw us, but, as we were mounted, they did not attempt to outrun us. They set a series of traps and ambushes for us to ride into, but most of these were so crude that it took no special skill to avoid them. Some were more clever, consisting of a very apparent ambush, avoiding which we would run into the real and hidden trap. On our right lay the dark Samabula forest and on our left some rugged ranges of hills and mountains. We rode as fast as we dared and yet conserve the strength of our mounts, and we scanned every rise for the famed flat-topped Mountain of the Chiefs.

Just before night we sighted a grassy vley and felt obliged to off-saddle and give our horses a chance to rest and graze, for good grass was scarce and our animals were tired. Vaversol held them on a long riata while I crept out on a point and lay with my glass, watching the natives moving to surround us. They, knowing us to be scouts, guessed the general direction of our course and carefully threw numbers of gun men across our line of march. This was easier than to come at us on a smooth vley, which would only make us rush to saddle and might expose them to a shot or two besides.

We led our horses for about two hours, until it was quite dark. The questions before us were: Would the ambush have patience to lie still and let us ride into it, or would the natives cross over to the forest and join their big camp there, or would they sweep across the vley by night, thinking we had laid up for a sleep? With my glass I had observed some deserted huts about two miles to the south. We decided they would never expect us to go in that direction, and, besides, we hoped we might find a store of Kafir corn for our hungry horses, so we cautiously approached the huts.

We found the corn and led our horses into a deep depression near by, where there was no possibility of their being seen against the skyline, and here we rested; rationing ourselves and the horses and sleeping by turns until midnight, when we mounted and rode northwest and then west again. This was slow riding, because small bushes seem like a forest at night and every few minutes we had to stop, use eyes, ears, and nostrils, and watch every inhalation of our horses and every turn of their ears. At each step the route must be infallibly registered on a scout's mind, for it may be necessary to backtrack in broad daylight at a gallop over the same ground. In such a country, at such a time, a scout would be lost only once.

The critical hour of dawn found us still in fairly open country with many kraals in sight and natives moving about. Evidently we were behind the big army that lay around and ahead of our little column with its twenty-two ox wagons, its weak horses, its wounded men and miserable artillery. Near the kraals we noticed a few warriors and gun men who should have been at the front. Luckily for us, most of the good and fast fighters were away, but there were a number of old men and ex-warriors and they nearly all had muzzle-loading rifles. There were also a good many swift-running youths with spears.

We rode slowly, saving our horses and searching constantly for the Chief's Mountain, as a shipwrecked sailor watches for sight of land. Where could it be? Vaversol himself had seen it once, on a trading trip in old days to Lobengula's capital, but from another direction. At last the situation became so uncertain that we made up our minds we must capture a native and get information.

We allowed a group of young spearmen to crowd us slowly into some bush; then we skirted it and dashed past them at a gallop out on the open lands, riding toward two isolated huts where we had seen smoke. We found an unexpected deep donga in our way, with a trickle of water in it. As we rode along its banks, suddenly two old black women, each one with a great jar of water on her head, stepped from a sunken path out on the level ground right in front of us. When they saw us, each woman let out a scream and slid from under her jar so quickly that it hit the ground in the same position as it had rested on her head. One woman darted toward the donga, but Vaversol jumped his horse between her and the bank, shouting to her to stand still, and I came out of my amazed trance and headed off the other woman, who had started to run for the kraal, about half a mile distant. Vaversol's command of the language and knowledge of the natives now stood us in good stead. The women soon got over their fright, and when Vaversol began to name some of their chiefs and spoke of incidents of his visit to their country, they became very talkative, in the soft, polite language of the Zulus. One of them had a son in the war. She herself did not favour the war and said the king had already been fully paid in gold and arms all that he demanded for Mashonaland.

Vaversol asked in a casual way about certain landmarks.

"Ah! There, right on the horizon, was the Chief's Mountain—Thabas Induna."

We had been looking at it for an hour! I was fairly angry at the miserable little molehill and wanted to blow it off the map. It was like going to meet a famous hero, who, according to boyhood dreams, should be at least six feet four, only to be patted on the head by a little fat, bald-headed man, scarcely five feet high.

"And where might Matchum Slopé, the White Rocks, be?" we asked.

They were "a little farther on." And, of course, that smoky haze was Bulawayo.

Would Aunty advise us to call on the king to-day?

"Not exactly to-day," she advised. Then she added that the king was already gathering his ox wagons and treasure and trekking toward the Shangani River, Shiloh, and the north; but there were still many warriors in Bulawayo who would be delighted to spear us or feed us alive to the crocodiles, as it was the king's pleasure to do with his captured enemies.

This information lifted a load from our hearts. There was an open road to Bulawayo and the king did not dream how small and exhausted our force actually was; otherwise, he would have led his last regiment against us instead of trekking to the north. We could save our people yet, if we could get back to the column and guide them into the open country. These withered old black women seemed like angels of light to us. We hastily bade them adieu. Vaversol tossed a coin to one and I gave the other a "sure to goodness" pocket knife which I could ill spare.

Already there came running from their kraal a number of men and boys with guns and spears. We cantered off a few hundred yards, and concluded we had better ride to Matchum Slopé so as to get a good view of Bulawayo and be absolutely sure of all our bearings. Then, if need be, we could bring in the column without fail and escape any possible chance of being caught in a thick belt of bush and cut to pieces by expert spearmen, as many a patrol has been in African wars.

Avoiding another kraal, we worked up over some rough ground to gain a vantage point where we could use our glasses. We dismounted and led our horses. As we cleared the rim of a small mesa, we found a Maholie slave boy herding a flock of goats. He was sitting on a rock with his back to us, playing a sort of tune by beating two sticks together. I slipped my bridoon to Vaversol and glided up quickly behind the boy, Vaversol warning me that he would bolt like a rabbit. I stepped directly in front of him, ready to seize him if he moved. It was unnecessary, as every faculty of his body except the horrified, staring eyes, failed to function. "Frozen" is the only word to express his state. Vaversol said: "He is a Maholie, too ignorant to give any information, and you have him so scared that we could do nothing with him for hours, anyway." He added that the Maholies sometimes actually die of fright. Every minute was precious to us now, so we mounted and rode away. For all I know that boy may be turned to stone, like the figures on Superstition Mountain, Arizona. According to the legend, they were petrified by the sight of demons. I suppose our appearance was as horrifying to the youth as it would be to one of us if we were to rouse from a pleasant nap in a country church and gaze into the red mouth of a Bengal tiger not two feet away.

From a little rise we saw through our glasses the great capital of King Lobengula—Bulawayo. There were great numbers of beautifully woven Matabele huts that could shelter twenty thousand guests and huge magazines for storing ivory and goods. Thabas Indunas now loomed up more importantly on our skyline. We were in possession of news that would lift a load from the commanders of our column. We dared not waste a moment. But our horses must be fed and we must have food and sleep.

It is often difficult to control the impulse to drive spur to horse and spare nothing, but this way lies certain failure. Restraint is very necessary. To be on foot, pursued by fast-running spearmen who can bring fresh runners into the chase every hour, means the end of all. Fortunately, the natives had exaggerated ideas of the endurance of a horse. Because he could gallop a few hundred yards at great speed, they supposed he could go on indefinitely, so they would prematurely give up the chase. In this the Negro differs from the Apache Indian, who is a keen judge of the condition of a horse. Many times the swift-running African warriors could have closed on us if they had known how weak our horses were. Now we asked ourselves if the wonderful luck that had passed us around so many obstacles still held good. Would our faculties endure for the return march through this hostile land?

We camped in front of the kraal of the captured ladies, on a wide open vley where there was some green grass that had sprung up after a burning—a godsend to our ravenous horses. Vaversol watched while I slept for an hour; meantime, he prepared hot coffee and biltong for our hungry selves. When he woke me he said he had seen several runners going to other kraals, and that the natives were forming a big circle around us. We ate heartily, and then I told Vaversol to lie down. It would be time enough to saddle up and be moving when any one crossed into the open ground. He was enough of a fatalist to drop to sleep at once. I watched the warriors steadily running from the kraals to tighten the circle around us. Every little depression and bushy point held a group. Finally, I knew the ring was complete because about a dozen of them had come in full view, brandishing their shields and shouting most uncomplimentary remarks about all our ancestors in general and our near relations in particular, adding most prejudiced opinions of ourselves. All this meant it was time to saddle up.

I woke Vaversol and, as we swung into the saddle, we saw group after group of blacks step out into the open. We were very thoroughly surrounded, but the natives had sent most of their guns to the south, as they believed we would ride in that direction. We therefore rode south slowly, thus preventing any general movement in the circle, as they thought we were running into its strongest part. The savages stood still for some time, watching us. The kraal of the old women was to the west of us, and in front of it were many women and children and a few old men and herd boys. Just before reaching a point where we might come under fire, we suddenly turned west, set spur to our horses, and galloped directly at this kraal. It had never occurred to the blacks that such would be our tactics. Unarmed people, even in great numbers, are harmless, so we dashed in among the huts, through the midst of wildly excited and screaming natives. One old half-blind warrior fired an antiquated muzzle-loading elephant gun, with more risk to himself than to us. We added to the pandemonium by letting loose a few shots, to keep any young spearmen from approaching near enough to hurl an assegai.

In a few moments, we were through and beyond the demoralized circle. The warriors, seeing us gallop away so easily, came trailing back to the kraals when the whole trap had dissolved. We rode north into rather heavy bush, slowed to a walk, then dismounted and led our horses quietly for an hour without seeing or being seen. After that we rode into the open and to the south, passing through the very gap which had been closed against us. We picked up our incoming trail and followed it till dark, very much elated, as every hour our peril grew less.

Suddenly, there sprang up a cold wind. We both knew its import and dreaded the mists that might come with it, for they often restricted vision to a range of twenty feet and made night travelling exceedingly difficult. In a few moments, we felt the first moisture on our faces. With such intensity as a condemned man might gaze for the last time on sun and sky, we tried to fix in our eyes the outlines of the rolling hills and the direction of the black lines of bush. To each, as we rode on in silence, came maddening fears for our column and thoughts of our lost settlements if we should fail. I searched my brain for all the lore of the great scouts it had been my good fortune to serve under in the American plains and deserts. I longed for the skill of McIntosh, Al Sieber, Sterling, or Lee. Our horses would not back-track unguided. The map stored in my mind for the past forty-eight hours unrolled, but not as vividly as I required. I was enraged at myself for not having turned in the saddle every fifty yards to gaze backward.

Vaversol now produced a little pocket compass and declared we were moving due north. This would land us in the Samabula forest. We dismounted, placed the compass on the ground, covered it carefully with our hats, and lit a fuse to read it. Sure enough, we were headed directly north. Yet so strongly did I feel that I had not lost my bearings, that I insisted on continuing. Vaversol was an experienced man, but he had been taught to rely on the compass. I had been brought up in another school among the Indians of our Western frontier and depended on accurate orientation by means of memory pictures. So we agreed that each man should save his own life in his own way and reach the column if possible. We separated and were soon lost to each other in the mist. The sound of hoof beats grew fainter and died away.

In a few minutes came a "Coo-ee!" I answered and halted. Soon I heard the horse again, and Vaversol rode up. He had decided to disregard his compass and follow me, although I was almost a stranger to him. I had been confident of my ability to back-track to the column when I felt I should never see him again, but now that he had returned I felt a strange responsibility for his life and the first real doubt of myself crept into my mind. Could it be possible that I was confused and the compass right, and that if Vaversol should continue to ride by its direction he and the column would be saved?

We rode on together. Once, during the night, we swung too far north and suddenly heard voices all around us. We had ridden into the edge of the forest and almost upon a regiment of the king's warriors. For an hour, we found ourselves riding parallel with moving regiments evidently being rushed to attack our column, and it was only by acute use of ears and nostrils that we avoided their camps. We nearly fired into a flock of stampeded goats, thinking we were being rushed by assegai men. The scares were not all on our side, and Vaversol could tell by the excited shouts that many of the natives were new recruits who had never been in war and were terrified at the thought of the strange white men they were marching to meet—those terrible whites who fought at any hour of the day or night.

A little past midnight, my horse suddenly stopped, sniffed the air, then put his head close to the ground. I was filled with hope and dismounted instantly. We were at a point where we had lifted our saddles and rested on the westward march—the odour was of our own horses. I said nothing to Vaversol of thus positively locating our trail, but just before day we rode under the shadow of the abandoned huts where we had fed our mounts on the way out. They loomed large and strange in the mist. We listened, circled, and then entered, finding the store of Kafir corn just as we had left it.

Vaversol now fully realized that his compass had been wrong, and I confessed to him that I had identified the trail several hours before, and that my gaiety during the latter part of the night had been due to my childish satisfaction in being able to crow over a lucky accomplishment. We fed our mounts and ourselves, but were too keyed-up for our last lap to sleep even a wink. We knew exactly where we could cut the big trail from here, but we did not know the movement of our troops. They might be in a big attack and unable to move, or they might be on the march. They might have kept too far to the north and be buried in the edge of the Samabula forest. The question was raised whether we should cut in by riding north toward the forest, knowing that if the column trekked it would be westward. This would save distance and spare our horses, yet might bring us into instant contact with the fiercest regiments of Lobengula. On the other hand, if we back-tracked to the last known point and then trailed the column, we would come in contact with great numbers of new recruits, spearmen, and camp followers. We decided to ride north until the thick bush became too dangerous, and only in the event of failing to get in touch would we back-track and follow the wagons.

Inside of two hours, to my relief, I spied through the glass one of our mounted scouts. We hurried on and reached the moving column just before noon. Riding at once to Major Forbes, we reported that we had been within sight of Bulawayo, that we had found a passable road avoiding the forest, and that if the column continued to march in its present direction, it would soon be entrapped in heavy bush and many regiments of the king would pounce upon us. While we were making this report, our scouts were rushed back by waves of warriors in the bush ahead. Forbes reluctantly ordered Captain Charles White to take charge of the scouts and the advance guard and to change the line of march.

We had barely time to gain the open ground discovered by

WHEN THE COMPASS FAILED

Vaversol and myself and take position on a rising knoll when thousands of the Matabele burst out of the forest and rushed our rapidly formed laager.

This was the battle of the Imbembezi, on November 1, 1893.

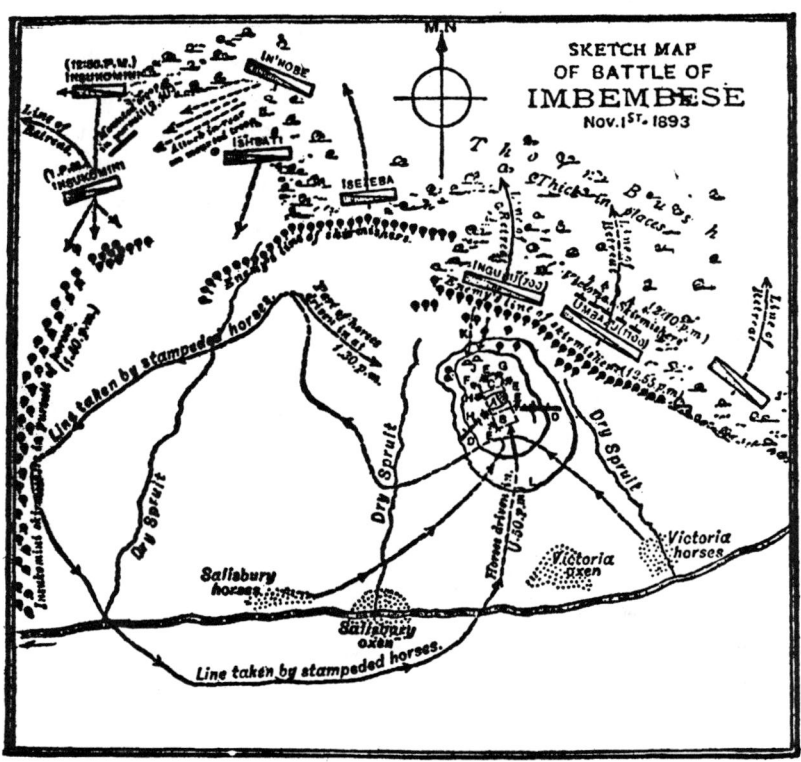

BATTLE OF THE IMBEMBEZI

The decisive fight of the Bulawayo campaign. This map shows the skill with which the natives were handled by their indunas, but the advantage lay with the British, owing to superiority of position.

It proved to be the decisive fight of the campaign—a battle of Gettysburg in miniature—with the king's Imperial Guard going down in magnificent defeat, as Pickett's "Flower of the South" fell that day in the 'sixties. Had this attack been delivered while we were in the forest, the fate of the entire column would have been that which overtook Major Wilson and his command just thirty-four days later in this same forest, far down the Shangani River.

Unfortunately for the Matabele in the present battle, their failure to prevent our carrying information of the open road to Forbes had allowed him to form laager on what was probably the strongest position between Victoria and Bulawayo. In this fight their rushes did them no good, and in broad daylight, with our six hundred marksmen, we annihilated every company of Matabele that rushed out of the forest and up the slopes of the hill. The king's executioner, a giant standing at least six feet six and weighing probably two hundred and fifty pounds, led one of the most heroic charges, running with his spear and rifle directly through our hail of lead until within a few yards of the laager He dropped the closest to us of all who fell that day.

Even then, Lobengula might have saved his capital at least for a time had he taken advantage of his opportunity. During the height of the action all our horses, which were held just under the knoll, stampeded for several miles over the rolling grass-covered hills. In the Salisbury part of the laager there were a few saddle horses belonging to the officers and these were quickly mounted for pursuit. A sally led by Sir John Willoughby and the gallant Captain Borrow (who perished in Wilson's last stand) succeeded in recovering the demoralized herd. Had the Matabele turned their entire attention to continuing and perfecting this stampede of our horses and to destroying about a dozen men, they would have had us all afoot in the middle of their country and probably not one of our expedition would have escaped. But as one of the Matabele prisoners remarked after this fight: "The medicine of the white man is always stronger than the medicine of the king."

The day following the battle of the Imbembezi, we were within sight of the famous Thabas Indunas or Mountain of the Chiefs. Lobengula's impis made a rally and attacked our right flank; this necessitated the forming of another laager and the deploying of our mounted men.

Just before the fight, we heard a great explosion and saw huge columns of smoke rising into the air in the direction of Bulawayo. Major Wilson ordered me to go in and find out what was happening in the town and if the king were still there. I took with me my friend Ingram and a noted colonial frontiersman and pioneer by the name of Poselt. By taking advantage of every contour and making use of every trick of scouting known to us, we managed to avoid the notice of the enemy, and at last rode up to within a few hundred yards of the huts of the traders just outside the main stockade of Lobengula's capital. We found the town burning and no natives visible.

While we were sitting on our horses, using our glasses carefully, I saw a man come out of one building and climb to the top of a big shed. At the same time, another tall figure appeared and started in our direction. Thinking, of course, they were Matabele, Poselt and Ingram dismounted and were about to fire when I discovered through my glass that the man advancing toward us was white.

We learned that he was a trader who had been held a prisoner by Lobengula during the war. Together with his companion, the man on the shed, he had been under the protection of the king, and, at the last, orders had been given to the warriors that these two white men should be left in the capital and not killed. It was a very generous act on the part of the king. From these men we got a complete history of the events of that short and sharp campaign from the Matabele point of view.

The traders told us that a messenger had rushed into the presence of Lobengula and described to him the advance of the British.

The king asked, "Where are the white men?"

"O Father, O King, they have crossed the Shangani!"

The king asked, "Why have you not defeated them?"

"Because," the messenger replied, "they move like the snake; the head goes under the grass and comes up again and they are always moving. We attack them at one place and they move on to another and never stop marching."

CHATPER XV

CARRYING DISPATCHES

LOBENGULA had fled into the jungles of the north; his capital was in smoking ruins; the power of the last of the Zulus was crumpled. When we entered Bulawayo on November 3d we found that the king on retreating had not only set fire to his huts but had also burned up an immense amount of ivory and treasure, along with valuable hides, horns, and skins that he had accumulated in his storehouses. We made a great effort to put out this fire, but it was impossible to do so, and we saved very little of what must have been one of the most extraordinary collections ever made. One trophy that we managed to salvage was the great knobkerrie of Lobengula himself. This was a single white rhinoceros horn, probably one of the finest existent, with a knob at the end as large as one's fist. The horn was fully four feet in length and had been straightened and beautifully worked. Bain, the Canadian scout, afterward secured this knobkerrie for Cecil Rhodes. It seemed peculiarly fitting that this emblem of authority should pass from the grasp of the most powerful black monarch of Africa into the hands of the strongest white ruler who ever dominated that continent.

Upon the fall of Bulawayo, Jameson was extremely anxious to get important dispatches to Rhodes, and to discover the whereabouts of the Imperial forces which had been sent by way of Mafeking and the Matoppo Mountains to aid us in our attack on King Lobengula. This reinforcement numbered about four hundred men under Major Goold Adams and was guided by the famous hunter and naturalist, Frederick Courtney Selous. It was understood that King Khama of Bechuanaland would assist Adams with a large force of friendly natives. During our entire march from Victoria we had received no tidings whatever from Adams, but were told by captured natives that Gamba, Lobengula's son-in-law, had been sent with an army of thousands of Matabele to intercept and annihilate this force; that this had been accomplished and all of Goold Adams's men were either killed or scattered in retreat through Khamaland. Should these rumours prove true, it would mean that our little command could not hope to maintain itself, even though we had captured the capital and driven the king into the jungle.

It was decided that I should be sent to find out the whereabouts of Goold Adams, if possible, and to carry very important dispatches to the nearest telegraph station. This was an outpost called Tati, one hundred and twenty-eight miles from Bulawayo through the rugged Matoppo Mountains by way of the Mangwe Pass. I chose my friend Ingram to ride with me, as we had already accomplished several difficult missions together in this campaign and I knew his splendid mettle. We took with us one native who spoke the Matabele language and who had been well tried out by us, both as to his personal courage and his ability to ride.

We reached the head of the difficult Mangwe Pass just as it was being abandoned by Gamba's regiments. Their camp fires were still burning. Fortunately, we spied two natives who were packing their belongings to follow the retreating army and, by a little stratagem, succeeded in capturing them. By holding our guns to their heads, we prevented their giving the alarm to the regiments. It was extremely necessary that we should find out the location and disposition both of the natives and of Goold Adams's forces. Our black scout was an adept in extracting information from prisoners and was far too wise to use force, which nearly always defeats its own ends. He elicited from our prisoners that there had been a big fight, that Gamba's impis were abandoning the Pass—glad tidings indeed for us!—and that King Khama's forces had fled back to Khamaland on account of the curse of sickness (smallpox), leaving Goold Adams without support and with only the original four hundred men under his command.

The Matabele also cheerfully volunteered the statement that the friends of Goold Adams as well as other white men who were coming into their country would soon be roasted like pheasants before the fire. Our black countered with some "big talk" of his own, declaring scornfully that their king, Lobengula, was neither an elephant nor a lion, but a miserable jackal fleeing before the great white Doctor Jameson, who knew how to draw medicine from the sky, who carried the moon in a box, and could at night throw the very stars into the king's regiments, and that these stars, exploding, would kill all within a radius of many yards. All Negroes are endowed with a vivid imagination, and I could never record adequately the duel of wits that took place between our native guide and his Zulu antagonists as to the occult resources of Doctor Jameson and the magic powers of King Lobengula.

We were in a desperate hurry to get through the Pass, so we forced our captives to the double-quick at the end of a gun. We had several close calls from attack and ambush, but our native scout, adopting the costume of one of the captured Zulus as a disguise, slipped ahead and found and reported the exact position of the enemy. By devious routes through the granite domes of the Matoppos, we avoided his neighbourhood and then climbed back down the steep walls into the Pass, finally reaching the bush country at the base of the mountains. As our horses were becoming exhausted, we paused here long enough to give them a chance to graze and rest while we stole a little sleep ourselves, always leaving one man on guard. We allowed our prisoners to lie down with only their wrists tied together. It was our intention to halt for two hours, giving each man about half an hour's guard duty while the others rested. When it came to the turn of our Kafir to stand guard, he fell asleep; whereupon the two prisoners managed to release themselves and escape. On arousing and finding them gone, we feared they would carry the news of our presence to the natives immediately around us, so we at once saddled and pushed our jaded horses in the direction of Tati.

At break of day we struck the spoor of horsemen and finally

CARRYING DISPATCHES

ran upon some natives whom we found to be friendly subjects of King Khama. Only the day before, they had advanced with Goold Adams into the Mangwe Pass, and from them we learned of the engagement with Gamba and his defeat.

Our horses' shoes were very thin when we started from Bulawayo, and a rainstorm that we had ridden through had softened their hoofs until our mounts had cast their shoes and we had been obliged to ride them barefooted over the rocky Pass. From this, the animals became so lame that it was almost impossible to proceed. Fortunately, in a deserted Matabele hut, we discovered some bull-hide shields which I soaked and cut into moccasins of a form in familiar use in Western America. These we stretched tightly over each hoof, and, with our horses thus re-shod, rode into Goold Adams's camp, where our Yankee method of shoeing horses greatly interested the commanding officer. We found that Selous had been wounded but was still capable of guiding the forces on to Bulawayo. After getting some assistance from Goold Adams, we continued our journey toward Tati, where we expected to meet messengers from Rhodes.

Shortly before reaching our destination, the way led through thick thorn bush. I was riding considerably in advance of the others, when the sound of horses' hoofs reached my ears from the road ahead of me. Pulling my horse into a clump of thorn bush, I waited. There was no approach. All was silent. This stirred my suspicion. I moved my horse a little farther into the bush, slid from the saddle, and listened. In less than a minute, I heard a short whistle. This I answered. Then came a white man's "Coo-ee" which I also echoed, but fearing the natives might have imitated the call to deceive me, I took the precaution of tying my handkerchief to the muzzle of my gun and waving it above the bush. A few yards away, around a bend in the road, rose a similar signal. Upon my shouting in English, "Who are you?" the same challenge was shouted back. We then exchanged a few more words to satisfy each other and advanced openly.

Thus the day was made memorable to me by my first meeting

with the Boer scout, Johann Colenbrander, one of the most noted characters of South Africa, as well as with the equally famous Frederick Courtney Selous—men so dissimilar yet so alike in many ways. Little did we then guess how the threads of our lives were to be interwoven in war and peace on the continent of Africa for years to come!

The works of Selous are standards and his name is well known to thousands. In the country where he had hunted with Roosevelt, he made his last campaign against the Germans. By that time, the Boers, who had once been his enemies, were fighting with him fifty thousand strong under their famous commander, Johann Smuts. Johann Colenbrander was of mixed English and Dutch blood. He possessed military skill and a remarkable knowledge of both Kafir and Boer. For many years, it was not possible to follow the trails of South Africa from the Zambezi to the Cape without at some point coming in contact with his doings. In the Boer War he fought with the English, believing that their victory would lead inevitably to the union of South Africa, which was a part of Rhodes's dream. Under Kitchener and Lord Roberts, Colenbrander was rapidly advanced and given a separate command with the rank of colonel. At the close of the war, high honours were justly bestowed upon him, for his efforts contributed greatly to a wise and final settlement of that great racial struggle. Unlike Selous, Laing, and a hundred other famous men of that time, a soldier's death was denied him. His end recalls that of Rostand's hero, Cyrano de Bergerac, who, after escaping the thousand dangers of a soldier's career, met an ignominious death through accident or petty enmity in the streets of a quiet town. Colenbrander, who had swum a thousand rivers, perished in crossing a bit of rough water in a Zululand stream to please a motion-picture director who wanted action. He knew well that no frontiersman would select such a crossing. It would have been a bad moment for that director if some of Colenbrander's old command had been within shooting distance.

When I first met him, Colenbrander was carrying dispatches

from the Government to Goold Adams and also to Doctor Jameson. I convinced him that I could return to Bulawayo as swiftly as he himself could ride; so he gave me the dispatches for Jameson, upon my promise of all possible haste, while he continued on his way to Goold Adams, whom I had just left. Before we parted, Colenbrander obtained for me an Arab stallion at Tati, and upon the rapid accomplishment of my mission there, I mounted this fine horse and started on the return trip. By riding with the utmost speed and caution, constantly watching the nervous shoulder muscles to gauge the condition of my horse, and frequently loosening and shaking the saddle, I was able to deliver the dispatches to Doctor Jameson at Bulawayo thirty hours from the time of receiving them at Tati, a distance of one hundred and twenty-eight miles over the route taken.

This Arab horse, Mahomet, seemed to have almost human intelligence. It has been my fortune in life to own and ride many splendid animals, but when this stallion finally perished of the deadly horse sickness in my camp at Gwelo I felt in my heart as though I had lost a very dear personal friend. So courageous was Mahomet that, when his malady was far advanced and any ordinary horse would have been lying down to die, he persisted in remaining on his feet, demanding affection and sympathy by nuzzling my sleeve with his foaming and swollen lips. This gallant creature seemed to understand thoroughly the spirit and conditions of native warfare. Many a time, by the dilation of his nostrils, the pointing of his ears, or the turning of his head, he seemed to be taking pains to warn me of an impending ambush. No matter how tired he was, how footsore or leg-weary, how wounded or thirsty, he never refused in a crisis to bound with all his strength at the lightest touch of my heel.

Many of the men in our column had similar experiences with various horses and dogs. Since, in a war of this character, the horse was our salvation and our greatest means of equalizing the differences between our handful of pioneers and the overwhelming masses of the Matabele, it was only natural that there should grow up between our men and their mounts such mutual affection and comradeship as that between the Arabs and their famous steeds. To this day I recall with a thrill the Fourth Reader tale of the Arab horse that rescued his tightly bound master from the tent of the enemy by carrying him off bodily with his teeth.

One of the strangest mascots of our column—the prime favourite with Major Allan Wilson—was a big African sheep. While we were drilling the troops on the open field adjoining the town of Victoria, this beast insisted on charging splendidly back and forth with the Major's big buckskin horse, and when the column started for Matabeleland, he faithfully followed the Major and the buckskin through all the marches and countermarches, and was gathered into the laager at the Battle of Shangani. Not long after this, he perished on the banks of the same river where his master was doomed to die.

On delivering my dispatches to Doctor Jameson in Bulawayo, the information was given me that Major Forbes had moved toward Shiloh and the Shangani River. A report that King Lobengula, after his final abandonment of Bulawayo, had taken seven wagons and his personal belongings and trekked north toward the Zambezi River, had caused much earnest discussion among the officers commanding the troops and especially between Majors Forbes and Wilson. They decided that the force should leave its position on the Imbembezi River and re-form an attacking column with Shiloh as a base.

Forbes was ordered to try to overtake the king and, if possible, to capture him and bring to an end the last resistance of the Matabele nation. It was pretty well understood that, because of exhausted horses and small supply of ammunition, the chances of success were slight. The king's regiments, although somewhat scattered and demoralized, were still quite capable of turning on so small a force as ours and suddenly annihilating it. Doctor Jameson decided that he would not take the responsibility of ordering any men on such hazardous military service, yet so great would be the achievement that he called for volunteers. To the credit of the pioneers, be it said, there was no lack of response. It became merely a matter of choosing those who seemed to be strongest, out of an already well-selected force. Two hundred and forty men were finally accepted to make the final dash to capture the king.

After my long ride from Tati, Doctor Jim was loath to ask me to follow Forbes and Wilson, but I knew he wanted me to go if I felt fit. After a few hours' sleep, I reported to Jameson that Ingram had arrived and we would both take the trail and overtake Forbes at Shiloh or Inyati. Doctor Jameson gave us a short, quick examination and pronounced us about fifty per cent. rawhide and fifty per cent. biltong, but added that, when we reached Forbes, we were to tell him that we were under orders to take it easy for a day or two. He then made us a valued gift of a tin of cocoa, and we rode into the veldt. Darkness fell. Often we had to feel with our hands or use our precious fusees to pick up the trail. We found the column, not at Shiloh, but en route to Inyati.

All the next day, we advanced to a position on a branch of the Bubi River. It was my duty to scout ahead of the column with a Boer and two colonials. While grazing our horses for a short rest we came on two ducks swimming in a small pond. I killed one of the birds by aiming directly under it, and brought it back and presented it to my commanding officer, Forbes. As any dainty morsel of this kind was now at a premium, he thanked me warmly, taking the duck in his hands and examining the plumage to determine the variety. Finding no bullet wound, he asked me how I had killed it, and on being told it was done with a Martini rifle, he laughingly accused me of trying to put over a "Yankee trick." My assurance that it was no great feat to kill a duck on the water with a heavy rifle without a wound, he would not accept. Neither would he credit my tales of our frontiersmen who, with the old muzzle-loading rifle, drove nails, snuffed candles, barked squirrels, split bullets on ax blades, and occasionally shot mugs of whisky from one another's heads, William Tell fashion; all of which were perfectly true. It seemed odd to have to asseverate what to me were commonplace facts.

Night found us with our two hundred and forty men, without wagons or means of forming a strong laager, in the immediate neighbourhood of several thousand Matabele warriors. Evidently, there had been some mistake in the story of the dispersal of these regiments. While it was true they had scattered to some extent and were driving vast herds of cattle to the north, it was also true that several of the trusted regiments of the king were still intact and quite able to pounce upon and annihilate our little force. Scouts reported that the enemy were preparing to attack us.

Major Forbes and Major Allan Wilson, the second in command, asked me to make use of some stratagem to prevent or delay until daylight the probable attack of these impis on our unprotected camp. In the daytime, when mounted, the accuracy of our rifle fire and the quickness of our movements made us feel little fear of the superior numbers of the natives, but at night, in a country rather thickly wooded and close to a force outnumbering us probably twenty to one, there was grave peril, and the experienced fighters in the column well realized this fact.

In 1893, explosives had not reached the perfection of the present day. Old artillerymen will remember that our bombs had a hollow core lined with coarse sand set in glue. The firing pin, which was about six inches long and the size of a lead pencil, was also dipped in glue and covered with the same sharp sand. In order to fire, this sanded pin, which was attached to a three-foot cord, had to be very gently inserted into the equally well-sanded hole without striking a spark. Any little unsteadiness of the hand would cause a premature explosion and the absent mark after one's name at roll call.

I took from our stores some bomb rockets, constructed after this fashion, and a brass firing tube about ten inches long. The tube had a square brass base which was supposed to be bolted to a timber, but in the present emergency it would be merely tied to a bush with an African "rim" or halter strap. This would make the insertion of the firing pin as precise a performance as the ceremony of dispensing high tea. Ingram and I

CARRYING DISPATCHES 161

were given two horses that were used to travelling together and could be depended on to stand quietly without neighing or stamping about. They belonged to Captain Coventry of the Bechuanaland Border Police, and were named Brandy and Soda. Hiding the horses in a clump of bush, we advanced cautiously in the enemy's camp, slipping between his fires. Then it was decided that Ingram should return to the thicket and sit his horse, holding mine ready for me to mount as soon as the rockets should go off. I crept under the sheltering banks of a little spruit or brook along which the main body of the king's impis were encamped, securing a position close to the centre of what appeared to be the largest impi. Attaching the firing tube to a small sapling, I inserted one of the huge bomb rockets and pulled the lanyard. A terrific crash followed. The final explosion, a thousand feet in the air, threw a shower of flaming stars in all directions through the black night and caused one of the greatest hubbubs among the savages that it has ever been my good fortune to witness. Quickly inserting another bomb, I fired again, and by this time men were leaping on all sides, guns were going off, and a general stampede was on. Having one rocket left, I clapped it in the tube, but the previous explosions had tilted the tube so that, instead of throwing the bomb straight up, it burst out at an angle into a large Kafir kraal occupied by many of the warriors. The result was particularly gratifying.

It must have seemed to the blacks that the very stars of heaven were combining with the white men to destroy the Matabele nation. No wonder they were completely upset. They did not even make an attempt to find out the source of the explosions; they simply stampeded. I slipped back to Ingram, and we rode straight up to the kraal that had been exposed to full view by the illumination of the last rocket. Lighting the huts and setting the kraal on fire, we then dashed off in the opposite direction. By the light of the burning village we were able to fire about fifty rounds from our rifles at the darting figures of the bewildered warriors. We learned afterward that the Matabele were convinced that all the forces of the whites led by the great Doctor Jameson himself with his strongest medicine had come to crush them. Instead of returning the attack on our exposed column of only two hundred and forty men, the thousands of savages fled through the night and did not pause or rally again until they reached the main stream of the Bubi River.

We were now so short of rations that, upon reaching Shiloh, some of our men and the weaker horses were returned to Bulawayo. We continued the march with one hundred and sixty men and only two Maxims and no wagons or oxen.

CHAPTER XVI

THE DASH TO CAPTURE THE KING

WHEN our column of volunteers started on the king's trail, it was quite easy to follow the track of the seven royal wagons, but by the time Shiloh was reached, this trail had become thoroughly obliterated. Behind the king had been driven at least fifty thousand head of cattle; the whole country was trampled by them. In addition, the rainy season was just coming on, so that altogether, the marching impis, the trampling cattle, and the hard rain every day blotted out the king's spoor almost entirely. Under Major Allan Wilson, the best trackers of Africa—Hottentots and Masarwas from the desert, whose existence largely depends on their ability to follow an antelope or recognize the faintest trace of small game—were put to work to discover the trail of the king's wagons. We had also in our force others especially trained in trailing: Boers of the Transvaal, Australians, and frontiersmen from all parts of the world. The final tracking, however, depended upon Ingram, an American, Bain, a Canadian, and myself. We found that we could outtrack the black scout even at his best. Many times we lost the spoor, but we always found it again.

I was asked by Major Wilson to verify a native report that the king's wagons had crossed the river about seven miles below where we were camped. I took with me a black, a Fingoe called John Grootbaum. He might better have been named M'Slopogaas, for he had many of the characteristics of that black hero. He was well known in the country, could speak good English, and was one of the pluckiest Negroes I have ever seen.

We started at dark and soon found ourselves riding through thick thorn bush and were compelled to dismount and hunt the trail for openings—an extremely difficult proceeding. About three o'clock in the morning, we reached a Kafir village on the banks of the river at the point where the king's wagons were supposed to have crossed. Everything was quiet around the place, and I decided that, as it was still dark, the best way to find out about the crossing of the wagons would be to capture somebody from among the native huts and force the information from him.

Selecting a hut that was nearest the river, we crept up to it and listened. We could hear the heavy breathing and snoring of several inmates. The natives, when not under immediate alarm, sleep like the dead, and it is quite possible to walk through and among a thousand of them and not stir or wake one. Grootbaum suggested that the best way would be to crawl into the hut, where he would take one native by the throat while I could wrap my cartridge belt around his legs and drag him outside. He said he would hold the fellow so tight that he could not make a sound, and the slight shuffling noise of his withdrawal would probably not be noticed by any one in the hut. This we accomplished and carried the struggling wretch out into the bush some fifty or sixty yards away. I placed my rifle on his chest and Grootbaum released his clutch on his neck sufficiently for the native to recover his voice. After explaining in whispers that we did not wish to kill him, we told him that if he would answer our questions truthfully and tell us everything he knew concerning the passing of the king's wagons and where they were, we would let him go. We assured him that we simply meant to prevent his shouting and giving the alarm to the sleeping natives in the huts. He informed us that in these huts were sleeping more than two hundred of Lobengula's warriors, and that these constituted the extreme rear guard of the king's personal fighting men. He said that the villagers had fled several days ago with all their cattle and that the king's spoor could be seen crossing the bed of the river within a few hundred yards of where we were.

We decided to slip along and verify this tale. The natives are most artful liars, even under extreme pressure, and I did

THE DASH TO CAPTURE THE KING

not propose to carry back information that I had found the king's spoor, on the mere word of a black held by a long leather thong fastened around his neck. The terrible maze of the thorn bush made riding perilous, and it was already getting gray in the east when we finally found the track of the king's wagons. Then, having proved his testimony true, we released our captive. We followed the trail until we found the charred remains of a wagon, showing plainly that the king was destroying whatever impeded his rapid retreat.

We now turned toward the column and retraced our way. As we rode along through high grass and thick bush, we came suddenly on a band of herders who were driving a large number of cattle bearing the earmarks of the king. We were within a few yards of them before they saw us or we them. Grootbaum shouted to the herders that, although he was with a white man, he was friendly to the natives and their cause. He told them the white man beside him could not understand the Kafir language, but, as there were many other white men near by, he advised them to rush their cattle out of sight with all possible speed before they were killed. The Matabele thought they were looking at the advance guard of a large white impi and rushed their cattle off as fast as possible into the bush and away from us. But for Grootbaum's strategy, the thirty or forty of them could easily have bowled us off our horses.

As soon as we reached the column and gave our information, the troops marched. Our weakest point was that we had no remounts, and the terrible campaign to which we had subjected our horses had reduced those splendid animals to mere skeletons. The rainy season was on, and before us lay an unknown country where night found us without protection, either of artillery or the laager of the wagons.

Nevertheless, by the first of December, we had trailed the king to within a few miles of the Shangani River. Ingram, Bain, and I, with our Kafir, Grootbaum, were several miles ahead of the column when we found immediately in front of us a large body of armed natives. While ascending a steep hill, Ingram's horse gave out completely. This was a very serious matter. All our horses were weak, but for a man actually to be dismounted was perilous. Ingram decided to lead his horse slowly back to the column. Bain and I concluded that we must scout out the ground a little more closely and find out just how strong this impi was, so that we could warn Major Forbes as to the danger of an attack on this timbered hill.

After Ingram left us, Bain and I determined to take an hour's time and, by working our horses into the high grass, find a place where we could slip the saddles from their jaded backs and give them a few mouthfuls of grass. The tracks of Lobengula's forces were everywhere about us and we had even seen a good many of the warriors, but up to this moment none of them had made a hostile move toward us. Scarcely had we slipped off the saddles, and while Bain stood holding his horse by the bridle, his gun resting against a tree not more than two feet from him, there rose up out of the grass and surrounded us about fifteen armed Matabele, with their guns at full cock.

Tribute should here be paid to Grootbaum, the coolest and bravest black of all my African experience. Bain and I knew a few words of the Kafir language, but our interpreter could speak excellent English. During the next few exciting moments he never for an instant betrayed, either by tone, gesture, or the quiver of an eyelash, the slightest fear of the encircling enemy. He interpreted my first shouted command instantly, and turning to the leader of the natives, roared at him in a tone as strong and fierce as my own, "How dare you advance with weapons in the presence of the Induna? Put down your guns!"

This, coming from the lips of victims whom they expected to see pale with fear, astounded the Matabele so that some of their warriors obeyed and actually lowered the butts of their guns. But their leader merely gave a leering grin and sidled along toward Bain, who stood motionless, still holding his horse by the bridle rein. When he thought he was near enough, he made a grab at Bain's gun, leaning against the tree, but Bain was too quick for him and with one sweep of his hand pressed the cocked rifle against the black's belly. This was an unexpected move. The black leader's rifle was in his hand, but he held it somewhat crosswise as he reached for the other weapon and this had given Bain his opportunity. Whatever hostile command was now given, it meant certain death to the savage leader, at least. Taking advantage of this, my own gun was instantly levelled at the breast of the man whom I thought to be second in importance, the oldest of the warriors. We knew what the feelings of those fifteen blacks were. They could easily shoot us, but their leader and at least one more would be killed, and our Kafir, who had his gun in his hand, would probably finish a third; all of which made them hesitate.

The leader concluded to try a bit of talking to help him move his precious belly out of line with the muzzle of Bain's gun. This he manœuvred by imperceptibly stepping a little to one side and ordering our interpreter to assure the white man that he had no intention of attacking him. But wherever he moved, Bain also moved the muzzle of his gun. The Kafir and I followed suit with our opponents. Both sides were seeking with their wits to gain some advantage before anybody should touch a trigger. I ordered our Kafir to tell the black leader we had been sent by the great Doctor Jameson as messengers; that we had been looking all day for their chief; that our horses had become tired, as the natives kept running away from us. Why, I asked, had they run so far? Why had they forced us to march so far to catch up with them? We wished to see their king to urge him to surrender, since the war was now ended. Other valuable fictions flashed into my mind, all promptly and faithfully repeated in the loud, imperious voice of my interpreter.

The two leaders, still under the muzzles of our guns, kept stepping back inch by inch, arguing all the while. The other warriors stood where they were, waiting for the word of command to shoot us. Their guns were at full cock, but, as some of them had placed the butts on the ground, they would have to lift them before they could fire, and doubtless they guessed that if they made any hostile move their leaders would instantly fall under three deadly bullets.

Our interpreter was now ordered to tell the chief that we were going to saddle up our horses and ride slowly back to the column, and that he must accompany us to meet our induna, who, with a very large impi, was just below us—almost within rifle range. He was told that it would take him only a few minutes to come with us to our chief and that we commanded him to do so. As he was still covered by Bain's rifle, the leader did not dare order his men to fire.

I quickly placed the saddle on my horse with one hand, meantime keeping my eye on the blacks. Then, swinging my gun upon Bain's man, I told Bain to saddle, which he did. The savages asked the interpreter why the other white man had gone back. The answer given was that our impi was so close that the white man had probably heard his induna calling him and had gone back under orders. But this question showed that the savages had been trailing us for some time and had kept us under observation. This they could easily have done, as the grass was high and the bush thick. When Bain and I had saddled our horses, we stood by them, still covering the black leaders with our guns, and ordered our interpreter to saddle his horse exactly as he had seen us do, which he safely accomplished.

Now came the critical moment of mounting. Unless we used extreme care, this would give the chief an opportunity to order his fifteen men to fire at us. I told our interpreter, Grootbaum, to mount, assuring him that I would cover him and that I would kill any man who raised a gun. As soon as he was mounted, I told him to ride into the grass a little to one side, then turn around and cover the black leader. The manœuvres between this interpreter and the chief were like the passes of two tigers or the sparring of expert swordsmen. Our Kafir carried out every detail as instructed with splendid speed and apparent unconcern. Never for an instant was the Matabele leader out of line with the muzzle of at least one of our guns. The next move was when I mounted my horse. I must confess that, as I put my foot in the stirrup, I fully expected to hear a crash and feel the sting of lead—and then all

THE DASH TO CAPTURE THE KING

would be over. Once in the saddle, still talking through the interpreter to the natives, I reached forward and, seizing the reins and driving my spur sharply against the horse's flank, I jumped him full among the natives, then as quickly jerked him back so it would appear that the whole thing had been unintentional on my part. This leap of the horse made two or three blacks immediately in front of me spring to one side and turn the muzzles of their guns in other directions. I at once wheeled my horse around and rode out beside our interpreter. Bain was still covering the savage leader and was in the greatest danger. I now covered his man while Bain mounted with the utmost coolness, telling the Matabele leader to shut his mouth, as he had done entirely too much talking. He ordered the black chief to follow him straight to the white induna and motioned him to come and take his position behind Bain's horse, which the chief did, followed by his reluctant men. Such insolence on our part probably confirmed the suspicion in the hearts of the savages that our interpreter might be right, and they were really in the neighbourhood of a large white impi which would certainly, at the crack of a gun, rush up and overwhelm them.

Whatever the thoughts in their minds may have been, we managed gradually to increase the distance between the blacks and ourselves, while turning in our saddles to keep our guns pointed at the leaders. We kept urging them to come on and report to our chief at headquarters. We declared that, if they did not come promptly, he might become angry and kill them all. We insisted that we had been searching for the Matabele all day and could not understand why they were afraid, and so on. Noticing that we were all the time moving away from them, the leader evidently gave the sign to his men to drop off into the grass. One by one, they melted into the brush and disappeared, while the chief himself walked on, as Bain had ordered him to do, behind the horse. As he followed, his gun was still held at right angles, for he knew well that, if he pointed it, Bain would instantly kill him. He kept up a continuous conversation with our interpreter, Grootbaum, telling him to wait, that he was coming. Suddenly he, too, disappeared into the high grass.

We immediately made a sharp turn to the right and a detour, so as to avoid a certain hill on our back-track, where the enemy might be lying in ambush. Our horses could travel only at a walk, and held in reserve could not exceed three hundred yards at a gallop without falling down. Bain and I were haunted by the fear that Ingram, leading his worn-out mount and not aware that we had been followed by a fast-running party of natives, might cling to the exact back-track and be overtaken and killed. But he was too wily for that, and while he kept in clear country as much as possible, he crossed and recrossed his trail and avoided all natural ambushes from force of habit. Soon we espied him on the side of some lagoons opposite our trail of the morning. Overtaking him with a great sense of relief, we all returned to our marching column with the news that the enemy were directly in front of us.

There was an immediate consultation among the leaders: Forbes, Wilson, Lendy, and the Boer Colonel Raff. They decided we must bring this terrible march to an end, and all were glad that the king appeared willing to give battle, rather than to penetrate deeper into the wilderness, drawing us with our nearly exhausted horses each day farther from Bulawayo. In front of us lay a rough, hilly country covered with rock and bushes and scrub mapani trees. It was difficult to see more than fifty yards in any direction. Great care had to be taken in the disposition of our scouts, advance guard, flankers, and rear guard.

By noon, we had advanced almost to the crest of a high hill when I saw dark figures moving between the trees and sent word to our commander that the savages were coming rapidly on our right flank and we might expect an attack at any moment. A halt was called. The next instant, a solitary elephant gun was fired by the enemy. We waited eagerly for the expected onslaught, but it did not develop. A half hour passed. Our scouts were ordered to advance. We did so cautiously. However, for some reason then unknown, the enemy did not

THE DASH TO CAPTURE THE KING 171

attack, and we went forward without molestation as far as the banks of the Shangani, following the spoor of the king.

Yet, on this very afternoon, all unknown to us, fate was preparing the death warrant of Major Wilson and all his men, as well as of many others in our command, and of five hundred of King Lobengula's warriors.

Lobengula, who was a monarch of far more intelligence than the average black warrior, doubtless realized that he was facing his last battle. Evidence received later on shows that he kept asking his scouts, "Is the white impi still following me?" He was assured that it was and that the message had been sent that his life would be spared on condition of his immediate surrender.

It is reported that, on reaching the Shangani River, Lobengula said to M'Jaan, his commander-in-chief, "It is not my surrender but my life that the white man wants. I will put him to the only proof that is of any value with the white. I will put him to the test of gold. Call some scouts. Give them a sack of one thousand gold sovereigns and send them to the white induna with this message: 'This gold is my guarantee that I will camp on the banks of the Shangani and enter into negotiations for my surrender, provided you halt where you are. If you keep the gold and advance, I shall know that it is my life you want and I shall therefore fight.'"

M'Jaan called two faithful scouts, gave them the gold, and made them, after the manner of the Kafirs, repeat word for word the message that they were to deliver to the white induna. Meantime, a large force of warriors had taken up position on a steep hill with instructions to attack should the whites advance.

The black scouts moved swiftly, and on the afternoon that we reached the hill I have mentioned, they met us. Owing to the adventure of Bain, Ingram, and myself in the morning, when we had discovered the position of their armed force, our column had deployed in fighting order and was spread out more widely than the scouts with the king's gold had anticipated. This forced them to make a detour, and instead of crossing our advance guards and flankers, they moved swiftly around our little column and approached from the rear.

Among our men were some members of the Bechuanaland Mounted Police. On this particular day, two of these troopers had lingered about a hundred yards behind the rear guard. One of them, who had formerly been a trader, spoke the Kafir language, and when the king's scouts appeared and shouted to him, he answered them in their own tongue. On learning their errand, he told them to come in and they would not be fired upon. The black scouts drew near and delivered to these troopers the sack of gold and Lobengula's message, and were allowed to retire unmolested.

It is said that, on their return, these natives passed through one of their own regiments fronting us and told the black commander that the whites had accepted the gold and would meet the king; therefore, the Matabele should not attack. This was contrary to Lobengula's orders, for he had told his indunas to attack if the whites advanced. Thereupon followed a division of counsel among the blacks. This was the reason why, when the signal gun to begin fighting had been fired, action was halted and we escaped attack for that day.

As soon as the messengers of the king had left our column, the two white troopers who had taken the gold concluded that, as no one but themselves knew of this transaction, it was not necessary to report the reception of the money or any message from Lobengula to their commanding officer. Instead, they divided the gold and that very night began playing for high stakes among themselves. Their gambling reached the ears of a petty officer, who made inquiry as to where all this wealth had come from. He was given an elaborate explanation, only to be equalled in ingenuity by some of the inventions of Kipling's Mulvaney. They made the officer believe it was some hidden loot found among the buried treasures of Bulawayo, and his suspicions were lulled. Had this officer followed the scent a little more keenly and brought the troopers to account before their commander, a message would have been dispatched instantly to King Lobengula and negotiations would have been opened on the Shangani that would have prevented the loss of many brave and brilliant white men as well as the leading warriors of the Matabele nation.

The English law is extremely strict as to the responsibilities of a soldier in time of war. Eventually, the two men who had appropriated the king's gold were court-martialled, but the death penalty was not inflicted, in consideration of their ignorance and their lack of intent to betray their country deliberately for the sake of a sack of gold. Each soldier was sentenced to fourteen years in the penitentiary.

In the light of the king's offer and our acceptance of his gold and consequent seeming bad faith, all that happened later on the banks of the fatal river becomes clear. Had there been scouts at the rear, as well as at the front and flank of our column, this lamentable incident could not have occurred. On many other occasions during the Boer War, disaster came to small columns of the British for this same reason. De Wet, the wiliest of the Boer generals, declared that the rear guard was the post of honour and often assigned it as a mark of distinction to his favourite scout, Danny Theron.

CHAPTER XVII

WILSON'S LAST STAND

ON DECEMBER 3d, Colenbrander, McMullens (his brother-in-law), and I were ordered by Major Forbes to try to capture a native from one of the impis directly in front of us. Forbes wished to cross-question him for verification of our belief that the forces of the Matabele were daily growing larger and more aggressive. The task assigned was not easy in broad day. Several times we were almost surrounded, but late in the afternoon we succeeded, by stratagem, in capturing a young herder who was tending a drove of the king's great oxen at a little distance from the black impi. He was a courageous young Matabele, and I could see that he would give an outcry if I should take my cocked revolver from his lips for one instant. Colenbrander did not wish to risk this, so he fastened an ox-rim around our prisoner's neck, and in this way we led him quietly out of range of the guns of his impi and back to our camp. This brave and crafty youth proved to be a nephew of King Lobengula, and he totally misled Major Forbes as to the positions of all impis and their ability to attack us. Colenbrander told Forbes, "This native is lying to you. I know his statements regarding Gamba are false," etc., etc., but Forbes could not believe that a savage youth scarcely eighteen years old would be able to conceal essential military facts from the cross-questioning of a British officer. In fact, Forbes proceeded to act as if the native were trustworthy and Colenbrander mistaken.

The exhaustion of our men and horses made it impossible for the whole column to continue the pursuit of the king beyond the Shangani River. The spoor showed plainly that only two wagons had crossed the stream, and we had information that the king was in camp on the opposite bank. So it was decided that Major Wilson, with fifteen volunteers, should make one last effort with our strongest horses to capture Lobengula.

After turning over the native we had captured, I had been sent by Forbes on a scout along our right flank. On my return, just before dark, I saw Major Wilson leading a file of men down the bank of the Shangani River.

Forbes said, as I rode up to report, "There goes Wilson. I want you to go with him." As my mount was plainly exhausted, he added, "Take my horse."

I did so instantly, and joined Wilson just as the lead horses splashed across the Shangani, then a shallow stream not more than six inches in depth. Wilson, with his quick observation, seeing me on Forbes's horse, said, "Burnham, I see you have a new mount, but you have left your coat."

It was a cloudy night and darkness was already upon us. On topping the bank, we entered a mapani forest, consisting of trees from a few inches to a foot or more in diameter and thirty to sixty feet high. As this is a very hard wood, there was little fallen timber, and all that did fall was promptly eaten by the white ants. The trees were not very close together, so there were vistas of from thirty to two hundred yards, and we could see on our right many camp fires of the hostiles.

Wilson gave the order to gallop, and before the astonished natives could gather themselves together, we were among them. In stentorian tones, Wilson shouted to them, in their own language, "Put down your guns! Put down your guns! The war is over. We want your king to meet our induna."

Some of the warriors leaped away from the camp fires in fright, but most of them seized their weapons, and we could hear the click of the hammers on their old-fashioned guns as they were brought to full cock. There we were, in the midst of their regiment and in the full light of their camp fires, fifteen mounted men who could all have been killed by one volley, but the suddenness of our approach and the audacity of our demands made the chiefs hesitate to give the order to fire.

Again Wilson shouted, "Where is your king?"

A young warrior replied and pointed the way.

Wilson said to him, "Run on. We will follow you." To me he said, "Keep him covered. If he misleads us, shoot him."

In a few seconds, we were moving at a trot into the forest and out of the light of the fires, leaving the first regiment still holding their cocked guns and waiting for a command. Soon we saw more fires and more regiments ahead of us. Instead of scattering, as Forbes had been persuaded to believe, the Matabele had concentrated in thousands. We rode through camp after camp as we had ridden through the first one, except at slower speed as we were now following our running guide. There were only slight variations of procedure. Each time we encountered the same surprise, the cocking of guns and the babel of yells as we rode on. These camps extended for a mile and a half in the mapani forest. Beyond them was a grassy vley from two to four hundred yards wide, and there we saw no more fires.

At last, our guide, whom I kept under my gun, said, "The king is here."

Out of the darkness loomed a circular enclosure of mapani palings a few inches thick and six or eight feet high. The enclosure was not more than twenty yards in diameter and was on the edge of the vley with rather heavy forest just behind it. By the light of very dim fires inside the palings, we could see the outlines of two big wagons. Here, indeed, must be the king we had trailed so far.

As we lined up, Captain Napier, who spoke the Zulu language excellently, shouted to the king. He addressed Lobengula in the grandiloquent native style, giving him all his titles and assuring him that we were distinguished messengers sent by Doctor Jameson's fighting induna to escort him suitably to Bulawayo and there conclude a treaty of peace; that his life would be spared and all honour shown him, etc.

There was no answer. Not a sound came from within the palings. Then we heard the cocking of rifles a few feet from where our horses stood. Napier told me afterward that he

WILSON'S LAST STAND 177

heard a youth whisper, "Father, shall I shoot?" and the answer, "Not yet. Not yet."

Napier said to Wilson, "They are about to fire on us."

Wilson gave the order to fall back into the vley, but while Napier had been shouting greetings to King Lobengula, I had been watching things to our rear. I had heard much shouting and saw a ring of warriors closing in on us along the edge of the vley. I told Wilson that the forest was our best way out, so he gave orders for all to follow me.

I shook a white handkerchief as a guide and led them quickly into the inky dark forest. In a few paces, we were lost to the sight of the natives around the enclosure, though I was dimly conscious of crouching men among the trees. Still, as no order to fire on us had come from the king's wagons, we were allowed to pass.

Soon we came out of the forest into the open vley. We rode in silence for a few moments and then halted, taking shelter behind a big ant heap. There a consultation was held as to our next move, Captains Judd, Kirton, Napier, and Fitzgerald all taking part. Major Wilson explained in detail Forbes's orders, which were: first, to give the message to the king and, if answered, to capture him forcibly, tie him on a horse, and bring him in. If this proved impossible, we were to keep him under observation until Forbes should come up with the column and the two Maxims and force the issue.

It began to rain, so we decided to retire across the vley into the timber on the farther side. There we huddled together in a small circle and continued to discuss the situation. Our officers decided to stand by orders and to send someone back to Forbes, asking him to hurry with the promised column and the Maxims.

Wilson inquired who could back-track to Forbes. I told him I could, but he said, "No, I need you here. I will send Bain." He then ordered a trooper named Robinson, a fine Kafir fighter but not a tracker, to go with Bain. As they were about to start, Wilson called Napier to him and said, "Captain, I think you had better go along to impress on Forbes the fact that we are confronted by big impis and that our entire position is bad and he should bring up the Maxims without delay. If he finds the timber too thick, take the guns off the carriages—but bring them at all costs."

Bain took off his boot and with his bare foot felt across the vley until he found the wheel marks of the king's wagons. As the recent rains had softened the ground, the wagons had left a track two to six inches deep, and Bain followed this, detouring around the big camps and finally mounting when he sighted Forbes's camp across the Shangani, at a distance of about three miles from us.

As soon as Bain, Robinson, and Napier were gone, Wilson turned to me and said, "We have lost Cahoun, Bradbury, and Hoffmeyer. I ordered them to act as rear guard and turn back some of the blacks who were trailing us through the camps and threatening to shoot. I saw them last just before we reached the king's wagons. We must find these three men. Hoffmeyer will get out somewhere on the back-track, in the open, if possible. Can you take the back-track to the king's wagons?"

I answered "Yes," but added that I would need someone to lead my horse.

Wilson said, "I will lead him. I want to see how you Yankees work."

We led away a few yards, and as there were cattle tracks in the soft earth, I had to crawl along on the ground and use both my hands to get the imprint of the curved horseshoe. We were too near the enemy to use a torch or even an occasional fusee. I was now working directly under the eye of my commander, and one who knew all the ways of the veldt—and now, of all times, my faculties balked! I beat about like a pup on his first fox scent. My stiff and numbed fingers conveyed nothing to my mind.

Suddenly, on my wet back, I felt a gentle slap and heard Wilson say, "Burnham, you are excited. Stand up."

I did so and warmed my fingers by chafing them. Wilson wanted to put his big cape around me, as he knew a thin shirt is not a good protection at night, even in a tropical country. The kindly, steadying tones of my commander did more to send the warm blood to my finger-tips than all my chafing. I picked up the first shoe track and from it soon got the direction and stride of the horse, and back-tracked across the vley to the great ant heap, twenty feet high, behind which we had first halted. Then we left the track and moved by direction until we heard voices and again saw the outline of the king's enclosure of palings. Rain had dimmed the fires. We listened a few moments but could make out nothing. From the forest we could hear some shouting.

Wilson said, "It is here we lost our men. Hoffmeyer will take them into the vley and wait till dawn to pick up our spoor. We must go down the vley a little way and shout for them."

This we did. Wilson with a great voice gave the Australian "Coo-ee" and I the cowboy yell. In a moment we got a faint reply from far down the vley. Guided by our calls, the three men soon joined us.

Meantime, our strange yells had stirred up the native camps, and there was much shouting in the darkness of the forest. After the war, a chief told me that many of the young men became afraid of another night attack like that on the Bubi River, and that, on this occasion, the leaders quieted them by telling them it was only wild animals they heard, and not white men.

We now back-tracked and found our companions crouching on wet ground, holding their horses by the bridoons and awaiting the result of our search for the lost scouts. We were all very pleased to be united again. Wilson said we must now snatch a little sleep before the column and the Maxims arrived. As I had been in the saddle almost constantly for more than sixteen hours that day, I lay down at once. Wilson lay beside me and insisted on spreading his big cape over both of us. In about an hour, he touched my forehead with his finger and said, "Burnham, do you hear anything?"

I sat up and listened, then took the billy from Captain Judd's saddle and tried the ground, but heard nothing. I lay down again and slept, but only for a few moments.

Wilson again woke me with a touch and said, "Burnham, I wish you would go out into the bush a little way and listen."

Once out of the sound of deep-breathing men and horses, I could hear faintly but unmistakably the splashing of human feet moving through the wet forest very slowly and quietly, but in great numbers. I came back to Wilson and reported that the sounds were moving toward the river between us and Forbes.

Wilson said, "I thought so."

Again I lay down. A little before dawn, Wilson woke me once more. He was sitting up in the rain but had covered me entirely with his cape. He said, "Burnham, can you go out on the trail where the king's wagons crossed the bush and meet Bain? He will be bringing in the column and might easily miss us there, and if daylight finds us here and no Maxims, it is all up."

I led my horse along the edge of the vley and, by good fortune, quickly picked up the trail. A few hours' sleep had quickened my sense of touch. There was no blundering around as when Wilson led my horse to find the three lost men. At the glint of dawn I heard a faint sound of heavy animals, and as the natives could never move their cattle so silently, I knew it must be our men. I whistled and got a reply. Then the figures of mounted men showed against the gray sky. I stepped forward, expecting to greet Bain, but found Ingram instead. Telling him to halt where he was, I dashed away to Wilson with the news as fast as the now faint light would allow.

Wilson and his men were up and mounted in a moment. We all felt immensely relieved, though sure there would be a big fight almost at once. As we rode up to the spot where I had left Ingram, instead of finding the column and Maxims, we found Captain Borrow and twenty-two troopers.

All of us who had ridden through the great camps and spent the night in the bush knew then that the end had come.

Borrow and Ingram quickly explained to us what had happened to Bain. He had back-tracked the king's spoor successfully, arriving with Captain Napier and Robinson a little before midnight. On reaching camp, Bain had fallen from exhaustion and an attack of African fever. Napier had at once reported to Forbes, who made no decision. Napier urged upon Forbes the fact that Wilson had relied on being reinforced before day by the entire command, with Maxims, and that every moment counted, as there were thousands of natives in front of him. Finally, at 1 A. M., Forbes reluctantly gave the order for Captain Borrow to reinforce Wilson. This was in reality no reinforcement: it merely sent Borrow and his twenty-two troopers to die with Wilson. As Bain was too ill to take the trail back, this duty had been assigned to the only other man in the column who could do it—Ingram.

It had now stopped raining. Captains Judd, Kirton, Fitzgerald, Greenfield, and Brown gathered with us around Wilson. The first three were experienced colonials, and Wilson asked each what he thought to be the best move.

Kirton, with a bitter smile, said, "There is no best move."

Fitzgerald said, "We are in a hell of a fix. There is only one thing to do—cut our way out."

Judd said, "This is the end."

Borrow said, "We came in through a big regiment. Let's do as Fitzgerald says, though none of us will ever get through."

When all had spoken, Wilson said, "We are surrounded. Between us and Forbes are the young regiments. Why throw ourselves away by fighting these? The royal Imbezu regiment and most of the indunas will be with the king. Let's ride on to Lobengula, and if we don't get him, at least we will try to kill his leaders and save our men in Bulawayo."

We formed roughly in sections, Wilson leading. I rode beside him until we reached the vley, when he ordered me to lead on to the king's camp. It was now light. All the distances that had seemed so long in the night dwindled. We rode at a walk along the edge of the forest. In front of the camp fires of the night were lines of natives with shields and guns. They were within range of us, but as we were already inside their circle and riding toward their strongest regiments, they stood still watching us without firing. We rode thus for more than a mile.

The king's stockade now came in view. It stood in a little cove off the vley, nearly surrounded on three sides by rather heavy mapani timber and a little scrub. Not a sound could be heard or a native seen. Wilson deployed his men. We advanced on the enclosure. With the bravado of the doomed, Wilson shouted to the king to surrender.

The wagons were empty, the enclosure deserted, but from behind a big tree an induna shouted, "We are here to fight!" and fired his rifle. This shot was followed by a scattering volley from all around. I was riding Forbes's horse, a rather young one and not used to fire. He jumped sidewise with me and brought me up as the extreme right-hand man and very close to the timber. Out of the forest leaped a splendid specimen of a warrior, a Martini rifle in his hands. As he ran toward me he shouted to some spearmen who were following him, "*Buya quasi!*" (Come and stab!) He had an enormous chest and a voice like a bull.

He fired at me and missed. I headed my horse toward him, holding my rifle with one hand. He was slightly disconcerted and halted to reload. His bandolier was carried across a leopard skin which he wore over his shoulder. I could see that in his haste he was tugging at a cartridge to pull it out instead of lifting it with the tip of the finger. Every second I was coming nearer. The failure of his rifle unnerved him, and quick as a flash the warrior threw it down and with one long sweeping movement drew from the inside of his shield his stabbing spear. We were now only a few yards apart. Having very strong wrists, I can easily poise a Martini rifle in one hand much as I would a revolver. As I saw him draw back his right arm to drive the spear through me, I put a shot directly into his left side, which crumpled him. Instantly, all the spearmen jumped back into the bush, on seeing their leader fall in such a duel with a Martini. If they had but come on, they could have avenged the fall of their induna during the precious three seconds it takes to reload. I afterward learned that my opponent was the son of M'Jaan, the commander of the king's forces.

I now had time to spare a glance to my left. Our men were being swept back by the fire. Two horses were down. I saw Ingram pick up Fitzgerald, as the captain's horse was killed. As we fell back, I heard Wilson shout: "Cut those saddle pockets off the horses." At that, little Dillon, our wonderful helio scout, dashed back and cut off the pockets containing the precious ammunition. I think it was Captain Kirton who held Dillon's horse.

Wilson gave the order to fall back to the ant heap. When we reached it, we dismounted and used the ant heap as a barrier. As it was twenty feet high, it was quite big enough to screen all our horses. Wilson stood on the top of it and directed the fight.

The Matabele now charged out into the open, firing as they ran. Wilson shouted to us, "Don't waste your shots. Pick your man." Sometimes when one was about to pull the trigger, the man aimed at would go down under a shot from some other rifle and one had to draw bead on another farther back. The charge was broken. We killed many of the royal blood that day.

While this was going on, some of the regiments along whose front we had insolently ridden in the gray morning came running up. Had they been patient, they could have come close and poured in a single volley that would have done for all of us then and there. As it was, a thousand rifles and muzzle loaders cut loose at us wildly from the timber on our left flank, making our position untenable. Wilson gave the order to mount. As I obeyed, a bullet knocked my rifle from my hand, and sent it spinning. It dropped at the feet of Captain Judd. He smilingly handed it up to me, saying, "Burnham, I think you lost something."

Wilson now gave orders to fall back into the timber on the opposite side of the vley, in the direction of our halting place of the night before, where we had waited in vain for the Maxims. This move compelled the natives to come out into the open. Wilson delegated several of us sharpshooters to protect the rear until our men could march across the vley and take position in the timber. Several times, a mild rush was made, but we dropped so many of the savages that they evidently concluded it was needless to take undue risks to rush the end, since they had us in a circle of spear points. When we reached the timber, the firing ceased.

Wilson now re-formed our little column. We had several wounded men, besides dismounted troopers leading wounded horses. These were put in the centre. Captain Judd and I were told to lead slowly toward the Shangani and Forbes's column. Major Wilson, Captain Borrow, and Ingram brought up the rear. We marched unmolested for about a mile. Then Wilson and Borrow galloped up to me, and Wilson asked me if I would try to get through to Forbes. I told him I did not think it possible, as I knew a big impi lay between, but I was perfectly willing to make a try. Borrow said, "Gooding will ride with you. He is an Australian and a good man." He was the trooper riding just behind me. He was a stranger to me, but he spurred his horse alongside, and seemed game to ride and fairly well mounted, as mounts went in our emaciated troop. Just as we turned away, the thought came to me to ask for Ingram. We had done many things together, and it seemed fitting that in this last fight we should also be together. Wilson said, "I will send him up at once."

As Ingram galloped up, I turned to tell Trooper Gooding that he could return to his place in the column, but he seemed still willing to ride. As the end for us all was at hand, it mattered little where we should fire the last shot. The three of us rode away and soon came up against the other wall of guns and spears which I knew hemmed us in. The enemy had seen us first and were waiting, crouched on the ground, until we came within fifty yards of them. On my right was comparatively open forest; on my left a clump of young, tough mapani trees about the thickness of my wrist. It seemed as if no horse could move through this thicket. My natural judgment would have been to turn into the more open ground where we had a bare chance of finding a thin spot in the enemy line. But some inner voice seemed to ring in my ears the sharp command, "Turn left! Turn left! Turn left!"

Setting spur to my horse, I plunged him into the thicket as the heavy fire from the Matabele broke over us. Once he fell to his knees, but rose again and partially cleared a way for Gooding, who was right behind me. Ingram's mount refused to jump into the heavy bush and turned on him, but Ingram was a skilled rider, and by bringing a free foot along the horse's jaw with a terrible blow, managed to turn him and plunge through behind us, in time to avoid being stabbed, as the natives were almost upon him with their spears. After a minute or two of struggling through the bush, the growth thinned and gave us a chance to move our horses more freely. We had actually met the tip of the right horn of Gamba's impis that had been thrown between Wilson and Forbes and formed part of the circle surrounding Wilson.

The custom of the Matabele is to form a charging regiment into a crescent, putting the strongest warriors in the centre and the young men and fast runners on either tip. Using the figure of a bull, they say the old warriors are the head to crush; the young warriors are the horns to gore. An enemy caught on either horn, if he stops to fight, is doomed.

It so happened that this very heavy patch of brush was the only part of the circle around Wilson not held in force by the enemy. As we broke through it into fairly open forest, we were pursued by about two hundred agile young warriors. Until our exhausted horses could get their breath from the rush through the thicket, we held them to a pace just a trifle faster than the warriors could run. Then we galloped out of sight toward the Shangani and afterward slowed to a walk. Soon we heard shouts behind us and knew they were again on our trail, so we hastened on. Reaching a narrow vley about three hundred yards wide, it occurred to me to try a trick that would never have worked with Apache Indians, but might work with the African natives, especially with the young and less experienced warriors.

The vley after the heavy rains was soft enough to leave no distinct shoe marks, only a black streak of mud three or four inches deep, as we rode through. On reaching the opposite side, we spread out and rapidly made two or three separate circles, each one trying to put his horse over as much dry ground as possible, to baffle trailers. We then came together again in single file and carefully waded our horses along the back-track across the vley, leaving a very distinct black trail. On hitting the dryer ground, we left the trail singly and cached ourselves in clumps of bush where we could dismount and give our panting horses a breathing spell. We had not been hidden more than a few minutes before we heard the guns of Wilson's men and the shots and shouts of hundreds of the enemy in attack. Along our trail came runners followed by about a hundred warriors. We could easily have killed a number of them, but feared to fire lest it bring other hundreds to their aid. The Matabele ran on to the edge of the vley, which we could see through our screen of bush. With the black trail of mud directly in front of them they were misled and overran our return tracks just as we had hoped, and all crossed to the opposite side, where the trailers beat about confusedly with much shouting and cursing. We were glad to see that some of the warriors sat down to rest while the trail was being worked out. Finally, there came an exultant yell, and we saw them all running back on our tracks.

It was high time for us to move. We rode swiftly and silently toward Wilson's fight. A fight, like a camp fire, draws all men to it, so it can be approached with certainty. We rode to a point where the zip of bullets sang through the trees and, knowing that the young warriors armed only with spears would not follow our trail into the line of fire, we made a small loop and waited until our trackers should again draw near. This gave our horses another rest, and when, after twenty minutes, no one appeared, I felt hopeful that they had abandoned our trail, believing that we had either gone back to rejoin Wilson

WILSON'S LAST STAND

or had been killed by the old warriors now firing on him. At any rate, they could reasonably suppose that we were included with the doomed white impi.

We again retraced our tracks and crossed the vley a third time. It was clear that, by our manœuvres, we had entirely shaken off our trailers. Now we could hear the Maxims firing and knew that Forbes, too, was under attack, so we pushed on to the river.

When we reached its banks we found that the little stream of the night before had become a swift yellow torrent, two hundred yards wide, with much floating grass in its swirling eddies. The noise of the firing increased. I judged that we had hit the river about a mile above Forbes, but I did not know which side of the river he was on. He might have crossed to aid Wilson or he might have sat tight where we left him the night before. My judgment of the man was that he would sit tight. This is no reflection upon Forbes's courage or any implication that he would shirk movement. But I always thought his courage was largely physical. Forbes's eyes were not trained to see at night, nor his feet to step in darkness, and unconsciously he felt that no one else could do a thing if he could not. He would be apt to consider it poor military tactics to undertake to move his Maxims and entire force at night. Later, on the retreat, I noticed that, whenever Forbes reconnoitred native positions with me in darkness, he frequently stumbled or bumped into stumps and bush.

Believing that Forbes was still on the left bank of the Shangani, I told Ingram and Gooding that I was for swimming the river; but I might be entirely wrong, and if they did not agree with me, they could stay on the right side and try to find him that way. They both thought it seemed best to cross the river, so, taking off our bandoliers and holding them above our heads, we plunged our tired animals into the water. Once I saved my horse by pulling a mass of floating grass from his head in the nick of time before he went under. We drifted far downstream, but finally landed on a sand pit on the opposite side and waited there for our horses to regain breath. The bank was about ten feet above us. Looking cautiously over it, the ground seemed level and the way clear, though we could hear shots downstream. After a few minutes, we led the horses up the bank and mounted, riding at a walk.

Soon we saw hundreds of the enemy standing in the edge of the bush about four hundred yards away, watching us. There was no cover near us. We continued to ride slowly in the direction where we thought Forbes was fighting, though we did not yet know surely that he was on our side of the river. Ingram, who was the tallest, was the first to see the horses of Forbes's column. We now began to draw a scattering fire from the edge of the timber, so, setting spur to our mounts, we took the last little gallop out of them and reached Forbes. I reported to him that we were what was left of Wilson's command. Dismounting, we took part in beating off the last attack of the morning made on Forbes.

We learned afterward that Wilson and his men were all killed. There, where they had taken their stand, they fired their last shot, and Nityana, the Matabele, told Le Seuer (a secretary of Rhodes) that seven were left standing together, singing "God Save the Queen," until they, too, went down before the assegais.

The dust of Wilson and his men is gathered with that of Cecil John Rhodes in Rhodesia and is a point of pilgrimage for great numbers of their reverent countrymen.

CHAPTER XVIII

FORBES'S RETREAT

WE CAMPED that night of December 4th on the left bank of the Shangani River. We were still surrounded by the enemy. There was a decision of great moment before us. Should we retrace our route over the rough hill where the single shot had been fired on December 2d, or should we follow up the unknown length of the Shangani River to a certain point south of the post of Inyati? There was a division of counsel, but the final choice was for the left bank of the Shangani. The river was in flood and could be depended on both for water and as a protection to our left flank, though its windings might nearly double the distance of our retreat.

It was also vital that some news of the present plight of the column be sent to Rhodes. Bain was too greatly weakened by fever to make the ride, and I was ordered to act as advance scout for the column up the river, so it fell to my friend Ingram and Billy Lynch, a noted colonial scout, to attempt to carry the word through jungle and veldt to Rhodes at Bulawayo.

Only oral messages were given; for, if the scouts should be killed by Lobengula's warriors, any papers found would be carried to the king, who had half-breed interpreters able to read English or even an ordinary code. The two famous horses belonging to the Bechuanaland Mounted Police and ridden, I believe, by Captains Coventry and Tancred, were again called upon to do this bit. These high-spirited animals, Brandy and Soda, were now emaciated wrecks, but seemed possessed with the indomitable spirit of their gallant masters. That night, at eight o'clock, a tropical storm of great violence burst upon us. Even our jaded horses began to surge on the picket lines, and every man had to stand by and hold his horse. Choosing the hour when the storm was at its height, the two scouts, Ingram and Lynch, passed out of our lines, leaving us with the hope that they would elude the enemy and make their way to

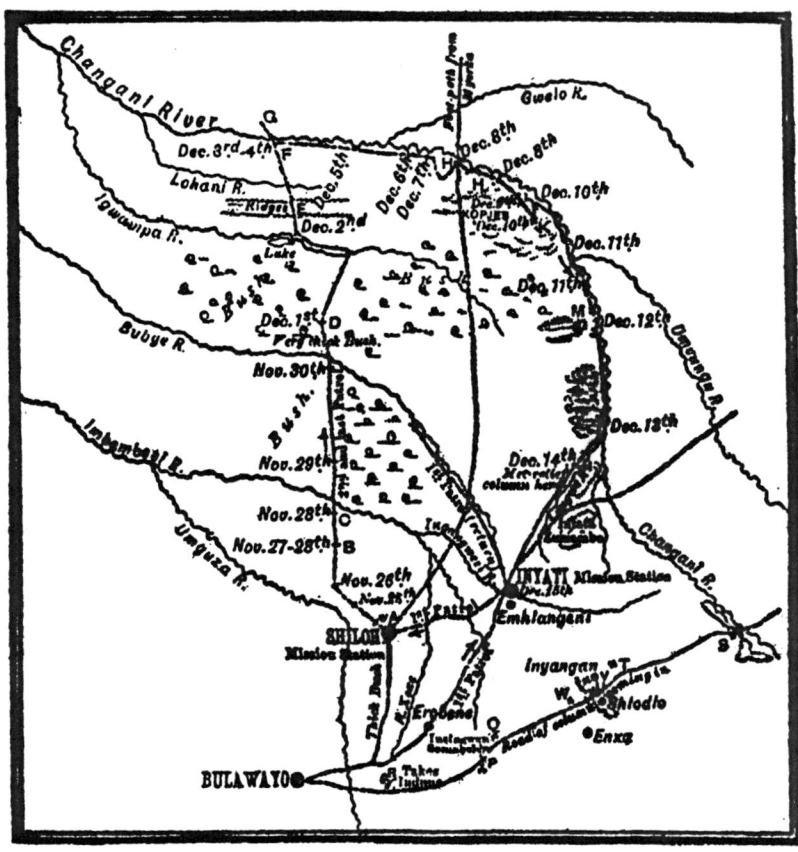

THE PATROL IN THE BULAWAYO CAMPAIGN

This shows the line taken in the attempt to capture King Lobengula after the fall of Bulawayo, and also Forbes's retreat along the Shangani River and through Inyati to Bulawayo. Major Allen Wilson and his men made their last stand on the right bank of the Shangani (at G) on December 3, 1893.

Rhodes and Jameson in Bulawayo and that relief would meet us somewhere on the bank of the Shangani.

The next morning, we began our retreat. The terrible storm and the flooded river prevented an attack by the natives. We found at daybreak that they had withdrawn to some shelters and huts several miles away, leaving only a small force of young warriors to hang on our flank and rear. About two miles from our camp I found the hoof marks of our scouts, so we knew they had successfully passed through the lines of the enemy. This spoor was shown to Forbes and reported to the little column as a good omen. It cheered every one.

I followed up the tracks until they left the river, as the two scouts intended to strike almost due south for Bulawayo. Just where they entered among the larger trees, I saw the prints of two sandals over the spoor of the scouts. This showed that the Matabele were tracking the horses within half a mile. Evidently one warrior had been sent back for help. Soon afterward, I saw where ten or fifteen savages, some of them barefooted, had joined the trail. This looked ominous for the scouts, whose horses were going only at a walk, which must continue to be their pace except when attacked. I rode back to the advance guard led by Johann Colenbrander, and he returned with me. We examined the sign carefully and then sent word for Colonel Raff to come up. He did so, and it was agreed that none of this information should be given out in the column. Raff would report it to Forbes only. In our present condition, such news might lead to extreme dejection, even in ordinarily confident and gallant men. It seemed highly improbable that two worn-out horses and two tired men could escape a fast-running band of fresh young warriors.

From this time on, Raff, Colenbrander, and I had little hope of aid reaching us, and another fear grew: that Rhodes and Jameson, hearing nothing from our column, would in a few days lead a strong patrol with their ablest men and horses along our line of march toward Shiloh. Should this be done and the natives make even a feeble rally to the king, they would have our forces divided into three parts, each one completely out of touch with the others. Then all the settlers left in Salisbury and Victoria would certainly be wiped out. It would be the Day of the Blacks.

The only ray of hope was held out by Colenbrander, who

knew the native so well. By careful reading of the spoor, he learned that many of the trailers were young spearmen who were running light, without sandals. Colenbrander said: "The Negro is not tenacious like your American Indian. If these youths fail to get Ingram and Lynch the first day, they may lose heart, especially the barefooted ones, as the rain has softened their feet." This was a precious crumb of comfort to those of us who knew.

For the next eleven days, the scouting devolved almost entirely upon Bain and myself. It was our duty to advance along the river in front of the column, feel out the presence of the enemy, and select halting places that would not be advantageous for enemy ambush. At first, while Bain was ill with fever, Colonel Raff, the Boer, often went with me, although as the real responsibility of command and the safety of our column depended more and more on his judgment, it seemed a great hazard to risk so valuable an officer on a dangerous scout. He was probably the most experienced Kafir fighter in Rhodesia at that time. Most Boers are large men but Raff did not weigh more than one hundred and twenty pounds. It was jokingly said of him that he had engaged in a Kafir fight for every pound of his weight.

After camp was made each night and all guards posted, our duty was to make the entire march of the coming day during the night and return to the column before dawn. After resting until nine or ten o'clock, Raff and I would move on foot through the grass and jungle and thoroughly scout out a strip of country ahead of us over a distance that we hoped the column would be strong enough to cover the next day. With this knowledge of the ground in our minds and the next camp selected, we would throw ourselves on the ground for an hour or two of sleep before returning to the column. The only criticism I could ever make of Raff was not for lack of courage in action or stoicism in defeat, but that he had not sufficient control of his mind to be able to sleep when under great responsibility. This was a talent which Lord Roberts possessed notably. Often when I awoke from our impromptu bivouacs I found that

Raff had not closed his eyes, but had been revolving plans for the next day's march over and over in his mind. I think it was lack of sleep that ultimately caused his death quite as much as physical exhaustion and privation of food.

On the night of December 10th, Major Forbes ordered me to make a scout around our camp, which was in a small basin surrounded by rocky kopjes and heavy bush—a most difficult camp to defend. Only on account of the utter exhaustion of the men did we stay there. I found that there were large numbers of Matabele on three sides of us and that they were preparing to attack, probably at dawn. On one side the kopjes were very steep and rugged. The Kafirs evidently believed it would be impossible for us to move our wounded men or induce our worn horses to drag the Maxims over these, so on this side they had placed no pickets. Upon reporting to Major Forbes, he discussed the situation with Colonel Raff and other officers and it was decided that Raff should go over the ground with me. When we returned and convinced Forbes of the extreme gravity of our situation, he reluctantly allowed Colonel Raff to arrange the full disposition of our force.

Word was quietly passed around that, after we had eaten our horse meat and slept and rested for five hours, we should saddle all except the weakest horses, tying the stirrups so they could not click, and destroying all the saddles and equipment that we were forced to leave behind. We should then take the Maxim guns off their carriages and bring the screen of bush around our camp to the height of several feet, so that whatever was inside should be well hidden from the eyes of the enemy. We were now obliged to destroy seven of our faithful dogs, who had followed us so loyally through storm and flood and war into this wilderness of trouble. They were knocked on the head with choppers and dispatched without a sound. To kill such friends is one of the most trying ordeals a soldier can experience. But there was only one way to escape from the trap in which we were caught, and that would have been closed for ever had a single yelp or bark reached the ears of the alert enemy enclosing us.

That night, at two o'clock, we started in single file up the rocky kopje. Our wounded were lifted on the shoulders of the men, and our Maxim guns, having been removed from their carriages, were transported in like fashion. It was a terrible strain on the exhausted muscles of even our strongest. All orders were given in whispers, and although the wounded suffered most excruciating pain, not a groan escaped from one of them. The greatest danger was from the noise of the horses' feet pounding on the rocks, and for that reason we led them step by step, a yard or two at a time, whenever we passed very close to the enemy. Two hours elapsed before the last man of our little column managed to slip by the last armed camp. Fortunately, the night was inky dark and it probably never crossed the minds of the natives that the horses and guns of this last white impi would even attempt to escape from the trap in which they held us.

As a last precaution before leaving camp, we arranged a piece of wood, resembling the outline of a Maxim gun, where it would be visible to the enemy by daylight. The tops of the wheels of the gun carriages could also be seen over the screen of bush. Natives told us after the war that they were suspicious of a trap of some sort, as several horses could be seen in the camp and our fires were burning slowly. They hesitated to attack, even after daylight came, and waited for us to begin to move about. It was two hours before any of them plucked up courage enough to make a closer investigation, and then, to their amazement, they discovered that by some miracle we had slipped away from them during the night.

By the time they discovered our trail, we had reached a broad, sparsely timbered flat and had taken up a position where the Maxims and even our feeble, starving and wounded men would be able to give a very good account of themselves before the finish. Moreover, we reaped the benefit of the moral effect of the recent brave death of Wilson and his men. The Matabele knew that here was a still larger impi than Wilson had with him, and since it had cost them hundreds of their bravest warriors to overcome Wilson, who had no Maxims, they were naturally reluctant to attack our larger force. Nevertheless, on this long and dreary march up the Shangani, they did attack us eight times, but each time, by some stratagem or good fortune, we succeeded in beating them off.

Another incident of this retreat illustrates the value of able officers. We had reached a point on the river which we believed to be about north of the missionary stations of Shiloh and Inyati. Up to this time, no matter when attacked, we nearly always had access to water, with the river to form on as our left flank. But now there was a chance of our being entirely surrounded, as we were in thick jungle away from the water. The scouting was extremely difficult, and the men were growing weaker every hour. In a thick bit of bush I discovered several hundred armed natives drawn up, evidently preparing to attack. By various manœuvres I learned that they were occupying a drift (or ford) across a tributary river, and that they expected us to attempt to make a crossing there. Working down this river to the northwest I found a shallow about thirty yards wide, with sandy bottom, where the water was not more than knee deep. But to reach this point we would have to march through very thick bush, which is always dangerous. After testing the drift, I hastened back to Forbes and reported the condition of things and the position of the enemy. Forbes advised an immediate attack on the natives. Raff, Lendy, and other officers, on the other hand, advised a quick crossing by the main column through the heavy bush to the new drift I had found, while a handful of our strongest men should advance along the expected line of march and attack the force known to be ahead of us. It would be their duty to continue the fighting until the main column had time to complete the crossing. There was a heated argument among the officers, but it was finally decided as Raff advised.

When men are already falling from exhaustion, it is almost impossible to increase the speed even as much as one mile per hour, but the impossible was done that day. The post of honour was the rear guard, where it was the task of the strongest men and officers to urge on the exhausted men by appealing to their sense of duty and their racial pride, and sometimes by stinging personal abuse.

When all had crossed the river, including the precious Maxims that now had none but human carriages, it was discovered that the Maxim ammunition, weighing about one hundred pounds, had fallen or been left on the far bank of the stream. Already we could hear the shouts of oncoming natives who had discovered our ruse and might at any moment make the recovery of the ammunition impossible. Nearly every man of us was sitting or lying down, exhausted by the great effort just made. Major Forbes, seeing the plight of the ammunition, called for volunteers to go back across the stream and bring it over. For a moment no one responded, each man feeling, for once, that this was some other man's job. Then the response came from one who was probably the most emaciated and exhausted man in the column—Captain Tancred. As I remember him now, it seemed as if his slender legs must break with the weight of the ammunition when he picked it up, but, nevertheless, he brought it successfully across the river, and it was with this ammunition that we beat off the final attack of the natives. Tancred's deed was a sheer triumph of mind and nerves over a weak and worn-out body. Very often this astonishing quality exhibits itself in long, hard campaigns. Other things being equal, the man with the strongest physique will obviously endure most; but there are times when he is outdistanced and outdone by some weaker man who possesses the intangible, unseen spiritual force that carries a human beyond ordinary physical limits.

On the fourteenth of December, we saw two horsemen approaching from the south who proved to be scouts from the relief patrol. One of them was Frederick Courtney Selous. They informed us that Rhodes and Jameson were near at hand with food and medical supplies, and the news sent a thrill of joy through our weary men.

Selous told me that Ingram and Lynch had arrived in Bulawayo and were recuperating there. On the night when they passed out of our lines in the terrific storm, they rode through a great camp where the enemy were huddled in groups under skins and blankets. The horses, guided by lightning flashes, picked their way among the natives without rousing them. The reason why the warriors who later took their spoor did not overtake them was that, before stopping to rest, Ingram always back-tracked a little on the trail. Several times, when screened in the bush, the scouts saw armed natives after them, but as these men simply followed the trail step by step, Ingram and Lynch always had time to mount and move away. This simple ruse would not have deceived an American Indian, but it was sufficient to enable the scouts to elude the Matabele. They had many close calls owing to sudden contacts with moving bodies of the enemy near the Bubi River—the same forces that later attacked our column. When they left our camp, Surgeon Hogg gave Lynch and Ingram a few ounces of food from our scanty medicine chest, and this, plus some wild leeks which they boiled, had been their only ration for the ride of four days.

Long afterward, Rhodes told me of his first meeting with Ingram. Neither he nor Jameson had received any tidings of our column, and their anxiety increased each day On a warm evening in December, Rhodes and Sir Charles Metcalfe rode out a few miles on the Shiloh road in the hope of meeting some natives and obtaining news through them. Looking across the veldt, Rhodes saw about a mile away two horsemen riding very slowly.

He exclaimed, "Metcalfe, I believe those are scouts from Forbes and Wilson," but Sir Charles said, "No; they are Mounted Police on patrol."

Rhodes, who had a wide knowledge of African veldt life, said: "Those men are dead tired. Their horses are worn out. Let's canter over."

They found two stumbling horses in the last stages of exhaustion, ridden by emaciated men with hollow eyes and stubbly beards, clothed in rags and barely able to sit their saddles.

On being questioned by Rhodes, who was in civilian clothes

and unarmed, Ingram bluntly told him to go to hell. "Why should I report to you?" he demanded. Then he added: "If you want to know anything, go to Bulawayo and ask Rhodes after I have reported to him."

Rhodes assured him that he was indeed Rhodes, but Ingram quickly retorted: "Rhodes wouldn't be such a damn fool as to be riding around Bulawayo unarmed. I think you are nothing but a trader up from Joburg."

Rhodes laughed and quietly followed the scouts into Bulawayo where he was properly identified to them by Doctor Jameson.

The promise of rest and rations brought by Selous cheered everybody in our column. The rear-guard duty was now light, and we decided to march a few miles toward the relief patrol rather than lie down and wait for it to arrive. So we moved on slowly to Inyati Station, where we were given food, rest, and the shelter of thatched huts before marching on by easy stages the remaining forty miles to Bulawayo.

We had been on constant patrol or fighting for twenty-three days on five days' rations. When we started for the king, we cut the rations in order to increase the supply of ammunition we could carry, and we had made up the shortage by eating our starved horses. Now, a fat horse, as is well known, is very nutritious, fine-grained, and well-flavoured, but a starving horse, like starved beef, is almost worthless as food. The meat issued to us was full of little air bubbles, and it was stringy and tasteless. After roasting it on the fire and eating two or three pounds of it, or all the stomach would hold, intense hunger would return within two or three hours. Bain and I, knowing the diet of our American Indians and their endurance, willingly accepted the horse's head as our portion. None of the English or colonials would eat the horse's brain, although, as a matter of fact, the last bit of nourishment in a starving animal is in the brain. This ration enabled Bain to recover from his attack of fever and even do some scout duty at night. It also, plus an inherited endurance, must have accounted for my still being comparatively strong at the medical inspection on our return

FORBES'S RETREAT

to Bulawayo, when Doctor Jameson declared that I was the only man left in the column able to march another forty miles.

There was great sorrow over the loss of Major Wilson and his officers and men, yet we all realized it was the fortune of war to meet death in a good cause—a fate that might come to all of us at any time.

A sound and healthy young human soon throws off fatigue, hunger, and sorrow On the whole, we had accomplished the impossible. Our little column of youths from Mashonaland had taken Bulawayo. Major Goold Adams, led by Selous as scout, had captured Mangwe Pass and joined our forces. He had defeated Gamba, the Matabele general, in spite of the fact that King Khama with his three thousand friendly Mungwatos had deserted Goold Adams in the Pass. The key to a country as large as all Western Europe was now in our hands.

CHAPTER XIX

AFTER THE WAR

THE closing months of 1893 had filled out the measure of my boyhood dreams with a sharp and desperate war, long hard rides, and the pitting of the white man's skill and courage against savage cunning and ferocity.

Then Rhodes came up through Mangwe Pass and called us all to a great endaba (council) at Bulawayo, and on Christmas Day threw open the whole country to land entry; giving every soldier and officer the same rights—to a farm of six thousand acres, a mineral right of twenty acres, and an equal share in the king's cattle, amounting to two hundred and fifty thousand head—a fine stake for any young pioneer. Vast as this grant seems, it was less than ten per cent. of the country conquered, and the captured cattle did not touch the private herds owned by the natives. Great reservations of land were set aside for the natives and thousands who had been slaves to the Matabele were freed.

This was my first personal contact with Cecil Rhodes, and he measured up to all my enthusiastic expectations. He told us much of what he hoped to do in this new land and seemed pleased with the type of settlers it was his fortune to be associated with. He seemed always to assume that we were really doing all the work, and he was merely pushing a little now and then from the base of supplies and keeping the Little Englanders from attacking us too annoyingly.

In a letter home dated January 1, 1894, is a brief account of our return to Victoria:

> To-day I am home from the wars, and Ingram, my young American comrade, has ridden back with me for good company. There were four Americans in the Scouts and they were no disgrace to their country. Victoria is on

picnic. . . . There is to be a great "surprise" and a royal reception and all the trimmings that go with a reunion of friends. Add to that the éclat of a soldier from the front loaded with all the latest news and fortunate enough to be in line for promotion, and you can picture how happy I am to-day! . . .

It is a delightful change to have sight of white women once more and to hear the laughter of children. There is even a regulation picnic swing to celebrate with, and tables loaded with all the luxuries dear to the heart of a campaigner—real butter and milk, sponge cakes, coffee and sugar, spices and jams—in fact, a civilized "feed"! And only a few days ago the sombre forest was around us, full of fierce savages, and we ourselves were a hungry band, eating our skeleton horses and boiling grass to keep soul and body within hailing distance of each other!

'Ninety-three is gone. I will make no resolves, oaths, or promises for 'ninety-four. It is here, and what I find to do, I shall do, but it cannot by any possibility prove as eventful a year as the one just past.

Lobengula held his camps in the jungles of the Shangani for a few weeks, but his death occurred in January. True to tribal custom, his burial place was kept secret, as was that of his father, M'Silikatze. In his tomb are doubtless hidden the treasures of gold and diamonds which his young warriors for many years brought from the mines of South Africa, where they worked by thousands and loyally paid their head tax of one diamond a year, or a piece of gold, to their king. None of this treasure has ever passed out of the kingdom in trade. Like that of the Pharaohs of Egypt, it must have been buried with its royal owner.

The Matabele, in spite of their victory over Wilson, were in a mood to make peace; so when Jimmy Dawson, a white trader who had known most of their leaders for years, was sent to them with the olive branch, it was accepted by the whole tribe. The surrender of their spears and arms was duly arranged, and peace was formally declared by Jameson on behalf of the British Government, and by all the surviving chiefs and commanders of regiments on behalf of the Matabele. M'Jaan, who succeeded Lobengula, was a very old man. His only son had been killed in the war. In making the final appeal to his tribe on behalf of peace he said: "If thirty-five young white warriors can kill five hundred of us Matabele before we can kill them, how can we expect to win when the bearded white men come from over the sea to ask who killed their infaans (youths)?"

Another letter, written in February, 1894, records several accounts of that day in December given by natives as they came in to surrender. I quote at some length from it:

The first actual narration of Wilson's end was given by a Matabele chief who lived on the Shangani River about one hundred miles above the point of battle. This is his story:

"The king's orders were that Gamba with four thousand men and I with the other three regiments of the king should attack the white impi at daybreak [on December 3d]. The night was very dark and stormy. My young men did not do as they were told but lay in their skerrams [thorn-bush barricades] to keep out of the storm. In the meantime, the white men took witch medicine, and a few of them came out of the black night right up to the king's wagons, the last he had saved. They were hidden in the bush on the edge of a vley. The white men talked but did not shoot, and then rode away.

"Our hearts were weak, but at daylight we got brave, knowing the white men were few and that we had thousands. Some of our young warriors attacked the [Maxim] guns and when the Induna with thirty-five men again rode up to the king's wagons, a long way from the big guns, we rushed at them saying, 'We will see if white men are afraid to die.' We fought them. They killed many of us, but we drove them back. Their horses could not run. Our young men came up and rushed after them, but they got off their horses and killed many of us.

"Then we sent for all of Gamba's army. The white men went into the bush, carrying their wounded and leading their horses. We followed on both sides, but three men ran ahead on horses. One man was small and wore a wide, stiff hat that they say is worn only by a great white tribe far beyond the kingdom of the English. He rode a big horse. Some of my young men knew him. He always rides at night and is the white induna's eye. We call him He-Who-Sees-in-the-Dark. We sent our best runners to ambush him. Some never came back, but the three men got away.

"Now we swore to eat the hearts of all the rest and attacked them again, but they fought hard. Again we killed more horses. Some of the white men ran to their horses to mount, but a tall induna with a big hat in his hand shouted to them and pointed to the men who were bleeding. They all got off and tied their horses in a ring, head to head. I urged on my men to rush at once but the white man's medicine was very strong and my men fell. I could not get them to close up and rush. They said, 'These are not men but magicians with guns that never get empty.'

"We now waited for Gamba, and from behind the trees we watched the white men. They killed all their horses and dragged them end to end. They tore up their shirts and tied up the wounds of each other. Many were dead, and the Induna carried the guns of the dead to the living and laid the belts of cartridges with them. Then he took off his hat and the others stood up with bare heads. They sang a chant and some put their hands this way [crossing or clasping them] just as they do in Victoria when the white man prays to his God for strong medicine. We watched but did not fight. We waited for Gamba's men. Gamba's men came and we shot and shot at the white men until we thought they were all dead, but when we crept up to them, several of them got up and shot at us. They fought with the little guns [revolvers] and some put them to their heads and went so [snapping], but they had shot all at us and had to die at last by the Matabele spear.

"But the Induna was *umtagati* [bewitched]. We shot him with six rifles and he still fought. A wounded man passed a new gun up to him all the time, but we killed him at last, and the wounded men who could not fight just put their hands over their eyes while we ran the assegais into them. Ah! they do not die like the Mashonas! They never cry or groan. They are men. No, I will never fight the whites again. They are not afraid to die. They are men!"

On being asked what he thought when the little white impi surprised them by a night march he said, "We did not know what to think. They did not kill women and children, only shot the young men who had rifles. We thought the white men hated death, but now I know it is not that. When we fight, we kill everything, even dogs, unless we take slaves."

Another who was present at the end of the fight on the Shangani says of the white Induna [Major Wilson] that he was the last man to stand up and that he was bleeding all over and had no more cartridges to shoot, so a young warrior rushed up to him with an assegai in his hand. The white Induna stood still and looked straight at him, so the warrior put down his spear; then he raised it again and plunged it into the Induna's chest and drew it out dripping with blood. The Induna staggered toward him, and he threw the spear again, leaving it sticking in the Induna's breast. The Induna fell forward dead. He could not raise his hands to pull out the spear.

On being asked why the Matabele did not mutilate the bodies after their usual fashion one said, "The white men died so bravely we would not treat them as we do the cowardly Mashonas and others." They stripped off the clothing from the whites and left the bodies behind those of their dead horses. Then they carried off their own dead, those who had friends, and there were very many dead.

Another Matabele said: "It is no use wounding a white man for, if he is hit in the leg he lies down and fights; if he is hit in one arm he shoots with the other. We saw a white man with arms flopping and bleeding. He carried a belt of cartridges in his teeth from one who was dead to another who was still fighting."

So much for the account given of these men by their enemies. Now these men of ours were not regular soldiers but volunteers: men who had business interests, homes, and families in Mashonaland. They were England's *real* pioneers, who built the brick and iron towers of Victoria and Salisbury and did not forget in the meantime to endow hospitals and churches. In fact, they made peaceful towns of which any Englishman might be proud. They could not stand to have the tongues of their servants cut out and dried as trophies by the young warriors of the savage king who lived on their borders. They have taken that king's country as a result of the inevitable conflict that must always come between barbarism and civilization when the two meet. Lobengula was not capable of ruling under the British flag in any way materially different from his own former despotic sway. . . .

History is making fast in this part of the world. Poor Captain Lendy, on whom the vials of wrath have constantly been poured by Labouchere and his adherents, now lies under the sod at Bulawayo. His patient heroism on the retreat from the Shangani and during the time when our diet consisted of our starved horses will long be remembered by all of us who took part in that terrible patrol. Colonel Raff, the most experienced Kafir fighter in Africa, lies beside him. The privations of the campaign worked their deadliest mischief with many exhausted men after we were safe in Bulawayo. But thank God! Lendy and Raff both lived to know that their services were fully appreciated by those who are honestly and intelligently interested in colonial affairs and prosperity! Africa may now be considered conquered as far north as the Zambezi River. . . .

The golden age of Rhodesia now began. England showered honours upon Rhodes and named the country after him. There was a wonderful exhilaration in the air. As the natives came in and surrendered their guns and spears, Captain Heyman promptly had the tough spear handles sawed into very handy survey pegs which were used for marking out the present town of Bulawayo.

Speculators and concession hunters by the score came into the country. They lived in thatch huts or tents and cooked over camp fires with the aid of naked savages, and it was a toss-up whether the savages or the speculators were the poorer and the dirtier cooks. It was the belief of these men that, by paying cash to the British South Africa Company (known as the Chartered Company), they could buy up all the choice valleys and most of the rich gold reefs at once, before the pioneers could exercise their rights and select and peg out their farms and gold claims.

The difficulty confronting the pioneers was that horses, oxen, and all grass- or grain-fed animals take months to recover, once they become as poor and exhausted as ours were, while men and other meat-eaters can be reduced almost to living skeletons and regain their strength in a few days. Very soon after the fall of Bulawayo our men had fully recovered and were able to ride; even the survivors of the dash to capture the king

AFTER THE WAR

either died or became strong and vigorous within two weeks after their return.

Doctor Jameson, the British Administrator, brought on his head no end of criticism by declaring a moratorium of four months for the pioneers to roam over the country and select any farm or reef they chose. Owing to the lack of transport, the whole four months were necessary for the men to march on foot, with native carriers to peg off their claims.

There was a scarcity of paper for keeping records. An old ledger that had been used as a ration book by one of the commissary officers was torn apart and each page cut in two. When a pioneer registered his farm, a description of it was written and drawn on one of these little pieces of paper, which then passed under the keen scrutiny of Doctor Jim and was marked by his big blue pencil with the magic initials "L. S. J." Simple as the method was, its power to convey title has never been broken, although the effort has been made by some very clever lawyers. They have been confounded to find that titles to a million acres could be passed without ted tape, sealing wax, notarial seals, or flub-dub of esoteric phrase. The "L. S. J." title is still the soundest in Africa.

Once in so often, some writer jots down his Utopian dreams of youth in a world where everybody has a fair start. All the groundwork for such a volume was there in Rhodesia. A thousand healthy young volunteers were given the freedom of a new land, with ample acres and money to develop them. But the same old laws worked out the same old results. Within thirty days, some of little faith had sold their rights and farms and trekked away. Others gambled them off in a night, as Pizarro's soldier gambled away his Golden Sun of the Inca before the sun of the heavens cast its first gleam over the gaming table.

A Boer named Zeederburg was the Ben Halliday of South Africa. He imported from the United States a number of Concord coaches carrying twenty-two passengers each, inspanned ten mules to each coach, and employed Hottentot herds to graze the spare spans. Brush huts were established for stations, and soon we had a non-stop stage line to Johannesburg, five hundred miles away. These coaches were driven by hardy young Boers trained in handling mules with a fifty-foot whip. When the roads were dry, the coaches travelled nearly as fast as our famous Pony Express. What little sleep the passengers got, they took sitting up, but every coach was full.

For two years Bulawayo enjoyed uninterrupted prosperity. Thousands of heavy Dutch oxen appeared, dragging across the veldt and through the Pass supplies that included everything required in a modern town, from Bibles to whisky. Prices soared; eggs sold for five dollars a dozen, jam for two dollars and a half a tin. Potatoes were auctioned on the public square of the new town in lots of from three to six, and very moderate-sized spuds brought as high as a sovereign (five dollars). One bright colonial trekked into the country with a wagonload and had the nerve and vision to resist the high prices: he took up a farm near Bulawayo, planted the entire lot, and inside of two years cleared up $75,000 on his crops. Another gathered up all the empty beer and whisky bottles—a goodly number—broke wild native cows to milk, and started a dairy. He made canvas panniers that fitted over the shoulders of native carriers and amassed quite a fortune selling bottled milk.

Brick blocks replaced mud and thatch. Churches, schools, a club, a Masonic Lodge, went up rapidly. I remember watching the Master of the Lodge as he marched with stately tread through the streets, shoe-top deep in the red dust. He was in full evening dress and was gravely followed by a tall, solemn, naked Matabele carrying on his head an iron box containing the jewels of the Lodge about to be opened.

Dynamite and mining machinery arrived, and it was a dull day that some prospector did not announce the discovery of a new gold reef and produce a pocketful of rock that yielded the magic grains by horn spoon or gold pan. Rhodesia is dotted with thousands and thousands of ancient gold workings, and every pioneer pegged his twenty claims on some dump or vein that might easily have been worked in ages past to furnish gold for the temple of King Solomon.

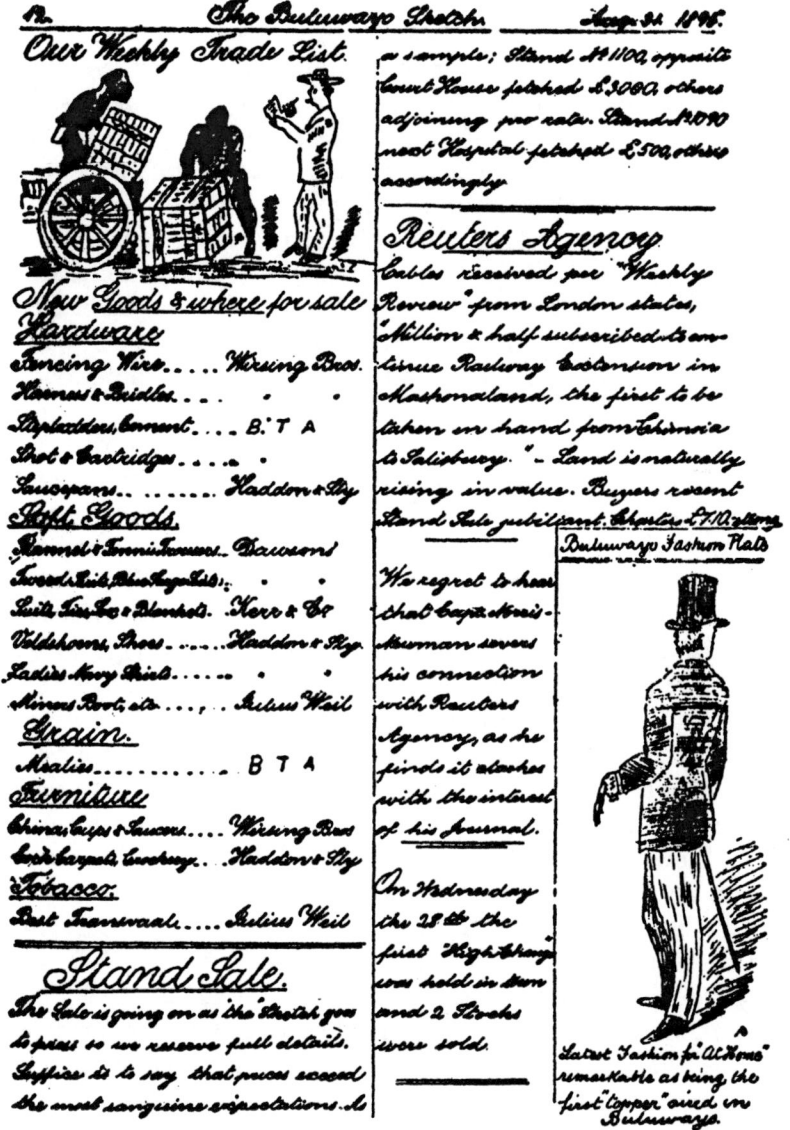

A PAGE FROM THE BULAWAYO "SKETCH"

A hand-written and mimeographed newspaper published in Bulawayo in 1895—a frontier *Vanity Fair*.

For Ingram and me, the year 1894 was one of fast, hard riding, and, when our mounts gave out, of swift marches. We bought the best "salted" horses we could get, paying five hundred dollars apiece, as these rare survivals of the African sickness became extremely valuable. We traced up every tale of ancient ruins and old mines that came to our ears, and found great ruins of towns and cities laid up in walls of granite many feet in thickness, and all along the streams we encountered countless grinding pits in the boulders where the ancients had crushed the quartz and washed out the gold. Afoot, we pegged out more than a hundred farms for soldiers. We drove the first peg in the town of Gwelo and rapidly opened up the Scout's Reef there, which cost us a lot of money.

This Scout's Reef that we thought so valuable turned out to be a "frost," the gold being only along the cleavage planes and not distributed through the rock. But there were plenty of other veins that were good, so I left Ingram to close the Gwelo camp while I trekked with the big ox span to Bulawayo, one hundred and ten miles to the east, taking my wife and Roderick with me. The rains made the veldt boggy, so we camped one night right on the battlefield of the Imbembezi. Our black servants were very nervous because the bones and skulls lay all about, and they dodged and ran past them very gingerly and at night huddled under the big bucksail in terror of ghosts; but our small son insisted on my showing him just where I had fought and just where I had shot a certain Matabele leader, and was not satisfied until he found the skeleton and brought in the skull, much to the horror of the black servants and drivers. They used to call Roderick "Little Chief" and would do his bidding instantly. To scare them, he built a little mound of skulls on an ant heap. All this may seem strange and unnatural, but perfectly normal children become accustomed to war as a common thing and will amuse themselves by very gruesome imitations, as we did in Minnesota by scalp dances and the like.

When we outspanned on the edge of the new town of Bulawayo, we found it all agog with new life. Rhodes, Jameson, and many of the officials came out to see us under the bucksails and accepted the Bedouin-like hospitality my wife could extend, in the spirit of the times.

We arrived at Bulawayo in the midst of the great real estate boom, when a lot, or stand, as it was called, might even in that wilderness rise in value as suddenly as in any of our American mining camps or our optimistic Western cities. Building material was still scarce. I built the first brick residence in Bulawayo, a house of four rooms, and floored it with small boards (salvaged from whisky cases) for which I paid one half dollar a surface foot. I felt that my wife, after living under the stars, or at best under thatch and bucksail for more than a year, was entitled to a real roof and a board floor.

We were all so full of bright hopes and great plans that even now, in retrospect, it stirs my pulses to recall those wonderful days. Three of my young brothers-in-law who had been with me in the West were clamouring to join me in Africa, and not long afterward they came out, bringing with them A. Kingsley Macomber of Pasadena. In a home letter dated the following year, I find this reference to him:

> I must write a letter to Doctor Macomber of Pasadena concerning his son Kingsley. The young man has done so well and shown such boundless energy, I think his father may well feel proud of him, and as to his personal courage there is no question. . . . Young Macomber shot and followed up in tall grass and killed a lion on the Guay; and, what is of more importance, has shown courage, patience, and tenacity under great difficulties. Many men can rise to an occasion of extreme danger, but few can stand the dreary monotony of duty with no spice of adventure.

The trek fever even stirred up my father-in-law, who thought he had definitely retired to a peaceful old age in Pasadena. The South African adventures of his boys fired his blood again and at the age of sixty-five he joined us and did valuable pioneering in Rhodesia before the call of home drew him back again to California. A tall, powerful man of few words, unconsciously he influenced all our actions. Later on, when long past the allotted span of life, he had the energy to leave his home in Pasadena and follow his boys on a new adventure, this time into the High Sierras where, true to form, he bravely answered the last call.

Reports began to be whispered about that the thousands of ancient workings burned by fire had struck the bottom of the ore chutes and that Rhodesia, as a mining prospect, was a failure. No one wanted to find out the truth about this geological possibility more earnestly than Rhodes, so he brought up with him the engineer who stood at the head of the mining world—John Hays Hammond—to make a very thorough geological survey of the region. This took several weeks, and every broker "within the chains" of Johannesburg was in a cold sweat for the entire time, fearing an adverse report that would burst the whole mining boom. Even the Kafir Circus in London shook with a chill, and all the little boomers of Bulawayo gibbered like Kipling's banderlog—and to just about as much purpose.

The one man who took things calmly, as well as the one who had the greatest personal interest, was Rhodes. He seemed to be merely enjoying life on the veldt, but all the while was looking far beyond the end of this boom to goals we could not see. At last Hammond's report was made: Rhodesia did not possess the rich gold deposits of Johannesburg, with its wonderful banket. Rather it was a land similar to Hammond's native state, California, with countless veins of gold-bearing quartz that would produce gold for generations. So it has proven, and, in fact, it is still producing each year a little more than Alaska and California combined. This report gave us all fresh hope and started the country on a career of sane and steady development which continued without halt until the bursting of the stormcloud in 1896.

My contact with Smithsonian scientists exploring among the cliff dwellings of our own Southwest, as well as my search for lost mines in Mexico during my boyhood, had always kept me keenly alive to the tales of African natives about great huts of stone and deep holes in the rocks made by people who burned the rocks with fire. This led me to the finding of the Dhlo-Dhlo ruins and their gold treasure and the granting to me by

Cecil Rhodes of the right for their further exploration. Some of my enthusiastic friends formed a company and bought my interests for a few thousand pounds, all of which is set out in a most entertaining manner in a large book written by Hall and Johnson, who took over the exploitation. Again, when my eye alighted on a certain curious bracelet worn on the arm of a slave, I was eager to discover whence the ancient ornament came; and further inquiries started me forth to cross the Great River of the North, the Zambezi, in a quest for lost mines such as have been so colourfully imagined by Rider Haggard. At the same time, Rhodes happened to want the route to the north explored. In his far-reaching schemes, the Cape-to-Cairo Railway was never entirely absent from his mind, and I was sent out on an expedition to look for a possible railway crossing of this great river, and with the hope that in these regions a new mineral field might be found.

During an expedition which I led in 1895, after some months of adventure and some successful hippo hunting, we continued north toward the Congo and came into the country of the Matokas and the Mashukalumbwa. Famine was raging in the land, and the natives were reduced to feeding on wild roots and a species of bitter lily bulb which grows on the dry veldt and has to be soaked in water several days to remove its poisonous quality and fit it for human nourishment. This bulb poisons the pools where it is soaked and makes it particularly difficult for passing caravans to obtain safe drinking water.

The scarcity of game made the crocodiles extremely hungry and vicious, so that even in daylight it was dangerous to approach a small pool without caution. The whole caravan was delighted to reach the Kafuwe River at last and forget the terrible sights in that land of famine and drought. Along the Kafuwe, the food and beer were plentiful and the natives plump and happy. It took but slight occasion to cause their black faces to break into smiles, displaying rows of shining white teeth; though the Matokas always show a gap of two incisors, their tribal mark.

On our return from the Zambezi River to Bulawayo we decided to explore as much territory as possible, so we divided into three parties, each taking a few natives and going by a different road. I chose eleven natives, one of whom was a Masarwa belonging to the tribe which lives in this part of the Kalehari desert and who was supposed to know all the water holes and to be able to act as guide. I found his case to be like that of other savages I have known. Their knowledge may be most accurate in detail, from tree to tree, from rock to rock, and from pool to pool, yet the moment they are out of sight or touch of the last familiar landmark they are quite helpless, lacking that wider knowledge of geography which a world traveller acquires. Not only that, but the keenness of memory and understanding which seems to stand them in stead in their own locality utterly deserts them, and they are left in a puzzled mental state wherein they may do most foolish things.

This proved true of our Masarwa guide on this expedition. After marching a day and a half from the Zambezi we reached a water hole which, he said, was the last water we should find for two days. We accordingly filled our water calabashes at this point and, as the loads the men were carrying were rather heavy, there was much grumbling over the additional burden. We marched on about seven miles through heavy sand and thorn bush. Then, as night came on, we suddenly ran across another pool of water which had been unknown to our guide and was a source of surprise to our men. We rested there a few minutes and then continued on our way.

The following evening, I was very thirsty, and after having recourse to the canvas water bag which my personal servant carried for me, it occurred to me to walk around the lines of men and see what supply of water they now had. To my astonishment, I found that every calabash was dry and the men already extremely thirsty, although they made no complaint. I learned that when they had left the last water pool they had said among themselves, "What is the use of carrying all this extra water when there are pools every little way? This guide is simply loading us up so we shall travel slowly and make it easy for him." Whereupon they quietly poured the water out of their calabashes into the sand.

After resting only a short time, I ordered them to push on again, and during the night we struck a belt of the most terrible thorn bush. My servant, in shifting my water sack from his shoulder to his hand, caught the bottom of it on a heavy thorn and ripped a hole through which the water gushed out almost instantly and was lost. This was the last drop of water in the caravan. I had reserved as much of it as possible, having taken only one drink since leaving the last water hole. Now we were all equally thirsty. The necessity to push on was obvious, although our guide really knew nothing of the country. I believed that the pools on the Gwelo River would not yet be dried up, and that, by striking due south, we might reach it before any of the men should perish of thirst.

All that night we marched through the sand or across rocky ridges and belts of thorn bush which seemed to reach out to tear us, like the claws of wild beasts. At daybreak we rested for a short time. My men presented a truly pitiable sight. Thorns had scratched and punctured their skin until little drops of blood could be seen all over their naked legs; their arms were lacerated and their hands bleeding. Their legs were beginning to swell, and in their eyes appeared the little hollow cast which denotes intense suffering from lack of water. But since to stop now meant certain death, we continued to push on. The heat became intense, and the men staggered farther and farther apart. By four o'clock that afternoon, my own vision began to fail. There seemed always to be two horizons before my eyes—one of green hills and streams, the other of the actual thorn bush and sand through which we were travelling. Thinking that I could never make the Gwelo River, I took my knife and scratched upon the stock of my rifle some messages which I fondly hoped might some time be carried to my family. As I marched along, I remembered an old Californian in a little mining camp of the Mother Lode, named Tarlock, an inventor of valuable mining machinery. He once said to me, "If you are going to South Africa, I warn you to beware of the Kalehari desert. It seems so easy to cross that many are misled. My own son has just died there, and he thought he knew all about deserts." And now here was I caught on this easy desert that seemed so harmless. I recalled that when a man goes mad from lack of water he tears off his clothing and throws away everything he has and then tramps round and round in a circle until exhaustion and death follow. I fought for a long time against the desire to do these very things. At last, I lay down under a clump of thorn bush and lost consciousness for some hours.

When I came to, dusk was just falling. Of the eleven blacks of our party, only four were left who had yet not lost their reason or given up in despair. Weak and haggard, we stumbled along together, partially revived by the coolness of evening. We had marched only a short distance when, to our great delight, we saw ahead of us a vley of green grass. Hurrying into this, we found traces of animals, such as the wild boar, whose tracks never extend any great distance from water. The country around was so level that it was impossible to decide from the appearance of the ground which way the true drainage lay. The contour of the sandy ridges bore to the west, while I knew the real watershed to be toward the east. When I started in this direction the four blacks hesitated and halted, declaring that my path led to death and that water lay in the opposite direction. Knowing that their minds and faculties were now impaired and at best not as keen as my own, I persisted in my course, leaving them free to go toward the west if they chose. After I had marched some three hundred yards to the east, they turned and followed me; concluding, I suppose, that, as the white man had been right in every decision of direction since leaving the Zambezi, they would do well to follow where he led.

Within a few minutes from the time they joined me, we found a damp sandy spot where, by digging with their hands, they quickly excavated a small muddy pool. Fortunately, during the time of our delirium I had not reached the stage of throwing away my belongings, or the natives of discarding the utensils to which they had clung all through the dreary march, so we were able to strain this liquid mud through a kerchief into some tin billies. After we had all taken a good drink, we went back to see what had become of the rest of our exhausted men and succeeded in finding four of them lying in the sand and bush. Three out of our caravan had perished of thirst.

I learned later that Ingram and my brother-in-law, Judd Blick, who were together travelling a route parallel to mine, were at that same time enduring equally frightful thirst. They clung to a pet burro until both of them were so exhausted that they decided the only way of prolonging their lives was to kill the faithful brute and drink his blood. They had thrown away all their weapons except a common case knife, and found that, in their weakened condition, they were unable to penetrate the tough hide of the burro's throat. Fortunately for them, as for us, the cool of the evening brought respite from the burning sun, and with returning strength they managed to push on until they reached a little water hole, which saved their lives and the life of the faithful burro as well. This animal had made the entire trip from the Zambezi to this point without water. They then retraced their spoor and brought in their exhausted blacks.

I arrived in Bulawayo alone from the Zambezi, August 14, 1895. My last day's march as I was nearing home was forty-five miles None of the blacks could keep up with me. They were left behind in a Kafir kraal to come in by easy marches the next day or two.

Bulawayo was booming. Houses of iron and brick were going up in all directions; property was selling at great prices; money was plentiful, small change not given; the times were good to live in, and the wolf had been driven a long way from every man's door. The only thing to mar the outlook was the positive knowledge that such conditions could not last, for all booms are bound to burst. Now was the time to lay aside a few pounds for rainy days and old age. So for the next two months I turned into a regular money grubber and sold and cashed and bought and sold again—farms, mines, interests, stocks, etc. I never took my eye off the glint of gold. It was hard work and exciting, but not calculated to bring out the best in a man. Business is a ferocious game, and while it goes on, all thoughts of things of real beauty and lasting value are forgotten; calm resolution and continuity of purpose are laid aside. This was the day of gold, and this my opportunity to gain it; so, although I hated the slavery it entailed, I did my best to gather it for the sake of my children and those dependent on me. It seems to me that, in one way or another, nine tenths of our proud race must bend the knee to the power of money.

I packed carefully a very fine bow with copper work on it and some poisoned arrows taken from a hostile chief in the north, along with many of the horns, skins, etc., gathered on my expedition, and sent them to Cecil Rhodes. I also gave him some of the gold inlaid work and gold ornaments found in the ruins of Dhlo-Dhlo, where Ingram and I had obtained the wonderful lot of gold—six hundred and forty-one ounces. In another ruin, later on, some prospectors found two hundred and eight ounces. From the beads washed from the Zimbabwe ruins I had a jeweller make a ring for my wife, a unique thing, but spoiled by his soldering the beads together solidly. That goldsmith should have been a blacksmith!

CHAPTER XX

THE JAMESON RAID

UPON the safe return of my expedition from north of the Zambezi, a complete change of scene seemed in order. Ingram, who had worked as a unit with me in Bulawayo, and my wife's sister Grace, who had come out that year from California, now decided to be married. Financial success enabled us to plan a vacation together. We decided to go to London by way of Cairo, Athens, and Paris.

Leaving our affairs in the capable hands of our brothers, Judd and John Blick, and our little Nada in the devoted care of our friends, the Cummingses, we invited our father-in-law, Mr. Blick, to go with us on his way home to Pasadena, where he would have every convenience and comfort for his old age.

It was a joyous party that clambered on the Concord coach the last of October, 1895, to travel across Mashonaland to Salisbury, then to Umtali and Beira. At Beira, the town of tin and sand, we loitered for twelve days waiting for some steamer going north and finally went bouncing over the waves in a little boat called the *Patna*, of the B. I. Line.

Reaching Zanzibar November 25th, we stopped at the Afrika Hotel for eight days. Each morning at dawn, we enjoyed being wakened by the Arab priest calling the faithful to prayer in that strange, weird tone peculiar to Mohammedan usage, and so penetrating that, no matter what noise on the streets, it is heard above all. It was the height of the shipping season, and the ordinary stench of the three-foot alleys of the queer old town was deadened to a comfortable degree by the pleasant odour of cloves. There were thousands of tons of them awaiting shipment—but, alas, no apples in which to stick them! We saw tons of ivory—huge tusks weighing a hundred pounds or more—billed to America to make piano keys and knife handles.

We had a pleasant visit with the American Consul, Mr. Mohun of Virginia. He told me he had been sent up the Congo when the Belgians were in hot water with the Arabs. The Belgian ammunition was reduced to ten rounds per man when Mohun arrived with reinforcements of 150,000 rounds and took command of their artillery. They had hard fighting for several months but finally defeated the Arabs, killing about two thousand of them. The last fight continued for fifteen hours without let-up. Mohun estimated the force in front of them at about twenty-five thousand; their own at about twelve thousand. The balance of power, he said, lay in the last handful of able Belgians, about fifteen men.

One day, the Sultan sent his steam yacht for us, and we dined with him at his palace above Zanzibar. There we met Tippoo Tib, famous for many exploits long ago chronicled by Stanley and other writers. He was without doubt a very shrewd man, with many excellent qualities. It has been a good thing for white supremacy in that part of the world that others of his race were not like him.

On December 2d, at an early hour, we sailed away from this ancient city, past the palaces showing white against the palms and mangoes and past the harbour thronged with quaint old teakwood dhows in strange contrast to the four big white men-of-war lying among them. The Cross and the Crescent have each held sway twice in turn since 1250 A. D., but the palm groves, the coral strand, and the Negroes are now as they were then and probably will continue the same after the history of both is forgotten. This, my second visit to Zanzibar, has lasted for many years as a bright spot in memory and is a picture to recall when the brain is weary and sleep needs coaxing.

We reached Aden on December 9th and passed the hours quickly by taking a long drive through that wonderful basalt mountain, tunnelled and walled and mounted with monster guns. Rock, sea, and sky have there an austere beauty all their own. There is not a tree or a blade of grass. Long lines of camels with slow and ponderous tread wind away from the white-walled town to the stretches of Arabia. Once in from three to seven years it rains a few hours, and under the basalt cliffs there were ancient reservoirs walled up to conserve the water supply. The British Government enlarged and strengthened these so that at the time of our visit they held several million gallons of water and were a sight well worth seeing. The garrison was kept very strong, as Aden is considered one of the most important coaling stations on the India route. While coming off to our ship, the *Irrawaddy* (M. M. Co. boat), we had a very narrow escape from being run down by a small steamer, as our idiotic boatman had blown out his light to save the candle. So I pitched him and the candle overboard—about as much punishment to an Aden nigger as wetting a duck.

We touched at a small French station in the Red Sea and thought the place fitted well some of Dante's descriptions of the Inferno. Next came Ismailia and the news of an Italian defeat in Abyssinia; twelve hundred men killed. Latest wires reported the British fleet off Salonika and all Turkey seemingly on fire, with the boundary lines of several nations in peril from the blaze. No man could tell the hour when millions might leap to arms, and Europe be plunged in chaos.

At last—Egypt! Cairo, the Nile, the pyramids, tombs, donkey-boys, bazaars, dahabeeyahs, mosques, camels, tons of curios, photographs, Joseph's well, Mary's tree, Mary's little lamb—St. Patrick's day in the morning!—Ah! I see even yet my mind is wandering, but why should it not? The fulfilment of such great desire—to drink the water of the sacred river, to look into the eyes of the Sphinx in the land of myth, the cradle of the race! Years ago, lying wrapped in my blanket on the Mexican frontier, I had passed many hours in contemplation of this land, unknown and yet familiar, and had secretly resolved that, penniless though I then was, I should see it all. And after years of privation and adventure, I was having my reward and feeling well repaid for all my efforts. There is but one Egypt.

One of my guides was a Bedouin of striking appearance, dressed in rich robes and the owner of many camels and women. He spoke excellent English and was a great admirer of Charles Scribner, the publisher, who had spent much time with him on the desert. I soon found that in the mind of this Bedouin all Americans were divided into two classes: gentlemen like Scribner—and the other kind.

Standing one day on top of the great pyramid, as we looked down on the khaki tents of British soldiers and saw the red coats moving in perfect line across the sandy parade ground, I said to the Arab: "You who are so proud—how do you feel toward the Unbeliever with the strange eyes and uncouth ways who rules over you?"

After a silence, he answered, with a far-away look in his eyes: "For our sins Allah has seen fit to punish us by setting the foreigner over us. When in his judgment we have paid, we shall rule again. The English came yesterday. They are here to-day; they will be gone to-morrow. We were here before they were known. We shall be here when they are forgotten."

He took me out on the desert among his nomad people. He told me his Arab grandfather had upbraided his father for wearing Turkish slippers on his feet and for living in a walled house, and that his own father in turn had railed at him for wearing silk robes and becoming soft like a woman. "Now," he said, "I am chiding my young son for using Christian utensils, such as your kodak."

This Bedouin was both just and courageous. If Egypt had many such men, there would be no need of soldiers to govern it.

Paris revisited! Beautiful, alluring Paris! There, in January, 1896, we heard the first news of the trouble in South Africa. Doctor Jameson had marched south with five hundred men. Johannesburg was in revolt against the Boers, and he had gone, as a brave man should, to help his countrymen in time of need, even though the odds were all against him.

Ingram and I were wild that we were not with him, and cursed the day we started on our pleasure trip. I left for London within an hour. The next morning came the news of Jameson's

THE JAMESON RAID

utter defeat. I felt like a deserter as I realized that we had not been with our brave Doctor Jim and that we were unable to raise a finger to help him. I knew the ways of the frontier so well and could have done so much had I been on the ground. Who knows but that I might have found some weak point in the line of the Boers where all the British could have cut through to Johannesburg? Then, as if it were not enough that Jameson was downed, all the secret enemies of this royal-hearted man crawled out of their dens like hyenas and snapped and snarled, ready to crunch the bones of what they thought to be the dead lion. My teeth were sore from grinding them in rage. I wanted to kill!

Ingram jumped on the first steamer leaving for Africa. We decided that I must wait for the next, so as to get some clue to the political moves and a better understanding as to what strategy would be needed. But before the week ended, Johannesburg had surrendered. A miserable failure—a revolution that did not revolutionize, a mob without a leader, a blot on England's shield!

Before I left London, Jameson was brought home a prisoner. The morning I sailed on the *Grantully Castle*, I took breakfast with him (he was then out on bail, awaiting trial), along with Sir John Willoughby, Bishop Galt, and a Mr. Wolf, an American. Jameson and Mr. Wolf were in animated conversation on the political outlook, and I remember how Doctor Jim paced round and round the large breakfast room of the Old Burlington, his hands behind him, and at every pace energetically striking the calf of either leg with the instep of the free foot. His head was thrown forward and rested on his chest, while he drew from the storehouse of his mind incident after incident that revealed him as a master of the political history of many nations and different ages.

The pity of it all! My heart went out to him, and I knew the hopes of many strong and progressive men must sink with his setting star. It is only a sip between the sweetest draught of life and the bitterest dregs. The falling of a spark, the cackling of a goose, the loss of a horseshoe nail may blot out the most brilliant man of his time and change the history of empires.

It had been an open secret for a year that trouble was brewing in the Transvaal. The Boers were arming, and so were the Uitlanders. The history of the dealings of the English with the Boers and with the natives in Africa is too long and tedious to recapitulate in these pages. The mistaken policies of various British officials planted in the country by a blind Home Government many years earlier were bearing their inevitable fruit, and the enmity between the English and the Dutch had grown to such a pitch that only a struggle by arms could decide the issue. Sometimes a broad-minded, just, and determined official would almost bring about complete understanding and agreement between these two powerful strains of white men in Africa; when another turn of the political wheel would land in the country some pompous, vacillating, irritating, small-hearted successor who would upset all the good previously accomplished, turn the black men against the whites and the whites against one another, and throw the whole country into turmoil. And all the while the politician would bleat of "Peace" and "Harmony" and fatuously insist that all his moves were made solely to prevent the bloodshed he kept on inviting.

If it had not been for the unholy crop of diplomatic errors already sown in Africa and ripe for the harvest, Rhodes would have been able to amalgamate the Dutch and English settlers slowly and quietly, without having to suffer the throes of the Boer War. It was but another case of the inevitable fruit of blunders, like the American Revolution or the Wars of the Roses. The crash was unavoidable; though, as Roosevelt prophesied, a kindly destiny was yet to mould these two strong bloods into one great nation.

The overt act which led directly to the Boer War was probably the Jameson Raid into the Transvaal, which corresponded somewhat to the John Brown Raid in the South prior to the Civil War in America. Nearly all great struggles have a premature flash before the grand explosion of the magazine.

THE JAMESON RAID

So threatening and so important had the Transvaal war cloud become on the political horizon, and so careless and shortsighted were the colonists of Rhodesia that all available mounted police, as well as Doctor Jameson himself, had withdrawn from Rhodesia and taken up headquarters on the borders of the Transvaal. Rhodesians were naturally eager to help their countrymen obtain the franchise and fair treatment by the Boer Government, although the Boers seemed determined to exclude them from both. Jameson intended to cross into the Transvaal with two thousand men—and fine fighting men they were, too. The first advance of five hundred arrived on the border of the Dutch Republic when things were bubbling in Johannesburg. Under the Boer clique—a small minority, it is true, but in possession of all political and taxing power—conditions were intolerable. Jameson believed that there was just a fighting chance to remedy the situation; that with five hundred men he could turn the tide of events and get control. But realizing the danger and uncertainty of the attempt, Jameson did not order a single man to follow him. He simply explained the condition of things in Johannesburg and called for volunteers. *Not one man failed to cross with him.* Everyone knows the disastrous result.

There are those who say Jameson went over the border from sordid motives and backed by a handful of capitalists. They did not know the man! He cared little for money. He could have made himself a millionaire by a gesture, so great was his power in the North. He already had honour, influence, and whatever wealth he desired. Why should he hazard an advance with but five hundred men, knowing that failure would mean the grave of a splendid career and the dragging down of a big circle of faithful friends as well? I say nothing of personal danger, as a man of his stamp does not take that into consideration. He had more at stake than any man under him, and he generously pledged it all, not for money or power but to help his countrymen.

The first gun of a revolution should be carefully loaded and full-cocked before it is fired. Jameson pulled the trigger at half-cock and landed in Bow Street instead of Johannesburg. Dim echoes of that fiasco could still be heard even through the crash of the World War.

So perished the career of a splendid man. To most of the world he has been painted as a land pirate, a reckless swashbuckler, but to us who have fought under him and really knew him he will always be the genial Doctor Jim, kind and just even to his enemies. All the men who were with him declared they would gladly follow him again. Like Walker of Nicaragua, he was a warm-hearted, generous, and courageous leader. As evidence of these qualities, witness the renaissance of Doctor Jim, not among his old Rhodesians, for they never lost their love for him, but among the hard-headed Boers who had looked upon him as a national foe, yet welcomed him before long as the leader of a great Boer party. He was even made Premier of Cape Colony by the votes of his former enemies. Botha, his determined antagonist, became his firm friend to the end of his days. All the revolutionists forgave him his error of judgment. His integrity of soul triumphed.

I have seen Jameson in many turbulent times. As viceroy for imperial Rhodesia he was the true spiritual and temporal representative of royalty. Rhodes could not be physically present with us very often, but Doctor Jim was, constantly. He shared our bully beef by our camp fires, or crouched with us under sodden bucksails without fire or food, as our fortune might be. We felt that he was the genuine friend of every man in the column, and yet, somehow, in spite of his simplicity of manner, he maintained good discipline. His photographs do not show the man as he was. No one could ever look at him without seeing his strength of will and character. He was modest and unassuming, or rather had an air of self-forgetfulness about him that put a man instantly at ease and enabled him to utter his thoughts freely, knowing they would be followed rapidly, surely, and with sympathy. A highly educated man, he hated bloodshed and misrule by white or black. He was small-boned, slightly round-shouldered, with short, heavy neck, thick chest, large head, and very beautiful and expressive eyes. Although careless in dress, yet under his unconventional attire and way there was an innate dignity marking a line over which no one dared step. In conversation, he was, like Rhodes, much given to walking about the room, and was totally oblivious of everybody around him except the one to whom he was talking.

The job of handling the temperamental Rhodesian pioneers must have been about as hard as that of managing a company of opera stars; for, unfortunately, high resolves and heroic intentions in the presence of danger do not banish the little bickerings and jealousies that crop up hourly in an army. We had our full share of such troubles, and Jameson would sit in his tent far into the night settling the hundreds of complaints as best he could. Many times I have seen delegations of irate stalwarts, with perhaps an extra shot of "Cape Smoke" inside them, march up to Jameson's tent fully loaded in their minds to lift the lid off things in general and the blankety-blank Chartered Company in particular. Such occasions used to give me a sick feeling at heart, for, being an American, I did not quite comprehend how far a South African delegation might go. To judge by looks and language, I could well believe that Jameson was about to be shot or hanged. So at first, since I thought highly of Doctor Jim, I used to slip my old six-shooter under my coat when trouble seemed imminent and casually hang around headquarters for a while. But I soon learned that Jameson needed no volunteer gun man to protect him. In a few minutes, he would have that delegation either split into two argumentative factions, or, more often, laughing at their own preposterous demands.

Each man in his heart thought that he should be an officer of sorts, and every one who rode a horse to the water trough privately considered himself a superior cavalryman. I recall one delegation that came to Jameson demanding that a certain young man be made a captain. Some of the women had taken a hand in the promotion of this embryo officer, and for once Doctor Jim was ruffled. He sharply told his adjutant to make every single soldier a captain *but to see to it that he carried a gun.*

If these little souls had realized how much vitality they were sapping from a great leader by carrying all their small woes to him, they would have blushed for shame. They annoyed him more than if they had thrown dust in his eyes or filled his shoes with sand, and yet they expected of him calm demeanour and clear decisions at all times.

Jameson's superlative quality of kindly patience endeared him to all. Rhodes could not have picked, in all Africa, a better warden for his northern holdings. It is well that his gentle dust rests in Rhodesia where he was known and loved, rather than in the Abbey, where lie the bones of some who wholly underrated and misunderstood this great soul.

CHAPTER XXI

THE SECOND MATABELE WAR

ON THE 25th of March, 1896, I stepped off the steamer at Cape Town and met Ingram, who had two cablegrams in his hand from Lord Gifford on behalf of the British South Africa Company, ordering us to rush off to Bulawayo with utmost speed, regardless of expense. The Matabele had risen; their black soldiers had turned on the white officers and were murdering men, women, and children. The papers were publishing the names of many of our friends already killed. We were off for the north within a few hours.

The condition of affairs in Bulawayo at this time was so peculiar that some explanation is necessary for an intelligent understanding of the famous events that so soon took place.

The swift and easy conquest of Matabeleland by a handful of pioneers in the first war had misled the new colonists into believing that the black question was settled for all time. The scorn of discipline—a weakness of all frontier peoples—made the situation especially perilous. The English pioneers considered it an acknowledgment of fear to carry weapons and for that reason, even when rumours of a Kafir uprising were thick, it was a common thing for solitary prospectors, ranchers, or miners, to wander over that wild country absolutely unarmed. If they possessed any guns, they were most likely stowed away in the bottom of an ox cart, while their cartridges were tied up in some dunnage box whose location was unascertainable except through inquiry of a black servant.

This same disregard of caution prevailed among the early English colonists on the American continent, and it took more than one hundred years of tragic warfare with that wiliest of all savages, the American Indian, to instil into the minds of our frontiersmen the fact that it is always wise to have ammunition handy and a gun loaded. Thousands of settlers were massacred and scalped, their homes burned and their families tortured, before our pioneers fully learned that first lesson of self-preservation—preparedness. So, too, in Africa, when we rode over the country at the end of the second Matabele war, we found evidence that often the colonists had given up their lives because they were wholly unprepared to meet a solitary foe. This seemed pitiful when we realized that if the settlers of Rhodesia had at that time made a practice of carrying their arms with them, the lives of five hundred colonists might have been saved at the outset and a long and costly war forestalled.

It is almost impossible for the white race to grasp, even in a slight degree, the motives actuating the black. Under the terms of peace made with the Matabele at the close of the first war, the natives were given generous reservations of land; also certain allotments of cattle, seed, etc., and ample employment for all who were willing to work on the farms, in the mines, or for the Government. But there was one inscrutable factor in affairs that even the wisest of the officials did not fully take into account.

Ever since the time when Lobengula perished in the jungles of the Shangani, the ancient power of the priesthood had been increasingly asserting itself among the blacks. In his lifetime, Lobengula, like many another monarch, had experienced the bitter struggle between Church and State. The king had triumphed, but after his death and secret burial the priesthood steadily preached to the natives that Lobengula had been defeated only because he had forsaken their counsel and had not made medicine as his father, M'Silikatze, had done. Secretly and continually it was instilled into the minds of the blacks that the whites had become weak and weary; that their great chief, Doctor Jameson, had already left the country with all his armed men; and that the hour had struck when the blacks should reassert their sovereignty and again establish the kingdom of the Matabele, fulfilling the prophecy of Lobengula that eventually every white man should be driven into the sea.

Here were people given more liberty than they had ever known before; the slaves all freed, labour paid in coin, lands held in safety, and taxes lighter by far than those levied on any white man in the empire. But let one cabalastic word be whispered in the ear of a servant by an emissary of the M'Limo (the Mouthpiece of God), and he became as a bit of grass swayed by an invisible wind. All the white man's kindness and the benefits of good government were swept from his mind.

Faint rumours drifted into Bulawayo that the Kafirs were restless and gathering in great numbers in the hills. Native servants were absent at night and red-eyed and listless by day. It became known that great dances, like the Ghost Dances of the American Indians, were going on in the mountains and caves of the Matoppos. But the officials discredited or ignored this information, and matters drifted along until the news of the defeat and capture of Jameson and his force in the Transvaal began to sift down to the Kafir. When the natives learned that the dreaded Doctor Jameson was actually a prisoner of the Boers, they became convinced that the star of the white man had set and that their turn had come. One day, a woman entering the town of Bulawayo with what purported to be a load of faggots was halted by the guard, as her burden seemed suspiciously heavy. It proved to be a load of assegais, evidently designed for arming the servants in the town against the whites.

We know now that the M'Limo, or great high priest of the Matabele nation, had commanded through the smaller chiefs in each district that, on a certain night of full moon, all servants should rise against their white masters over all Rhodesia. The instructions were that in every case the entire family should be killed. The massacre was to be complete; not one white man, woman, or child was to be spared. Further to incite and encourage the warriors the M'Limo promised them that if they would bring all the treasure to him, after looting the white men's goods and stores, he would give them a medicine and a doctoring that would make them immune from harm and would turn the white man's bullets to water.

Such an uprising was sure to be very serious, because the white population was scattered and totally unprepared, while the natives for three years had been quietly accumulating quantities of rifles and ammunition from the south and from local dealers, hunters, and prospectors. The Government had made the initial mistake of arming, drilling, and training some of the Matabele in a police force, thus teaching the blacks the very methods by which the white man maintained his superiority. This black military police, well drilled and armed, immediately joined the uprising and became able leaders of their own people. It is probable that the bulk of the British losses in the fighting that followed was due to the accurate shooting of these men, so carefully trained at low wages by the whites, in order to save a few dollars from their treasury.

It was all ancient history over again. Thus the Romans, absorbed in their own affairs and trusting to their great prestige, had armed and trained the wild Goths and Vandals—our own forbears—until those barbarians turned upon them and sacked Rome. The policy of equipping and drilling the blacks in South Africa was one of the worst mistakes the white man could make, if he expected to hold the country permanently. Again and again, experience has proved the folly of placing the black man over the white man with authority and power as an officer of the law. It has invariably brought trouble. So long as the white race dwells in Africa, it must hold the country by the sword or by the fear of it.

Among the Rhodesians was a percentage of Boers who for generations had lived and fought among the blacks. These sensed the coming trouble from very minute signs which would never strike an English official new to the life. Many of these Boers trekked south to safety, but the average settler was like our own people in the Indian wars—careless, cocksure, rather boastful. Many refused to believe that the servants they had treated so well would turn on their good masters. Some were even trusted to carry their masters' guns and ammunition.

THE SECOND MATABELE WAR

Such assurance may be all right just after the savage has been thoroughly beaten, for if the vanquished has lately felt the sword, the victor may for a time carry an empty scabbard with impunity. Yet, in the end, to rely on the scabbard alone brings more bloodshed than to have the sword always ready within.

So well were the plans of the natives laid, and so weak were the colonists that, had the orders of the M'Limo been carried out, it is probable that all the whites in Rhodesia would have been killed within twenty-four hours from the hour set, and every town left a smoking ruin. Fortunately, the black brain cannot be trusted to carry through quite so comprehensive a measure, although its secretiveness is ample. It is indeed a strange fact that while no white community can be trusted with any military secret whatever, the childlike Negro can hold one as deep as a well. The Mashonas, who were the slaves that had been set free from the Matabele, joined with their old tyrants in the plan to exterminate the people who had freed them, and in no instance did a Mashona give warning to the whites, although certain other colonial blacks did betray some intimation of trouble.

What upset the M'Limo's plans was the zeal of certain young warriors on the Insesi River, forty-five miles from Bulawayo. Instead of waiting for the full of the moon, as ordered, they began killing the settlers three days in advance. The whites, taking alarm, hastily fortified themselves or formed into strong patrols and gathered in the outlying settlements. But in spite of these three days of grace, it was a desperate situation and hundreds were massacred.

The enemies of Rhodes, like jackals, could not help showing their cowardly satisfaction at this terrible turn of affairs, for this whole country was essentially the creation of the genius of Rhodes, whom they had envied until their envy turned to hate.

When we arrived at Mafeking—the end of the railroad—I was much astonished to meet there Doctor Sauer, with Captain Wools-Sampson, Lieutenant Hook, and young Swinburne (a grandson of the poet), who were all hurrying to help Rhodesia in her hour of need. Doctor Sauer's brother, a high official at the Cape, was a bitter opponent of Rhodes, and I had always thought Doctor Sauer himself one in secret. His financial methods were considered those of a pirate. But such times show up both the good and bad qualities in men and sometimes reveal virtues we never dreamed they possessed, and Doctor Sauer in wartime proved to be a brave and forceful man. With all his financial dubiety and shortcomings, he must have had a love of country so strong that he would take any risk and make any sacrifice for it. As for Captain Wools-Sampson, the leader of the Imperial Light Horse, he was such a splendid type of man and so well known that I need say nothing to add to his brilliant reputation. Ingram and I expected to serve under him during the war, but he was called down country to his trial, to answer for his part in the Jameson Raid. He pledged himself to return and did return later, for his word was like that of a knight of old and could not be broken.

Our wives had accompanied us as far as Mafeking, but the government officials would permit no woman to come up on the coach, although the ladies wished to go and pleaded earnestly that they would be of more use in the hospital, and even in a fight, than some of the silly boys just out from home and clamouring for what they called "a little sport," but who hardly knew which end of a gun to put to their shoulder.

We left Mafeking at five in the morning, by coach heavily loaded with mail and passengers. At Gaberones we met the down coach with refugees from Rhodesia, among them a writer on a Bulawayo paper who filled us with all the latest horrors and said we would only add to the list of the doomed by going up. He told us there was no ammunition, very few guns, and that any night the savages were likely to spear every living soul. Clearly the man had an overdose of funk, but it made Sauer and myself very uneasy, for we both had children in Bulawayo.

We were carrying Her Majesty's mail, weighing more than a thousand pounds. What was the use, we asked ourselves, of lugging letters to dead people? If they were still alive, they would want cartridges far more than bills or patent-medicine advertisements or even love letters. At this time, Gaberones was not under the control of the B. S. A. Co. It was British, and ever since the Jameson Raid, we were told, all the petty officials had been as domineering as possible to any official of the Chartered Company, because they were foolish enough to think that Rhodes was dead politically and the charter would be taken away, and then they would be installed over the settlers of the North. So, when Doctor Sauer and I suggested leaving the Royal Mail behind and taking on cartridges, a mighty howl arose.

"No orders, sir, you know," and "Can't be done, you know," etc.

But since it happened that the armed force representing Her Majesty consisted of two soldiers poorly mounted, and we were six determined men bound for Bulawayo, we concluded it *could* be done. We held a consultation, and Doctor Sauer suggested that we make one honest effort to see the Resident Magistrate and explain things to him before resorting to force. Fortunately, he was an old colonial and knew the meaning of Kafir wars as well as he understood our present temper. He gave us the order for the cartridges, and the subordinates had to give way.

We drove triumphantly up to the post office, chucked the mail, loaded up with Martini cartridges, five thousand rounds, and the coach moved on to the veldt. This was all done in one hour. Quite a jolt for Her Majesty's official servants in that part of the world, but they were destined to have many jolts before that war ended, not the least being to see Rhodes again master of the situation and of them.

Night and day, we travelled along the dry, sandy road, flogging our jaded mules. There was no more news from the North, but the evidences of rinderpest were everywhere. Stranded wagons laden with provisions lined the road, and the stench of dead bullocks was scarcely ever out of our nostrils.

Pelapswe, a huge kraal of more than 20,000 Kafirs and King Khama's capital, was the last place where we could procure salted horses, and we bought from the white traders their all—six in number. I paid one hundred and twenty pounds in gold for a sorrel pony worth in England about ten pounds and in America three pounds—war prices with a vengeance! We desired to save our mounts as much as possible, so we still rode in the coach to Tati in order to have our horses fresh for the hostile country, where we might have to abandon the coach and make a dash for Bulawayo over a trail that Ingram and I had travelled in the first Matabele war.

At Tati we met Mr. Vigers, an ex-official of the Chartered Company and now in command of the Tati concessions. Here we were among friends and received every assistance, including saddles, belts, and various war supplies. We heard that the natives were all around Bulawayo in thousands, and were being directed in their movements by their M'Limo, whose signal they awaited to make the final rush on the place. We also learned that Mangwe, just at the entrance to the Matoppo Hills, was in laager and that a lot of Dutch families were gathered there under the leadership of Hans Lee, the noted hunter.

When we reached Mangwe, we found that a circular earth fort, well palisaded, had been built, and outside this was drawn up the circle of large wagons, with a still larger circle of thorn bush surrounding all; making such a very strong position as only a full regiment would venture to attack. From Mangwe to Fig Tree, a distance of thirty miles, we travelled through those strange, fantastic kopjes and jagged granite peaks known as the Matoppos. Here a whole impi could come unseen within a few yards of us, in spite of all our precautions, and we were kept wondering why the coach had been allowed to travel unmolested up and down this narrow pass. Men at Mangwe who had lived among the Kafirs all their lives were at a loss to find any plausible explanation for us. The fighting had been fierce and very close to Bulawayo; the hills were full of armed and hostile blacks; yet, for some unknown reason, they had not yet held up the coach. We could do no less, therefore, than go on with our load of cartridges and hope to

From sketches and descriptions by Mr. H. J. Hirschler.

The attack of the Matabele on Cummings's store, where about thirty-eight settlers, including women and children, had taken refuge. Thanks to the timely arrival of Gifford with reinforcements, the savages were driven back and most of the settlers made their escape.

reach Bulawayo. In case we were attacked all we could do would be to make as hard a fight of it as possible and then blow up the ammunition so that the enemy could not, after wiping us out, use our cartridges to kill our own people. Several times we sighted savages and looked for an attack, but it never came.

At Fig Tree, Bulawayo was only thirty-five miles away, and the country between was fairly open. If necessary, we could outgallop an impi, and, unless the town was very closely invested, we believed we could slip through. It was with an acute sense of surprise and relief that we rode unmolested on and into Bulawayo.

Now, for the first time, we got the real facts about the uprising and learned how many of our people had been murdered. Doctor Sauer's children were safe, as well as my own little daughter Nada, who had been left in the care of our good friends, the Cummingses, while my wife and I were in England. The town was in laager. The market building was used as a huge bedroom for the women and children. My brothers-in-law, the Blicks, had just come in with the Gifford patrol from Shiloh. Captain Lumsden had been killed during a hot fight of two days. Gifford, one of our very best, had lost his arm in the first day's fighting and lay at point of death in a hospital.

There were none of the recognized leaders in the country when I arrived. Jameson, with all his officers, was imprisoned in England. Rhodes was over on the East Coast trying to get to our aid. There was a conflict of authority as to who was the senior commander. Duncan, the Surveyor General, was acting as Administrator. Napier was the oldest captain in the Rhodesia Horse; Spreckley and Gifford each claimed rank. It was finally arranged that Napier should be colonel commanding, so Ingram and I served under him, I as Chief of Scouts.

It would have been small wonder at that time if the whole population had left the plateau and marched down country to Mangwe or Tati, out of reach of the Matabele, but such an idea was suggested by only a few weak-hearts. The rest would fight—die, perhaps, but would never retreat. It was not in their blood to abandon the country on which the British flag had once been planted.

In the district along the Insesi River the murders started. A mild-mannered old man who had always treated the blacks with especial kindness, a Mr. Maddox, was the first to have his brains beaten out with knobkerries.

Mr. Henry Cummings rode over one night on his way to Bulawayo and stopped at the Blicks' farm, warning them that the Matabele had risen and counselling flight. As a number of families lived up the river, it was quickly decided that, since Cummings must carry the alarm to Bulawayo, the two Blicks should go up the valley and warn all the settlers there and get them to concentrate at Cummings's store, only a few miles from the Blicks' farm, and fortify the building.

It was then eleven o'clock at night. As they had just graded a new drift or ford across the river a mile from their house, the Blicks thought it best to put Cummings on this new route to Bulawayo, as it would be considerably nearer for him. Their horses had recently died of the Dikop sickness, so, picking up their guns and ammunition belts, they walked with Cummings down to the drift, intending to return at once to their house and take away what few valuables they had, including sixty-five pounds in money locked in a medicine chest. But, a moment after leaving Cummings, they heard the howl of their old hound, and then the yells of a horde of savages. Their house was surrounded, and the dynamite the Blicks had bought for the purpose of sinking a well was used to blow up their own buildings. To this day, my bachelor brother-in-law laments the newly darned socks he lost on that occasion, and in memory of that cruel event has refused steadfastly ever since to darn a sock.

The Blicks debated quickly whether the people up the river would already have been killed, for the valley was full of Matabele kraals. Between them and Bulawayo was open, rolling country, and they could easily make a run to safety —but what if their friends were still sleeping, as they themselves had been less than an hour ago? They could not take

THE SECOND MATABELE WAR 237

this chance, so up the valley they ran, warning and gathering the people together. Arriving at Captain Rickson's farm at daybreak, they snatched breakfast and started through the hills to Cummings's store, twelve miles away. By this time, there were several women in the party and one child in arms. The sun was hot and progress slow. At the store they knew were a few people and some provisions, and if it had not already fallen they could fortify it and try to hold out until reinforcements could come from Bulawayo.

When the party reached the store, the entire garrison was counted and found to number thirty-eight, including women and children, armed with an assortment of weapons, mostly shotguns and revolvers—some of little use—and with only five hundred rounds of ammunition. They did not yet realize that the whole Matabele nation had risen, and so they thought they could stand off the neighbouring Kafirs until help should arrive. The building was not in a commanding position, but was overlooked by a high hill; and while the walls were of iron the roof was thatch and could easily be fired. They laid up meal bags and goods boxes against the walls, and took the precaution to remove the thatch roof. All that day, not a Kafir came in sight. At night, about nine o'clock, Gifford arrived from Bulawayo with twenty men, in response to the message from Cummings. They were just in the nick of time, for before morning, one of the hottest little fights of the war was on.

Gifford at once ordered more loopholes made, posted pickets close by, and made every man lie on his arms. At about five o'clock, just before dawn, the house was surrounded by savages who rushed the pickets with a yell and a fusillade, and in spite of all precautions, almost succeeded in taking the place by storm. But the blacks were unaware that Gifford and his twenty men were there. They thought they had only their own neighbours and masters to kill, and as these Kafirs lived and worked on the farms, they knew every gun inside that store and could gauge pretty accurately the amount of ammunition. So it was a great surprise to them when the little tin fort belched so much fire. The blacks did not flinch but came right against the building. They stabbed one man through a loophole, wounded John Blick slightly, and killed Lieutenant O'Leary. One old induna shouted for the young men to bring axes and chop through the building and stab the women in a certain frightful manner so that their screams would shake the nerve of the white men. The fort replied with fire. In about ten minutes, it was all over and the baffled savages retreated to their kopjes. Numbers lay dead on the ground and even against the building. Homer Blick recognized one man whom he had befriended and doctored and who had always seemed truly grateful for any favours. But there is no telling what passes through the brain of a savage under tribal control. Beneath their thick skulls lurk such uncertain emotions that a trusted servant of years may suddenly burst out in a frenzy for war and kill even his own master, though he may owe him everything.

Gifford was now convinced that if the settlers were to get into Bulawayo they must start at once. This they did, and although the Kafirs hovered around for a time, they abandoned the chase when the little armed band reached open country.

Meantime, another brother-in-law of mine, Judd Blick, had missed Gifford and joined Captain Spreckley in his first patrol to rescue the miners and prospectors in the Fillimbusi district. But here, alas, they were too late. The whole camp had been massacred and Bentley burned alive in his hut, as he was sick in bed and could not get out. The Cunningham family, three generations, were butchered and mutilated in a horrible manner. All over the region, men, women, and children were slaughtered and little patrols under such leaders as Napier, Gifford, Spreckley, and others rode night and day and fought big odds to save such settlers as they could. The Salisbury coach was attacked and the occupants forced out. Fortunately, they were armed and had no women along, so they tried a running fight and, being good shots, made it hot for the blacks, but they were nearly dead from lack of water and exhaustion when they met Napier with thirty men. In the Belingwe district the miners and prospectors gathered under the gallant Major Laing—Terry Laing, formerly of the Black Watch—and held their fort successfully for several months.

At times, during the war, the troops would reach a stage where a singular jumpiness possessed the nerves of all. On the exhausting march to the Insesi the commanders, Napier and Spreckley, carried in the supply wagons two barrels of good brandy and at times when it looked as if everybody would blow up with the strain, officers included, the dop call would be sounded and a stiff drink given to each man.

Before long, they would be laughing, playing jokes, singing, relaxing mentally and physically, or else lying on their blankets with all the sorrows and ills of life wiped out for a sweet hour or two. This relief by stimulant seemed to be demanded by about eighty per cent. of the men. There were about twenty per cent. of us who did not draw our dop ration. We neither felt the urge nor received from it the expected result.

The mild native beer, while not strong enough to affect a white man unless taken in great quantities, did seem to relieve both thirst and the parched and dry state of the skin, as well as the lack of moisture in the eyes with which both whites and blacks were afflicted at certain seasons of the year.

We are "but children of a larger growth," and an issue of a ration of cigarettes will often turn glum and cursing troops into columns of docile and smiling men, ready to obey orders cheerfully. There seems to be something mysterious and soothing in watching the curling smoke. The first call of the wounded, after water, is for a cigarette. Then, too, the courtesies of offering, receiving, and lighting a cigarette, like the amenities of Japanese tea drinking, introduce that precious element of time that, by its mere lapse, tends to modify or prevent the sharp reply or biting sarcasm which would lead to trouble.

To try to put on paper the tales of hardship, endurance, and heroism of those days would fill a volume. There were scenes pathetic enough to melt a heart of stone, and others so awful in their shocking cruelty that the blood surged with the craving for vengeance. There seemed but one thing to do—to fight and die; and this resolve sank deep into the hearts of many.

CHAPTER XXII

RHODESIA'S DARKEST HOUR

THE situation of Rhodesia was desperate. Egypt's ten plagues came in succession, but the plagues of Rhodesia were simultaneous. The pest of political dissension came up from the south; the locusts, from King Khama's country and the western deserts; the native uprising sprang over night from the soil around us; the drought fell from the brazen sky above. Deadliest of all, down from the north swept the rinderpest. For a time our whole lives seemed subject to the caprice of this disease. It closed our lines of communication with the outside world more effectively than a besieging army could have done.

Rinderpest is endemic in Central Asia, and was brought to Africa by the Italian forces in their war with the Black King Menelik of Abyssinia. The deadly germ got into the Italian transport, perhaps through some infected sheepskin or saddle pad stuffed with hair from a sick animal, and triumphantly survived its six-thousand-mile journey to the Cape of Good Hope. The malady attacks all cud-chewing animals and is fatal to probably ninety per cent. Great herds of buffalo were exterminated by it; millions of antelope of all varieties, from the lordly eland to the tiny dick-dick, died of it; and vast numbers of domestic cattle were wiped out. Many native wars blazed up in its wake, and the resultant financial cloud continued for years to hang over the great colonial governments of Africa. Science eventually found a way of combating the disease, although strict quarantine is still the first and best line of defence.

At Bulawayo, we were a frontier community of a few thousands shut up in a wilderness five hundred miles from a railroad.

Our sole means of transportation was ox teams. A span of oxen in Africa is eighteen head. These are yoked two abreast and attached to a monster rope of rawhide, or in later years to an iron chain or steel cable fastened to the disselboom—a timber of hard wood corresponding to the tongue of an ordinary wagon. The African wagon is a huge affair with buck-rail bed eight feet wide by sixteen feet long and covered with tarpaulin well soaked in paraffin wax, or in the old days in beeswax and tallow, and thus made impervious to tropical storms. With more than ten tons of bone and sinew tugging on the trek-tow, those ponderous wagons delivered in Bulawayo most of our food, as well as every stick of timber, sheet of iron, and pane of glass used in that country. All the miscellaneous supplies required by an embryo nation had to be drawn slowly through the wilderness, across flooded rivers, and through the long rugged passes of the Matoppo Mountains. About five hundred of these carriers were required to supply the normal demands of the colonists.

Is it any wonder the officials of the country were filled with anxiety when runners came in day by day reporting the ravages of the plague? Whole spans of big, strong Dutch oxen dropped dead in the yokes, and their precious loads were left to be looted by hostiles. The scavenging hyenas and vultures could make no impression on the thousands of huge, swollen carcasses that blocked the roads for miles. More than eight thousand animals died in three weeks along our only line of supply—the road to Rail Head at Mafeking. Some of the last of this great line of wagons managed to reach Bulawayo with staggering, dying oxen, just before the native uprising. They were loaded with the precious Boer meal on which the whole town depended for food. The war began just at the time of year when the merchants' stocks were lowest, owing to the lack of grass that, apart from disease, determines the condition of the animals used in hauling. We had four thousand whites to feed, besides about two thousand friendly blacks—Cape boys and servants from the Colony mostly. To eke out the food supply, the cattle and oxen, though stricken with plague, were slaughtered and the diseased meat dried in the sun or salted in casks. Three thousand rotting carcasses lay around the town, and for weeks there was an unremitting stench, as we had no fuel with which to burn them. Hordes of armed savages were besieging us, and our men, exhausted by sorties at night and fighting patrols by day, could not be spared to go out and cover those carcasses with earth.

Nearly all the good horses, indispensable in Kafir wars, had been lost at the time of the Jameson Raid. Since it had not been the custom of the whites to carry arms, and if any one had them it was mainly for the purpose of killing game, there were few cartridges among the outside farmers and miners. In Bulawayo itself there were only three hundred and eighty rifles, and in the whole of Rhodesia not one sound fort. The old forts of 1890 had been abandoned and had fallen in decay. The natives surrounding us had thousands of guns. But, thank God, the settlers of Rhodesia were not made of the same stuff as the Little Englanders! Never for one moment did we think of abandoning the country.

From the Intelligence Department, now fairly well organized, the native commissioners, such as Taylor and Thomas, and experienced campaigners like Colonel Napier and Collenbrander, gained tolerably accurate knowledge of the situation in Rhodesia from the native point of view—and the news grew more and more ominous. It was learned that every night in their camps the black chiefs were eloquently haranguing their warriors and people, declaring that no real defeat of the Matabele had occurred since the M'Limo had been accepted as their oracle. The white man no longer swept over the country scattering the Matabele with the stars of heaven as he did during Lobengula's reign. The invincible Doctor Jameson had become a miserable prisoner, and the great Rhodes had left the country. All the police of Bulawayo had been captured by the Boers. The strong magic of the white man was certainly failing, for even though it had brought the cattle plague and the locusts to harass the natives, yet were not these curses,

RHODESIA'S DARKEST HOUR

intended for the blacks, now turning on the whites themselves? Were not their wagons stranded on the veldt and their oxen lying bloated and dead? Even the horses were so poor they could not gallop, for the locusts had eaten the grass, and there was drought besides. Was it not true that, from Manicaland to King Khama's country, all the whites were huddled in a few small towns with almost nothing to eat, and that every day many dead whites were being put in holes in the ground out near Government House? Did not the native women from Bulawayo report that the white women were crying in secret every time their men went out to fight? There was no longer any singing, dancing, or music in the towns, because the magic of the M'Limo was striking fear into the hearts of the whites. Soon they would hide their heads in the straw and squawk with terror like chickens. Then the hour would arrive for the blacks again to wet their spears in blood as they did in the good old days of M'Silikatze. The warriors were urged to be doctored by the M'Limo for immunity against the white man's bullets. They had been assured by their High Priest that, if they would but leave an open runway down Mangwe Pass, as if they were catching rats, many of the whites in Bulawayo would flee and those left behind would turn blind with fear and could be stabbed by the warriors when they rushed the town. They were repeatedly warned not to touch the white man's wire that ran through the Pass for this was indeed strong medicine and had been put there only to poison the natives.

As this information reached us from time to time, many means were planned to save the town. We recalled that, at the great fight at Rourke's Drift, in the Zulu war, the savages failed to take the drift because they foolishly set fire to several outlying houses, and under that blazing light, the deadly aim of the white defenders beat off the attack. So we prepared oil-soaked bundles of faggots and placed them on roofs where they could be fired as soon as the warning bell on the market building should ring out. Blasting gelatine was then laid in layers between boards, and these improvised mines carefully placed every night. By arranging rifles sighted on these mines and covered by sandbags, we could fire a mine at any time by inserting a loaded cartridge and pulling the trigger.

The wagons were drawn up in laager entirely surrounding the brick market building in the central square of the town. The wheels of the wagons were chained together, with a barricade of sandbags between the spokes, and the buck-sails were lined with sandbags. As a further protection, we gathered up all the empty bottles around the town, broke them, and threw the fragments in a mass several inches deep and about twenty feet wide in front of the wagons. Barbed wire was skilfully used to add to the defence. By day, all this fortification seemed quite brave and sufficient, but in the darkness of the night, when the fires of the enemy could be seen for six miles around the town, we who knew the acuteness of the situation felt in our hearts that our existence only depended on whether the Matabele should decide to rush us or not. Certain of us were given orders each night that in case a rush was made and the laager broken, we were to kill our own women and children and not let them fall into the hands of the savages.

Fortunately, the inner councils of the Matabele had not read the mind and heart of the white man aright. They believed that if we besieged and starved we would finally attempt to escape through Mangwe Pass, always left open to us by the M'Limo's orders. Once in that rocky defile, sixty miles long, they might indeed attack and destroy us, even as Cæsar destroyed the Helvetii in their fatal passes. Not one of us would ever reach Khamaland and the railway.

Desperate patrols to rescue settlers were sent out in all directions. These troops were badly mounted, poorly armed, short of rations, but led by men famous in colonial history. The only thing they possessed in abundance was daring. Often they arrived too late and found the settlers all killed. We discovered that spies of the Kafirs were buying ammunition from our servants, and some foreign traders were suspected of selling cartridges to the blacks.

One of the first bits of work assigned me by Colonel Napier

was to try to destroy the enemies' rifles—the Martini-Henry, a weapon using a bottle-necked shell and a .45 calibre bullet. The gun was constructed to withstand the force of black powder or even certain grades of cordite, but we figured that it would blow up if the shell were loaded with blasting gelatine, which contains eighty per cent. nitro-glycerine. Of this high explosive we had quite a supply, as it was used in gold mining, and we thought, by loading some of our own shells with this gelatine and distributing them among the enemy, we might put a good many of their guns out of commission. It would be futile to allow this deadly ammunition to be captured all in one place; it must be widely, secretly, and simultaneously placed to tempt a great number of our enemies.

I was ordered to make this distribution. First I chose an old cowboy named Tex Long and an American named Baxter, both familiar with dynamite and weapons, to aid me. We carefully pulled the lead from five hundred rounds of our precious rifle shells, removed the powder—leaving only enough to cause an explosion—filled up the space with gelatine, and then replaced the lead bullet. It was night before our task was finished, and by that time the fumes of the gelatine had given Baxter and Tex such severe headache and nausea that they could not sit their saddles.

During the day, I had gathered up from a Kafir camp bits of old belts, canvas, and calico, and in each I carefully tied up or inserted a few of our special brand of shells. This was done in exactly the same way that the natives usually carried their ammunition. My plan had been that at night Tex, Baxter, and I would slip into the camps of the hostiles along the M'Gusi River and drop here and there a belt or a little package tied in calico, so that the warrior finding it would not report to his chief but would immediately appropriate it for his own use. Our cartridges in Bulawayo had to be guarded with far more care than gold to keep enemy spies among our "friendly" natives from stealing them. But at the crucial moment here were Baxter and Tex too ill to stir.

Swinburne (the poet's grandson, and a very plucky young

fellow) offered to accompany me. We worked long and carefully, but Swinburne was handicapped by having to rely on a compass at night; so I had to use him chiefly as a base of supplies, hiding him in the bush in charge of the bulk of the ammunition while I made trip after trip into the enemy's lines with a few belts at a time. Fearing that daylight would catch us on foot in sight of the Matabele, we slipped back rapidly to Bulawayo by way of Cummings's farm, having disposed of only about two hundred rounds of ammunition. To be effective, the remaining three hundred rounds must be distributed at once. A force of seventeen men was quickly mounted, including such well-known fighters as Stewart, Ingram, Bain, Art Cummings, and the McMullens. We were to sacrifice to the cause one poor old horse already past riding. The plan was to load the glycerine cartridges on his back and ride in broad daylight in front of one of the enemy's big regiments, draw their fire, retreat, and leave our wounded or dead horse to fall into their hands. It sounded easy.

We rode away toward Colenbrander's farm, a few miles from Bulawayo, and soon could see the camp of the enemy. The Matabele watched us deploy to attack, but instead of rushing us at once, they sent out swift runners on either flank to surround us. Our horses, at best, were very weak and we might easily have been surrounded, but just as they were closing on us we got a chance to open fire. They answered as I had hoped they would and came at us with a rush, firing as they ran. I was very pleased to give the order for retreat, shooting our ammunition horse as I did so. We then galloped out of the fast-forming circle of hundreds of blacks and saw a big squad of warriors eagerly dividing up the ammunition from our abandoned horse.

Colenbrander told me later that the natives complained bitterly that their guns burst or jumped out of their hands after knocking them flat. Their induna accounted for it by saying that the white man's bullet entered their gun barrel just as theirs started out and the meeting of the bullets "killed the gun."

RHODESIA'S DARKEST HOUR

A few days later the battle of Colenbrander's Farm, famous in Rhodesian history, took place. Captain Grey, brother of England's Premier, who held the command, distinguished himself and so did many others. It was a day when Boer and Briton fought side by side.

Among all the memories of the treachery and cruelty of the natives, it is well to recall some of the redeeming traits and virtues that help to reconcile one to black humanity. One of our servants in Bulawayo was old Longwan, an ancient Zulu "boy" who had in his youth been a warrior and, though now old, was much feared by the natives, as he was of gigantic frame and could still throw an ox without help. When I was away on patrol or scouting inside the enemy lines at night, he always camped faithfully on the doormat with his great knobkerrie and an assegai sharpened to razor edge, to guard my wife, who, with the persistence of her sex, had soon persuaded the authorities to let her enter the besieged town.

Just after the first war, we had built a new house on the outskirts of Bulawayo. Among the articles of furniture to be moved from the old house to the new, a distance of about half a mile, was a very heavy table of native hardwood. Glancing from the window, my wife saw Longwan coming down the main street, stepping wide and high, with the table balanced on his head, its legs in air. Inside the legs of the table were jangling all the pots and pans of the kitchen, while running along behind, empty-handed, were two black boys who had been sent with Longwan to help him carry the table. As he put down his load, my wife said:

"Longwan, you have been drinking. Tell me this instant who sold you liquor."

(Sale of liquor to natives is illegal in Rhodesia.)

"No one, Missus. You leave fire-bottle on shelf, bottle-magic to curl hair. I drink him all.'

My wife expected to see Longwan drop dead, as he had drunk about half a pint of wood alcohol, but aside from stimulating him to an exhibition of his great strength, nothing happened.

After the loss of our little daughter Nada, not yet three years old, from the hardships of the siege, we moved again into a small brick shed near the centre of the town. There Longwan formally brought before my wife several infaans or youths who had at various times taken care of the child. For each of these youths he acted as interpreter and expressed in a most wonderfully poetic way why each one of them was individually grieved over Nada's death and how all felt deepest sympathy for my wife.

On the night when I rode away to Mangwe on my mission to capture or kill the M'Limo, Longwan, sensing that I was going on some very unusual mission and might never return, said to me earnestly: "Master, if the Matabele come to this house there will be many dead with me around the door."

CHAPTER XXIII

THE M'LIMO

ONE day in June, 1896, a young man came through the lines and knocked on the door of the small brick house we had dubbed the "Rat's Nest." He asked for the Chief of Scouts, as he had something to tell me.

On seeing my wife inside, he said shortly, "I prefer not to talk before women." I told him if it was anything concerning the war, he need have no fear, as my wife knew well the rules of the Intelligence Department of the army and that even her own brothers, who were all with the troops or on guard, would never learn from her what might pass between us.

Then he told me his name was Armstrong and that he was a Native Commissioner stationed at Mangwe, in the pass through the Matoppo Mountains. He said that a certain Zulu who had a Matabele wife had betrayed to him the location of the M'Limo's cave in the Matoppos. The reason for this treachery, he explained, was personal hatred of the M'Limo; for when the Zulu had neglected to pay tribute to the great high priest, the M'Limo in retaliation had bewitched the Zulu's family and killed them all. In spite of this, the Zulu had gone on to declare that he did not believe the magic of the M'Limo to be as strong as that of the whites, for he remembered vividly what had happened to his own people after their terrible war with the whites in Zululand. Armstrong had come to propose to me that we go together, find this cave and kill the M'Limo, and put an end to the source of all our troubles with the natives. His account, including the location of the cave, seemed so clear and definite that I considered it worth reporting to Headquarters. Armstrong demurred at this, fearing his plan might miscarry, but finally agreed that we should report together to Earl Grey, who was then Administrator.

Earl Grey gave us immediate audience and promptly decided that knowledge of the locality of the cave was of military value and required immediate action. He instructed us to

A SKETCH OF MAJOR BURNHAM

Made in June, 1896, during the Boer War by another scout, now Lt. Gen. Sir Robert Baden-Powell, K. C. V. O., K. C. B., who sent it to the authors for use in this book.

report directly to General Sir Frederick Carrington, the Commander of all our forces. The General called in his Chief of Staff, Baden-Powell, then a major. It was arranged that Baden-Powell, who was keen to go, should leave that very night with Armstrong and me, in command of the enterprise

THE M'LIMO

to capture or kill the M'Limo; but before we could start, news came in of important movements of the enemy near the Bembesi and Baden-Powell was ordered to that section instead.

General Carrington then gave his instructions to Armstrong and me and impressed upon us that we were not ordered on this enterprise, but that it was entirely a volunteer venture on our part. He had been in many Kafir wars and knew well the cunning of the natives, and he pointed out to Armstrong that his information might prove to be incorrect and only a trap to get us into the M'Limo's hands. His final words were, "Capture the M'Limo if you can. Kill him if you must. Do not let him escape."

There was small need for that last injunction. Constantly before my enraged vision rose the picture of my wife vainly holding to her breast our dying Nada.

I walked quickly home from Headquarters to tell my wife of the honour conferred on me by Grey and Carrington in allowing me to volunteer for such an important mission. There were not a few keen scouts and gallant officers who would have jumped at the chance. The door of our little shelter stood ajar. A small lamp cast a light on the features of my wife, sitting rigid and tearless beside a small box we used as a table. Her face told me that she had already reasoned the whole project out to the end. She had foreseen that the Military would be impressed by Armstrong's information, and that I would be sent to the M'Limo's cave. In her vision I was already dead; there was but one chance in a million for me. On questioning her, she admitted that her reason had indeed told her all this, and yet she declared she held an abiding faith in that millionth chance, and she did not ask me to renounce the venture. I strengthened her faith all I could by reminding her of the hundreds of times in the old wars when I had all the odds against me and yet managed to come through. I warned her that in about two days the usual dismal rumours would reach Bulawayo by the native underground, but urged her not to consider me lost before fully six days had elapsed. Then Longwan appeared at the door with my horse, and the moment of farewell, dreaded in all wars, was upon us.

The blackness into which I rode was no darker than the thoughts that ebbed and flowed through my mind during that night, as Armstrong and I silently turned our horses toward the Mangwe Pass. Many gruesome pictures of tragedies to settlers at the hands of the natives rose before me. The dark canvas stretched from the Mazoi to the Insesi, a district larger than a dozen of our states. And now, by a strange turn of fate, I was setting out in the hope that I might meet the artist who had inspired all those horrors. This thought made me immune to sleepiness, that dread foe of the scout, harder to combat than hunger or fatigue and is only less perilous than thirst, with its ultimate doom of insanity.

Riding cautiously over the only road left open through the lines of savages besieging Bulawayo, we reached Mangwe. There a handful of English and Boer settlers, bound for the north and left afoot by the death of all their oxen, had formed laager and put themselves under the command of Van Royen, a noted Boer trekker and hunter, and his son-in-law, Hans Lee, who had also been caught in the pass. Van Royen was a crafty scout and knew the natives well, yet he acknowledged it was baffling to him why some great impi did not destroy the laager and close the pass. He said the laager was under keen observation by the enemy every day; that the Makalakas, a slave tribe under the Matabele, who lived in the little glades and valleys of the mountains round about, constantly reported the moving back and forth of armed natives; but for some unknown reason they did not fire on the miserably mounted white patrols moving along the pass. He told us the telegraph line could easily be destroyed, as well as the stages still hauled through by their skinny mules, at any moment the leaders of the Matabele should give the order. Meantime, the whites in the laager could only sit tight and await developments. It was indeed a strange war, and the immunity of the stages could be accounted for only by the stories we had heard of the M'Limo's intention to leave this runway open so that he might eventually trap the whites and destroy them all in this defile, with the minimum of loss to the natives. This curious condition of things gave considerable freedom of movement to those in the laager, though no man knew when he rode forth whether he would ever return.

Armstrong had secretly arranged a rendezvous for us with his mysterious Zulu informant. By turning a rock in a certain way, he arranged a sign indicating the time and place for the meeting (a method of communication also in vogue among our American Indians). After the sign was set, we undertook the difficult task of a preliminary scout to locate the M'Limo's cave from the description given by the Zulu. There are many caves in the Matoppos; fortunately, the one we sought was not many miles distant from Mangwe. The country was full of trails among the rough granite kopjes and over mesas covered with high grass, thorn bush, and scrub. Here the Matabele kept large herds of goats which were a source of meat supply for their fighting men, now that most of their cattle were dead of plague. Their slaves, the Makalakas, stored in the mountains the Kafir corn and mealies that, with native beer, completed their ration.

Our first effort, made at night, failed to locate the cave. So at break of day we tried working along on foot, screening ourselves from observation with bunches of grass when in the grass and with branches when in the scrub. In this way we got a general idea of the mountain that held the fateful cave. It was a rough granite pile, perhaps a thousand feet high and three quarters of a mile in length. Over its dome-shaped mass great boulders lay scattered, many of them the size of an ordinary house. Bushes, scrub, and grass grew in every crevice where there was a handful of soil, though there were many masses of granite as devoid of vegetation as the Pyramids.

At last we found the entrance to the cave, about halfway up the mountain, in a mass of detached boulders among some scrub, and from it a zigzag path descended to the base of the mountain where there was a level space of hard-beaten clay used as a ceremonial dancing floor and wide enough to accommodate a thousand natives at one time. In front of this floor we saw about one hundred Zulu huts of a shape used for ceremonial purposes and not ordinary dwellings, for, unlike the Matabele and Mashona living huts, these were thatched with grass clear to the ground.

The prospect of ever gaining entrance to this cave unobserved appeared hopeless. Over the numerous trails were passing many goat herders and women carrying grain and supplies to the villages that lay farther on. At any moment, we might run into a party of fully armed warriors. Our method of procedure was for Armstrong to hold the horses well hidden in a clump of scrub or deep in the six-foot grass along the spruits while I worked out on foot a route for the next advance and another safe spot to hide the horses. When this was done, I would return to Armstrong and we would advance carefully, brushing out our horseshoe marks as they crossed the trail. In this way, we kept our mounts available for quick escape in case we should run into a band of warriors. We observed the boulders and the bush that marked the end of the zigzag trail, and we believed that by coming in from the southeast end of the mountain and covering ourselves with grass, we could then slip from boulder shadow to bush screen undetected. Favoured by a breeze that would make all things quiver slightly, we could even cross certain bare spots that were in full view of the village at the base of the hill.

Having ascertained so much, we returned to Mangwe and awaited with keen impatience the arrival of our Zulu informant. He duly appeared, having read the rock sign, and he then gave us the promised details of the M'Limo's plans. I may say here that Armstrong could extract more truth from a native than any man I ever knew, unless it was the great Johann Collenbrander, who went into the last hostile camp with Rhodes and helped to make an honourable peace with the Matabele that is unbroken to this day. Armstrong was only a boy at this time and was a character of most peculiar moods, but with boundless nerve and loyalty to the settlers' cause. He did Rhodesia a stupendous service by exploding the myth of the cave and destroying the M'Limo's power.

Our Zulu reported no suspicious changes in the programme that had been outlined. He told Armstrong much of the history of the M'Limo; some of it was new to us and some already known. He repeated the story that, at the beginning of the war, the M'Limo had promised that he would so doctor the warriors that the white men's bullets would turn to water, provided the plunder of the slaughtered whites were all brought to him. This was wise, as he knew well that the black man cannot resist loot; it is like a smokehouse with the door open. So, when some of the natives reported that his medicine was weak and that many of their number had been killed, the M'Limo would shrewdly exclaim, "Where is the man who kept the loot? Bring him to me!"

Then the M'Limo declared that more medicine must be made and a new regiment must be doctored and made immune to bullets. An ox must be skinned alive and the meat eaten raw, and a great ceremonial dance should take place in front of the cave where we had seen the huts. This regiment of warriors, the Zulu said, was already in camp close to the cave and there was to be a preliminary meeting in the afternoon of the next day when a number of Ring Kops (Matabele warriors and councillors) would be present for a special ceremony before the M'Limo's cave. This cave, we were told, was not the residence of the M'Limo but his temple, and the god would certainly strike dead any man except the M'Limo who should put his foot inside it.

Our Zulu now held us in the hollow of his hand. Was he a genuine enemy of the M'Limo, we asked ourselves, or a cunning spy sent to trap us, to prove the further potency of the black medicine? We decided to act upon his information. The following day, when the Ring Kops were to have their special meeting, we must be inside the cave, for to be certain of the identity of the M'Limo we must find the man who alone dared to enter the holy place.

We left Mangwe before dawn, following the route scouted

before and repeating our previous methods. We hid our horses in a clump of scrub and high grass as near the village below the cave as we dared. We tied their heads high and left no metal to clink or gleam on the saddle. From this cache, by utmost caution and favoured by the hoped-for breeze, we gradually worked along the side of the mountain to the cave above the zigzag path. Though often in plain sight except for our grass coverings, we were unnoticed by the numerous goat-herds or by the women who were preparing the huts for the feast to come, fetching quantities of native beer and filling the earthenware jars. After two hours spent in slowly working along the short distance from our cached horses, we managed to slip inside the great cave; moving at once into deep shadow, so as to see out clearly without being seen. Soon we would discover whether or not we had been duped. After watching for more than an hour, we saw the Ring Kops coming from the huts at the foot of the kopje, just as the Zulu had said they would. The path leading to the cave made several turns and at these turns were poles smoothed off to serve as seats. The Ring Kops stopped at these stations.

Then I saw with surprise that a man striding in advance of the others was not a Matabele at all, but a pure Makalaka, one of the ancient people of the country. He separated from the Ring Kops and kept on alone, moving higher and higher up the path to the cave; pausing at certain points along his ascent to make cabalistic signs and utter prayers, as if he were a high priest preparing to meet the god supposed to dwell inside the cave and for whom the great M'Limo acted as mouthpiece. We learned later that, when any one would speak at the entrance of this cave, those outside would hear a booming of the voice, faint at first as if at a distance, and then growing much louder. This echo or ventriloquial quality was used by the crafty M'Limo to awe the Matabele into deadly fear and the implicit belief that they heard indeed the very voice of their god.

Now I gazed fully upon the M'Limo as he was about to enter the cave. He was a strong, active man, perhaps sixty years old, with short cropped hair; rather sharp-featured for a Negro, and of a mahogany tint rather than the Nilotic black. His face was forceful, hard, cruel, and very wide between the eyes. He was not dressed in snake skins, charms, or any of the ordinary equipment of the witch doctor; neither did he have about him any article whatever of white manufacture.

Here was the author of all our woes. Because of him, my little daughter was dead and the bones of hundreds of brave men and good women were scattered on the veldt by hyenas. Carrington's command, "Capture him if you can; kill him if you must," rang in my ears. The moment had come for action; but after all, it was young Armstrong's skill that had located our arch-enemy, and I knew Armstrong intended never to ride back to Bulawayo until the M'Limo was dead.

I whispered, "Armstrong, this is your work. When he enters the cave, you kill him."

"No," he replied. "You do it."

So, as the M'Limo came in I made a slight sound and gave him his last chance to turn the white man's bullet to water. I put the bullet under his heart.

It would have been impossible to capture him alive, even if we had chosen, for we were almost within gunshot of a black regiment, and the country swarmed with armed natives. At the crack of my rifle, we sprang out of the cave, stepping over the M'Limo's body, and ran down the path toward the huts, the nearest way to our horses. There was no further need for secrecy in our movements.

The roaring echo of the shot within the cave, booming and bellowing after us, and the frightful apparition of two armed white men dashing out of the temple of their god were too much for the old Ring Kops. They sat for one instant frozen with terror at their stations and then fled. In their excuse, be it said, they were armed only with knobkerries, and the young herders who were helping the women prepare the dancing floor for the next day's ceremony had only their assegais. Our real danger was from the armed regiment in camp at the north end of the kopje, about half a mile away. Running toward our horses, I shouted to Armstrong to help me fire the huts. Pulling out a bundle of thatch and lighting it, we set fire right and left and sped on. The yelling of the natives having stirred up the fighting regiment, we circled around our horses, fearing an ambush, but found our mounts still concealed and undisturbed. Fortunately for us, the African native is far less observant than the American Indian.

Yet for two hours we were hotly pursued and had a long hard ride and a running fight over rough ground, until we were nearly exhausted, but the savages abandoned the chase after we had crossed the Shashani River. On looking back we saw a huge sheet of flame and volumes of black smoke rolling over the granite dome above the cave and knew our work was well done. We arrived at Mangwe at 6:30 P. M., caught the military wire, and sent our report in to Headquarters.

It is commonly supposed that, once a savage country is conquered, all troubles are ended. The spectacular and dramatic may be; but the silent, constant labour of the real administration of a new land is more like that of the chemist in his laboratory, experimenting with T. N. T. With the expensive military establishment cut to the last possible unit, the civil official must face the task of handling thousands and thousands of highly explosive savage human entities that lately were armed enemies. Adding to his difficulties, a new stream of his own and kindred races pours in to complicate matters. These are not subject to military control and are often of a type one is ashamed to acknowledge as belonging to the same blood. Then the problems of peace are often as heavy and exhausting as ever the strains of war. So it was in Africa when peace followed the downfall of the M'Limo.

CHAPTER XXIV

KLONDIKE

THE great strike of gold in the Klondike was really made by George Karmack in 1897. It was several months before the news escaped to the end of the nearest wire; then, within twenty-four hours, it was flashed to the frontiers of the world and thence passed swiftly by word of mouth to the remotest corners of the earth.

When the news reached us in Rhodesia, Ingram made the first jump, and thirty days later I followed with my two brothers-in-law, Judd and John Blick. It was not long before we found ourselves at Seattle, the great Pacific outfitting point for Alaska.

It seemed as if the world had been in the doldrums for a few years and needed just this shot in the arm to stir its sluggish blood. The grandsons of the Argonauts of 'forty-nine were now given a chance to find out whether the high spirit of adventure was still a ruling passion in their blood. The sons of those who wrested the silver hoard of a thousand million from the Rocky Mountain states had also an opportunity to prove their mettle. Adventurers from far and near joined the rush. Two things favoured this new Eldorado: It had been discovered under the flag of a friendly nation, and there were no savages to contend with. Yet to reach this Promised Land roused the fighting instincts of every searcher for its wealth.

I shall never forget the directions for reaching the Klondike offered by a veteran sour-dough to a group of wide-eyed cheechakos on the wharf at Seattle. They were substantially as follows:

"Yes, I went up the Yukon in 'eighty-four, with the Dick Schiefflin outfit and the little steamer *Boss Racket*. But now you can go quicker. You take passage on one of these floating coffins lying around this harbour. Put aboard her a thousand pounds of grub and a thousand pounds of outfit. If you're not wrecked on the coast, you'll be chucked off on the beach at Dyea—a little burg at the head of the big fjord they call the Lynn Canal, that cuts into the Alaska Mountains like a knife for ninety miles but is a tricky bit of water. Hurry your dunnage up on shore, for there is a twenty-foot tide here and the Almighty won't hold back the flood for you to make a dry crossing.

"Now, put on your sled a load of a hundred to two hundred pounds and haul it up to the foot of Chilkoot Pass, eight miles or more. Then form it into packs of fifty pounds, or more if you are strong; by hanging on to the rope and keeping the ice steps carefully chopped out, you can climb the last five hundred feet to the summit of Chilkoot. Establish your cache there and keep on packing and climbing until you have carried all your outfit to the top. If you haven't fallen off the glacier and broken your neck you will meet a Northwest Mounted Policeman there, but he'll be mounted only on Shanks's ponies. Don't be afraid of him—he is your best friend in all the Yukon. Give him your *true* name and address, so your folks at home will know which rapid you were drowned in.

"Now, you begin sledding your outfit down in instalments to the shores of Lake Linderman—or better, to Lake Bennett—miles away. When this little job is over, you will find yourself on the true headwaters of the Yukon. There will be many thousands of you there. You will have nothing much to do till spring, when the ice goes out. Of course, you will find a husky partner and you'll have to get up in the dark long before dawn; cook, eat, wash dishes, set the sour-dough, sharpen a saw, and then go out into the pine forest about a mile away. You'll cut down a pine tree, and roll the log over a pit that you've dug, and then you'll climb on top of it and pull one end of the six-foot saw while your partner pulls below. The saw must start at daybreak and not stop till dark, because the days are only a few hours long. The object of pulling the saw is to

KLONDIKE

saw out a board an inch thick and ten or twelve feet long and about a foot wide. Saw as many as you can, for it takes a lot of boards to build a boat that will carry two men and outfits down the Yukon to Dawson.

"In case you get tired of sawing, take a few days off and go over the White Pass to Skagway—forty-three miles—and pack over nails, rosin, tallow, oakum, augers, planes, and other tools, also several good ash oars, some canvas for a sail, and a couple of boat hooks and some poles.

"As the days lengthen, you can work longer hours until, by April, you can put in about sixteen hours, besides cooking and washing. When the first rush of ice leaves the lake, you can load your outfit on your wonderful craft and follow the ice down the lake. The first stretch will be Thirty Mile River—it's swift and full of big boulders. You'll see a lot of wrecks. Assuming you miss these boulders, you will now find yourself on Lake Tagish—a treacherous, windy lake. Some of you that fail to caulk the boat tight will be drowned here—but thousands will pass on. In Miles Cañon the waters will bow up like a barrel hoop and you will glide past its black walls on top of an arch of water. When you hear the roar of the White Horse Rapids, snug down everything, for you sure will get wet. If you are a tee-totaler you will swallow your Adam's apple, but if you are a drinker—swallow about four fingers. You'll need them. Assuming that you pass the White Horse and bail out the water successfully, you will now float idly and peacefully down the broad and mighty Yukon to Dawson—unless you get wrecked at Five Finger or Rink Rapids.

"Maybe you'll be in a hell of a hurry; if so, don't camp on the shore, but take turns steering in the middle of the stream while your partner cooks over a fire built on a box filled with sand, in the middle of the boat. This will be the most restful part of your summer in the Yukon, and when you arrive at Dawson you'll be ready for active prospecting and real work.

"Now you will pole or pack up the Klondike River and then up its many creeks or pups, carrying your pick, shovel, and gold pan. You will spend your time grub-testing, washing, and digging, and if by fall you have not taken the last steamer down the Yukon to go home to your wife's folks, you will probably have staked a five-hundred-foot claim on some pup. In that case, you buy of the Alaska Trading Company at Dawson a winter's grub supply, a dog team, and some shaft equipment; and you build a log cabin and again prepare to hunt the elusive nugget, which lies close to bed-rock under ten feet of frozen mud and ten to forty feet of frozen gravel. You thaw this by building a fire on it and then shovelling out the muck, and repeat till bed-rock is reached. The wood for your fire you haul by dog team off the near-by mountains. You scrape the pay dirt carefully off the bed-rock, and the following spring, when the snow melts, you shovel this dirt into sluice boxes, where the water washes away the gravel and leaves the gold—if any—lying behind the riffles."

One of the cheechakos said, "You don't talk like a boomer. Maybe you didn't find any gold."

But the sour-dough took a number of us over to the hotel and showed us in the safe five elk-skin pokes filled with gold dust whose total weight was a little over one hundred pounds. Such great weight in so small a space is hard to realize. A ton of gold, if melted into a solid ball, would be only fourteen inches in diameter, and would be worth, at U. S. standard, more than six hundred thousand dollars. After seeing this gold, it would have made no difference to some of us if there had been a hostile Indian behind every rock and a grizzly bear in every thicket.

Gold hunger, like land hunger, will move whole peoples. From every harbour on the coast, old craft were dragged forth and overhauled in a superficial way. Smugglers, tramp steamers, pleasure yachts, Indian canoes, and four pirate ships of the China Seas—all were used. They were loaded to the limit with passengers, and then, often poorly equipped as to sails and engines, turned northward along one of the wildest unlit shores in the world. Many were wrecked. One stream of prospectors came two thousand miles up the Yukon in boats; others crossed Canada from Edmonton with dog teams:

KLONDIKE

but the great rush was over the two passes, the White and the Chilkoot, both made famous by such writers as Service, London, Beach, Joaquin Miller, and others. The great North has had many volumes written about it by able writers, yet each of us who has gazed at its cold, silent, flaming banners carries in his own heart emotions that no written word can ever express.

Judd, John, and I did not quite agree with all the old sourdough told us. We intended to improve upon methods in the North just as we had done in the tropics. But in some ways we found the sour-dough was right. There were countless thousands going, many already gone, and more coming. By no possibility could there be enough gold claims to go around, though the Government of Canada limited each man to one claim of only five hundred feet. Therefore, the winners in this rush would surely be the swift.

We, being horsemen, took very little of our outfit over Chilkoot. Later, we joined with an experienced Oregon packer and chose the White Pass—though down its icy cliffs nearly three thousand horses and not a few men fell to a mangled death. Not only did we carry our outfits by pack train over the pass, but we carried also thin cedar boards with which to build a light boat along the lines of the best practice of Canada. We trusted to lightness and ease of handling in swift water rather than to strength.

In crossing the passes every means of transport was brought into play: oxen, horses, and even goats. Indians with their head-band method of packing were hired at fabulous prices. Large bets were made as to who could carry the greatest load a given distance. Many men bet on the Indians, but a husky young giant came along and carried the Indian's load and the Indian on top of it! Little Lucien Marc could have won money very fast here by betting he could carry a horse and rider, as he did for years at every performance in the circus. A green farmer boy from Iowa stood looking at a plough that some enthusiast had unloaded at Dyea; the bystanders got to bantering him about packing it in. The upshot was a big bet, but not liking the carrying rig his backers were putting on his shoulders, the youngster picked up the plough with one hand—it weighed a hundred and twenty-five pounds—and holding it high above his head, carried it the distance of the bet.

You had to be sure you were backing a champion of champions to lay a bet safely on anything or any one. If you got to boasting in Red McConnell's saloon in Dawson what a good man you were in the squared circle, Jack O'Boyle would promptly introduce you to Slavin, or Peter Jackson, or the terrible Ketchel would be glad to put on the gloves with you.

It was no place to flourish a gun or shoot out the lights. Those light-stepping, clean-shaven, unarmed young fellows sauntering through the dance halls and saloons were the famous Northwest Mounted Police and would have you in the hoosegow before you could say scat. You could do anything except destroy life or property. In those times, we seemed to live quietly under two commandments: Thou shalt not kill, and Thou shalt not steal. If you broke the former, you were sent by dog team and canoe thousands of miles to be hanged; and if you broke the latter, you were sent thousand of miles to prison. In either case, you started a power against you that was as silent as the Aurora and as relentless as the glaciers. Not one murderer escaped in those days—and gold lay in every tent and cabin and was carried in tons, unguarded, down the creeks. I saw eight tons put on one steamer going down the Yukon and only one policeman (of the Northwest Mounted) to guard it. Like Rhodesia, it was a land of the greatest personal liberty, yet the strictest observance of law.

Thousands of hardy men and hundreds of equally hardy women foregathered there from all nations of the white race —with a sprinkling from some others—and their superlative qualities were not confined to physical prowess. Among those who called on the editor of our favourite paper, the *Midnight Sun*, were many whose names were mentioned in the great journals of the world and whose books ran into many editions. Art and the drama sent a contingent that would do credit to any community; there were engineers of international reputation and military men of every nation, some of whom were to win distinction in the wars to come. Major Steel was then in command of the Government of the Yukon. A military observer for a great foreign power, on looking over the material there for forming an army, said, "With such men, even a poor general could win every battle."

With the approach of spring, avalanches roared off the mountains along the shores of Lake Bennett, and its twenty-five miles of ice became so slushy that dog teams could not travel and one outfit was drowned. This whole mass of ice might begin to move any hour. Thousands of us were ready, at the first clear water, to follow it through lakes, whirlpools, and river to Dawson, six hundred miles away.

One morning, I noticed a new camp had been made not more than a hundred yards from ours and nearer the lake. A broad-shouldered man standing by the tent seemed to have a familiar look to me. I stepped over—to find that the newcomer was Major Terry Laing, my old Rhodesian friend and respected opponent in many a hard stampede when we were hunting the elusive Oof Bird of Rhodesia or pegging out its pioneer farms. This broad-chested Highlander was of the famous Scottish regiment, the "Black Watch," and took great pride in beating a certain Yankee scout whenever possible; and I am sorry to say he quite often succeeded. There were a number of Rhodesians scattered along the lake, and many of them laughed to see the two of us amicably foregathering in this far nook of the world. Laing promptly challenged me again to a race, this time to Dawson.

He had come via Canada and had picked up on the way a man named Ferguson who was a splendid boatman and rough-water pilot. Like the Blicks and myself, they had a fine, light boat. In camp a few yards north of us was another Rhodesian named Andersen—a Scandinavian by birth and therefore a born sailor. With him was an American engineer named Coffey, a six-footer with muscles like whalebone. They had a good boat, but rather heavy. They offered to accompany us in the race, pacing us until we hit the smooth water when we could row and sail to a fast finish in our own light boat. This was to be a use-your-own-judgment, depart-at-your-peril-any-hour-you-choose race. If you started too soon, you would get in an ice jam and be wrecked, if not drowned.

We watched each other pretty closely for a start. About two o'clock in the morning I heard sounds of crunching ice in the lake and slipped out to look at Laing's camp. He was gone. I stirred up our two camps at once, and inside of an hour we were off, with acres of floating ice all around us. Just as we pushed off, Andersen said, "I tank we better put in these little poles"—a precaution remembered from experience of ice jams in his Norwegian home. We were soon in slush ice, and presently there was a solid jam in front of us. By using the poles on the ice as rollers, we were able to slide our boats along quickly on the surface, though every now and then a seemingly solid cake would dissolve in the water right under our feet, or break up in long slender needles with a tinkling sound like the ice in a mint julep glass in the good old days! Rolling and plunging and sliding and often dropping *plunk!* into the frigid water, by daylight we cleared Bennett.

Judd Blick, who was the best boatman in our craft, steered us through the terrible Thirty Mile River. Thousands of others were now following, and some boats manned by powerful oars and stout sails were passing us. Before us lay Lake Tagish, which had a fleet of its own that had been built during the winter. The day we entered the lake, all who had a sail set it, and if they had no regular sail, they hung up blankets or clothes to catch the breeze.

I recall there were two women on one boat who gained the lead over many of us by sewing their undergarments together and stretching them between two oars. In those days, such garments were voluminous and helped the boat quite a bit. Late in the afternoon, a sudden squall struck this mass of boats, and many persons were drowned We were nearly wrecked; Judd grasped the steering oar from my hand just in time to save us.

The main fleet was glad to camp that night at the foot of Lake Tagish, but we pulled straight on, and gradually, by steady rowing and use of sail, passed all the other boats and had the river to ourselves. But no Terry Laing was to be seen! We whizzed through Miles Cañon, halted to register at White Horse Rapids, jumped aboard again, and in a few moments, well drenched and half full of water, we bobbed into the pool below—and there on the bank were Laing and Ferguson. They were patching a big hole in their frail craft. Ferguson's skill had saved Laing and the boat, just as they were capsizing.

However, I knew Laing too well to rest easy just because he was behind me. Many times, in Africa, I had been awakened by the thud of his horse's hoofs and had jumped into the saddle in the darkness—and not always to win, at that. So, as we rushed along down this wonderful arctic stream, I was always listening for his paddle stroke to overtake us. Andersen's great skill and steady pulling, together with Coffey's giant strength, kept their heavy boat even with our light one, and with Laing behind us, we reserved the final dash for our little cedar until the beach of Dawson was in sight. We won the race by several hours.

I am not yet sure in my mind that Coffey and Andersen could not have beaten us. Andersen was a very wise chap and had reasons of his own for wanting to be one of the first to arrive at Dawson. He had slipped into Ottawa and obtained a concession from the Government for ten miles of Hunker Creek as a hydraulic claim, while the rest of us thought only of sluice boxes, Long Tom's cradles, and gold pans. He had the signed document in his pocket, and as it did not dispossess prior locators, he was naturally in haste to get it recorded at Dawson and therefore very glad to help us win our race against Terry Laing.

We had brought a single copy of the Seattle *Post-Intelligencer*, the favourite newspaper of the Northwest. Several thousand Dawsonites had not heard a word of the outside world for months. This copy was given to the Gold Commissioners, who read it aloud to the assembled crowds, even to the advertisements. Then a shrewd speculator got hold of it, hired a dance hall, and filled it that night at fifty cents per head, and the paper was read through several times before morning—when Laing arrived with more papers. The silence was broken!

Among the new arrivals that touched the shores next day were Jack London, Joaquin Miller, and Jack O'Boyle. Red McConnell and Swift Water Bill were already sour-doughs. Miss Marooney, whose name is woven into all the early rush days, arrived in one of the first boats and was initiated into the sour-dough fraternity about one minute after landing. As she stepped on shore under the eyes of the great crowd, this gallant young woman stood irresolute for a moment, then drew from her purse a silver dollar and, with a whimsical shouting laugh, cried, "This is my last dollar; I will throw it into the Yukon for luck!" She won all hearts in that moment, and before night one of the miners had staked her to a half interest in a mining claim and a hotel that became the financial and social centre of the region for years.

After we had helped Andersen and Coffey get some supplies up the Klondike River to their concession on Hunker, we struggled hard to obtain some claims for ourselves. We finally located three and bought a couple on French Hill, adjoining the discovery claim of Caribou Bill, a noted prospector in those days. From this claim, George Burke and I took one hundred pounds' weight of large nuggets to England—the first arrival there of the actual gold of the Klondike that was to pour its flood for so many years to come.

I showed this gold to my friend, Lord Gifford, who was the representative in London of Cecil Rhodes. He took me right over to the Rothschilds, whose offices, where so many things of grave import to the British Empire happened, were just across the little street called St. Swithin's Lane. There on a table the gold was displayed, and a plan was discussed to bring in water and hydraulic and dredge the entire stream bed and benches of all the bonanza creeks of the Klondike. The plan was not attractive to the bankers at that time, although it was afterward put in operation and is the main source to-day of all the gold taken in that country.

While Burke and I were carrying out this gold over the pass, news reached us that Soapy Smith's gang, of Skagway fame, had posted scouts on the lookout at Bennett to watch for gold arrivals. Two good friends and two owners of Eldorado Creek claims joined up with us to protect our holdings. We secured arms and placed two men well in advance and two in the rear, leaving the gold to be carried by the other two, turn about. But the very night we were to have been held up, Reed, heading the citizens of Skagway, killed Smith in a duel and himself received a mortal wound. Both men now lie in the little plot behind the town. The reign of Soapy Smith in that little seaport would make laughter for the millions if it were not for the very real tragedies with which it was darkened. Soapy's sardonic jokes, his generosity, wit, ferocity, and suavity are now all part of the Northern anthology.

Upon my return from my trip to London, I found the winter upon us. It was very necessary that I reach Dawson at once. John and Judd Blick were cleaning up the French Hill claims. They had built a cabin and their elder sister, Madge, having much the adventurous temperament of her brothers, had come up from Pasadena and joined them. My wife was only detained in Pasadena by the arrival of our second son, Bruce.

In Skagway, I purchased two splendid dogs, weighing a hundred pounds each, a light running sled and outfit, also a silk tent, fur robes, and food for both dogs and myself. The distance over the ice to our cabin on French Hill was six hundred miles, and most of the travelling had to be done in darkness, with a temperature of from 10 to 35 degrees below zero. Part of the way I had to break trail for the dogs, and, by keeping moccasins on their feet most of the time for the last three hundred miles, arrived with them in fine condition.

With all our haste, the clean-up took much more time than I had expected. Timber had to be hauled for fires to thaw the gravel and the fires burned, like those on the ghats of India, without ceasing. Labour was hard to get, and wages were fifteen dollars per day. It required rich ground to pay. Yet that wonderful winter in the Klondike has left many images in my memory that can never fade: the strange stillness of the air where one could carry a lighted kerosene lamp from cabin to cabin without a flicker and where the blue smoke from the cabins rose, vertical as a plumb-line, until it faded into the sky; the snow so dry and light that it would pile up inches high on twigs or telegraph wire, though the faintest breath or slightest jar would send it tumbling down; and the singing of the sled-runners and the tinkling of many bells floating up the cañons incredible distances in the still, clear air, as the dog teams passed endlessly to and fro. It took fifty thousand dogs to keep the camps of the Klondike going—half-blooded timber wolves, most of them, fierce and strong. After sleeping in that dry snow, the dogs would give themselves a good shake and no moisture would be left clinging to their thick coats; but in working them at very low temperatures, care had to be taken that they did not pant heavily, or the cold air, striking their lungs, would freeze them. The effect on the lung is practically the same as if they inhaled a breath of hot air from a blast furnace. Many a cheechako killed his dogs by not having in his mental kit this little item of knowledge.

We melted the gravels that had been frozen for millions of years and sometimes disturbed the tombs of ancient monsters whose ivory tusks were still white and solid. The mastodons, without taking thought, had hidden their graves more successfully than the Pharaohs of Egypt; but in the search for gold we uncovered them.

There were rumours of great quartz strikes on the Alaska coast, so, in 1899, I came out to Skagway, built a substantial house there, and sent for my family. We were joined by several women of our adventurous tribe; Judd Blick's wife going in to the Klondike while the rest stayed in Skagway with mine. I made numerous and arduous expeditions in and out along the rugged coast of Alaska and far inland. In the early winter, I taught my son Roderick, then thirteen years old, how to make torches of birch bark and how to camp and travel in the snows of the great mountains, to drive dogs and fashion moccasins. Finally, I sent him alone to blaze trails in the high mountains and forests. Seattle and Tacoma, my two big dogs, were first used; then the fierce half-wolves. Seattle had such a winning way with him that I pensioned him off the big sleds and gave him to my tender-hearted sister-in-law, who killed him with kindness by overfeeding in less than one year. In this she was abetted by her children. More robust Klondike dogs were killed in this way than by starvation, though some were flogged to death by irate cheechakos.

The Alaska interlude was now soon to end. Rumours of trouble in Africa had been reaching me from time to time. Major Terry Laing rushed out of the Klondike, headed for South Africa. He said to me, "You beat me to the Yukon, but I will beat you to the Boer War. It will come and all our friends will be in it." This was Laing's last race with me, and he won. It was also his last race with Death, who stopped him near Johannesburg by a Martini bullet in the heart.

I had already made my start when a cable reached me:

Lord Roberts appoints you on his personal staff as Chief of Scouts. If you accept, come at once quickest way possible.

At that message, all the gold of the Klondike was no more to me than to the frozen monsters whose tombs we had thawed to obtain it. Within an hour, I was on my way to Africa.

CHAPTER XXV

AN OPINION OF THE BOERS

IN THE latter part of the 19th Century, the Boer Republic occupied a large part of the world's attention. The two opposing forces were clearly typified by the personalities of the two great men who faced each other in South African affairs—Cecil John Rhodes and Paul Kruger.

Harsh, primitive, and as strong and deliberate as his own ox wagon, Kruger wished to preserve the trek from the Zambezi to the Cape exclusively for the Boer. He desired no growth of population that would prevent an allowance of a farm of 6,000 acres to each Boer family and he approved no education for the people beyond the ability of the elders to read the Bible. For himself, he was content to believe the earth was flat. His was the restricted vision of the peasant, but in many respects he was a great and powerful character and worthy of remembrance.

But the boundaries of Kruger's vision stopped with his own holdings. There he found facing him a giant, a man of his own race but of different breed, Cecil John Rhodes; schooled at Oxford in the highest culture, trained and informed by all that time and thought and experience could offer to the student, and spending his knowledge with genius toward great ends as only a superman can. Rhodes saw Africa as a vast unkempt field, calling to him to be cleared for the planting of those flowers of civilization that are cultivated and enjoyed by the whole white race—a vision far beyond the Boer's limited dream, for it has been well said that "while Kruger thought in Dutch farms, Rhodes thought in continents."

Those of us who know South Africa well can understand the charm of the wild, open, trekking existence that Kruger hoped

AN OPINION OF THE BOERS

to perpetuate. Once a taste for that life gets into a man's blood, it is hard to shake it off, and I, for one, would not willingly exchange it for the most magnificent residence to be found in the West End of London. The Boers felt that they had fought for and earned their country. When these men came from Holland they were small, short of stature, and blessed with the extreme tenacity, patience, and industry of their Northern forbears. They were proud, deeply religious, crafty, unscrupulous, corrupt in government. Their struggle for existence in this huge black continent, unsupported by the army or navy of a home country, makes one of the most romantic pages in history Two hundred years of open veldt life developed them into tall, self-reliant, big-boned men, fine horsemen and good shots, though at the expense of much of their original painstaking industry. Every inch of territory they gained was won against almost overwhelming odds—always some mere handful of men holding out against hordes of savages. Through all the struggle with fierce and warlike tribes, the Boer had at the same time to contend with the most ferocious wild beasts and with almost equally savage and antagonistic natural conditions. Then, as a climax to his difficulties, he found himself threatened by the invasion of another race, similar to his own in blood and tenacity of purpose, but far superior both in numbers and in wealth.

Much that has been written about the Boer has been false or misleading He has been depicted as a sort of nomad mongrel, part Dutch and part Negro, with the additional blood of any other nation that has happened to be in Africa during the last few hundred years. He has been accused of being uncleanly, treacherous, and of such negligible courage that a handful of trained European soldiers could easily defeat any number of Boers. Some ill-informed folk even supposed that a body of police would be sufficiently strong to upset the Boer's peculiar form of government. On the other hand, he has been represented as liberty-loving, patriotic, and red-blooded; willing at any time to die for his country. He has been painted as possessing all the virtues of childlike innocence in commercial and political affairs, and as the pathetic victim of a certain harsh and tyrannical empire, cruelly seeking to wrest from him his hard-won little republic. Phenomenal tales of the Boer's prowess at shooting, riding, hunting, and of his feats of prodigious strength and endurance were widely circulated immediately following the defeat of the first British regiments in the Boer War. Out of the mass of contradictory literature on this subject, it would be almost impossible to form a correct idea of the Boer; but as he has bulked so large in African affairs, I shall venture to add a little personal testimony from my contact with him for a number of years in various parts of Africa.

Many of the young Boers settled in the dorps or towns scattered through South Africa were graduates of colleges and law schools in Europe and differed in no marked way from the descendants of the early English settlers who have taken similar courses of study preparatory to similar occupations. I first came in contact with the typical farm Boer when on a hunting expedition north of the Limpopo River. I found that his ideas of frontiering corresponded very closely to those of the early Mormons of the Territory of Utah. Like the Mormons, the Boers possessed singular ability to make a living in hard, lonely, barren surroundings. Their principal reliance was on their stock. In the early days of the founding of the republic, the Boers moved their herds from section to section, and their subsistence depended on their skill in killing game and on growing here and there little patches of mealies or Kafir corn. Given a few rough tools, it was astonishing on what meagre resources these sturdy pioneers would develop a self-sustaining community. With an outfit so scanty that it would make a European mechanic throw up his hands in despair, the Boer would repair his wagon or, if necessary, build one outright from the raw wood of the forest. From hides, he made leather for his footwear, and his women-folk were quite competent to spin wool and weave it into cloth for the use of the entire family.

A little later, I spent a most interesting time with a number

AN OPINION OF THE BOERS

of Boer hunters. From them I learned a good deal of the peculiar kind of woodcraft that one must know in order to get along in Africa. They taught me all the spoors of the different kinds of game; their habits, their food, and their enemies; as well as all the things I was not to do in this new land. The "Don'ts" would take pages innumerable to jot down, but careful remembrance of them was often essential to survival. Some should never be forgotten, such as, "Don't mingle white blood with black." The shooting of the average Boer is more accurate than that of the average American frontiersman, though perhaps not so rapid. The Boer is taught to conserve his ammunition, to make careful estimate of the glaring sunshine of the open veldt, and to sight game and other objects that are the exact colour of the veldt over which he shoots. In warfare, this gives him a tremendous advantage over the unfortunate soldier who has never fired a shot from his rifle except at a black spot surrounded by a large white ring, set at a certain distance. I believe the Boers would make poor showing for accuracy at the national rifle ranges or at Bisley, yet their method and practice would be hard for a British marksman to surpass. Their targets were often such objects as a clod or a rock, the top of a bush, or an old skull lying on the veldt. For their sharpest contests they used empty bottles set up on an ant heap at from one hundred to two hundred yards. Another favourite target was an egg at one hundred yards, when every shot was either a hit or a miss. Such shooting as this, begun in boyhood and practised into manhood, made it possible for a hundred ordinary Boers to be more than a match for five times their number of ordinary soldiers such as are recruited in any European country or the United States.

Another great advantage to the Boer was his ability to move easily at night. This also had been constantly practised from youth. The country Boers of Africa are expert drivers of wagons hauled by oxen, mules, or horses. On account of the heat of the country, it is their custom to do nearly all freighting at night. Their food is cooked in the dark, their beds are laid down and put up in the dark, their oxen are inspanned in the dark; and they travel all night in all directions, from staat to staat, from farm to farm, and become so accustomed to moving about either in moonlight or darkness that they are bound to have an overwhelming advantage over any body of troops whose manœuvres can be made only by daylight. If a night march is ordered for practice, by the British, it generally consists of marching a solid column of men a set number of miles down some lane or well-beaten road in good weather. This is quite another matter from setting out across country in all kinds of weather and degrees of darkness. I have found that when night comes there is a wide difference between the procedure of the Boer, or the American Indian, or the American frontiersman, and that of the European soldier. These characteristics must all be reckoned with by the scout.

A third great advantage that the Boer has over men raised in cities is that he knows almost instinctively the utmost limits of endurance of whatever animal he may be using and can obtain from a given number of oxen or horses the maximum amount of labour and still have the animals in condition for further service. One of the heart-breaking experiences of the Boer War was to note the thousands and thousands of magnificent American mules brought into the country by the British but destroyed by ignorant and improper treatment, while the enemy were trekking all around us with far inferior stock.

The mistakes of the British Army have been thoroughly aired by many correspondents, both foreign and British, who took part in the South African War. A fair criticism will show that the Boer, in spite of his unusual ability as a marksman, the wonderful mobility of his commandos, and the long, tenacious resistance which he offered against overwhelming odds in numbers, was not free from the gravest military mistakes. While it is true that a nation in which every man carries a gun and is a brave fighter is bound to be a hard nation to defeat, yet the Boers lacked two qualities which might have made them as invincible as Cæsar's Tenth Legion. The Boer was never willing to sacrifice his personal property for the common good, neither would he instantly and implicitly obey the orders of his commanders. He was a shining example of the ultra-individualistic idea, which is both a fault and a virtue. In the early days of the war it was almost impossible for the Boer commander to exact obedience from his men. Every project of any importance had to be talked over and argued about at such length that the moment for its successful execution often passed. Not until near the close of the war did leaders like Del Ray, Botha, and De Wet, by the brilliancy of their tactics in eluding or defeating many British regiments, prove that the Boers had at last learned the soldier's vital lesson of obedience to orders. Their raids, attacks, marches, and counter-marches make a most interesting volume for the student of military history; showing, as they do, what damage a small body of men can inflict upon a great power when the minority are united, determined, and obedient, as well as thoroughly skilled in the use of the rifle and the management of the horse, as the men who fought under these leaders certainly were.

But by the time the Boer was roused to make a truly heroic defence of the remnants of his country, it was too late; for the railroads, towns, and supplies of his nation were already firmly in the hands of the enemy. The condition of affairs at the fall of Bloemfontein illustrates the lack of necessary discipline and self-sacrifice. Lord Roberts's army was marching on half or quarter rations, having lost one large commissary train of more than two hundred wagons when five hundred miles from the nearest base of supplies, Port Elizabeth. Although we had just captured General Cronje and his forty-five hundred men, there were still present in the country fully twenty-five thousand well-equipped and active Boers who, had they been trained in discipline, would have placed themselves promptly under the command of one of their ablest generals, and undoubtedly could have cut off our supplies at the station of De Aar, which was defended by only a few hundred men. It was not for lack of knowledge that this was not done, for De Wet and many others, through their numerous spies and scouts, knew almost to a man the British defenders of De Aar and all about the enormous and valuable stores that were held at this base. The failure of the Boers in this instance was simply because the orders sent out by their commanders for the concentration of the commandos were not obeyed. Each commando was intent upon saving some pet span of bullocks or pushing some little raid of its own, practically carrying out an independent campaign. Nor was the Boer of the dorp any more manageable than the Boer of the farm. The town Boers refused positively to obey orders to burn and destroy their stores and supplies in front of the advancing British Army.

When the town of Bloemfontein was surrendered to us, the Boers deliberately allowed some three hundred thousand pounds of their precious meal, stored in one mill, to fall into our hands. Instead of driving before us and out from our reach every horse, cow, sheep, and goat they possessed, they supinely allowed us to capture hundreds of heads of cattle, and a great many horses which we utilized at once as remounts. The officials in Bloemfontein even turned over to us all the shops and stores, which were immediately paid for at full price by the British, who used Bloemfontein itself as a base of equipment and recuperation before marching upon the next Boer town. Had the spirit of the Russians when they burned Moscow prevailed in the republics of Transvaal and Orange Free State at that time, or had the self-sacrifice vital to the salvation of any nation existed among the ranks of the Boers, we should have found nothing in Bloemfontein but a mass or smouldering ruins without one animal or one pound of food left in sight to cheer the foe. This would have stopped our advance into that country, and the presence of an active mobile enemy of twenty or thirty thousand men would have frustrated any small raiding parties, so that not a single head of beef could have been procured or a single remount captured. A retreat to De Aar would have been in order, and if this base had been seized by the Boers, a retreat to Port Elizabeth on the coast would have been almost inevitable. The war would have had to begin all over again.

Even after the fall of Bloemfontein, the Boers still seemed

slow and phlegmatic in thought. Having inherited both the strength and the weakness of their remote Dutch ancestors, they obstinately refused to learn this fundamental military lesson of sacrifice, which should have been seared into their brains by the fall of this one town. They allowed the same thing to happen when Kronstaat capitulated, and again on our capture of Pretoria and the other towns. There was no power of government among them strong enough to enforce this military law of removal or destruction of supplies necessary to the enemy. The result of this folly was that within six months from the time that Lord Roberts crossed the boundary of their territory, their capital and all their towns were in the full possession of the British. The Boers had failed to destroy even the railroad, except in a half-hearted fashion—by dynamiting portions of the right of way and the numerous steel bridges across the rivers. The foundations and piers were often left intact, and even many of the spans could be repaired and used again. Water tanks, telegraph lines, buildings, and even much rolling stock fell into our hands. Within a few days from the fall of Johannesburg, Sir Percy Girouard was delivering more than twenty trainloads per day to the army and civilian population. Slowly and steadily the British wrested from this people the last vestiges of their power. Their final surrender was inevitable, and the flag of the Transvaal was furled for ever.

The Boer is worthy of admiration for many qualities of value. He is a peculiar product of colonial Africa, and is probably destined to influence its history for all time to a very marked degree. The fact that his flag has been lowered and that his land is now an integral part of the British Empire is only a political incident, and for his ultimate good. The recent World War showed how important a part this new member of the Empire could play. Yet I would not wish to see my own country relying for security wholly upon such qualities as have made the Boer famous.

CHAPTER XXVI

PAARDEBERG AND MODDER RIVER

THOSE of us who knew Lord Roberts can never forget the change from gloom to confidence that came over all when he took command of the armies in South Africa. After forty-one years of service in India he had retired home to a well-earned rest. His son had ably represented him in the new war in South Africa, but had been killed in a gallant attack on the Tugela. A series of defeats to the British arms in Natal, and the failure of Methuen to relieve the garrisons beleaguered in Kimberley and Mafeking, led the responsible ministers in the Imperial Government to call upon the aged general to take active and supreme command. This was asking service and sacrifice from a soldier sixty-eight years old, who had just lost an only and greatly beloved son; yet, with splendid nerve, Lord Roberts accepted command of the defeated armies. Sparta at her best could not have produced a truer hero or a nobler example of valour than this gentle, soft-spoken little man of iron as he reviewed the troops on his wonderful Arab war horse, Valonel. All defeats were forgotten by the cheering ranks. The enthusiasm roused was like that inspired by the fiery Russian, Skobeleff, when on his great charger he swept along the wavering lines in the passes of the Balkans. Truly the Boer War was already won the day "Bobs" took command.

His first great action was the relief of Kimberley, accomplished by a force of nine thousand cavalry under General French. From my position on a ridge on the high veldt, I could see far away to the north faint flashes rising on the horizon from the besieged town. Our signal men could not read the message, so I was ordered to scout farther north beyond the Boer lines and try to jot down on a piece of paper the dots and dashes flung in code against the starlit sky. All night I lay upon the veldt between the hostile lines, able to do so little, yet burning to do my utmost; for inside that ring the Boers held our mighty Rhodes, their chief foe, yet really their truest friend, whom they were trying desperately to kill or capture. They had brought up a big Krupp hundred-pounder to shell the town to atoms. Meanwhile, inside the town with Rhodes was an American engineer named Le Brun, from the old Silver King mine of Arizona. Rhodes asked him if he had ever built a cannon. Le Brun replied, "Yes, once when I was a boy, to shoot firecrackers on the Fourth of July—to celebrate the time we licked the British!"

Rhodes smiled. "Well, build one now to celebrate the time you are to save the British. It must be as big as the Krupp that is bombarding us. Its range must exceed two miles."

In the great machine shops of the De Beers Mining Company there was some big steel shafting. This Le Brun bored, making a marvellous gun carrying a one-hundred-pound shell. The gun was christened "Long Cecil" and soon shot a lengthy message into the laager of the astonished Boers. Because they knew the British possessed no big guns and certainly could get none up country, the Boers had laid their siege lines just outside the range of the few seven-pounders that for months were the only British guns to bother them while they were slowly tearing the town to pieces with long-range Krupp fire. So out of their clear sky came a genuine thunderbolt when a brand-new one-hundred-pound shell feel into their laager! It surely raised havoc! Then occurred some of the fastest trekking ever done by the Boers. But the eccentric Goddess of Fortune gave the wheel a new turn, and a great Krupp shell picked out the exact square foot on which Le Brun was standing and landed there. In the twenty-six million feet of area under fire, on that particular square foot at that particular instant, the bursting shell and the engineer met. Some actuary can wear out a pencil figuring the odds against the Krupp shell being able to kill Le Brun in a city one mile square, but the fact remains, and the American was buried under the great gun he had built and which did so much to prevent the capture of Rhodes and Kimberley during the Boer War.

Not long after this, another prominent American engineer, Seymour, was killed by a random Boer shell fired at a bridgehead over a river, and still a third was killed at the fall of Johannesburg. Ordinarily, it takes a trainload of artillery ammunition to kill one man, but this average does not seem to hold true of American engineers. They seem dangerously attractive.

At this time the eyes of the Empire were focussed intently on a little town named Mafeking on the frontier five hundred miles to the north. Here the famous Baden-Powell was holding out month after month with a handful of police and volunteers against an overwhelming number of Boers under Snyman. This siege had resolved itself into a test struggle between the endurance of the British and the tenacity of the Boers. The surrender of this town and its popular commander would have been felt as a greater disaster than the loss of an army division in ordinary war. The relief of the siege led to nation-wide rejoicing.

At one time I had been under orders to act as scout for a strong column that was to be sent to Baden-Powell's relief, and it would have been a keen delight again to be under his command. But other things of greater importance prevented. Lord Roberts was throwing his coils around the wily General Cronje, who with four thousand five hundred Boers retreated down the Modder River, a crooked stream in the middle of an alluvial plain about two miles wide. By forced marches, General French hoped to close the gap in the circle Lord Roberts was throwing around the Boers. One afternoon the scouts of the advance guard cautiously crested a small hill. In front of us lay a plain several miles wide and almost surrounded by a crescent-shaped line of kopjes; both plain and kopjes were covered with tawny grass from a few inches to a foot high. Across this plain the Modder River wriggled like a huge brown snake, and along its left bank trekked in

PAARDEBERG AND MODDER RIVER 283

orderly disarray the entire Boer commando under Cronje. The hundreds of big canvas-covered wagons, each drawn by sixteen or eighteen oxen, were being rushed at a speed such as only the South African ox can show. The cruel pole whips in the hands of the drivers, more than thirty feet in length, were kept cracking on the flanks of the great beasts like rifle fire, while other mounted Boers rode alongside the trotting and galloping spans and with heavy hippo-hide sjamboks flogged the maddened and sweating oxen. Only a few miles more, and Cronje would be in a position in the hills to check the pursuing regiments by a strong rear-guard action and give his cattle a chance to outspan and feed while his weary troops rested. At first, it seemed impossible to overtake Cronje, as our own horses were showing the hard strain of the race, and our commissary wagons were miles and miles behind us. But even as we looked, we saw his advance wagons suddenly halt, and an immediate concentration of all forces took place on the banks of the Modder in the middle of the plain. It took sudden shape like a white cloud that grows from the blue on a summer day. We could see the screen of mounted men thrown in all directions and the heavy advance guard retreating on the central mass. This was all very puzzling to us, as Cronje did not seem to be forming laager. Soon, with our glasses, we observed squadrons of cavalry following this retreat of the advance guard and now the strange manœuvres of the Boers were suddenly made clear to us.

Lord Roberts, with his swift movements and their surprising results, looked a new kind of British general in the eyes of the Boers, and they now realized that they must take choice of position and fight, either in the low hills or on the great plain. According to the books on tactics, General Cronje should have taken his position in the hills and used the river only as a source of water supply and a barrier to the enemy; yet he chose neither the hills nor the plain, but in an incredibly short time buried his entire commando and nearly all his wagons and oxen in the bed of the crooked Modder, eroded to a depth of from ten to twenty feet and with many little side cañons running into the main river bed. These made excellent rifle pits and would permit the Boers to pour severe cross-fire on the British whenever they attacked.

When our forces came up, the hour of the artillerist seemed to have struck, for soon we had more than a hundred cannon in position. Our heaviest pieces were some naval guns sent by order of the Admiralty under Sir Percy Scott—one hundred-pounders, if I remember rightly. When the first fire opened, we found the Boers had failed to get all of their hundreds of wagons into the stream bed and some of their cattle were exposed on the level plain, along the fringe of willows bordering the stream. The fire of the British gunners was very accurate; every living thing on the plain was killed, and the Boer wagons were reduced to kindling wood. Into the river bed, by plunging fire, we threw much good ammunition, until it seemed that the stream must be choked with dead horses, cattle, and wounded Boers. Day and night it was drenched with fire—yet from the river bed came never a sound. We wondered how the Boers could stand such punishment and not surrender. The delay began to draw upon our resources of supply, for we now had a force of seventy thousand men to feed.

Lord Roberts was not willing to sacrifice men when time would bring Cronje's surrender. Yet the delay might cause disaster, should Botha and De Wet bring up a mobile army and break the ring of iron thrown around Cronje. It was now raining heavily and steadily every day, putting the supply trains in great peril. I was directed to find out the actual conditions inside the great Boer laager along the stream bed.

Reconnoitring within our own lines, I found that, owing to the storms, the river had swollen to twenty or twenty-five yards in width, with a depth of from six to ten feet. The water was red with mud, and many animals dead from starvation had been thrown into the stream by the Boers and were floated down from their laager. Besides these, there were the horses, mules, and oxen dead from exhaustion and wounds, thrown in from our own lines farther up the river. Recalling how a relative of mine, a scout in our Civil War, by sticking his head in a hollowed log had successfully floated by the Confederate batteries at Island Number Ten in the Mississippi River, I concluded that it would be possible for me to float down this little Modder River for two miles if I should put my head in an empty packing case, disguised by drawing over it a fresh green cowhide to make it appear like a floating carcass. I knew there would be no danger of crocodiles in this part of the stream, because of the bombardment. So I secured a green hide and a suitable box, put them in a mule cart, and taking along with me a trusty Cape boy, I made for the river within our own lines, where the experiment could be tried out. I found that, by cutting slits and holes in the hide, I could see out fairly well, but when I stood on the shore within a few feet of my device as it floated on the water in daylight, I came to the conclusion that some sharp-eyed Boer would be pretty sure to suspect that under that crinkled hide was something else than a dead cow; so I decided it would be wiser to drift through the Boer laager by night and make what observations I could. I slipped into the river above the Boer lines a little after dark. The Cape boy who helped me off was very much interested and, at the last moment, very much frightened. "Good-bye, Baas," he said. "I think dem Boers shoot you sure."

As I slipped into the stream, I found it was not cold, and by resting my arms on some cross-pieces in the box, my head was quite clear of the water. I had removed part of the sides and bottom of the box and had cut corresponding flaps in the green hide, but the silence and the darkness and the pull of the current gave me a queer feeling of falling down, down, as in a nightmare. At times it took all my courage to keep from diving under my unsavoury hood and swimming to shore. Fortunately, the current moved only about two and a half miles an hour, so there were no whirlpools. Before long I heard voices of Boers close beside me and occasionally caught a glimpse of their little flickering camp fires. At one point, I bumped against a partly submerged ox wagon, and at another came up against a muddy bar that gave me a sudden horror of quicksand and smothering. It was starlight, so time could be measured, but it seemed as if I drifted many miles. As a matter of fact, my Cape boy met me, as I had commanded him to do, below the Boer laager a little over two hours from the time I entered the water. I had drifted by all their pickets, as well as our own. At times I had seen the Boers cooking and eating within a few feet of me as I floated along.

The total result of the night's work made me downcast. The knowledge gained was of so little real value to Lord Roberts that it was not worth reporting. My friends, Colonel Hume and Colin McKenzie of the Intelligence Department, knew of my effort, but I had brought no answers to their questions, "Was the river bed full of dead horses, cattle, and wounded Boers?" "Were the Boers really starving?" "Would a determined attack be likely to bring the white flag or another repulse?" All I had seen, dimly in the darkness, were various groups of men. Had I not known Cronje's actual numbers, I would have reported not more than one thousand Boers in the laager, which would have been a totally misleading estimate. That night's work showed with what care a general must sift and discount the reports of his scouts. We found afterward that the Boers had dug far under the banks of the river and also had camped chiefly in the little short side-breaks or cañons. At night, my eyes, being near the level of the water, missed those camps entirely as I floated by. Our heavy artillery fire and all our sallies had resulted in only about fifty casualties to the Boers, so wonderfully had Cronje protected his men in their rabbit warren on the Modder River.

At last, after a heavy bombardment, the British decided to attack, as the Boers were believed to be greatly exhausted as well as to have suffered many casualties from our constant shell fire. To the Canadians—a splendid body of men under General Otter—and the famous regiment of Gordon Highlanders, was given the post of honour. The orders were to attack at eleven o'clock. Then the silence of the Boers was broken. The river bed woke up. A ragged fire leaped from every side cañon, and along the river bank, and over the flat

PAARDEBERG AND MODDER RIVER

plain, rose the peculiar, indescribable whine of the steel-jacketed bullet of the German Mauser rifle. In a short time, the Boers had crumpled up the first attack with hundreds of British casualties and demonstrated that the bombardment had not silenced their rifles.

The British troops re-formed under fire; the Highlanders resorted to volley fire and alternate advance. Again they were mowed down. The fight continued. All guns were in action. A great storm broke, and the thunder and lightning crashed and flashed as they can only in Africa. By the flashes, the stretcher bearers worked constantly, gathering the dead Highlanders who, when they fell, were laid out on the veldt by their companions face to the heavens and feet to the foe, thus carrying out the famous tradition that so shall their brave meet Death.

Just out of the zone of fire a trench was dug, where the dead, wrapped in their blankets, were quickly buried. Beside this great grave marched back and forth all night without pause the pipers of the Black Watch, skirling for their dead. The wild defiance and sadness of their notes pierced the roar of cannon, the rattle of rifles, and the crash of the storm.

The next morning I was standing near Lord Roberts when the wounded passed on their way to the field hospital, and for the first time I witnessed the salute of the Commander-in-Chief to the private, instead of the private to the Commander-in-Chief. Such a little thing may seem non-essential and outside the science of warfare, but I realized that an American was witnessing what Bismarck would call one of the "imponderables"—the sort of thing that has made the wheels of the British Empire go round for a thousand years.

This attack on Cronje at Paardeberg cost the British seventeen hundred casualties. The officers of the high command were wild with chagrin at its failure, and begged Lord Roberts to let them lead their troops into the river bed, cost what it might. The Boer, in his practical way, had discovered just what the Rhodesians found in the Matabele War when, under Maurice Gifford, they took position in a deep donga surrounded by a plain and so brought the flat trajectory of their rifles into most effective use. A rifle pit on the top of a hill is dangerous and ineffective; but one at its base, covering a level plain, can, if constructed for delivery of cross-fire, stop the charge of the bravest troops. After the Paardeberg fight, many changes were made in the tactics of both British and Boers.

It was known that Botha, the Commander-in-Chief of the Boers, was holding General Buller in Natal, yet making heroic efforts to send relief under De Wet to Cronje to break the iron ring in which the Boers were held. In making the supreme effort to capture Cronje, Lord Roberts had risked the destruction of his supplies at a station called De Aar. De Wet could attack either Lord Roberts or De Aar. Fortunately for the British, he chose the more gallant and romantic effort to relieve Cronje rather than by indirection to compel Lord Roberts to abandon his northern march as then planned.

While the bombardment on Cronje's laager was proceeding, a staff officer rode up to me and said, "There is a countryman of yours out on that point of rocks. He is an officer from your Military School of West Point."

So I galloped, on my diminutive Basuto pony, up to a natty officer riding a superb hunter sixteen hands high, which I learned he had imported for his own use from England. I found he was Captain Stephen Slocum, the United States Military Observer attached to Lord Roberts's staff. We discovered that as youngsters we had both campaigned against the Apaches in Arizona. Slocum was a remarkably keen observer. He had an uncanny instinct as to where there would be action, and, like old Melton Prior with his sketch pencil, he could always be found where the bullets flew thickest.

We had located a Boer commando in laager at two farmhouses southeast of Bloemfontein. I found that, half a mile away, about two hundred horses were being grazed at night in a rather damp vley where the grass was thick. Some of the horses were knee-haltered, and the whole herd was guarded by two young Boers who rode silently around them from time to time.

This seemed sufficient precaution, as the English pickets were fully fifteen miles away. After talking things over, Captain Slocum proposed to me that he and I should stampede these horses in regular Indian fashion. The horses were not very wild, and it was almost a certainty that I could slip into the herd and, with a nose-bag containing a little grain, lead two of them out a short distance, where I could tie securely to their tails a rawhide rope on which would be strung some empty tin cans—an excellent substitute for the old Apache rawhide rattles. A tin-canned horse, like a belled cat, will straightway seek his kind for sympathy, whereupon the hard-hearted herd will frantically stampede to avoid his distressed advances. For fear too much time would be spent in catching the Boer horses, Slocum suggested that we each take a lead horse and some old saddles and wrap the cans so as to make no sound; then, when we had our horses well into the herd, we could cut the cinch rope and set free the tin-can music. After the Boer horses began to stampede, it would be our job to keep them bunched and running as long as possible. If the country had been dry, we could conveniently have used a bundle of burning grass to increase the panic of the animals. It would then be the work of the mounted infantry massed at the nearest British outpost to make a dash on the Boer commando at the farmhouses and surround them before they could escape or get remounts. Lord Roberts listened to our Yankee scheme and had a good laugh, but as it did not fit into his general plan of campaign, we were not allowed to put it over.

Slocum helped me in many ways in my duties as scout and gave me a much-needed broadening of my comprehension of big military movements such as those Lord Roberts was carrying out. He foretold with uncanny accuracy military happenings of the future, and seemed to understand acutely the weakness of the Boers as well as the blundering carelessness of the British.

CHAPTER XXVII

THE PIETERSBURG FAILURE

LORD ROBERTS had been informed that a large force of Boers were gathering in Pietersburg. He ordered me to make every possible effort to enter this town and find out the exact number and disposition of the forces there and report to him immmediately.

A large part of the field of operations in South Africa was in a country very similar to the states just east of the Rocky Mountains—semi-arid yet crossed by dry stream beds that in season are swimming torrents. Between these streams are great mesas and rolling, treeless hills covered with scanty grass. Everywhere are scattered rugged buttes and deep cañons, called by the Boers kopjes and kloofs. The whole terrain is called the veldt. The high veldt is the country just described and the low or bush veldt is the forest and scrub region along the coast. Over the high veldt are dotted the towns and hamlets of the Transvaal and Orange Free State. On every meadow (vley) of size, or near every spring, called by courtesy a "fontein," is either a hamlet or a Boer farm, very similar in appearance to the ranches of Old California and marked by a clump of the Australian black wattle or blue gum trees. The whole country in the habitable part is crisscrossed by miles of barbed wire as in Texas and our own Southwest.

As I wished to get as close to Pietersburg as possible before night, I left Headquarters at Paardeberg about four in the afternoon. Usually about three miles of neutral ground intervened on these broad plains between the lines of the Boers and those of our own forces. Passing through our lines and out into this open space I saw only an occasional mounted Boer

General Sir Robert Baden-Powell, founder of the Boy Scouts. One of the few men of all time who have succeeded in establishing a world organization.

THE PIETERSBURG FAILURE

picket, so, by a little doubling, I managed to reach a point ten or twelve miles from our headquarters by nightfall. Inside a barbed-wire fence on a Boer farm I observed a stray horse, saddled and bridled, and thinking the animal might come in handy for a remount, I clipped the wire and moved slowly up to him. He proved to be very gentle, and I led him out of the enclosure and resumed the route to Pietersburg.

As it was now dark, I stopped occasionally to listen and take what bearings were possible. Moving over the veldt, I went down into a little depression where the blackness of the soil made the road totally invisible. Suddenly, out of the darkness shone a tiny spark that proved to be the lighted pipe of a Boer picket who threw up his gun almost in my face, shouting, "Hands up!"

I flung myself backward off my horse and hit the ground just as the Boer fired. Both horses wheeled and galloped back up the road. Two other pickets shot at the retreating animals while I lay perfectly still in the darkness within twenty feet of the Boers. They held a hurried consultation, and after listening a few moments and wondering audibly what had become of me—asking each other whether I had galloped away on a horse or was lying near them—they drew back toward Pietersburg. For some unknown reason, these three pickets were not mounted. Probably there was a farmhouse not far away where their horses had been fed and left for the night; otherwise, there would have been a fair chance of my catching the sound of horses or at least a faint odour of encampment.

I was now in the disgraceful position of being unhorsed and many miles from my own camp, as well as a long distance from Pietersburg. If I advanced to my destination, daylight would certainly find me in the town. Had I been familiar with the country, I might have gone to some farmhouse and perhaps acquired another gentle horse, as had been my good luck earlier in the evening. But as things were, there was hardly a possibility of my getting back with the information Lord Roberts needed. I discovered several dim roads and some barbed-wire fences, but I could hear nothing and find nothing that gave me any hope of securing a remount. If daylight should come upon me, the only thing I could do would be to lie still in some hollow throughout the whole day, to avoid being captured by one of the various Boer patrols beating back and forth all day long over this section between the British and Boer lines. Promptness was the essence of the value of the information required. I decided it would be wiser to return to Headquarters and admit my complete failure to accomplish the work as ordered, and this purpose I carried out.

It so happened that Lord Roberts had decided to wait for the arrival of some supplies before making the advance. He again ordered me to find out the numbers and disposition of the enemy at Pietersburg. This time I decided to take with me a black boy and to lead a spare horse. We followed closely my former tactics but changed the route somewhat. Leaving the road, we cut the barbed-wire fences and crossed some of the farms which were not far distant from Pietersburg. Just as we struck a poor road and were following along it slowly, a large farmhouse loomed up directly in front. Turning sharply to avoid the house, I rode straight into a tightly stretched barbed-wire fence of several strands. My mount, a high-bred mare from England, was not familiar with barbed wire and reared and plunged frantically. The saddle turned under her belly and threw me inside the fence, but fortunately free of the wire, except for a few slight scratches. The plunging of the horse and the singing of the wire within a few yards of the house roused the inmates, and from the little room inside and from blankets and beds out of doors about twenty or thirty Boers jumped out, calling to one another and deploying to right and left. Some of them came very near to me as I lay inside the barbed-wire fence. Meanwhile, my horse had rushed out into open ground and was circling around with the saddle still under her belly, kicking wildly and galloping close to some of the Boers and to the house, whence other Boers came running with guns in their hands. My black boy, with splendid presence of mind, dashed his own horse at high speed alongside my frenzied mare and, grasping

THE PIETERSBURG FAILURE

her loose bridle, raced off with her. The Boers kept shouting and calling to him in Dutch and Kafir, asking what in many thunders all the hubbub was about, who he was, and where he was going.

I climbed carefully through the barbed wire and wormed along on hands and knees, little expecting to find my animals or hear of my black boy again, when, to my astonishment, within two or three hundred yards of the house, my ear caught our prearranged signal. Answering it, I soon joined the Kafir where he had halted with the horses. I found the saddle still clinging to the belly of my mare, although both stirrups had been torn away and the equipment was generally much the worse for its entanglement in the barbed wire. I straightened the saddle and mounted, and we had gone half a mile when we ran into Boers—either some of those who had slipped out of the house after me or still another picket—who challenged us and fired a volley at us at about fifty yards. We turned and fled at top speed. After cutting two more fences, we were in what seemed to be free and open country, two or three miles away from the point where we had been attacked.

Our total progress toward our objective, Pietersburg, had been extremely slight. The fences had been numerous and, although we had used the utmost caution, our delays and accidents had come upon us so thick and fast that, as we saw by the stars, our time to reach Pietersburg and return was very limited. It was necessary to push on at any hazard and take the risk of putting our horses to a canter on the open road rather than to ride across country so obstructed by wire fences. In this way we had travelled another mile or so when we heard the barking of dogs and saw, looming up before us, Boer wagons on trek, with loose animals. To pass these without detection would be impossible, and again we were forced to return in the direction of our own camp.

I was much astonished and pleased with the behaviour of the black boy who was with me that night, and promised him that he should receive a handsome reward, and the gift of a good horse and saddle besides, for his splendid assistance in such a difficult situation. Then the extreme excitement of the night began to tell on him. He trembled from head to foot and was taken with violent nausea which lasted from fifteen to twenty minutes. Daylight found us still far from our camp, but as we had managed to cling to our horses, we did not feel any especial alarm and rode without mishap to Headquarters, ending our second vain attempt to reach Pietersburg.

It is always a most humiliating moment in the career of a scout when he is obliged to report to his commander and acknowledge that he has turned back from his objective and is defeated. In this instance, my whole scheme had resulted in utter failure. But Lord Roberts and the officers in command of the Intelligence Department were most considerate and passed no judgment except to say that I must try again.

The third night, I called for my good Kafir at his tent, but no inducement, not even the bribe of a handful of gold sovereigns, could persuade him to accompany me on another scout to reach Pietersburg. So, starting alone and earlier than before, I rode out into the debatable ground. After a while, a solitary horseman appeared, riding along almost parallel with me. He was mounted on a very nimble-footed horse and kept me in constant observation with a pair of glasses. This made me uneasy. His method was skilful and ominous, as he managed to keep drawing closer to me all the time. At a distance of about eight hundred yards, standing on a little knoll, the Boer turned his horse toward me and each of us viewed the other carefully through our field glasses. I could see every movement that he made, and he, likewise, could see mine. He carried a rifle slung over his shoulder, instead of the gun bucket generally used by the Boers to support their weapon, while mine was held across my saddle. Through my glasses I saw him unsling his rifle, and I wondered whether he intended to take a shot at me at such very long range from the back of his horse. But this was not his intention, for after a short pause he dismounted, and then I knew he intended to shoot at me with care. Thinking I had something more im-

THE PIETERSBURG FAILURE 295

portant to do than to stop and fight a single-handed duel in the open veldt that afternoon, I turned my horse and galloped swiftly in my intended direction—toward the north. As I turned, the Boer fired several shots at me, but at that distance there was no chance of their being effective. He then quickly remounted and made after me.

Seeing now that it was a case of attack and fight, and judging that his horse was swifter than my own, I glanced about to see if there was any possible advantage to be taken of the ground, and noticing a large ant heap on the slope of a little hill, I made use of it as cover. But quick as my movement was, his was equally so, for scarcely had I touched the ground before he lay flat on the veldt and I heard the ping of his bullets all around me. My horse, as well as myself, was partially protected by the ant heap. The Boer's horse was exposed, but he, lying flat on the veldt at a distance of probably four hundred yards, was invisible to me. I fired a couple of shots at the spot where I believed him to be. My horse flinched, and it dawned upon me that the Boer intended to slip a bullet into my mount and leave me afoot on the hills until he could get assistance and capture or kill me. I concluded it was better for me to dismount him and then gallop away. So, with considerable reluctance, I drew a bead on the fine horse he was holding by the extra thong the Boer always carries when fighting dismounted. At the third or fourth shot, I saw the horse rear and plunge and knew that the power of the Boer to follow me was ended. He sent several more shots at me, which were promptly answered. Then, slipping back to my horse, I mounted, giving him time for three more unanswered shots, one of which struck the ground between my horse's legs, one the ant heap, and the third went wild. A swift gallop soon put distance between us. The Boer and his stricken horse were left on the veldt alone.

Only a few more scattered Boers were sighted, and good time was made in the direction of Pietersburg. This third night's attempt bade fair to be successful. But just as the sun was perhaps half an hour high, three Boers, who evidently had me under observation, spread out and advanced toward me. Shots were exchanged with the leader, but as the other two were coming up on either flank at a distance of about a quarter of a mile, I knew it was a question of only a few minutes when I should be the centre of fire from three directions, with an extremely remote chance of ever reaching Pietersburg at all. It was now, until darkness should come to shield me, a matter of one long gallop, winding and twisting, seizing every advantage of the contour of the ground; a supreme test of endurance for all our horses. One Boer had a splendid animal that enabled him a number of times to ride within easy range, and we continually exchanged shots from our saddles. Probably none of my bullets came nearer to him than his did to me. Yet it was impossible to turn toward Pietersburg, where they would have been joined by other Boers and my end made certain. During this half hour I was forced back over most of the ground I had gained during the afternoon.

Darkness came at last; my enemies drew off, and I found myself with a tired horse many miles from Pietersburg. I rested my animal for half an hour and then tried another route into what seemed to be higher, rolling hills. The country here was quite free from barbed-wire fences. By making a circle far to the south, Pietersburg might be approached from a direction not so well guarded by Boer pickets. I must in some way shake off the persistent ill-luck that had beset me at every attempt to cross this wide plain. The turn to the south was far out of my course, and the faint gray light of morning found me miles away from Headquarters and the work unaccomplished. Under the circumstances, it would be wiser to abandon my horse, hide during the day, and make a certainty of getting into the town the following night to gather the desired information, trusting to luck to lay my hands on a Boer mount for my return run to Headquarters.

As I rode along slowly, just before dawn, I found a little donga well covered with bushes and grass, high enough to shelter me and to hide my horse as well. Believing this would be a favourable position and sufficiently near to

THE PIETERSBURG FAILURE

Pietersburg, I hid there, waiting for daybreak. There was a small hill on one side of me and along the donga to the south a few scattered bushes. A farmhouse loomed up about a mile away, on a commanding position overlooking my place of concealment. I tied my horse to the bushes so that he could do a little grazing and taking the billy from the saddle, made coffee in it at a carefully hidden fire. That, together with the condensed rations carried in my pockets, made a substantial meal. Creeping to the edge of the donga, I was able to view the country in all directions and concluded it was a rather favourable place to lie hidden during the day. Everything seemed quiet and deserted at the house and there were neither Kafirs nor stock in sight in the neighbourhood. Slipping up the donga fifty or sixty yards from my horse, I secreted myself carefully in the grass and took some much-needed sleep, to be fresh for the night's work.

I was roused, after about four hours, by the sound of voices not more than fifty yards distant. Screening my face with a bunch of grass, I rose slowly from my bed. I saw four Boer wagons loaded with meal and general camp equipment, followed by a commando of about forty mounted Boers. For some reason, they were not driving along the regular road, but were passing between my position and the little hill just mentioned. I thought they would surely discover my horse, and if so, they were likely to make a shrewd guess from the looks of him that the saddle and equipment and the rider as well were close at hand. But although they passed the point where my horse could easily have been seen, they did not notice him. Marching steadily on to the farmhouse, they went into laager, putting some Kafirs in charge of their animals. I held them under observation.

All went well unto two o'clock in the afternoon, when two small Kafir boys left the herd of stock and came down to my donga to play and hunt birds' nests. Several times they passed within a few feet of me. Finally, one of them spied my horse; they held a consultation and seemed very suspicious, but they did not untie the animal or even make any effort to hunt up the saddle or the owner. Soon, however, they started at a jog trot back toward the farmhouse and I knew it would be only a few minutes before some of the mounted Boers would come to investigate. There was nothing to do now but to saddle as quickly as possible and trust to getting a good distance away before they should start to follow, when they could force me to make a daylight ride toward our own lines to escape being run down. To my relief, although some of the enemy came out of the house and watched me galloping away, none pursued me. After clearing their neighbourhood, I rode quietly in the direction of our headquarters, roughly retracing my route. At one time it seemed as if an old abandoned farmhouse might afford shelter from detection until darkness, so I dismounted. Almost immediately, several Boers came into view, driving cattle across a ridge not far from me, and one of them rode directly toward the farmhouse, so again my horse had to be turned toward British Headquarters.

Riding over the crest of a little knoll, I dropped down upon a Boer who, with two mounted natives, was travelling ahead of me in the same direction I was taking. Evidently thinking I must be a countryman, since I was coming from the direction of Pietersburg, this Boer drew up his horse for me to overtake him. As I did not do so, but swerved off to the right, he watched me intently for some time, and then, becoming suspicious, sent one of his Kafirs galloping toward me with orders for me to come at once and report to him as to my identity. Seeing that the black was unarmed, I allowed him to ride pretty close. I turned my hat brim down so he could not tell whether I was Boer or British until within a few yards of me, and I held my rifle well hidden by the side of my horse. When the black was quite near me, I covered him and commanded him to ride along in the same direction I was taking and neither to look back nor pay attention to any summons from his master. The black was greatly frightened. I told him that if he signalled his master, he would be shot; that he must ride along with me quietly while I talked with him. He tried to lag behind, but on my raising my gun he quickly obeyed and we cantered steadily along without undue haste.

He told me that the man he had just left was his baas—one of the Boer commanders, named Danny Theron; that the commando I had seen taking possession of the farmhouse was Theron's famous scouts, and that De Wet must be near by. I knew of Danny Theron. He was, without doubt, one of the finest scouts the Boer nation produced. He repeatedly entered our lines and obtained most valuable information. Again and again he cut off our scouts and patrols, raided our stock, and did all manner of splendid military service for his people. I learned later that it was Theron who gave me a tremendous run for my life and about the closest rifle duel it was ever my chance to be engaged in, which I have already recounted. I was sincerely sorry that he was killed before the war closed. It would have been a pleasure to swap yarns with him after the hostilities—more so than with any other Boer. In this particular instance, Theron watched the native galloping away with me and could not see that he was riding with the muzzle of my gun as the impelling force. He must have thought it one of the vagaries of the Kafir, who had met another Dutchman and for some reason or other rode along with him. I kept the Kafir with me for about an hour of steady riding, and then ordered him to leave me. It was useless to keep him, as I had extracted all the information he could give me, and at any moment I might need to gallop at utmost speed toward my own lines.

Mental depression and physical exhaustion seized me at this time. Three attempts to reach the town of Pietersburg had ended ignominiously, when such a performance was ordinarily one of the simplest duties of a scout. Baffled, harassed, and defeated, I hated to return to Headquarters a third time with no information of the slightest value to my Commander-in-Chief. There are times when a feeling of weakness and depression will so benumb the senses that even strong eyesight and keen hearing will fail, and the most obvious signs on the road will be passed unobserved. My mind, wearily revolving the dismal picture of my reappearance at Headquarters with the admission of another defeat, had allowed my eyes to rest continuously on the ground in front of me for some time. Glancing up, there appeared within two hundred yards of me a well-travelled road along which were marching a number of Boers driving before them a few head of loose cattle and some mares. I had been riding obliquely toward them. They had seen me, but paid no particular attention to me.

It seemed very improbable that I should escape this troop if they once suspected that I was other than a Boer. The only thing to do was not to arouse their suspicion by turning aside from my course. It occurred to me that if I pretended to have suddenly lost a valuable spoor and kept slowly turning my horse round and working back on my own tracks, halting every moment or two, they would conclude that I must be trailing a lost saddle horse and might allow me to pass unchallenged. One man did wave his hat to me, shouting something that was not understood and would not have been understood by me at any price. I continued steadily on, weaving back and forth after my supposedly lost spoor. The Boers who were driving the stock were dust-covered, no doubt from a hard march, and were not inclined to come over to investigate the doings of a solitary and extremely impolite and unsociable countryman who refused to answer a salutation. I could imagine them muttering that they did not give a damn whether he found his lost horse or not. Within the next fifteen minutes, my lost spoor had been followed a sufficient distance to allow me to sit up straight in my saddle and give a little attention to what was going on around me. It was high time for me to return to Headquarters or else prepare to become a free boarder in the prison at Pretoria, or food for the vultures on the veldt. Resolved to face for the third time the unpalatable acknowledgment of defeat, I rode with a heavy heart into Headquarters.

The only satisfaction I ever had to compensate me for these vain attempts was when, after the fall of Pretoria, the head of the Intelligence Department informed me that, of all the efforts made by scouts in different divisions of the British Army to obtain this special information for Lord Roberts, not a man had been successful. It is one of the fortunes of war that sometimes the thing that seems easiest to accomplish proves to be beset with insurmountable difficulties. Here was a little Boer town within twenty-five miles of our headquarters, and only rolling prairie, a few dongas, and scattered farmhouses, lay between. Under ordinary circumstances, a commander-in-chief could have obtained positive information regarding that town inside the first twelve hours of darkness following his order to scout. In fact, not only was I turned back on three separate occasions, but a dozen other independent efforts by skilled men were equally unsuccessful.

At other times, problems that seemed impossible to solve reached a rapid and happy solution; even when the enemy pickets were known to be lying silently behind their guns, waiting without the slightest move, sign, or challenge until the foe should come close enough to be killed without fail; and with videttes, constantly alert, posted behind this vanguard of silent pickets. In spite of all these things, a well-trained scout was often able to obtain valuable information—provided skill was aided by good fortune. To overcome the keen wits of hundreds of able men alert to prevent the acquisition of just the particular knowledge which the scout is after, is the joy of the game and compensates for days and nights of strenuous effort and physical hardship. The scout must work where there is no cheering regiment or the eye of the commander upon him. He must find within his own mind the vision to spur him on. The darkness of night is his best friend, for it will hide his secret movements—although it is at night that physical exhaustion is most apt to breed the cowardice that comes creeping into the bones of every man at times. It is then that the supreme effort must be made to overcome fear and force one's self relentlessly to gain the information so vital to his commander.

CHAPTER XXVIII

CATTLE LIFTING NEAR BRAKPAN

NOT long after the battle of Paardeberg, Lord Roberts ordered me to find out the exact position and strength of a large Boer laager said to be encamped at a place called Brakpan, to the north of our position at Paardeberg.

Taking a Cape black with me, I reached our extreme outposts just at dusk and struck across country in the direction of Bloemfontein. Night came on and the veldt was rough. We were obliged to use our wire nippers to cut the fences as we progressed, owing to the danger of pickets. About two o'clock in the morning, I scented the faint odour of burning embers and discovered that we were close to Brakpan. Dismounting, I left the horses with the Negro well hidden in a little hollow, and creeping along, found myself on the edge of the Boer laager. Evidently the Boers considered themselves far enough from the British to disregard the necessity for pickets, and there was only one man posted on the main road from Kimberley and a second on the road toward Bloemfontein. It was evident that the Boers had just reached the place after a hard trek. They were lying around their wagons in large numbers and looked extremely tired and worn. At no fire did I see a soul awake. Circling around from wagon to wagon, I made estimates of the size of their camp; the number of sleeping human figures, and of horses and loose cattle grazing on the north side of the laager; and lastly of the herd of knee-haltered horses guarded by two young Boers who sat drowsing on their saddles, only moving slowly around now and then to turn back the heads of straying animals toward the centre of the herd.

By three o'clock, the mist had lifted slightly and a few stars were showing. I returned to the place where I had first en-

CATTLE LIFTING NEAR BRAKPAN   303

tered the laager. There was a splendid span of sixteen oxen lying tied to the trek-tow of their wagon, so gentle that they allowed me to walk close by them. Under the hind wheels of the wagon three Boers were snoring heavily. The happy thought occurred to me that it would be a good thing to transfer this fine span to our headquarters' staff mess wagon. Their oxen were exhausted and fresh ones would surely be welcome. I cautiously examined the faces of the drivers and found one to be that of a heavily bearded old man who carried no arms. The other two were young men whose rifles rested against the spokes of the wheels. I lifted their guns noiselessly and laid them on the ground to one side as deftly as if playing jackstraws and began to cut the rawhide rims that tied the oxen to the trek-tow. The animals by this time began to stand up. I drove them gently out toward the south, taking along with them from the last wagon as I passed two milch cows that I thought would make a pleasant addition to the officers' mess at Headquarters—provided I should succeed in passing the lines of the Boer pickets lying between us and Dreifontein. I regained my black boy, who was guarding our horses about half a mile from the laager, and with his assistance drove the stock rapidly toward the British outposts. I thought of Vasquez, the bandit hero of California, and of his one-time prophecy as to my own latent talents for banditry.

The mist thickened again and hung heavily over the lowlands; it was still dark, and we were not able to retrace exactly the route by which we had come. Suddenly, our lead animals ran into a Boer picket of several men, who could easily tell by the sound of the oxen's feet that they were being driven, not simply grazing across country as free animals do. Quietly the pickets spread, fanlike, to find out who was driving the stock, and I saw the crouching forms of several Boers just in time, as they were endeavouring to discern our figures against the skyline. By dismounting instantly and taking our horses by the bits and turning diagonally, we escaped betraying ourselves by being silhouetted against the sky. Now it looked as if we must lose our precious loot, and for a short time we did abandon the cattle. Taking the tin billy from the saddle and using it as a sounder on the ground, I could hear their footsteps still moving in the direction in which we had headed them. Evidently, they were not being rounded up by the pickets after all. Either the Boers had become suspicious and had shifted their ground, or else they had concluded that it was merely some Kafir stealing a bunch of stock—at this stage of the war a common occurrence.

By slipping along gently on foot and quietly urging the cattle in the proper direction, we soon had the satisfaction of clearing the neighbourhood of these pickets and had no further difficulty until we reached the British lines. Our method of picketing was entirely different from that of the Boers. Our men marched back and forth until they met the opposite picket, and any one making good use of his ears could hear them for a long distance, sometimes as much as half a mile. The Boer method was to observe the skyline; two men lying side by side and one watching while the other slept. As we approached the first line of our pickets, we left our horses in a little donga and drove the cattle slowly, letting them spread out fan-wise. Softly throwing rocks and pebbles at them, we kept the cattle moving and headed toward the British lines. The animal first to arrive at a point about fifty yards from one of the pickets received a most peremptory challenge to "Halt!" A moment later, two or three men down the line were also sternly challenging the supposed enemy. They mistook the clumsy tread of the oxen for an advancing Boer commando. To add to the confusion, one of the stones we threw to urge on the animals happened to miss the ox at which it was aimed and struck the foot of a soldier. Thoroughly convinced by this fact that it was a hostile attack, the picket fired. This alarmed the others to the right and left and they also fired. A moment later they realized that it was merely some cattle moving across the veldt, but it was too late, for already the guard had turned out. The Kafir who was with me fired off his gun, for no reason whatever. As this shot was in the direction from which the enemy would be supposed to come, it instantly drew the fire of half-a-dozen pickets and a rush for reinforcements. But by now the cattle had made their way through the line. I got my Kafir in hand, and we retreated to a point about half a mile away, and then, by the simple stratagem of dismounting and slowly grazing our horses along, we succeeded in getting through the British lines and brought in our prize successfully—the span of oxen to haul our commissary wagon and the two milch cows to contribute to the comfort of the headquarters' staff.

I reported my information, which proved very satisfactory, and then enjoyed an hour and a half of good sleep preparatory to starting on the next day's march. Just before marching orders were given, I was informed the Commander-in-Chief wanted me. Pleasant visions flashed through my mind of new and more important trusts. Instead of which I received a cold statement that the information was valuable but my work was very unsatisfactory. That I was trusted to gain information of importance; that I hazarded this mission by wasting time and taking chances to recover stock and by harrying the guards for no purpose except to prove my ability to do so. That if I was useful to the army, I was too useful to act as a small raider, even if I should always be successful. I was told that I was not to kill the Boer sentries even if I found it possible, nor engage in desultory fire with their scouts, along with much more that did not contribute in the slightest to my vanity. My feeling of elation over my feat came to a sudden end.

As I came out from the tent, the only ray of hope visible in my darkened sky was that Lord Roberts would not waste five minutes of his valuable life on what was really a reprimand unless he secretly believed there was a possibility of quick reform in my conception of duty and trust. From that time on, no more pranks were played that could remotely jeopardize information needed by my Commander-in-Chief.

On another occasion, we were very close to the outposts of the enemy, with a small river called the Rhinoster between us. It was extremely desirable to find out the disposition of the enemy's batteries, as a fight in the morning was almost a certainty. The drifts (or fords) of this river, several in number, lay between deep pools of water about half a mile long reported to be swarming with crocodiles. The importance of the mission was fully impressed upon me. The best native scouts had been selected to cross the drifts at night, and during the six attempts made, five scouts were killed by the silent Boer pickets posted at the drifts.

My success hung solely upon the fact that I decided to swim one of the deepest pools, first taking the precaution to beat the water with a stick, as the crocodile, like the hyena, is not only ferocious but cowardly. The shore at that point was unguarded by pickets, the Boers trusting to the deep water and the crocodiles to protect their lines from entry by scouts. Creeping carefully up the bank, I entered the Boer lines and gained the information needed, locating exactly the enemy artillery. After reswimming the river that night, I reached the British lines held by the Canadian contingent commanded by Major Beaver, from whom I received much-needed assistance and food, as well as the latest reliable intelligence, after my own report had been forwarded to Headquarters.

I then pushed on to the north by a detour and found that the commandos of the Boers, with their heaviest supplies, were in rapid retreat. Their best mounted men were moving to the rear and evidently preparing for a determined stand against the pursuit of Lord Roberts's oncoming army. After meeting many difficulties during the night I found myself at break of day still close to a retreating body of the enemy who, by their movements, gave every indication that the British were following rapidly and that a battle was imminent.

Seeing some huts on a little eminence I went up to them and found only an old Kafir woman. As soon as she realized that I was not a Boer she fell into a terrible stew for fear she would be accused of harbouring an enemy. She was quite sure the Boers would punish her by burning her hut and eating up the last goat and chicken she possessed. So strongly did she urge my immediate departure that I feared if I remained she would betray me to the first Boer who came along, but as I was convinced it was only her dread of personal loss that moved her,

I gave her two gold sovereigns to compensate for any injury the Boers might inflict upon her. This comforted and quieted her and we entered one of the storage huts together. She placed before me a small bowl of goat's milk and went out, fastening the door in Kafir fashion from the outside. It was very hot, and as I could hear the guns of both British and Boers firing rapidly, I poked little holes with a sharpened stick through the dirt walls of the hut, which gave me some air and enabled me to look out on the Zand River fight from an excellent point of vantage. The whole scene of action was spread like a panorama before me. With large gently rolling hills crossed by dry dongas, the country was treeless except for willows lightly bordering the Zand.

By about ten o'clock, some of the Boers began to retreat, and the hill where my hut was perched was selected for temporary headquarters by one of the principal commandos. Several Boers rode up to the hut and dismounted, making the old Kafir woman and one of her children fetch water from the spring and kill and roast goat meat for them. One of the generals and his son sat for some time just outside my hut. They were using a field glass and I could hear them making comments upon the advancing British. They were plainly astounded that the continuous march of the enemy had never ceased since daylight and that, as far away as they could see, the British Army still kept coming. One old Boer officer expressed his firm belief that it would be impossible for his forces to hold this position and that they must all retreat that night. Then another Boer commandant rode up, very dusty and travel-stained, and as it was now exceedingly hot, ordered the Kafir woman to take down the door of the hut in which I was hiding, that he might find shelter from the sun. Of course, the old woman was compelled to obey, but she managed to take an unnecessarily long time in pulling down the braces with which the door was laid up from the outside.

Having been in the dark hut for some hours, my eyes were well accustomed to the dim light, and I had found that there were two or three sheepskins and some sacks lying near the wall. I now drew these toward me and crouched down on the side that the entering Boer would be least likely to choose. I pulled one sheepskin across my knees and another over my head, wondering as I did so where the Commandant would take up his position. Fortunately for me, he sat down about four feet to my right. As the interior of the hut was quite dark to him on entering, he must have supposed himself the sole occupant. The Kafir woman brought him food, and two other officers joined him in the hut, eating goat meat and discussing the likelihood of maintaining their position, also deciding where they would make their next stand against the advancing British, who were now in full march to the south. After about half an hour they went out.

I lifted myself up and, resuming my outlook through the holes I had poked, I watched the Boer artillery rapidly retreating from the Zand River fight. I made a count of their equipment and guns, and with the other valuable data I had gathered I slipped out that night, successfully evaded the Boer pickets, reëntered the British lines, and laid my information before Lord Roberts.

CHAPTER XXIX

TAKEN PRISONER AT SANNA'S POST

THE plan of campaign of Lord Roberts, from the time he took command in 1900 to the fall of Bloemfontein in the same year, should win the praise of all true soldiers. That it was not immediately successful roused the ire of those valiant fireside warriors who imagined that our cavalry were all mounted on thoroughbred Irish hunters and could gallop right up to Mafeking and relieve General Baden-Powell without more ado. The easiest thing during the war was that Easy Chair in London from which armies were directed and their misfortunes damned.

At Bloemfontein, the capital of the Orange Free State, a military action took place that even now, after twenty-five years and the immensely larger campaigns of the World War, can start arguments as hot as the hinges of Hades and as inconclusive as a debate on "How long is a string?" At the time of its happening, it smothered with black criticism the military fame of two fine soldiers, General Colville and General Broadwood, and brought adverse comment upon nearly every officer under them. Upon this controversy, started in London and participated in by the military attachés of seven great powers and the war correspondents of twenty nations, I do not consider myself qualified to pour any new light. The present portrayal of events is based only on what my two eyes saw. There were thousands of others to bear witness. The keenest make mistakes, and at times the brain becomes fagged and fails to record truly the camera pictures taken by the eye. History must sift the evidence and pronounce.

A glance at the map of South Africa will show, forty miles east of Bloemfontein, a rugged mountainous country—Thaba

Nchu (pronounced Tabanchu, to rhyme with Manchu). I was given orders at about four o'clock in the evening of March 30th to scout the country rapidly between Bloemfontein and Thaba Nchu and report my observations to General Broadwood. It was rumoured that several Boer commandos under General De Wet were converging on Broadwood, who was stationed at Thaba Nchu with two thousand men.

This was all new territory to me, so in order to provide for some hard riding, I asked for an extra led horse. Two sorry nags were allotted me by the Remount Department. The officers of the Intelligence Department, Colonel Colin McKenzie, Colonel Hume, and Major Davis, had on occasion generously offered me their best mounts in order to allow mine time to rest; but at this stage in the war, good horses were very scarce, and to ask an officer for the loan of his horse was about as delicate a matter as to ask a schoolboy for an introduction to his first sweetheart. My mount was in no condition to make a hard ride, although I had repeatedly robbed the mess wagon of hardtack, sugar, and bread to provide him extra rations. A horse, like a man, requires a certain amount of sleep, and if ridden all night and kept awake all day by flies and the hot sun soon becomes useless, even though fed the strongest ration. To be poorly mounted in the enemy's country is like fighting a duel with a broken sword.

Saddling the weaker horse to cover the less difficult country, and leading the other in reserve, I rode toward Sanna's Post. A most disconcerting thing then happened. My led horse, startled by seeing a white animal pass suddenly in the night, broke away from me and I had to spend two hours of the precious darkness in recovering him. Being now hard-pressed for time, I reluctantly took to the regular road instead of following my usual procedure of riding cross-country, cutting the wire fences and swimming the streams above or below the regular drifts and bridges.

On my right rose dimly a farmhouse, and on my left a shed or rough barn enclosed by a stone kraal, with the road between. It was not the part of wisdom to ride between buildings, even at the early hour of 3 A. M. Hearing the faint slam of a door, I cut the fence, made a detour, hid my horses, and reconnoitred on foot. Voices sounded from inside the house. I prowled about and found that it stood on the brow of a hill overlooking a deep spruit. This, then, must be the Pretorius farm marked on the map, and Korn Spruit must be just east of it and west of the waterworks with their high chimney or tower. The drift must be scouted before chancing my horses. Cautiously approaching, I noticed first a faint odour, then many low voices and the click of stirrups. The Boers were in possession of the drift, although, as I did not at this hour know the position of Broadwood, I could see no object in their holding the crossing of Korn Spruit in force. I hastily regained my horses and determined to cross the spruit below the drift, but its banks were vertical and for more than a mile I was baffled at every effort to cross this seemingly insignificant barrier. It looked as if I were starting on my Thaba Nchu venture with about the same series of defeats ahead as attended the Pietersburg effort of bitter memory.

The gray dawn began to show the outlines of rugged hills to the east. Lower down, unmistakable Kafir calls drifted up from a small staat on the banks of the spruit. Only a few minutes more, and the kindly curtain of darkness would lift. It seemed best to retrace my route, ride around the farmhouse, and cross this pesky spruit to the south, where, if the enemy should see me, I could abandon my horses and hide for the day in the hills and kopjes whose outlines I could already make out. The sun follows the dawn quickly in these latitudes. While I was still on the ridge where the farmhouse stood, I heard a heavy gun far away to the east, then more cannon shots and rifle fire. In a few minutes, everything became visible.

Just in front of me, half a mile away, was the tower of the Bloemfontein waterworks, and near by the camp of General Broadwood, who was already withdrawing from Thaba Nchu toward General Colville's larger force that lay near Bushman's Kop. Apparently, Broadwood's whole camp was moving in retreat. His van consisted of the transport wagons, mess wagons, Cape carts, and Q and U batteries. The morning light penetrating the dark shadows of the spruit right in front of me showed it full of Boer horsemen—hundreds of them. They had dismounted and lined the bank of the spruit at the drift, and were in far greater numbers than I had expected to find in such a place. In the night, I had supposed them to be merely a strong patrol intended to dash in behind the British lines, gather information, intercept messengers, etc. But now I realized that this was an ambush on a large scale to capture or destroy Broadwood's entire command, which was unwittingly being driven into this trap.

Just below the Boers was a narrow path across the spruit that I had missed in the night. If I had a swift dependable horse, I might be able to dash across and dodge the screen of scouts which I now saw De Wet had thrown out. It was they who had slammed the farmhouse door, and now others appeared on the ridge between me and Bloemfontein and two more farther down to the north. I was inside their screen—sitting quietly in plain view on the hill! Clearly, up to this moment I had been taken for one of them.

By abandoning my horses, I might crawl through the screen and make my way to Bloemfontein. If I were to try to dash toward the oncoming British on my miserable mounts, I should last about a minute. Yet to sit idle and watch my comrades-in-arms ride blindly into an ambush was maddening. I rode at once very near to the farmhouse on the ridge. The nearest Boer scout was about four hundred yards away. I was in plain view of the British advance wagons and transport officers approaching the drift. I drew from my pocket a large red silk handkerchief, about two feet square, that I always carried for signalling. Sitting on my horse, I waved this frantically for about ten minutes, but there was not a single British scout to observe my warning, and no advance guard appeared in front of the oncoming transport wagons.

By this time, some of the Boers in the spruit below noticed me and sent two men galloping up to investigate. As I was already inside their lines, escape was impossible. My captors took me

TAKEN PRISONER AT SANNA'S POST

along the ridge to the stone kraals of the farmhouse, inside which there had been posted during the night a strong picket of Boers intended to catch and to hold just such scouts as myself who might come meandering down the road from Bloemfontein and discover the hundreds of Boers ambushed in the drift of Korn Spruit. Turning me over to this picket, my captors galloped down the slope and rejoined the enemy in the spruit.

The stone kraal was made of loose rock, and the walls were about four feet high and nearly as thick. They were laid without mortar but gave excellent protection from fire as well as a screen from observation. There were six Boer scouts inside. They took my horses and gun and told me to sit behind the wall and not show myself over the top. But between the large, loose top rocks there were many chinks that in the clear morning air gave me a perfect view of the entire panorama unfolding before me.

Broadwood was fighting a steady rear-guard action. Every mile of his retreat was bringing him nearer to Lord Roberts's great army and to all the cavalry forces of General French. The advance troops of General Colville's division were at Bushman's Kop, only ten miles away. Broadwood had sent messengers to Headquarters asking for reinforcements and could expect them at any hour. The extreme audacity of De Wet in cutting in behind Broadwood's well-ordered retreat and placing his small commando of a few hundred men between such overwhelming forces was something that had obviously never crossed the minds of any of the officers responsible for the operations of war in this area.

As the first wagons of the British dropped down the slope into the bed of the spruit, the guards were instantly disarmed by the Boers and each wagon driven up the opposite slope or headed up or down the stream bed. Soon the commotion in the drift warned the British advance. A shot was fired; an officer in the spruit refused to surrender; more shots; the long line of wagons halted; officers galloped up. Q and U batteries, becoming alarmed, turned their pieces out of the line of march. Lord Roberts's Horse, four hundred strong, galloped toward the spruit. I could see every Boer as they crouched under the bank ready to pour in fire. When the front ranks of the British were within a few yards, a Boer officer, whom I soon knew to be De Wet, jumped over the bank directly in front of the advancing troops, put up his hand, and shouted to them to surrender.

The British officer in command, seeing hundreds of rifles facing him from an entrenched position against which his own fire would be useless, shouted the order, "Files about: gallop!"

Both he and his horse were riddled with bullets instantly, but the order reached his men. For a moment there was a mass of flying horsemen, plunging animals, and falling men. More than one fourth of the force was destroyed in a few moments. Galloping horsemen on a smooth plain were subjected at close range to the bullets of Mauser rifles in the hands of excellent shots, amply protected and firing at will. There was no return rifle fire and at this time no artillery fire to aid Roberts's Horse. In war, much can happen in one hundred and eighty seconds.

The scouts in the kraal that held me prisoner fired steadily, a young Boer lad shouting to them the estimated range as the retreating horsemen fast increased the distance between themselves and the kraal and the deadly spruit below. Now all the fire of the Boers was poured into the helpless wagons that stretched for more than half a mile in front of us. Oxen, mules, horses, guards, officers, black drivers—all were thrown into a terribly confused mass at first and then scattered over the plain. Wagons were overturned, with the spans tangled and kicking in the harness and still being riddled by rifle fire. In the midst of all this confusion, I saw Q and U batteries take position near some buildings in front of the waterworks. Their shells brought the first effective answer to the Boer rifles. The shots came so fast and so accurately that they prevented the Boers mounting their horses and following up and capturing all the troops immediately in front of them.

This respite gave Broadwood time to re-form Lord Roberts's Horse and to make effective use of the 10th Hussars, who fought a long running fight to the north, protecting Broadwood's right flank. The Hussars were cut off from Broadwood, but finally worked through to the British outpost on the east of Bloemfontein. With Lord Roberts's Horse, Broadwood checked the Boer attack, thus saving the bulk of his command, and the main force moved off to the south and escaped the deadly Korn Spruit.

Meanwhile, the whole strength of the Boer rifle fire began to play on the two heroic field batteries, Q and U, standing on the open plain and ringed by riflemen. The batteries soon spotted our stone kraal and crashed many shells against it. By skimming the wall behind which we crouched, they burst their shells behind and over us. Both my horses were killed, but the Boers moved their mounts into one corner out of the line of fire and thus saved all but one. The flashes from the batteries decreased; then came a lull. More than once we in the kraal believed the British gunners all killed. Then someone would manage to crawl to his gun and send another shell and draw a further burst of rifle fire from spruit and hill. But at last the khaki-clad figures lay still. Q and U batteries had saved Broadwood and paid the price.

During a lull in the firing, some Boers, riding hard after their attack on the 10th Hussars, came up with orders from De Wet for the soldiers in the kraal to join them in pursuit of the "Verdomte Rooineks" who could still be seen fighting and galloping over the distant veldt. This my captors promptly refused to do, as the shooting was still good from their vantage point. After a local council of war and much vehement argument, it was decided that those who had been resting behind the wall, and whose horses were fresh, should go on as ordered, while the jaded newcomers should take their places in the stone kraal and rest and shoot from behind its walls. Their discussion gave me an insight into the peculiar, loose discipline that governed the Boer commandos and accounted for their singular effectiveness as well as for their strange failure at times to grasp a situation to their advantage. It would be hard to imagine a British officer reporting to his C. O. such an incident.

As my original captors rode away to chase "Rooineks," one of them turned to the new men and said, "Here is a prisoner. Look out for him." One of my new jailers declared that I should be shot but, fortunately for me, the others vetoed the idea. During the heated argument of the Boers over the chasing of Rooineks and change of horses, I had been thinking of several useful things preparatory to escape. First I slipped a shoe lace from my shoe and tied it rather tightly around my leg just below the knee. This was to keep me constantly reminded to limp. Over this I bound my silk handkerchief, covering the knee joint, so that my new captors would think me wounded.

When the British were all out of range, the Boers led me, now limping painfully, out of the kraal and down to the spruit where De Wet, the Commander, stood near the first captured wagons. He was still directing movements and giving orders. The Boer in charge of me asked where he should put a wounded prisoner. De Wet at once ordered me to climb on a wagon already being loaded with wounded. A Boer came up to me and asked, very kindly, if I wanted a surgeon, but upon my assurance that mine was not a bullet wound and that many others had more pressing need of a surgeon than I, he passed on.

The Boers were now gathering in the wagons, more than a hundred of them, scattered between the spruit and the waterworks. In an incredibly short time, they had cut out the dead animals, killed the disabled ones, straightened up the overturned wagons and untangled the harness, gathered up the prisoners and the captured batteries, inspanned, and by ten o'clock the order to trek was given. This started an arduous retreat toward Wynburg from Sanna's Post. The Boers commandeered all the black drivers captured with the British. The wounded, about thirty, were placed on ox carts. The four hundred prisoners were ordered to fall in and were marched to the limit of endurance before they were allowed to ride on the wagons. The sun was very hot, but the trek pressed forward even faster than soldiers can usually be forced to march.

I had climbed, with noticeable pain and difficulty, to the top of a captured wagon loaded with bright, gleaming biscuit tins. Once, when there happened to be a gap in the guards, a young Boer, evidently from the bush veldt, rode up close to me and began cursing me furiously. He raised his sjambok as if to strike me, but instead brought it down with a sounding whack upon a tin beside me. I shouted, "Look out! That is captured dynamite! It will explode!" He dug his spurs into his astonished horse and almost crawled over the animal's neck to increase his distance from the expected explosion. He did not pull rein until a long way out on the veldt. That morning, in gathering up the spoils of the camp, a half-dozen very ignorant young farm Boers found in an officer's mess cart a bottle and sparklets. As one of the bottles popped with a great fizz, some town wag called to them, "You have opened up the terrible lyddite! The gas will kill you! Grab your noses quick and run!" The rustics promptly seized their noses and ran until they were dizzy for breath, to the immense amusement of the town Boers.

At four o'clock that afternoon, after trekking about thirteen miles east of north from Sanna's Post, we outspanned in a place well suited for fighting a rear-guard action if necessary. Seventy thousand British troops of all arms were still within striking distance, and many of the Boer commanders wanted to continue the trek. They felt sure General French would pursue with his cavalry, just as he had followed Cronje and caught up with him at Modder River. Shortly before dusk, the Boer officers directed the prisoners to obey their own officers. They then told the British officers that their men must be prepared to march almost constantly, night and day, in view of the expected pursuit by the British. The Boers had been marching and fighting continuously for two days, so they cut down the guards on duty to about forty, to give the others opportunity for a little sleep. We were all duly warned that the orders were general to shoot instantly and without challenge any prisoner disobeying commands or trying to slip past the guards. To each guard was given a certain number of prisoners for whom he was held personally responsible.

I was sitting underneath our wagon of wounded when the

Boer officers came up, and as the count was proceeding, I slipped through the spokes and, by circling the wagon wheel, managed to escape detection. I thereby became a sort of "extra," not reckoned or missed by any one guard; a state of things that gave me great freedom among the wagons but made me very shy on rations. It appeared, subsequently, that I had forgotten the number of my mess and my meals were accordingly meagre. A little hardtack or a scrap of tough old trek ox or a handful of mealies was about all I got. In justice to the Boers, be it said that their own rations were none too plentiful. This retreat gave me a special opportunity to see the Boer commandos at their best and to realize the wonderful adaptability which enabled them, in spite of scanty resources, to contend with the great, well-equipped army of the British.

The fact that I had not been counted gave me a choice of wagons and the possibility of finding a chance to escape, but on the second day the vigilance of the guards increased, making it more difficult for any plan to succeed. I whispered to several of the captive British gunnery officers about my plans and offered to carry any messages from them to Headquarters. Major Wray, R. H. A., told me a written message would cause me trouble if I should be recaptured, so he gave me oral ones only. This officer passed to me, unobserved by the guards, his whole day's rations—a nice, big square hardtack, called dog biscuit by the British Tommy, and which the Major sorely needed himself. Captain Stewart contributed to my need his only cup of coffee. At another wagon, a Boer guard gave me an ear of corn just boiled. This and the biscuit I had in my pocket when captured comprised all the portable rations I could accumulate for my hoped-for escape and dash to Bloemfontein, now sixty miles away. I was still limping slowly about the laagers, and therefore the guards might not watch me quite so closely as the other prisoners, but the veldt was very bare, with scarcely a bush and almost no grass, and in that clear atmosphere even a small object could be seen at a great distance; so much caution was necessary.

Sunday morning, while we were outspanned, a Boer officer

came up and questioned me sharply. He said he had a suspicion that I was Burnham, the American scout, whom the Boers had boasted they would have inside the Pretoria prison within thirty days. He was sure he had seen me in Rhodesia, and was not at all satisfied with my plausible statements as to how I happened to be caught at Sanna's Post. He sent for a young fellow who belonged to the Boer Intelligence Department—one who had been at school in England and was of pleasing address. This young man began his investigation by suavely giving me the "once over" in the three R's. It soon developed that, while his physical information about me was rather accurate and checked up dangerously close, his card index of personal characteristics was a bit off. I was supposed to be a most ruthless character, born in the extreme Wild West of America and familiar with Indian warfare—my favourite practice of scalping being but a slight index to my general ferocity. I could read and write, and had no Indian or Negro blood in me, but I was believed to be uncouth in language and deficient in all the attributes of educated or Christian people. With this as a cue, I drifted the conversation to the exploration of Africa by Speke and Burton and to various other subjects that somewhat criss-crossed my investigator's data. Then I started an argument with him as to whether baptism by immersion or sprinkling was the one sure means of salvation. This, with a little poetry conveniently recalled from the declamations of my schooldays and some mental arithmetic by way of fireworks, convinced him that I was a sure-to-goodness highbrow who had never seen the wild and woolly West of Scout Burnham. The first officer, however, was not wholly satisfied, so, acting on his own convictions, he called up the wiry Hottentot servant who looked after his spare horses and commanded the native to keep a sharp eye on me, adding that I was a very bad man and would try to escape.

It is almost as hard to shake a "Totty" off a trail as a bloodhound. These yellow, beady-eyed, diminutive natives come from the southern deserts and are only a shade above the now extinct Bushmen in the human scale. Their hair grows in kinky tufts instead of covering the whole head like that of the Zulus and the rest of the Bantu race. They make good trackers, herders, and grooms, and, like a good dog, they obey only one master. As I limped from wagon to wagon and from group to group of prisoners, this Totty was always near. He was truly my shadow. For the first time since my capture, real fear gripped me. I could see that I might actually land in the Pretoria prison, useless to Lord Roberts and a disgrace to my profession, and all because of one wretched Totty.

CHAPTER XXX

ESCAPE FROM THE BOERS

ALL Saturday night and Sunday I carefully noted every turn and direction of the trek. Only at daylight outspans did I venture to sleep. The procedure at night was advance guard, wagons, prisoners, wagons, more prisoners, and at the end a large wagon drawn by eighteen oxen on which were loaded only the wounded, who by this time were suffering intensely from neglect, dirt, and flies. Most of the marching soldiers had become so exhausted that they, too, had to be carried in wagons. About one hundred yards behind the last wagon rode six or eight Boer guards, while along the flanks single horsemen were spaced from twenty to fifty yards apart, according to the darkness of the night. These had orders to shoot without challenge any prisoner trying to escape. My hope of a let-up in the vigilance of our guards as we increased our distance from Bloemfontein seemed to go glimmering. My own special guard, the all-too-faithful Totty, was ever near me. Yet I had promised Major Wray that I would escape that night—Sunday.

As the night trek started I was allowed, on account of my lameness, to climb on the lead wagon. Before long I fell off this conveyance and climbed on another just behind, watching always for a gap in the guards and trying to shake off my human bloodhound, all to no avail. We outspanned at about eleven and the tired prisoners were asleep on the bare ground in an instant. I crawled under a soldier's greatcoat and then left it hunched up as if there were still someone under it. But the Totty's tireless eyes followed my every movement.

The dreaded hour of 2 A. M. found the weary, cursing prisoners again on the move. Very many of them had to be lifted on the wagons and some actually fell off from drowsiness. I, too, fell off, but for a different reason. Finally, I climbed painfully upon the last wagon. To stir up wounded men in the small hours of the night is like poking a caged bear with a stick. Each soldier had his little nook on the crowded wagon and was bearing his own sorrows as best he could as he jolted on the buck-rail over rocks and ruts, while a chilly wind froze him at night in lieu of the burning sun which roasted him by day. At first, the wounded quite rightly wanted to knock my block off for scrambling on their crowded wagon, yet as soon as it was breathed to them that I was slated to escape and carry a message from Major Wray to Lord Roberts, I had their instant and hearty coöperation.

Especially kind were the two troopers on the front end of the wagon just back of the disselboom. I told them about the Totty, and pointed out that he was now walking beside the near wheel ox and had seen me crawl in among the wounded. One of the troopers, a big powerful fellow, said, "Just let me at him for a moment. He won't see out of his blinking eyes for a day or two after I have landed on him." But as this man had a bullet through the calf of his leg and his valour would only get all of us under special guard, I felt no enthusiasm for his well-intentioned plan. The other, who had a severe wound in one hand, was a light, wiry, plucky Englishman, not inclined to take orders or advice from a mere colonial as he thought me to be.

I began to surmise, from a careful study of my two-legged bloodhound, that he was using the outline of my Stetson hat as a sure marker, since by stooping to the ground he could catch its silhouette against the sky from time to time. The second trooper confided that he was "poison" on being taken to Pretoria a prisoner and that he, too, would make a run for it if the guards would give him a chance. So I gave him a star to bear on and told him when in doubt to head west to the railway and then south; to hide by day, etc., etc. I then suggested he should wear my broad-brimmed hat, for he intended to jump from the off side and, if he escaped, the Totty would then report to his master that his charge had run successfully through the guards and I would no longer be under special observation for that night. I saw that at times a little belt of darkness intervened between one guard and the next following, and the guards themselves were noticeably tired and sleepy. There was a chance that, in this blot of darkness, a man might slip through unobserved. Picking an instant when the guards seemed farther apart than usual, I whispered to the second trooper, "Now slide off the buck-rail; run close behind the guard in front and pass through—gently, on tiptoe—before you can come into the vision of the one behind."

The Tommy gathered his greatcoat around him. I had implored him to leave it lying on the buck-rail, but he said a trooper pays good money for one of these coats, and he knew some of the men nearly froze on the high veldt for lack of them; so, like the foolish monkey clinging to his handful of rice, the trooper clung to his greatcoat. Then, instead of slipping softly into the shadow behind the first guard, he ran straight out between the two—and made a noise like a galloping cow. Instantly the guard behind dashed up and the advance guard turned back. I held my breath for the expected shots, but the Boers were humane. One shouted, "Hands up!" and then began cursing, much to the relief of those of us on the front end of the wagon who knew what was happening. The harder the guard cursed, the less danger to the prisoner. The trooper was allowed to climb back on the wagon, quite convinced that the Pretoria jail might not be so bad as to leave one's bones bleaching on the veldt.

I had expected him to be rather upset when he crawled back on the seat beside me, but he took what he called his "narrow squeak" as all in the day's work, and within five minutes was offering to help me do anything I could think of toward my own escape. I told him the Totty paid not the slightest attention to his running off with my hat. Evidently, after all, his job was to watch *me*, not my hat. Had his orders been to kill me, I am sure they would have been faithfully executed. Things were now getting desperate. We were near Wynburg. There was less than an hour of darkness left. For myself, it would be better to die than to live a prisoner in Pretoria. It seemed, I thought, to be the Totty's life or mine. The only weapon available was my pocket knife. Most of the time the Totty walked beside the near ox, sometimes talking to the black driver, but seldom walking very far from the front end of the wagon where I sat. I meditated jumping to the ground and using on him the same stroke the Apache uses before his victim can make a sound. It would be ineffective to hit his thick skull with a rock or a club, even if either were available. I balanced myself on the corner of the wagon and waited for some rough ground or kopjes where mounted men could not quickly follow me, in case I succeeded in ridding myself of this bloodhound.

The moments passed; the hour seemed ripe; the guards were nodding in their saddles and far apart, but the veldt was as bare as a floor. Daylight was near and as doubtless even the Totty was weary, he walked up the span, alongside the driver. Then the idea suddenly came to me: Why not slip down on the disselboom between the oxen, drop off in the middle of the road, let the wagon pass over, and trust to slipping by the rear guard?

I acted on this in a moment. As I dropped, the off ox kicked at me but missed. The hind wheels rolled by me. I turned over a few times and lay still. The thud of the rear guard came closer. Would they see me? Would the horses shy at me? But fortunately even these iron men and tough horses were, like all the rest of us, weary and hollow-eyed. When their hoofbeats grew faint, I crawled away, then rose and ran until far from the creaking wagons and cracking whips. I had about twenty minutes left to find a hiding place before day would break.

A small native kraal loomed in the dim light. I chanced a word with a native. He promised to get me a horse, but I feared he might not stand a sharp quiz by a Boer if one should come along looking for me, and I knew the Totty would report to his master at daybreak, when he must become aware that I was no longer on the wagon of the wounded. So I told the native I would return for the horse in an hour or so and ran on toward a small kopje that was dimly outlined against the sky.

On nearing it, I found there was a Boer farm at its base and Boers on the kopje and much stock about. The barking of dogs in a kraal halted me instantly.

The morning light was breaking. I was on a bare plain; the horses of the moving commandos had eaten every blade of grass within sight. Near by was a small piece of ground recently ploughed. I ran out into this and lay down in a furrow, covering my face with my dust-coloured hat. The furrow was shallow, not more than four inches deep; my entire hat and the greater part of my body were exposed above the ground, but I had done all possible. Sleep overpowered me for a time, until the sun grew hot. All day long troops of alert, armed Boers passed along the road a hundred and fifty yards from me. I learned later that they had planned to use this very farmhouse and kopje as a base from which to repel the British and fight a strong rear-guard action, in order to allow the convoy of prisoners to be taken on to Wynburg. Many of the Boers were resighting and trying out the captured rifles of the British. They had a wagon load of the ammunition taken at Sanna's Post and were trying it in competition with their German guns and ammunition. On the kopje about two hundred yards away were guards with glasses. There was much commotion all day long. From under my hat brim I could watch most of their movements, but at no time did I dare lift the hat or turn myself over.

Thirst made strange fancies throng my mind. The ear of boiled corn given me by the Boer Sunday afternoon bulged in my breast pocket. As I lay on my back in the shallow furrow it seemed this cob must be a foot in diameter. I was sure the Boers would notice it, yet I dared not lift my arm to pull it out and thus lessen my bulk. Why had I not thrown away the corn when I lay down? What a fool to be such a glutton for food! If I should be caught, that would be the reason. I was not living up to the traditions of an American scout. Jim Beckwith travelled ten days with only the meat of one teal duck to sustain him but I, having one entire biscuit and a piece of another, must needs stick a great bulging ear of corn into my breast pocket—and Bloemfontein less than eighty miles away! I knew that my critical younger brother would say "Bah!" to such folly in a tone calculated to make me creep. Would I ever get out of this fool furrow? I was no Joshua about that sun; I wanted it to set right now and not stand eternally still. During the day I had systematically and repeatedly tensed every muscle and then relaxed, to keep my heart from pounding in the heat. The blazing rays slanted more and more, but even after they no longer struck me, it seemed hours before I dared turn on my side and move my hat.

As soon as darkness fell, I ran about two miles to a spruit where I had a good drink and ate the troublesome ear of corn with gusto, wishing now I had at least three more just like it. That night I felt fine. The chill night air, the twinkling stars, the sense of freedom, exhilarated me greatly. The terrible Totty and the shallow furrow were mere memories. As the dawn grew rosy, I sought out a little kloof between two small kopjes. During the night I had picked up an empty tomato tin; this I filled with water at a small spruit and carried to my cache in the kloof. I passed the day in sleeping and dined sumptuously on the biscuit which Major Wray had given me. As night came on again the country about appeared to be void of any living being, and it seemed safe to venture out before it was entirely dark.

I followed a cattle trail that led me over an embankment— and right under the shotgun of a tall Boer who was out hunting along the vley for karan, a fine South African game bird. He was a spare man of great frame and may easily have been one of the Boers who fought at Sanna's Post. He hailed me instantly as an escaped prisoner, and declared he would like to shoot me and be done with it, as it was such a damned nuisance to drive me to the Field Cornet, but since I had no gun and could not fight, perhaps he would bother to take me over to the Commandant. He made me walk about a hundred yards over a little swell in the land and there, tied to a wire fence, were two small ponies and a Cape cart. Ordering me up into the cart, he jumped in and we started off at a brisk trot across

ESCAPE FROM THE BOERS

the veldt and then along a dim road. I could see three Boer farms in the distance. We were headed toward them, and I also felt that I was again headed for Pretoria prison, as I knew this Boer did not intend to shoot me. In fact, he looked upon me as a weakling beneath contempt; dirty-faced, red-eyed, half starved, and unarmed. He did not take the trouble to care for his gun, but put it between us, loaded, while he plied the sjambok and handled the lines.

Again I thought fast, as I did when poised on the buckrail watching the Totty. My first idea was to seize the loaded gun and leap from the cart, covering the Boer with his own weapon; but I had observed that this giant of a man was like a bear— very agile. One grab of that big bony paw might get me before ever I left the cart. Or he might jump with me and land on top of me before the gun could be turned on him. My kingdom for a pistol, even a small one! I had acted, when captured, as if very lame and exhausted. The Boer did not know that I still carried my pocket knife, but I knew that I could open it unseen and kill him with a single blow. Yet that would never be done by me. This man had spared me, a national enemy. There must be some way to outwit this huge, powerful, but none too intelligent fellow creature.

Suddenly, there came to my mind an early California incident. Sheriff Morse of Alameda County had arrested many hard characters. He was a man of great strength and stature and once he got his grip on a man, he landed him in jail. One hot afternoon, with a prisoner beside him, he was driving a single horse and rig over the dusty road to San Leandro. His prisoner was leaning forward with his head in his hands as if asleep in the hot sun. Suddenly he caught Morse by the bottom of the trouser leg and threw him heels over head into the dusty road behind the rig, seizing the lines as Morse went out. When the sheriff came to, his prisoner was stirring up the dust a mile away, and so far as Morse ever knew he may be going yet.

I threw the big Boer out of his cart backward but missed the reins, which dragged on the ground. The horses broke into a gallop but stayed in the road. Their scare soon subsided, and within half a mile they had slowed to a trot and had to be sjamboked frequently. It was now getting dark and I was master of the gun, so I jumped out with it, taking a handful of shells with me from the jockey box in the cart. The enraged Boer would doubtless soon raise up a small commando to track me. To escape them and also to avoid the farms, I turned west and scouted along the back trail toward Bloemfontein. Once clear, I abandoned the gun, and making a detour to the south, I ran, during the night, many miles out of my direct course. After another slight adventure, I crossed the Modder River successfully and hid all day Wednesday until dark. That night I reached a little spruit about five miles from Bloemfontein.

The Boer had told me that the waterworks and Korn Spruit were still held by the Boers, and up to this point no British outpost had been seen or heard. Now the faint odour of a camp reached me on the cold air flowing down the vleys. I followed this for about two miles, scouting with care, and at four o'clock on Thursday morning, April 5th, reached the camp of the famous 12th Lancers, commanded by Lord Airlie, where every consideration was shown me. If I had eaten a tenth part of the food pressed upon me, I should have been done for, as were so many of our men and officers in Rhodesia from overeating after their privations were ended.

This was my last meeting with the dashing Lord Airlie. He insisted on riding a conspicuous white charger and was killed at Diamond Hill, on the march to Johannesburg. There was much skirling of pipes in Scotland when the cables flashed the account of his death.

At eight o'clock on Thursday morning, I reported to Lord Roberts at Bloemfontein.

CHAPTER XXXI

CUTTING THE RAILROAD

A FEW incidents of the advance from Bloemfontein to Pretoria may reveal something of the methods in use at that time, not only to gain knowledge of the enemy but to destroy his lines of communication.

I received orders to cut the railroad behind the Boer army that was being pressed northward toward Johannesburg by the advance of all arms under Lord Roberts. The British outposts were left at the little station of Smalldeel, forty miles north of Bloemfontein. Two sturdy Kafir boys, each carrying eighteen pounds of guncotton and condensed rations, were detailed to accompany me. We moved at night only, and without horses. The Boers were very alert and De Wet's famous scouts kept their line of retreat well covered. I decided to march rapidly west, then north, until we should hit the Zand River and thus get clear around De Wet's scouts. It was a trying march, mostly at Indian jog trot. We made a distance of forty miles that night, passing through three small commandos and the sleeping town of Ventersburg, whose pickets fired on us, unwittingly taking a chance of blowing up the little dorp by doing so. We eluded them and passed on north, but I had made careful estimates of their strength and position.

While we were under fire at close quarters, one of my Kafirs, carrying the explosive, crept up to me, trembling like a leaf, and whispered, "Baas, I don't mind being shot, but this mine powder might go off and my spirit would be blown to bits and never find my ancestors in the sky." So I took his load.

Morning found us near Kroonstadt, the position of which I carefully noted in the early light. We hid in a mealie field on the banks of the Valch River and watched the Boers. Late that afternoon, General French appeared with several thousand cavalry, brought up by forced march, and I reported to him all that I had observed. My orders had been to blow up the railroad at a certain point at a certain hour, but the movements of both armies had been much swifter than was anticipated and our chance of catching the Boers' big guns and rolling stock was lessening with every passing hour. So General French countermanded my orders, relieved my Kafirs, and ordered me to report to Major Hunter-Weston, Royal Engineer.

Our instructions had been to destroy the railroad at a point about fifteen miles north of Kroonstadt. A new plan was arranged in a few minutes. Hunter-Weston called for fifty volunteers and was answered by two hundred, in spite of the fact that for two days the men had known hardly a moment's rest and had had very little to eat. Every man of them knew that our present expedition most likely meant death or Pretoria prison, but there was any amount of nerve in the army. Fifty cavalrymen were selected, principally from the Inniskilling Dragoons, with eight sappers and Royal Engineers. The plan was to ride west and then north to a point where the pickets would be thinnest, and there charge through them. The cavalry would be left to fight their way back while Major Hunter-Weston and I, with the eight sappers and the explosives, would slip inside the railroad lines. It seemed a rather mean trick to desert the cavalry, but they understood it perfectly.

In the moonlight, we soon saw dimly the mounted pickets of the enemy. The Inniskillings under Captain Yeardly made the charge with swords—the only one of the kind I saw in the war. It was thrilling while it lasted, and the gleam of those bright blades and the suddenness of the onslaught paralysed the black pickets. In taking them prisoners, we achieved the first success of our plan. The spirit "For the Service" was clearly shown when the young commander said to Hunter-Weston, "I am awfully sorry to turn back. It would be the pleasure of my life to go on with you but I can easily see that it might ditch the whole enterprise. I would only be in your way." It takes more courage to deny one's self such a chance than it does to win the Victoria Cross.

CUTTING THE RAILROAD

With our eight picked men, we pushed on cautiously. Because I had the sharpest eyesight Hunter-Weston ordered me to locate the outposts in advance. We twisted and turned and were chased off by watchful pickets, but kept working in again until, by four o'clock in the morning, we were fifteen miles inside their lines and the outposts had lost us. Then came the most difficult part of all. We were within a quarter of a mile of the railroad. The moon had just set and we had only one hour in which to do our work.

It so happened that at the particular point where we were to strike, the Boers had posted a whole commando. There was a farmhouse with a small wired pasture by the side of the railroad, also a big wagon road. Men were walking up and down the track and others were sleeping beside the road. Convoys of wagons and mounted troops were passing along to the north. The horses of the sleeping soldiers were hobbled inside the pasture. I crept in among them and then returned to Major Hunter-Weston and reported their position. We decided to cut the barbed-wire fences on both sides and then lead our horses and men into the pasture, carrying our explosives; approaching the railroad line between the guards, and trusting to fortune for what might happen after we fired the charge.

When we were all three inside the pasture, we ran upon three Boers asleep in their blankets. Lieutenant Childs, R. E., held a gun to the head of one, Hunter-Weston did the same to another, and I put my hand over the mouth of the third to keep him quiet. We led our captives from the pasture, and finding that there were more Boers sleeping among the horses as well as beside the wagon road, we decided to bring in all our men from outside to hold our prisoners. We were very close to the wagon road and had just mounted when several companies of Boers came marching along the road and the leader shouted to us to halt. We never stirred but bent our heads on our horses' manes and waited for the expected challenge and volley. It was a critical moment. We were quite a solid clump of horsemen, purposely without formation, and the Boer leader was suspicious, but the men behind were impatient and swore loudly, so he moved on. Whether he concluded that an enemy would not be so foolish as to sit in front of three hundred men within pistol shot, or whether he inferred that we were some black servants leading horses, will never be known. But they all passed on, and we led the Boer prisoners and our own men successfully out of the pasture.

As we were now encumbered with our captives, Hunter-Weston decided that he and I alone should blow up the railroad line. He gave orders to Lieutenant Childs to hold the men and horses just outside the barbed-wire fence where we had opened it, and to await our return, but should we be killed, to cut his way back to the British lines if possible. Securing the guncotton from the sappers, Hunter-Weston and I crept back a foot at a time among the sleeping Boers and across the wagon road, slipping through a gap in the moving guards and wagons. By very cautious movements, we finally reached the railroad and adjusted the charge of guncotton. I covered the fuse with my hat while Hunter-Weston lighted it. We crept away. Soon there was a trembling of the ground and a roar that sent the sleeping Boers running to their horses in all directions. In the confusion, we reached our command and rode quietly away.

At daylight we picked up some Boer sentinels. Then we ran upon a Boer outpost, charged, and captured it. We could take no more prisoners as we already had seven on our hands, so we broke their six guns on the ground, took their four best mounts, and let the men go free. By this time, many Boers were after us with horses and rifles. We had a long running fight for two hours. One solitary Boer, well mounted, led all the others and clung to our rear guard. He wounded one man and killed a horse. Major Hunter-Weston dropped behind and dismounted. The Boer instantly did the same. The duel was over in less than a minute. Hunter-Weston was victor, the range about three hundred yards. We had other adventures and did not reach the British lines until about eleven in the morning. We had been in the enemy's country since six of the evening before. We had ridden more than fifty miles, lost one man wounded and one horse killed; had blown up the

CUTTING THE RAILROAD

railroad, cut telegraph wires, captured seven prisoners and four horses, and gained a lot of important information.

This happened to be my thirty-ninth birthday, so we called it a party.

It was now decided at Headquarters that it was necessary to cut the railway between Johannesburg and Pretoria in order to prevent the Boers from rushing the rolling stock out of Johannesburg. The acquisition of railway equipment of every kind had an exaggerated value, as the transportation for the army of seventy thousand under Lord Roberts was dependent upon it. The capture of engines was vital to success. Our instructions were to blow up the railway north of Johannesburg just as the attack on Johannesburg should begin, but not before. This was for the purpose of cutting off whatever rolling stock might then be in the switchyards and town, and it was the plan of the advancing British to rush the place as rapidly as possible and take possession of this rolling stock before it could be destroyed by the Boers.

My orders were to take my departure from Smalldeel, as before. Detailed to accompany me was a Kafir of tremendous physical strength and toughness, who had been with me on many a similar night march where horses could not be used. Of all the native scouts we employed, this man seemed best able to stand the strain of hard scouting. The point where we were to destroy the railway was distant about one hundred miles, so we filled our pockets with food tabloids and emergency rations, knowing we would be many days without other food. Each of us carried a quantity of the necessary guncotton, fusees, and caps. So bare and smooth was the country that to move over it in daytime was impossible. Large bodies of Boers were marching and counter-marching in all directions, as well as many natives friendly to the Boers. As a rule, the Kafirs of the Transvaal were more sympathetic to the British than to the Boers, but where personal risk was involved it was not safe to trust one's self in the hands of a Kafir if a Boer commando happened to be near by.

The Intelligence Department of the army has often been

criticized because of the dearth of information obtained as well as for various indiscretions, but it is not betraying any official secret to say that, when I was instructed to cut the railway at some point between Johannesburg and Pretoria, I was supplied with a map showing me every curve, grade, culvert, bridge, farm, spruit, and river of the entire route. Every detail of this map I proved to be correct. It was the result of the patient garnering of information, probably by some obscure young officer years before, who had thus made it possible for me to carry out the present orders. Should I find a certain bridge too heavily guarded to be destroyed, the exact distance and position of the next bridge and the size and thickness of the iron girders that sustained it could be ascertained from this map. My own experience as a scout told me precisely the amount of guncotton necessary, and how to place it so as to cut the girders without wasting any of the precious explosive.

We scouted north, avoiding the various camps and commandos of the Boers and meeting with adventures similar to those already related. During the day, we were forced to lie hidden to prevent discovery. We dared not enter a house or make a fire to cook food. One night we found ourselves in sight of the twinkling lights of Johannesburg—the greatest gold-mining city in Africa. It was girdled by an immense Boer encampment. Miles of huge quartz mills and well-lighted bungalows lay before our tired eyes. Having subsisted for five days on the concentrated rations we had brought with us, we were now so ravenous that we decided to take a chance on the fifth evening and try to get food from a neighbouring Kafir staat. Much persuasion and the glitter of a gold piece induced a native to give us the shelter of his hut, and we succeeded in purchasing and cooking for ourselves an elderly and resolute hen whose youth and beauty I judge were contemporaneous with the dove that flew out of the ark. Certainly, the twenty minutes we allowed her to boil in the pot made no impression whatever upon that obdurate female except to warm her venerable sinews. I envied the Kafir boy his powerful teeth, for although mine were strong there was severe risk of cracking them on that fowl. Then my friend the Kafir, armed with another coin, was persuaded to storm the near-by huts for eggs. He brought back twenty, and we did not cavil over their laying dates, but cooked and ate the lot with gusto.

We then approached one of the large quartz mills at the eastern end of the Rand property. As grazing stock had eaten the grass off close we were obliged to crawl into two ant-bear holes, not fifty yards apart, to hide. There we lay the entire day. The ant-bear in Africa makes a hole considerably larger than a wolf den and about equally deep. The animal itself is harmless, and while the hole is extremely annoying to horsemen, it is certainly a mighty convenient refuge for a scout. We found the nights here very cold, as Johannesburg is more than five thousand feet in elevation. At dark, we could come out of our hiding places and get some much-needed exercise. There was water at the nearest spruit, but hunt as we would, we could not find a single chicken or any place to get food. So much depended upon the success of our enterprise, however, that we concluded to starve it out awhile longer.

Two days and two nights we waited in the ant-bear holes, listening patiently for the roar of General French's artillery that was to be my signal to cut the railway. At last the distant boom of the cannon reached us, sounding as sweet to my waiting ears as any cathedral chime. We emerged from the ant-bear holes, skirted the edge of the city, and struck the railway above a little station called Zurfontein. Near the point that we selected for hiding was a field of unharvested maize. It was very dry, and the native and I did not dare make a fire, so, for the four days we were there, we had no other food than the uncooked maize. Again the strength of the black's massive white teeth excited my lively envy, for his could crunch and masticate the hard kernels at a speed about twice as fast as mine. My lips and jaws grew so sore from grinding this dry corn that my speech became thick and almost unintelligible.

We used our guncotton to good advantage and cut the railway on a curve between two culverts in such a way that it would take some time for the Boers to repair it. When they did manage to do so, we slipped down once more from our hiding place and cut it a second time. Our performance was essentially successful. A large quantity of most valuable rolling stock and many engines were captured by the British on entering Johannesburg and were put to immediate use in bringing up supplies for both the town population and the British troops.

There was no sign of the advance of the British beyond the town, and the Boers still hovered between Zurfontein and Johannesburg. It was necessary for us to get into the town, and in this effort we were obliged to seek shelter in a small blue gum grove. Within an hour of our occupancy, this grove became the camp of a large Boer commando. The soldiers came in considerable numbers to pick up the scattered dry leaves and twigs and whatever dead wood they could find, for fuel. As the gum trees were planted in rows, it seemed inevitable that the Kafir and I must be discovered. My method of protection was for each of us to take a branch of blue gum tree and use it as a screen behind which we could sit or stand in whatever portion of the grove seemed most advantageous at the moment. We spent an anxious and wearing day, and never was the darkness of night so welcome. We were not only very weak and hungry, but frightfully thirsty, as this day had been spent without water as well as without food. We had done all that we had set out to do. The railroad was cut—at just the right time, as I learned later, to capture four hundred cars and many engines. Now we were entitled to risk something to appease our own painful thirst and hunger.

I decided that we must at any cost get into Johannesburg and meet the British outpost. My Kafir boy became so miserable that he broke down completely and declared he was unable to go on. He was convinced that, if he should be caught with me, the Boers would kill him by flogging. We still had to creep through the pickets of the commando that was encamped above our immediate hiding place, and I realized that the best thing for him to do was to crawl off in the veldt alone and take no chance of being captured in my company. Then, at the worst, he could explain that he lived in Johannesburg and had been taken sick on the veldt. His looks would certainly bear him out, as his eyes were sunk far in his head, and he could hardly be recognized as the powerful black I had started with from the British lines only eleven days before. The constant marching and loss of sleep had told their tale. Kafirs stand certain kinds of fatigue to a marvellous degree; but there are others in which they cannot compete with the endurance of the experienced white, and the ability to forego sleep is one of them.

Having started the Kafir through the Boer lines, I began a long, tedious night scout through extremely alert pickets who were in close proximity to the British. The latter were not yet in full possession of Johannesburg, for it was a large sprawling city of more than a hundred thousand inhabitants and extended for many miles along the gold reefs. It was broad daylight before I worked through. I screened myself with bunches of grass and crawled slowly, at times, foot by foot, and sometimes compelled by weakness to move on all fours for a considerable distance; but at last I got safely inside the British lines.

The information I brought to the First Regiment was barely transmitted to Headquarters when the Boer commando that had camped upon my place of retreat made a sharp attack and killed two British officers, several men, and a number of cavalry horses.

At the headquarters of the 12th Lancers under Lord Airlie— a regiment whose officers had often been exceptionally kind to me—I stopped just long enough to clean up as well as was possible so as to make my report fittingly to Lord Roberts. This accomplished, I took a fourteen-hour sleep and was given an "off duty" for several days to recuperate.

CHAPTER XXXII

WOUNDED

BY JUNE 2, 1900, Johannesburg was entirely in the hands of the British. We had fully expected the Boers to destroy the great gold mills along the reef, whose thousands of stamps had been turning out tons of gold to finance the Boer cause. These mills were built and owned by the British and were the very life blood of commerce for all South Africa. No greater blow could have been dealt to the British than to destroy this entire city, but it fell into our hands uninjured.

I suspect that the Boer leaders must have decided that their long antagonism to the Uitlander—as the British and other aliens were called—did not require the sacrifice of such an edifice of human energy as Johannesburg, and that even through the clouds of war they could foresee the dawning of a better day for all white men in the land, although their beloved little republic should be swallowed up in the Union of South Africa. Intended or not, the sparing of the gold camp from destruction was bread cast upon the waters by the Boers, and came back to them in the final treaties of peace when their real friends used it as an argument to procure the Boers full citizenship, the equality of the Dutch and English languages, and the confirmation of all farm titles; as well as a valid reason for advancing them money to purchase seed, implements, and stock. There were those in England who had never lost a dollar or heard a shot in the Boer War who demanded drastic and humiliating terms for the Boers, but fortunately the policies of Milner, Rhodes, and other great statesmen prevailed, and to-day a Boer sits in the highest councils of the Empire. Nevertheless, considered from a strictly military point of view, the general Boer strategy was poor, although their tactics were often brilliant, elusive, and costly to the enemy.

By this time, there was organized a fairly good system of scouting under the Intelligence Department. Colonel Colin McKenzie, its chief, was made Governor of Johannesburg. Bennett Burleigh, the war correspondent who was attached to the Department, had a remarkable knack of picking up information within the town of Johannesburg itself, and I learned many important things from him. By night and day, natives, friendly Dutch and English colonials, and picked men from various regiments were sent out, until the information received as to the whereabouts of the enemy became far more exact and full than it had been during the early stages of the war. Meantime, no effort was made to change the common Boer belief that Colonel McKenzie, Colonel Hume, and Major Davis were asleep at the switch and that the English scouts were idling in the clubs or training bird dogs on the veldt.

Burleigh brought to light many facts concerning the working of the great gold mills at the time they were confiscated by the Boer government from their British owners, as well as many amusing tales of the hoarding propensities of some of the leaders under Kruger. In days to come, some of the tales of the buried riches of Johannesburg will have reached such magnitude that Captain Kidd's famous treasure will seem a mere pittance. Certainly, many tons of gold taken by the Boers to be shipped out of the country never actually left the port of Lorenzo Marques and were probably buried secretly.

Great problems confronted the British commander. The outside country was held by the Boers. The British army of seventy thousand men must be rationed, and the civilian population of more than a hundred thousand cared for, all by means of a Cape gauge railway, here a thousand miles from its base and that base six thousand miles from England. Fortunately, the sea route was free and the great navy had moved all troops to Cape Town in a wonderful way, maintaining them in health and morale en route.

Only experienced officers of the Quartermaster Department can fully appreciate the task of supplying and victualling this newly captured city which, up to this time, had had a base at Lorenzo Marques, about four hundred miles away, and the entire surrounding country to draw from. Again Lord Roberts called upon Sir Percy Girouard to meet the situation, and the seemingly impossible was performed by that able executive. Girouard's training in pioneer railway building in the United States under James J. Hill, and later in the great railway systems of western Canada, enabled him to perform a miracle in South Africa and to supply more than three times the transportation possible, according to the best German authorities, for a railway of Cape gauge, one thousand miles from base to railhead. As soon as Lord Roberts knew this supply of material and ration could be maintained, a new and final advance was made on the capital of the Transvaal Republic, and Pretoria is distant about forty miles from Johannesburg and was the last city of any importance to be captured.

After being baffled by the alert Boers in some minor assignments given me by the Commanding Officer, my duties again brought me under the command of my friend Major Hunter-Weston. It had been decided at Headquarters that the Boer line of railway which connected Pretoria with the seaport base, Lorenzo Marques, on the Indian Ocean, should be demolished. This line was about four hundred miles long, and over it all munitions came in for the Boers from Germany and elsewhere. The port was under the flag of Portugal. In addition to the value of this line to the enemy, there was danger of their using it to rush four thousand British prisoners of war from Watervaal, just north of Pretoria, to a certain pestilential point on the Portuguese East African border. As these men were already greatly reduced by imprisonment, it was probable that half of them would quickly die in the hot low veldt. This we were most anxious to prevent.

With this double objective, it was worth while to make a fast, hard ride, without hesitating to sacrifice our raiding party, in order to blow up tanks, bridges, culverts, and all curves, as

WOUNDED

fast and far as possible Two hundred men were selected from the Lancers and other famous regiments for this raid. We moved rapidly. Many times during the night I sighted the Boers and warned our troop to avoid combat, but at dawn we found ourselves in the presence of vastly superior forces with no hope of being able to cut through them to the railway, even by sacrificing heavily to do so. We therefore decided to retreat and save as many of our men and good mounts as possible. Most of the men were extremely loath to refuse battle, but after a hard night's ride, our horses were in poor shape to meet big commandos on fresh horses.

Our retreat was rather ignominious. At one time it looked as though we would surely be surrounded, so Hunter-Weston sent me through the Boer lines for help. I was mounted on one of the swiftest Basuto ponies I ever rode—Stembok, given me by Lord Roberts after the disaster at Sanna's Post. By means of constant zigzagging, my pony escaped being hit, though fired on several times at close range. Already a hundred times he had borne me out of hot fire, and this was another of his lucky days. He seemed to grasp the idea of dodging just like his namesake, the stembok or swift gazelle. This day he brought me safely into the lines of General Dickson, who rushed out reinforcements to meet Major Hunter-Weston and his tired men, but they had already accomplished a good retreat, keeping up a hot return fire all the way and with less than twenty casualties. But we had failed in our mission, which is always a dark hour for the scout.

It was then ordered that I should go alone and cut the line. The Royal Engineers furnished me with twenty-five pounds of guncotton and the supposedly unintelligent Intelligence Department gave me, as usual, accurate information of culverts, bridges, etc., along the railway. But as any destruction that I could effect alone would be but a temporary handicap for the Boers, it was necessary that it should synchronize with other general movements.

A reconnaissance in force by General French was planned, and a picked body of men under Major Hunter-Weston was sent far to the west to draw off the Boers and increase my chances of reaching the line. Again Stembok, my Basuto pony, was brought into action after a few hours' rest. Lord Downe, a most expert horseman, had given personal instructions as to his rubbing down and feeding. I mention this because I had flattered myself that I was a past master in the art of caring for and rationing my own horse, but one should never write *finis* even to the humblest department of knowledge. A raw savage may teach one a new thing, and the nation that has developed the wonderful modern horse has also developed its pundits on equine matters, and I learned much from Lord Downe.

I took some extra chances by starting my ride in daylight. Just at dusk, I ran across a cavalry troop sent by General French to reconnoitre toward the railway station of Irene. As this was in my proposed direction, the commander of the troop asked me to act as scout until they were in touch with Irene, his objective. I very much disliked delaying my special mission, yet I did not feel like refusing to help a fine troop of cavalry who happened to be without a scout or even a native guide, so we rode on together and successfully avoided several of the enemy scouts.

Some of the peculiar instructions occasionally given to junior officers by their superiors before sending them on patrol were brought sharply to my notice that night. When there was no longer even a dim glow from the sunset and the stars began to shine brightly, the Commanding Officer asked me what I was bearing on to find the station of Irene, now that the sun was down. I pointed to a star not far from the western horizon. He said, "Ah, yes! That is right; always use a star!" We rode on, winding in and out and changing course very often. After about two hours, the C. O. rode forward and said to me, "Burnham, I have been noticing for some time that you are not accurately bearing on the star you pointed out to me. Are you quite confident of your direction?" It took a little time to convince him that his instructions to use a star as bearing, if followed out literally, would soon reverse his direction.

But however faulty his astronomy, there was nothing lacking in his courage to attack the Boers or to do his best to cover my movements when in contact with them.

Near Irene there was a rising bit of ground overgrown with high grass. As this appeared to be a probable place for a Boer outpost, the cavalry troop was halted. Instinct urged me to scout it out on foot in the proper way, leaving Stembok and my explosive with the troop, but so much time of the precious darkness had been wasted that I decided to chance it by working along on my mount. The C. O. deployed his men to cover me should I draw the Boer fire. Working slowly up the slope as cautiously as possible, and striving to avoid the tell-tale skyline, I reached a point within twenty yards of the summit when, suddenly, out of the grass sprang a line of Boers, perhaps twenty or more, with guns levelled, and the sharp command rang out, "Hands up, you!"

I shouted the word "Frints!" (Friends), so for an instant the Boers concluded I must be a stray fellow countryman and lowered their rifles. Simultaneously with my shout of "Frints!" I slipped my hand close to the bit, threw myself on the side of my horse and turned, quartering away down the slope so as not to get in line of possible British fire. A hail of shots from the Boers was instantly answered by the British troop. There was a half moon to aid the Boers in their aim at my running horse, so I headed Stembok toward some burnt ground whose blackness would deprive them of this benefit. When I believed myself a safe four hundred yards from the Boers, I pulled Stembok to a canter and straightened in the saddle. But some Boer scout had paid no attention to the British fire and kept pumping steadily at my dim, retreating pony, and even at this great distance, in the moonlight, he managed to send one bullet true. My last vision of my good Stembok was his silhouette against the sky, legs in air, directly over me.

When I came to, the half moon was just setting, so I knew the time to be about two hours later. My guncotton was still in my knapsack on my back. The veldt was silent. A terrible pain burned in my spine and, like most numbed and wounded men, I believed my back was broken. The next half hour was spent in the same travail that every wounded soldier passes through and which is so familiar to all doctors and nurses. If there is anything worth recording of my ordeal it is the mental struggle that took place between the pain and that other unnamed higher element which exists in everyone.

During paroxysms of suffering the physical self took command and seemed a separate individual arguing, "Save your body! Shout! Light a fire! Call for help!"—whispering, "Even the enemy will aid you now that you are helpless. Tell your commander that you did your best and you may even be rewarded," along with other cowardly counsels that crowded my brain and that even now, after the lapse of years, I shrink from recording. But the instant the terrible pain slackened, another voice spoke, in the simple words of bygone ancestors who did the right thing in the right way without any heroics whatever. Would I fail them? Could I look men like Roberts and Rhodes in the eye with peace in my heart if I did? With every moment of these thoughts I grew stronger, but the lesson of that night has never been forgotten—not to judge too harshly what a man may do under intense physical pain suddenly inflicted.

Finding that I could manage to rise and walk, and even get some relief by holding my abdomen tightly with both hands, I turned toward the designated place to cut the railway. A strange elation came over me, and for some time the pain seemed to leave me. Just as I neared some hills, daylight began to break—that bad hour for the scout in the enemy's country. Before me lay a small marsh and at either end of it a Boer farmhouse. There was almost no cover. Both houses, distant about a mile, were occupied by Boer commandos, as I could see from the number of horses about. Before me, at the junction of two dim wagon roads, was a small stone kraal only ten or twelve feet in diameter and with walls three feet high, used by the Kafirs to hold goats. In this I lay down just before the sun came over the hill.

In an hour there were many Boers moving, mostly on horseback, and centring on the two Boer farms. By ten o'clock, intense pain again brought back all that troop of cowardly desires that had formerly beset me to save the body and gain a little human sympathy, even from the enemy. It would be easy now to walk to a farmhouse and surrender, and get medical attention as well. Intense nausea soon ended these shameful thoughts. As I was vomiting blood, I became convinced there was no use in worrying about a doctor, as I was already beyond his help. So I wrote a note to my wife and hoped the British advance would cover this ground soon, and that my end would not be as a miserable prisoner, dying inside the enemy's lines with three failures chalked up against my last three efforts to perform my duty as a scout.

Soon I fell into a profound sleep of several hours, from which I was wakened by the sounds of a commando of more than a hundred Boers passing within a few feet of my kraal. That afternoon more Boers gathered at the two farmhouses. I slept again and felt much stronger. At dusk I saw pickets being posted and observed that the enemy trusted to the swamp to prevent any from crossing their lines at that point. So I determined, as soon as it was dark, to try to wade it. Fortunately, the cold swamp water was not very wide or deep; it climbed above my knees, and when I emerged, I was wet to the waist, adding to the stiffness of my muscles and delaying my progress. The Boers were holding a religious service in each farmhouse; the chanting of psalms fell upon my ears. Their gathering for this purpose had left the country free, and by two in the morning I heard the whistle of an engine and saw the gleam of lights at the distillery of Esterferbraaken.

This was my long-sought objective. About a mile from it, I placed my first charge of guncotton, lit the fuse, and crept' away to a depression in the grass. Soon after the crash, I heard the sound of troops moving at the distillery. Repair men came out, and by four o'clock the rails were repaired and all was quiet once more. Evidently the Commandant at the distillery thought the job must have been done by scouts out of Pretoria, as he posted pickets only along the railway.

Watching every movement carefully, I saw a chance to fire my last charge of guncotton. This time, I chose as my hiding place a blue gum grove on the edge of a small spruit where I could get water. At the second explosion, the Commandant realized that the enemy scout or scouts were still near by, and an angry bunch of Boers boiled out of the distillery and spread out up the railway. They were evidently country Boers, used to hunting, and knew how to beat rapidly and accurately. My chances of escaping seemed small indeed, and there was also a probability that, being very angry, they would shoot me on sight. Strange to say, my high resolves and willingness to die of a few hours before all deserted me, and I felt as must a hunted rabbit before the hounds.

It was now light, and every move of that grim line of horsemen was of a kind familiar to me, and I saw how tremendously efficient at this kind of work they were. Soon they fired the grass and, by elimination, narrowed things down to the gum grove. It was planted in rows as usual and, being partially dry, might easily be burned. I had but a few moments left to act. Beside the spruit, the grass was about a foot high, not very thick, but too green to ignite readily. It happened that, on the edge of this strip of grass, a spindly, stunted little gum tree was struggling for existence. It was not more than three or four feet high, and had only a few branches and leaves on it. One could look clear through it in any direction. Two things must be done at once: I must escape the fire and break the outline of my body on the veldt. The tree and the green grass did both for me.

I wreathed my hat brim and shoulder straps in grass in the best way to disguise them, and changed the human outline by curling myself around the slender trunk of the little gum tree, lying on my side. The Boers passed very close to me and rode on but soon swept back again. The Commandant ordered them through the grove in line and shouted to them to examine every tree and then fire the grove, which they did, but it burned only partially. The Commandant sat on his horse within twenty feet of me while his men dismounted and

WOUNDED

walked along the bank of the little spruit even closer. Good fortune was mine again. The Boer artillery now thundered along from Pretoria in retreat, and all the commando that had been so interested in me personally forgot me and went off to join their army. Once more, I drew a full breath without fear. The Commandant had cursed his men for not finding me, yet I was under his own eye at the very time, as he sat his horse and shouted directions and reproaches.

A long day passed for me after this, drowsing and sleeping between periods of sharp pain; then a very cold night without fire. Another day dragged by while I watched long lines of Boers in retreat. I was getting too weak now to move, but the welcome sound of big guns reached my ears, and I knew that General French was marching and that Pretoria had fallen. I had cut the railroad as ordered. My one thought now was to hang on until the British occupied the ground on which I lay. But at dark I made up my mind to walk and crawl toward Pretoria. At times my brain seemed too weak to master my own plan, but I managed to flog my muscles into action by selecting a bush fifty yards away and giving them a promise of rest when the bush was attained; then on again to another visible objective.

Crawling along at about eleven o'clock, I overheard the voice of the Officer of the Guard making the round of the pickets. Far over the veldt came that familiar English voice, "Picket Number Nine, where in hell are you?" The language that followed was even more lurid, but it sounded to my ears like sweetest music. I crawled on and was soon near enough to call out. The picket was at first inclined to fear a trap and came forward with finger on trigger. Upon my making myself known, his kind heart prompted him at once to dig into his pockets for the "dog biscuit" (hardtack) which, short though his own rations were, he offered me. Fortunately, so the surgeons afterward told me, I could not eat it. I was soon taken to the Field Hospital; then my friend Hunter-Weston came for me with a tanga (bullock cart) and took me to staff headquarters in Pretoria.

A son of John Hay (McKinley's Secretary of State) was then American consul to the Boer Republic. He was extremely kind to me in hospital and gave me the political news of America and T. R., Rhodes and Rhodesia, Russia and Japan, and also of the critical French situation. He was a brilliant representative of our country, placed in a very important position at the age of twenty-four. On one of his visits he brought with him his charming secretary, Mr. Cooley from Boston, who in some subtle way managed to convey to me that the United States Government through him sent best wishes for my recovery. That day, a sudden surge of vitality seemed to stir in my blood, and by evening I was able to stand on my feet.

Lord Roberts's close friend, Surgeon Edwards, had patched me up, to be invalided home to London into the famous hands of McNaughton Jones, but it was not until two years afterward, after the Ashanti campaign, that this great surgeon straightened out the kinks between ribs and muscles and made me fit again for many more campaigns.

CHAPTER XXXIII

REWARDS

I WAS invalided home on the *Dunnotter Castle*. Pretoria had fallen, and Lord Roberts was due to return to England. There was much guerilla warfare before the final treaty of peace was declared, but the railway and all the principal towns and resources of the country were in the hands of the British.

On the voyage to England were many invalid officers, and some high in the councils of the Empire who were called home because the political clouds had shifted from South Africa to Fashoda, China, and Constantinople. I recall a graphic review of the world's condition given by young Winston Churchill, who even then had a clear premonition of the coming storm. He explained to me why, in his thrilling escape from the Boer prison, he had been compelled to do certain things which I, as a scout, had criticized. His moves were restricted by the handicap of physical weakness which made a twenty-mile run at night entirely beyond his power.

But the thing that marked him in my memory for life was his solemnly calling a meeting in the cabin and demanding that such men as General Colville, Lord Bentinck, and others should be brought to trial for misappropriation of the sport funds. There was a great buzz throughout the ship, including the crew. Churchill was amply cursed as a bounder, an upstart, a silly ass, a swell-headed "Leftenant," etc., etc. High Dignity appeared offended. Yet the trial had full attendance. Some of the famous legal talent on board was commanded to represent the accused. This play was all new to me, a Western American. We abuse our gods quite often, but we do not torment them in just this jocular way. I had a creepy, goose-flesh feeling for Churchill, such as one might have for a child innocently gambolling before an onrushing herd of cattle. I was so sure they would turn the tables on him. It was all wasted sympathy. The cabin was resolved into some sort of parliament and passed a vote of censure on the accused by a safe majority. It was either young Brooke (later Earl of Warwick) or Sir Byron Leighton who remarked to me, "Don't you worry about Churchill. K. of K. sat on him to no purpose, and all hell won't keep him from being Premier some day."

My arrival in England brought a very pleasant interlude in my strenuous life. The kindly letter given me by Lord Roberts was interpreted by the English as an imperative social introduction, involving almost a national obligation to the stray American scout who had been willing to do his bit for the Old Country. The charm of English country life was now known to us by experience instead of by hearsay or through books. My wife and I enjoyed every moment of our visiting and deeply regretted we could not enter all the hospitable doors that were so cordially opened to us.

There was one visit that stands out above all others, when I was asked to be the guest of some of the heads at Oxford. It was in my mind to avoid this invitation, for it really worried me. I knew the mighty Rhodes held Oxford in both love and awe. He sacrificed great financial gains and, what was of more importance, his invaluable time to obtain his degree there and to absorb the habit of thought that makes and rules the English-speaking race to-day. What could these men have to say to me or I to them? But the visit turned out a delightful surprise, and the days I spent there are treasures of memory. My hosts quickly found the limits of my mental horizon, and there was not an embarrassing moment. At this time, Rhodes had not, through his scholarships, made it possible for the youth of my country to swing wide the doors of this great cultural centre that through the centuries has so profoundly influenced the world.

The kind-hearted Queen invited me to visit her at Osborne, and everywhere we went we were treated as real friends—a

FACSIMILE OF LETTER FROM LORD ROBERTS TO MAJOR BURNHAM

A tribute from a commander who wrote few letters

contrast to the ordinary attention given for any unusual action either good or bad.

To all this cup of joy was added the great honour of being made a member of the Distinguished Service Order. The notification of this was a great surprise to me and its first effect was almost humiliating. I had already received two medals, several bars, the Thanks of the Sovereign, and many other kindly favours without feeling really conceited or, as the English say, full of bounce. But when I realized that the little enamelled gold cross of the D. S. O. was to be worn by me I found that I was no different from any other primitive man. I inwardly glowed and strutted with an exaltation which I sincerely hope was not visible to my friends. Perhaps my wife was the only one who knew the whole truth and the duration of my lapse into savagery.

The actual investiture took place in St. James's Palace in 1901, after the death of Queen Victoria. By this time my vainglorious mood had passed, and if there had been any lingering trace of that weakness it would have been swept aside that day. For I felt very humble and insignificant when my name and deeds were called aloud and I stepped under the critical eyes of grim old generals of the Sepoy Mutiny and many others of the most distinguished figures of the British Empire, gathered to witness the investiture. Somehow, the steps leading up to the throne seemed very high, and Edward VII looked every inch a king. At the instant the cross was pinned over my heart by the King, his left hand was placed on my wrist, and I touched the hand with my lips. After that I retired from the throne to receive the congratulations of brother officers gathered for the occasion. I confess their voices sounded far away and confused, but I realized at that moment why it is men so cheerfully die for the Empire and why the Anzacs and Canadians and all the others come hurrying from overseas at England's call. There was no desire now in my heart to boast or strut. I felt of no more importance than a grain of sand on the shore of the mighty sea.

Another unprecedented and most highly prized favour was

that King Edward, in confirming my majority in the British Army, was so gracious as to permit me to hold my rank without renouncing my American citizenship.

It was my intention, as soon as the surgeons had spliced me up and pronounced me able to take on another expedition, to go directly back to Rhodes; but some friends of his borrowed me and sent me, in 1901, into the hinterland of the Gold Coast Colony on the West Coast of Africa. I took with me my brother-in-law, John Blick, who had adventured with me in many lands and climes, and together we entered a region that from time immemorial has produced a vast quantity of gold; in fact, until the discoveries in California and Australia, probably more gold than any other field in the world. Sending John Blick to make an exploration of the Volta River, I then returned from the interior by the caravan route. We finally reached Cumassi and went on to the coast, bringing back only a little gold.

The details of our exhausting Ashanti expedition, as well as the long and fruitful explorations I carried on in East Africa, the wonderful mountain climbing above Navashi, and the many hunts after lions, elephants, ostriches, leopards, hippo, rhinoceros, and other game which I pursued from time to time, as well as the finding of the lost M'Gardi, have been reserved for another telling. Toward that end, I have already deleted from the manuscript of this book part of my youthful experiences, and of my recollections of the Klondike and of the Apache wars in Arizona, as well as the full account of my Mexican explorations, the great Yaqui Delta development, and the discovery of the ancient and curious Maya Stone. I hope the reader will gratefully appreciate that this has been done to help me avoid that high crime against his good-nature—the perpetration of the two-volume book.

However, I will say here that the results of our expedition and exploration of East Africa formed the nucleus for the first real settlement of the country. It is true we did not find either gold in paying quantities, or the excitement of diamond mines to give the country the feverish development of South

Africa. But our experiments with stock, coffee, Indian corn, and a hundred other products proved very encouraging, and to-day planters are encircling the great mountains with many prosperous homes. There are other assets, too, that will in time make this favoured land a great island of civilization in a sea of tropical wilderness. It is already the most famous hunting ground in Africa for all big game. Expeditions come from far and near to slaughter the wild animals in this their last sanctuary. The English are more careful than we Americans with game and other resources, but whether the officials can control the wholesale destruction when modern hunters with high-power rifles pursue the game in flivvers and even in airplanes, remains to be seen. This mode of sport is, to my notion, about as thrilling as sitting on the pasture fence and slaying the pet cow.

While my exploration was progressing along the lines laid down for it, the Government sent Sir William Garstin to devote the last great effort of his life to solving the problem of giving water to Egypt. The plan included building a dam at Murchison Falls to raise the level of Lake Victoria a number of feet. As this lake is three hundred miles long and nearly as wide, every foot of the dam's height gives an enormous volume of storage. For a man as advanced in years as Sir William to take on such work in that country in the rainy season was almost like signing his death warrant, but the great engineer went about his mighty task as silently and quietly as a farmer going out to plough. I met him in one of his camps on Lake Victoria and heard from him many tales of the great works of India and how Wilcox dammed the Euphrates by simultaneously felling two huge towers of masonry, one from either bank, which met in the middle of the river and controlled the flood.

On the completion of Sir William's work, we found ourselves fellow passengers on the steamer to England. One night, on deck, I said to him, "Sir William, now that you have disappointed your enemies and pleased your friends by not dying in the jungle and have given the Government most valuable information, you will certainly receive some distinguished mark of recognition."

"No, no, nothing like that," he replied quickly. Then, after a pause: "But some day, probably fifty years from now, they will want to know certain things about the Nile, and they will dig up the records and find a report by one Garstin—and it will be accurate so far as it goes."

I felt again that one of the secrets why the British Empire has existed for a thousand years had been revealed to me. Sir William returned to England as modestly and silently as he had moved about the border town of Nairobi, and not long after was laid away and forgotten.

There came a time when serious planning for a change of scene seemed advisable. My wife had endured every hardship without complaint; but I knew she longed to see and be near our son Roderick, who was at a military college in England, and I felt it my duty to take her there.

My part in the far-reaching plans of Rhodes in the march from the Cape to Cairo had consisted mostly in blazing trails and quieting the natives. This task was about completed. A great arch of steel carried the railway over the wonderful Victoria Falls. Other lines touched the Nile. Stamp mills were crushing gold ore from the lost mines of Ophir. South Africa was now a nation. The feud of the white race in Africa was ended. Cecil Rhodes, our mighty chief, had died, and all hearts were filled with grief. The natives held for him the sacred burial rites given only to their own departed kings. My boyhood dreams of Africa had all come true. I realized this with a sense of accomplishment and joy, although it had streaked the heads of both my wife and myself with gray.

In October, 1903, from our camp at Navashi, I wrote to my mother:

> In a few days, we are all off for Europe, but I will start this letter ahead of me. There will be little time for me to write in England and on shipboard I never feel in good humour for it—I am too restless and confined on a ship.
> It is with real regret I leave this lovely camp with its lakes and great mountains, its steaming old craters and solemn moss-draped forests. The

wild life is so varied and interesting. I shall miss the roar of the leopards, the wail of the hyena, and the soft calling notes of the bell bird. The nights are of matchless splendour when the moon is full, and my naked wild Kikuyu are singing some deep and lovely chant in perfect harmony with the sounds that come from forest and plain.

During the day, the valley below is dotted with thousands of sheep and herds of cattle tended by spears (Masai warriors) who stand about in little groups like ebony statues. A soft lowing, as continuous as the sound of running water, comes constantly and pleasantly over the boma walls—such a sound and scene as must have touched the hearts of the shepherds of old.

The wildest and sweetest land I have ever seen is, I fear, passing from me for ever. Sometimes I wish I had never learned to read or form any conception of duty, civilization, or religion; for then I might have been outwardly, as I am now at heart, a thorough savage, nothing more. As it is, I am to return to London—to swallowtails, clubs, soft carpets, soft food, soft life, soft men and women. I fear all these things will fit me about as neatly as Paul Kruger's plug hat fitted him.

But my boys must go into the army. I shall try to keep them in that branch of the human organization that is last to decay in a too luxurious nation. Fighting and bloodshed may be condemned by the good, but the army is the ark that carries the strong and enduring virtues far in the world's progress. Whether it will be so always cannot now be determined by any one. . . . You should not upset one's picture of you by jumping from one frame to another—jaunting to San Francisco! I had you firmly set in lovely, sleepy, sunny Pasadena, a safe nook hid away on the edge of the world; a place to which I may turn sometime, who knows? when old and bent with the deepening shadows. I may then see it again as in my boyhood days when I despised it a little as a mere safe retreat from savage winds and ice. . . . I saw so little of every one when I was home. I keep regretting I could not have stayed longer. Howard's visit was, I think, so characteristic of the Burnhams—a hasty lot at best.

I have just had a big hunt in a forest as dense and silent as Stanley Arumoi. In it I shot three bull elephants and came very near being snuffed out. The tusks are taller than a man and very beautiful ivory. We shall have a pair for our London house. I shot a rhinoceros also, and shall have a table-top made out of his hide, which is thick as a plank. Among other things are two Marabou storks whose plumes are worth over their weight in gold.

After some months in London, we returned to Pasadena in the spring of 1904, and built a new home there. About a year later, Sir Rider Haggard came to visit us and brought about a meeting with that great adventurous American, John Hays Hammond, who had also for years been a worker under Rhodes. Again we spent the summer in London. There a deep sorrow came to us in the death of our son Bruce from drowning in the Thames. I then went to Germany to meet Hammond, who now laid out for me long and difficult tasks on the deserts and in the jungles of Mexico. Mighty forces were stirring in that land: rivers were being tamed, deserts reclaimed, mountains washed away, harbours built, and an empire making. My own old Mexican frontier seemed the most active region left in the world, and by night and day it was calling me back. As the choice of assistants and skilled engineers had been left to me, I sought out my kinsmen and some of my South African friends to join me in this enterprise.

The World War brought this episode to a close.

CHAPTER XXXIV

THE GREAT WAR AND THE PROSPECTOR

WE WHO have lived in the day of great personalities like Rhodes and Roosevelt can hardly mention their names without bristling the hair and loosening the tongues of many otherwise peaceful and self-controlled people. As I have always been a sincere admirer of Theodore Roosevelt, it is but likely that some people may consider my statements concerning him biased and partisan. My first meeting with him was long before the Spanish War. As a learned naturalist, he was always keenly interested in the wild life of Africa, and as an American statesman, in what his countrymen were doing under Rhodes. So whenever I came back to the United States on a visit, Roosevelt always found time to see and question me. He was especially anxious that the Americans then taking part in the development of South Africa should be a credit to their native land. He well knew they would be sharply scrutinized and measured by the hard-headed Dutch and the subtle East Indians, as well as by the English, the greatest colonizers of all time. It was indeed refreshing to meet so broad a mind as Roosevelt's, so different from the "Little Englanders" and "Little Americans" who look upon that fellow countryman as almost an outcast who crosses the sea or even leaves the small town in which he has happened to be born. Roosevelt's idea of an American abroad was simply that he was a guest in the house of a friend and should do his best to make himself welcome. He, too, had a high opinion of Rhodes, and smiled sympathetically at my confessed conviction that Rhodes was the greatest man living. At the same time I secretly thought that, next to Rhodes, Roosevelt best filled my ideal of what a man should strive to be.

What I could tell him of the struggles of the Dutch and English in South Africa interested him greatly, and he was delighted to find me enthusiastic over the way John Hay, Jr., and his assistant, Mr. Cooley of Boston, had handled the delicate situation in the Transvaal during the Boer War. He twitted me a little about the prediction he had made many years before when I had argued strongly against the possibility of such a conflict, banking my opinion on the genius of Rhodes to avoid war. I remembered that Roosevelt said to me then: "Sitting here in Washington, I should not know the situation in Africa as you do, who live its life, but I shall nevertheless differ with you and with many other Americans I meet from South Africa. I have so much of that stubborn Dutch blood in me that I predict a clash at arms is bound to come. It can have but one ending, the defeat of the Dutch, yet the future of South Africa will still be in their hands, for theirs is the dominant blood. The outcome will be English laws and customs for a sturdy and powerful Dutch stock, insuring a great future for South Africa."

I was one of the eighteen officers chosen by Roosevelt for the proposed Roosevelt Division for service in France in the World War. The part assigned me was to raise a battalion in the Southwest. My superior officers were to be David M. Goodrich, Rock Channing, and Colonel Jack Greenway, all three Rough Riders. Within a few days from the inception of this movement, there were on my desk telegrams and cables from Mexico, Canada, South Africa, and other lands, many of them from men who had been with me in various wars and expeditions, but it was the magic name of Roosevelt that filled the lists at once.

At a time when both the Senate and the House had approved the sending of Roosevelt's Division to France, it seemed so near a certainty that Roosevelt summoned all eighteen of his lieutenants to a meeting at the Langdon Hotel in New York and there gave us an insight into the reasons he considered sufficient for our going. He told us also that criticism of himself seemed to fall under three heads, *i. e.*, many who knew nothing of war declared his purpose was to make a great parade along the Western Front, have a few skirmishes staged, and possibly a minor victory pulled off, so that his name would shine in all the histories of the war written in the coming years. Another group of critics who claimed to know all about war declared the raising of the division was a monumental piece of folly, a Balaklava on a large scale, and certain to entail annihilation of the entire division; that whenever we were sent into action the grim Germans would concentrate their offensive most heavily for our destruction, and that all of us who followed Roosevelt were silly dupes of a man possessed of such an exaggerated ego that, for the sake of a spectacular death, he was planning to sacrifice thousands of enthusiastic followers on the altar of his vanity. The third line of criticism, said Roosevelt, seemed to take the cynical view that he would seek only a modicum of danger on the battle front, and if sufficiently successful, would use it as a political club to bring the Administration into disrepute; then, grasping this new political power, would carry out his secret plans of becoming Dictator. He laughingly added, "Comment by me on all this among ourselves is time wasted, but I do want to tell you in all confidence something that is not a laughing matter, but what every military head knows. France, the keystone of the arch of defence, is in sore straits and bitterly discouraged. If we can go over at once, our one division may be to them and all the Allies like a sail to the shipwrecked sailor. But it will need to be something more than a mere landing. The common soldier, in this modern war, will not accept us as full comrades in arms until we have proven ourselves in contact with the enemy. So each one of us and every man under you must prepare himself to meet the enemy in such a determined way that he will be strongly aware of our presence. I may also tell you that I have assurance that we shall have with us on either flank experienced troops. They will have much to teach us. Yet I believe we shall find ample scope for using many of our own methods of war."

It was a dark hour for Roosevelt when the jealousy of those

THE GREAT WAR AND THE PROSPECTOR

in power denied him the taking of his division to France, but it was a blacker hour for this nation and for the world that lost the services of its most brilliant son, so needed both in the war and its terrible aftermath.

There came a time in the course of the war when it seemed as if vital supplies were almost exhausted—oil, bread, mercury, sugar. Then a whisper went out that two obscure minerals were sorely needed—tungsten and manganese, most essential in the making of tools to stand the terrific speed required by those machines turning out munitions and building ships to keep the submarines from cutting the lines of supply.

A. Kingsley Macomber, who had been with me as a young man in Africa, financed a systematic exploration of the Southwest to locate tungsten and manganese for the war, and asked me to take charge of the various units. The great manganese supply from Russia and that from South America had been cut off. Needless to say, our search was not shouted from the house-tops. Many keen mining engineers began turning their attention to old abandoned mines, and there was great ransacking of ancient bulletins issued by the United States Geological Survey's state mining bureaus and of old mining publications. But above all, we needed the prospector. Whether we believed in evolution or not, he was our missing link.

When a discovery is actually made, the trained engineer is a marvel of speed and efficiency, but to wander vaguely over the desert wastes with the patience of the burro and the imperturbability of the Sphinx is more than his precise and methodical mind can stand. It is as if you said to him, "Somewhere north of Mexico and south of Colorado I lost a large diamond. Being a mining engineer, you should be able to find it." But a real desert prospector would equip for the journey in the serene belief that he would eventually come up with the sparkler. He always feels that all eternity is his. Calendars, watches, clocks, and tooting whistles are but badges of slavery. He alone of all men is no slave of Time.

The origin and development of the American prospector of the Great West and his hoary passing are best typified by the few remaining groves of giant sequoias now nodding their bald heads on the shoulders of the Sierras. To find the prospector's blood beginnings we must glance backward along the trail.

When our seafaring ancestors landed on the eastern coast of America, they were confronted by one of the greatest forests of the world. Two generations passed before the full development of hunter, trapper, and scout. They learned nearly all their lore from the Indian, and having horses, oxen, and guns, within two hundred years they conquered the land of trees and paused on the banks of the big rivers. Beyond lay an appalling, billowy prairie, endless as the sky. In the forest, with ax, hoe, gun, and a handful of corn for seed, any settler could carve out a home for himself, but this so-called American Desert was for a time his End of the World. Beyond were only thundering herds of buffalo and equally fast-moving bands of mounted Indians; hostile, elusive, relentless; living on meat alone and with no fixed abode. No wonder the mighty onset to the West halted.

Great statesmen like Webster raised a clamour in Congress to stop further Western movement as madness. The day of Leatherstocking and Boone was drawing to a close, and along the border states of the great forest land a new type of man began to develop, or, rather, an old type redeveloped. What really happened was a harking back to the ancient steppes, and wherever this steppe instinct arose, the Western boy was turned into a fast-riding, meat-eating nomad and became the typical plainsman. The day of Carson, Bridger, and Buffalo Bill dawned.

Then it was found that the sod of the vast desert prairies could be broken and was indeed very fertile. The wheel carried the plough, and the long lines of covered wagons began to roll westerly; while the statesmen and pundits were still chattering in the halls of Congress that it could not be done, because everybody who was anybody still knew that everything west of the Mississippi was desert. But the covered wagons rolled on and on until on the Western sky they saw floating a cloud, first white, then blue; but on nearer approach it proved to be a sinister wall of solid rock, thousands of feet high. Here, then, was the real barrier, the Ultima Thule, the locked gate of the great desert. It is true this mighty wall did halt the pioneers. Many wise men in Washington smiled and said, "I told you so." But just then the car of state skidded into the Mexican War and a few plainsmen sifted through the desert sands into California. They found the Dons basking in the pueblos. They hoisted the Bear flag, had a few tussles, and finally insisted that Congress include the whole California coast in the treaty of Guadalupe Hidalgo.

Still the covered wagons halted behind the Rocky Mountain wall until Marshall chanced to pick up a nugget of gold at Sutter's mill in California. Like fast-galloping horses, the news leaped the deserts and mountains. With a mighty roar, the pioneers moved across the Rockies like the barbarians over the Great Wall of China. Up to this hour, the people of our race in their migrations across Europe and the New World had been essentially agriculturists. Now they were to embark on an entirely new venture. They were to become the most successful searchers and the greatest producers of gold and kindred metals. In those vast walls of the Rocky Mountains that had halted the covered wagons, there lay hidden wealth to gridiron the land with steel and to build a hundred cities.

Much we had learned from the Indian, but this time it was the Mexican who taught us. Mining had been going on in Mexico for hundreds of years, and we knew and cared nothing about it. We were so busy cutting down our forests and rolling across our plains that we never heard of Mexico until we found ourselves at war. But now we learned many facts that fitted like mosaics into our world of mountains and deserts. From the Mexican we borrowed the horn spoon, the gold pan, the batea, the sluice box, and rocker. We threw away the coon-skin cap for the sombrero. We took his faithful burro as our bosom friend; his diamond hitch, riata, lasso, spurs, and saddle—in fact, his whole method of handling wild horses and cattle; even his adobe house and many of his dishes, then so strange to us. His tortilla we transformed into our flapjack.

Finally, after living two hundred years next door to him, we began growing alfalfa, the lucerna of the Romans and called the "Gift of God" by the Arabs. Now, Kansas grows more alfalfa than Mexico, and some of its farmers have grown to believe that they invented it themselves, but this will probably be disputed by the good people of Los Angeles, who have a reputation for claiming all honours.

While the findings of Baron von Humboldt focussed the eyes of scientific men on the values of other minerals, yet at the cry of "Gold!" most of them started off to hunt that most alluring of metals and became that first generation of American prospectors who wrote their names with a flourish on the pages of Western history. When it was my turn to wander over the waste places, I came in frequent contact with these earlier pioneers, gray-bearded survivors of the first draft in a new kind of frontiering. A prospector, like a poet, is born, not made. To all the keenness of eye and sense of direction and much of the knowledge of the plainsman or the mountaineer must be added an indescribable spiritual quality, a perennial optimism like the sublime faith experienced by those who have just joined the church or been converted to a new cult. This faith does not prevent the prospector from taking advantage of every method to help him in his quest. Often he is a student of geology and mineralogy and carries with him an intricate, though tiny, outfit for assaying and testing the thousands of samples he is for ever collecting. A prospector may spring from any social class. An ignorant peon is sometimes possessed of an uncanny sixth sense as to touch, colour, weight, and crystal of a metal-bearing rock, and will trail it to its parent ledge or vein as a hunter follows the trail of a wounded stag. Occasionally, I see a painting in which an artist has managed to catch with his brush some of the strange moods and rare qualities that are concealed behind the sun-wrinkled brows and rough exteriors of these dreamers of the desert.

The prospector has something in him of the knight-errant, as he rides forth alone on his faithful burro and for months at a time is swallowed up in cañon walls and sandy wastes,

THE GREAT WAR AND THE PROSPECTOR 365

sampling, sampling, sampling; breaking a thousand hard rocks and aiding his keen eyesight with a powerful glass, testing the "feel" as a Chinese mandarin touches jade, moistening the surface with his breath to detect a certain sheen that may be gold camouflaged by tellurium, weighing his rock samples in water and out, burning by fire, and finally proving by the "Great Horn Spoon." The prospector's observation and memory of minute things must be abnormally acute. He has done his work well and has enabled us to make the last Far Western leap. The song of his desert canary now blends with the roar of the sea lions at the Golden Gate.

There is probably not a square yard of exposed rock from the 49th degree north down to Mexico that has failed to pass under the observant eye of some prospector during the last seventy years. We may be reasonably certain there are no great outcroppings of mineral wealth exposed in vain to the light of day. The prospector of the present must delve below the surface, and this at once calls for the training of an engineer. This sub-surface wealth may easily prove to be greater than all that has yet been found, but it will be discovered by men of a type different from the old prospectors.

It so happened that I knew many old prospectors and where to reach them, and I sent them quietly on the quest for that strange black metal, often found in small quantities and considered of no particular value, the now all-important manganese. I urged them to recall to memory some long-forgotten cañon with stained walls, or some crags and peaks streaked brown and black, crumbling in the blaze of the desert sun. There somewhere in the thousands of miles they had wandered, driving, riding, or following their desert canaries, they might recollect some jet-black outcrop rich in the now essential metal.

A little incident in this search for the lost manganese may shed some light on the ways of the Southwest. It was August. We were searching out some rocky buttes of the Chuckawalla Desert. I had with me an old desert prospector seventy-four years of age. He remembered that in prospecting this waste, thirty years before, he had found in one of the cañons of these buttes the peculiar little black nodules of high-grade manganese. He had traced this float to a little mesa and found a vein of the jet-black ore two or three feet wide, but in those days, gold and silver were the only metals sought, so he had made no indelible print of the locality on his mind. Yet he felt sure that in time he could unravel the long thread of his chartless wanderings.

This day, we had found the float but not the mesa and the big vein. The old prospector, who was suffering from a crippled foot, had gamely climbed all morning long over sand dunes and through cactus, with the terrible sun beating down hotter every hour; while I carried the canteen of water—a light weight at sunrise, but by midday, with the temperature more than 110 degrees, a heavy load. As we slowly climbed the hot rocks of a steep ridge to the summit, the burning wind of the desert struck us just as if it were blowing across a hundred miles of living coals. In a few moments, our dripping faces and sweaty clothes were parched and dry; but, strange to say, it gave relief from the awful heat, and if we protected the mouth and nostrils with a wet handkerchief and sat quite still, we felt comfortable as compared with our condition during the struggle of the morning. We sat silent for some time, each gazing over the strangely desolate Chuckawalla. All the mountain peaks seemed to be dancing, moving, quivering, waving, in the billows of air. Nothing seemed solid or real. The old prospector leaned toward me and said, "The mountains are all whispering to me. If I could only understand!" For an hour he sat there, oblivious to the hard rock used as a seat and forgetful of the strain of the morning and the long struggle ahead that night to the desert water hole. His lame foot, the cactus thorns that must again be endured, were for him non-existent. I considered myself fairly stoical about trivial annoyances, but here was a spirit beyond me. The old miner was actually enjoying it, while I was only enduring for a great cause.

A few days later, on a huge barren peak of this same desert, this prospector again sat entranced, gazing over lines of blue ridges in air as still as death and as clear as crystal. Beside him sat Dr. Harry Macomber, who had joined us in our quest for the lost manganese vein. The doctor is a trained athlete, but he told me in confidence that, on that particular day, he was profoundly thankful the peak was no higher. After a few minutes' silence, the old prospector turned to the doctor with a blissful smile, remarking, "I could sit here and gaze on these mountains for ever."

My task of gathering prospectors was about as difficult as "Bill Lightnin's" herding bees. They run mostly in flocks of one. Like the Indian, they belong to a vanishing race, and this last effort made in the war may well be their swan song. I rounded up all I could reach, and long-forgotten trails were retraced into the deserts. To avoid the burning heat, these long-beards often travelled at night. We passed many of their ghost camps, famous in bygone days, whose tottering buildings stood gaunt and grim under the light of the stars. If you but listen with the inner ear, you can still hear the tender strumming of La Paloma, the frou-frou of silk, the click of spurs, the tinkle of thin glass and soft laughter. But to-day we were searching for hard steel, so we dared not pause even to listen to the soft-toned bells of memory. We must snatch a few hours' sleep on the cool sands just before dawn, then rouse to battle heat waves mountain high that rolled over us like the surf of Africa.

But at last I was able to direct the engineers to long-forgotten mines. Soon, from the hills of Nevada, the old camps at Tombstone, the flanks of Mount Diablo, the Chuckawalla Desert, came out the precious manganese. By burro and mule it came. Even Henry Ford's brain child was pressed into service and rolled over the desert with loads that would have made the builder weep. A small but valuable tonnage was borne East by the trains to the gaping furnaces. Most of this effort was made at a financial loss to all concerned. It was certainly the desert people's best tribute to the nation, and remembered by them along with the breadless days and other deprivations common to all and cheerfully borne. It was the last fine rally of the long-beards.

THE LATEST ADVENTURE

WHEN I came back from Africa to California it had been with small fear that the Audubon Society would be lying in wait to accuse me of robbing the Oof Bird's nest—that feathered African whose song is believed to indicate the neighbourhood of gold. Yet, in spite of years, I had not grown deaf to its tantalizing and alluring note, should it twitter across my path. In my cattle ranch among the High Sierras above Three Rivers, I never even heard it peep, although I had the music of the tall redwoods and the rushing streams to console me. I began to conclude that one scout's life would end without actual capture of that blessed bird.

But with the close of the World War, I found myself listening again for those siren strains that call the world over to the hearts of men. Back on the mesa at Dominguez Field—famed as the scene of perhaps the first great aviation meet held in America (in 1910), on land where, as a lad, I had ridden my pony herding cattle nearly half a century before, dreaming my dreams of African adventure and keeping an eye peeled for a glimpse of the dashing bandit, Vasquez, who sometimes frequented that region—there it was that at last I caught the full-throated song of the Oof Bird!

Steadily and patiently I have tracked him down to his hidden nest far below the surface of the earth and at last I have him caged. A picture of my Oof Bird's cage will do to complete the illustrations of this long recital of a scout's adventures.

GLOSSARY

Aasvogel: large buzzard.
Askari: armed guard.
Assegai: throwing spear.
Baas: boss or master.
Boma: collection of thatched huts protected by thorn bush or palisades.
Caboco: Swahili word for heavy whip.
Disselboom: a timber of hardwood corresponding to the tongue of an ordinary wagon.
Donga: gully.
Dorp: town.
Endaba: council.
Frint: friend.
Induna: chief or general.
Infaan: youth.
Impi: regiment.
Insucomeme: ever ready.
Kloof: open basin against side of mountain.
Kraal: native hut or compound.
Laager: fortified camp, generally of ox wagons.
Minyot: Kafir village.
M'Limo: mouthpiece of God.
Ring Kops: Matabele warriors and councillors.
Safari: caravan.
Schoen: shoe.
Showri: palaver.
Sjambok: heavy Boer whip.
Skerram, scherm: thorn-bush barricade.
Spoor: trail.
Spruit: stream.
Staat: settlement.

Tanga: bullock cart.
Tom-tom: native drum.
Trek: journey.
Trek-tow: The chains or throngs attaching an ox wagon to the yoke.
Veldt: wild country.
Vley: hollow or valley.
Xanca: a ditch or reservoir.
Zareba: compound or fenced-in place.

THE END

CPSIA information can be obtained at www.ICGtesting.com
Printed in the USA
LVOW131249020812

292646LV00004B/70/P